The Abortive Revolution

Harvard East Asian Series 78

The East Asian Research Center at Harvard University administers research projects designed to further scholarly understanding of China, Japan, Korea, Vietnam, Inner Asia, and adjacent areas.

The Abortive Revolution

China under Nationalist Rule, 1927-1937

LLOYD E. EASTMAN

Harvard University Press, Cambridge, Massachusetts 1974

© Copyright 1974 by the President and Fellows of Harvard College

All rights reserved

Preparation of this volume has been aided by a grant from the Ford Foundation.

Library of Congress Catalog Card Number 74–75639

SBN 674–00175–3

Printed in the United States of America

For "a great guy," our son, MICHAEL ERIC EASTMAN

Preface

China has been undergoing a continuous process of revolution throughout the twentieth century. This fact is obfuscated by the outbreak of three distinct political upheavals: the Republican Revolution of 1911, the Nationalist Revolution of 1927, and the Communist Revolution of 1949. Underlying these discrete episodes, however, has been the continuing quest for a new political system that would bring prosperity, stability, and strength to the Chinese nation.

The revolution of 1911 did more than remove a royal family from power and more than topple the structures of a governmental administration. More significant, the revolution exposed the pervasive decay of the traditional political system. The state had become corrupt and ineffective. The always precarious balance between central government and the provinces had shifted decisively away from Peking. Ravaged by domestic rebellions, beset by foreign imperialists, and burdened by the payments of indemnities and debts, the dynasty was financially, intellectually, and politically bankrupt.

If this had been 1644 rather than 1911, the dynastic structure might have withstood the storm and been patched up by a new set of dynastic rulers. In the twentieth century, however, there existed new forces, and the old structures could not resist the added pressures. The growth of population from about 125 million at the beginning of the dynasty to 430 million in 1912 had imposed enormous strains on the administrative apparatus and had threatened to outstrip the economic resources of the country. And the presence of the Westerners constituted a new kind of challenge—even more perhaps because they offered social and political alternatives than because of their military and economic power.

The development of nationalism among the lettered elite also generated forces that were wholly new. Sensing a power vacuum as the dynasty weakened, and motivated by concern for the nation, the gentry were no longer content to have the officials mediate for them in the political process. Instead, the gentry began asserting their influence and control directly in the military and financial administration at the local level and actively demanded to participate in the political process even at the level of the central government. The Manchu response to this demand lagged behind the spread of political mobilization. And it was therefore the so-called reformers and constitutionalists who were even more responsible for bringing down the dynasty in 1912 than were the revolutionaries.

As the sentiment of nationalism intensified, the Ch'ing government was forced to undertake new tasks that had confronted no previous dynastic administration. It attempted to create a new army, to institute a national system of education, to suppress opium, to develop a modern economy, and to create a national system of transportation. It sought also to reestablish central control over the provinces. These reforms, essential if the Manchus were to satisfy the waxing expectations of nationalistic Chinese, generated new forces that ultimately contributed to the Manchu downfall. The fiscal requirements of these reforms, for example, could only be met by reasserting political controls at the local levels and increasing tax burdens, or by relying on loans from the imperialists. The Ch'ing tried both alternatives. And both so aggravated the political discontents of the Chinese non-official elite that they embraced the revolution that had been begun by persons more radical than themselves. Or, citing another example, the Manchus abolished the Confucian-oriented civil service examinations in 1905. This measure was long overdue and was crucial to the technological and administrative modernization to which the government leaders aspired. Yet it is probable that no other single measure was more destructive of the elite's loyalty to the dynasty, of commitment to the established social order, or, in the long-run, of the traditional value system.

Even at the local level, the foundations of the traditional system had crumbled. When the system had functioned at its best, local power interests and the state bureaucracy had worked hand-in-glove to tax and police the population at the village level. During late imperial times, however, real power had devolved into the hands of local elites. And, indeed, during the years before the revolution, even the lower gentry—the *sheng-yüan–chien-sheng* stratum, whose activities in the governance of the local areas had earlier been informal and often illegal—were displacing the upper gentry and were acquiring real and formal powers of government at the hsien and sub-hsien levels. This had resulted in a persistent and often sordid battle for power, with the bureaucracy being at least partially displaced by new elements which were only minimally responsive to the wishes of the state. The dimensions of this disintegration of the traditional political system at the local level have been trenchantly described by Philip Kuhn: "By the twentieth century . . . the problem had swollen disastrously. The disintegration of control mechanisms in the countryside had led to virtual anarchy in some areas, a collapse of local security, and rampant banditry. From the standpoint of the bureaucracy on all levels, an equally serious problem was sequestering the rural economic surplus for state purposes, because so much of it was being siphoned off by local sub-county functionaries, local elite long out of control."[1]

After the Revolution of 1911, the situation worsened. So badly had the administrative mechanisms broken down that

Yüan Shih-k'ai complained privately that he wielded less power as president of the republic than he had as governor-general under the dynasty.[2] Central authority over the provinces withered; sources of revenue fell into the control of local elites; the military authority of Peking was challenged by increasingly recalcitrant and independent-minded commanders. In this environment of political decay, even the moderately progressive reforms that had been initiated by the Manchus now faltered under Yüan. The weakness of the government also invited increased foreign intervention. Both Tibet and Outer Mongolia fell from Chinese suzerainty. And Japan, like a jackal scenting rotting flesh, laid extravagant claims to a dominant position in China by presenting the Twenty-one Demands in 1915. After 1916, the entire political structure progressively collapsed, and the nation sank into the depths of warlordism.

Even more corrosive of the political system, taken in its broadest sense, than administrative disintegration was cultural disintegration. Talcott Parsons has remarked that "a relatively established 'politically organized society' is clearly a 'moral community' to some degree, its members sharing common norms, values, and culture."[3] The strength of the traditional Chinese political system had been precisely this sense of moral community—the remarkable consensus both among the elite and masses regarding personal and societal values. This consensus had, however, become fragile during the latter years of the Ch'ing as China was assailed by both Western might and ideas. And, when the examination system had been abolished in 1905, and then even the emperorship was overthrown in 1912, the institutional underpinnings of the entire structure were jerked away, leading, as Lin Yü-sheng has put it, "to the final and complete breakdown of both the traditional political order and the traditional cultural order."[4]

Actually, the full extent of the cultural breakdown has still to be measured. Thus far, scholars have remarked mostly about the cultural iconoclasm of the May Fourth radicals. Important though the total rejection of China's ethical and social traditions by some of the nation's intellectuals may have been, however, this was but symptomatic of a more profound cultural crisis. For, with the general assault on the old certitudes, non-intellectuals too were confused about proper goals of action and about the standards of personal conduct. Traditionally the *li* (standards of social propriety) had been sharply defined; everyone could be fairly confident of what was expected of him in his particular status. To an increasing degree, however, the traditional *li* became meaningless, and it was no longer the Confucian literatus who was accorded respect and obeisance, but the possessor of wealth, the wielder of the instruments of violence, and the master of the ways of the Westerner.

Even in Yüan Shih-k'ai's day, a moral decline was evident.[5] A decade later, the effects were pervasive. Cities such as Shanghai, for example, appeared to the relatively tradition-minded as veritable sinks of iniquity. And in the villages, most of the former gentry were being replaced by men "with not one drop of ink in them." That is, many of the new local leaders were innocent of the traditional ethical indoctrination, they sensed no noblesse oblige regarding the commoners, and they provided no community leadership. They "had no political ideology to teach the villagers," C. K. Yang has observed about leaders of a village in Kwangtung, "except the silent message that these were times when the strong man won regardless of class background or moral conduct."[6] China's sense of moral community, in other words, had been replaced by confusion and contention.

Growing demands for political participation also exacerbated the disintegration of the political system after 1912. In ways more profound than the mere proclamation of a republican constitution would suggest, China had irrevocably entered an era of popular sovereignty. Now it was felt that government must not only rule for the people, but that the will of the people should somehow be expressed directly in government decisions.

Even Yüan Shih-k'ai recognized this change, and in 1915 he

rigged an election, hoping thereby to legitimize the reestablishment of the dynastic system. Thereafter the demands for political participation became more strident. Students during the May Fourth Movement (1919) constituted a potent political force. And during the 1920s, as the sentiment of embittered nationalism spread through the cities of the nation, tradesmen and workers also became a political force. No government in the future could function if it did not in some effective way take into account these new, politically mobilizing elements.

The decade of warlordism was not, however, a period of unrelieved regression and disintegration. Nationalism became a strong centripetal force that countered the disintegrating tendencies of warlordism and imperialism. Political ideologies, too, were coalescing, providing clearer images of means to raise China from its degradation. The industrial sector of the economy, albeit still minute relative to the traditional base, grew continuously. And, not least important, large numbers of youth were going abroad for study, so that a new intellectual elite, more or less informed about the technologies, institutions, and outlooks of the non-Chinese world, was brought into existence. In other words, the process of modernization—regardless of the conditions of political collapse—was inexorable.

The Nationalist regime, coming to national power in 1927–28, put an end at least nominally to the period of warlordism. It was a regime that spoke the rhetoric of revolution. In its lexicon, revolution carried a positive value, and anyone who opposed the policies of the dominant faction of the Kuomintang was a counter-revolutionary. But the revolution of the Kuomintang was not a revolution of one economic class against another, nor was it in any meaningful way a revolution of one ideology against another. It was a nationalistic revolution, whose destructive thrust was directed against warlordism and imperialism, and whose constructive thrust was directed toward the creation of a new and effective political system. The Nationalists endeavored, in other words, to restore political unity, economic plenty, and national pride and security to the Chinese people. This book is an analysis and assessment of that endeavor.

The decade of Nationalist rule in Nanking was of extraordinary significance for the Chinese people. During those ten years prior to the war with Japan, the Nationalists might have formulated a system of rule sufficiently viable that it could have survived the rigors of war—with the result that the communist revolution would still be a vision in Mao Tsetung's mind. As will be shown, the Nationalist regime did succeed in evoking considerable popular support after mid-1936. But it had not succeeded in creating an integrated political system; the administration continued to be ineffective and corrupt; the regime had not begun to cope with the problems of the rural masses; the process of cultural disintegration was not arrested, and the leadership's reliance on the New Life Movement gave little promise of promoting a sense of moral community; and the government never adequately resolved the problem of how to deal with the growing pressures for political participation. If the regime had been given more than a decade before it was drawn into the vortex of war, it *might* have resolved these problems. The investigations for this book do not, however, give cause for optimism. The government did not in the main comprise officials who were highly dedicated to the welfare of society. And political forces outside the regime were too weak to impose efficiency and accountability upon it.

This study lays no claims to comprehensiveness. It focuses on but one dominant theme of the period, the failure of the Nationalist revolution. The chapters of the work are intended to illucidate the causes and manifestations of that failure and to portray the responses of various segments of the nation to the failure. The strategy of the study, in other words, has been to essay a few exploratory but relatively deep probes into the history of the period, hoping in this way to penetrate beyond political narrative in order to discover the forces that aborted the Nationalist efforts to reconstitute a viable political system. This strategy precludes definitive statement, and the study probably raises more questions than it answers. But with research on Nationalist China in such a relatively primitive state, this may not be entirely bad. I hope, for example, that future scholars will go on to examine the *process* of factional interrelationships (for example, between the Blue Shirts and the CC clique), to test the hypothesis that the Nationalist regime did not rest on a class basis of rural landlords and urban capitalists, and to demonstrate more precisely than has been possible here how the Nanking government related to the provinces that were still largely controlled by residual warlords. And, in particular, I hope that future scholars will further examine the influence of China's political culture upon the political behavior of the Nationalist officials. No part of this study has provided me more intellectual stimulation and pleasure than the sections of Chapter 7 that treat of political culture. Yet I am keenly aware that I have not provided the final word on this subject, and that it is possible that scholars approaching the problem of bureaucratic pathology from different perspectives will discover more cogent explanations.

Acknowledgments

"I have considered it the *tao* of friendship," wrote one of the scholars who kindly consented to comment on the manuscript for this book, "to dig as hard and critically as I possibly could at all points." By this measure, I have many true friends.

I am most beholden to Philip A. Kuhn and John Israel. They meticulously read the entire manuscript, and their many criticisms, suggestions, and questions enabled me substantially to sharpen and strengthen the analyses in the study and to eliminate a number of factual errors. Other scholars who contributed time, energy, and expertise to improve or advance this study are David D. Buck, John K. Fairbank, Victor C. Falkenheim, Noel R. Miner, Andrew J. Nathan, Cheryl Ann Payer, Dwight H. Perkins, Peter Schran, Lawrence N. Shyu, Lyman P. Van Slyke, Ezra F. Vogel, and Wang Yeh-chien. My students at the University of Illinois also contributed intellectually to the work, most notably Parks M. Coble, Allan A. Gable, and Lai Jeh-hang.

Librarians and archivists are among a researcher's most treasured friends, and I never ceased to be amazed by the patience and good spirit with which they responded to my frequent displays of ignorance and helplessness. In particular, I am happy to acknowledge the assistance of Ernst Wolff of the Far Eastern Library of the University of

Illinois; Ichiko Chūzō and his staff, who contributed greatly to the facility and enjoyment of my research at the Tōyō Bunko; John Ma and David Tseng of the Hoover Institution; and Eugene Wu and his staff at the Harvard–Yenching Library. Others who materially aided the work for this study were Professor Kuo T'ing-i and my many friends at the Academia Sinica in Taiwan; Wu Ch'un-hsi of the Institute of International Relations, Taipei; and Virginia Briggs and her staff at the East Asian Research Center, Harvard University.

No one, however, helped more directly and continuously in the preparation of this book than Margaret M. Y. Eastman. Through each stage of preparation—from the original research, through typing of the successive drafts of the manuscript, and down to compilation of the index—Meya shared the burdens, anxieties, and pleasures of this study.

The research for this book has also been aided by grants from the Committee on Exchanges with Asian Institutions and the Joint Committee on Contemporary China, both of the Social Science Research Council; the Center for Asian Studies, the Center for International Comparative Studies, and the University Research Board, all of the University of Illinois; and the East Asian Research Center of Harvard University.

Finally, I am grateful to *The China Quarterly* for permission to reproduce here substantial portions of my article on the Blue Shirts that appeared in Number 49 of that publication.

Contents

The Abortive Revolution

The *yüan* was the standard unit of Chinese currency during the Nanking period. In the following text, it is designated by the sign ¥. Between 1927 and 1937, the value of the *yüan* fluctuated considerably, but generally speaking ¥3.00 equaled U.S. $1.00.

One catty is one-hundredth of a picul, or equivalent to 1.1 pounds.

Chapter 1 **"The Revolution Has Failed"**

"No governmental group in China," George Sokolsky wrote in 1929, "started under better auspices than that which composed the Nanking Government . . . The people wanted them to succeed."[1] And Franklin Ho recorded the feelings of young Chinese intellectuals at the time: "We in North China, I know, really looked forward to the Nanking regime. For example, in 1928, I, Tsiang Ting-fu and a few friends went to Nanking from Tientsin. On arrival, I recall how anxious we were to see the new national flag—a symbol to us of a new era of great possibilities."[2] Popular elation at the Kuomintang victory was short-lived. Indeed, the first and inescapable fact about the Kuomintang during the Nanking decade is that the revolutionary momentum and spirit of the Nationalist movement vanished with startling suddenness after the establishment of the government in Central China.

"The Chinese revolution has failed," Chiang Kai-shek admitted in 1932. "My only desire today is to restore the revolutionary spirit that the Chinese Kuomintang had in 1924."[3] Chiang Kai-shek frequently scolded his subordinates intemperately, and his repeated assertions that the revolution had failed might be interpreted simply as a means of exhorting the

members of the Kuomintang to even greater accomplishments. Yet the charge that the revolution had failed acquired
such common currency both inside and outside the party that
the contention cannot be easily dismissed. In a report to the
League of Nations, for example, Ludwig Rajchman reported
in February 1930 that "the Government . . . soon began to
lose its original driving force; eventually, after two years of
office, little remained of the early schemes of reconstruction;
the top-heavy machinery of the Central Government was
clogged by the defensive attitude of those holding doggedly on
to official positions, and real incentive to reform and reconstruction passed more and more into the camp of the Opposition."[4] And Charles E. Gauss, United States chargé in
Nanking and later ambassador to China, wrote in September
1934, "The impulse of the Revolution is dead . . . The revolutionary zealots now nestle in the comfort of public office and
concern themselves less with their public responsibilities and
the welfare and progress of their country and people, and
more with their personal fortunes and jealousies."[5]

The precipitancy with which it became apparent that the
Kuomintang had stumbled in attempting to create a viable
political system shocked contemporaries and puzzles historians. One explanation, or part of the explanation, may be
that, even before 1927, the Kuomintang (and its predecessors,
the T'ung-meng-hui and the Chinese Revolutionary Party)
had always been a loosely knit organization with an exceedingly disparate membership.

Some of the members, of course, were demonstrably committed to the cause of the revolution. Ts'ai Yüan-p'ei, for
example, had given up a highly promising career within the
Ch'ing government in order to join the revolution. Others like
Wang Ching-wei and Hu Han-min had fought and lived in
revolutionary exile much of the time since the turn of the
century. Among the younger members, there were the cadets
of the Whampoa Academy, whose life expectancy in a military revolutionary career was short indeed. And some of the

young university students had given up the security of the classroom to join the party or army after being fired by the selfless and emotional nationalism of the May Thirtieth (1925) Movement. So there were, incontrovertibly, men and women of idealism and vision in the ranks of the Kuomintang.

Yet the Kuomintang, prior to the assumption of governmental powers, was not a vital, tightly disciplined or uniformly idealistic revolutionary movement. Admission procedures had always been lax, so that undesirable types had not been excluded from membership. Prior to the 1924 reorganization of the party, for instance, virtually anyone who applied for membership was admitted, and party leaders had been more concerned about the size than the quality of the membership.[6] Sun Yat-sen, it is said, personally never turned down anyone who sought admission to the party. And just how little control over the doctrinal commitment and morale of the membership was exerted is suggested by the fact that the entire army of Ch'en Chiung-ming had been enrolled as members of the Kuomintang.[7]

One of Sun Yat-sen's chief purposes in forming an alliance with the Russian and Chinese communists in 1923 had been to take advantage of the communists' organizational talents in order to tighten the discipline and to renew the vigor of his own movement. As a consequence, Michael Borodin had quickly restructured the Kuomintang on the model of the Russian Communist Party, political commissars were introduced into the army, and Sun Yat-sen's lectures on the Three People's Principles were decreed the ideological font of the movement.

If these measures had been given sufficient time to take effect, the Kuomintang might have become an organizationally vigorous and unified political force. The pace of events, however, soon outran even the best intentions. As a result of the wild surge of nationalism that characterized the May Thirtieth Movement, and subsequently the sudden expansion of revolutionary territory during the course of the Northern

Expedition, there was a flood of new recruits into the party. Between 1926 and 1929, the party ballooned from approximately 150,000 to over 630,000 members.[8]

During this period of expansion, party headquarters was helpless to control the kinds of people that become card-bearing members. Most of these recruits had no real familiarity with party doctrines when they joined the party. And, as it became apparent that the revolutionary movement was successful, careerists and opportunists leaped onto the bandwagon. There was virtually no screening of the applicants. "Party headquarters at all levels," Ho Ying-ch'in remarked in January 1928, "are concerned only about the quantity, and pay no attention to the quality [of the members]. The spirit of the party therefore becomes more rotten by the day."[9] Sa Meng-wu, another old-time Kuomintang member also complained in early 1928 that "today when our party army reaches a place, it often admits members in excessive numbers. Many corrupt bureaucrats and evil gentry regard entering the party as a shortcut to *sheng-kuan fa-ts'ai*. The party branches are corrupt, and therefore capable persons do not wish to enter the party."[10] (*Sheng-kuan fa-ts'ai* is a term that might be translated as "to become an official and grow rich." Invariably the phrase bears the pejorative connotation that the riches are obtained through corrupt means.)

At the moment when the Kuomintang became the ruling organ of the nation, therefore, the party membership as a whole was perhaps even less cohesive and less dedicated to revolutionary goals than it had been prior to the reorganization of 1924. Party members, Ho Ying-ch'in declared, had inadequate training, they did not attend meetings, and they utterly ignored party doctrine. Worst of all, he stated, "Party leaders do not place the party in a primary position nor accept party control . . . they merely use the party as a cover in their plans to *sheng-kuan fa-ts'ai*."[11]

Chiang Kai-shek, too, expressed chagrin and disillusionment at the decadence into which the party had fallen. "Now," he stated in early 1928, "party members no longer strive either for the principles or for the masses . . . Many officials have become equivocal toward the party and toward the doctrine. Now there are not a few pseudo-military officers and opportunistic politicians who are concerned only for their own freedom and benefit, and who seek only to satisfy their lust for *sheng-kuan fa-ts'ai.*" Chiang then asked why the revolutionary forces had been unable to take Hopei and Shantung. "The reason," he replied, "is that the revolutionaries have become degenerate, have lost their revolutionary spirit and revolutionary courage. And the basic reason is that, after those individuals got to Nanking, they developed erroneous thoughts of struggling for power and profit, and are no longer willing to sacrifice."[12]

The recruits that proved most damaging to the revolutionary character of the party were the old-style militarists and bureaucrats. Warlords who turned colors and professed loyalty to the new regime were not only admitted to the party but were rewarded with party and governmental posts that were commensurate with the size of their armies. And the old-style bureaucrats who had hitherto served the various warlord regimes descended on Nanking in such numbers that people spoke of the "military Northern Expedition, bureaucratic Southern Expedition" (*chün-shih pei-fa, kuan-liao nan-fa*). These so-called "northern mandarins" were soon finding posts at all levels of the government, and at least four of the ten ministries in 1929 were headed by men from the ranks of the northern warlords.[13] Quo Tai-chi (Kuo T'ai-ch'i), a long-time member of the party, resigned his post as vice-minister of Foreign Affairs after witnessing this development, declaring that "conditions in our Party are not what they should be, that the Party is nearly usurped by the old mandarin influence even as it was usurped last year by the Communists."[14]

The absorption of the old-style mandarins and militarists into the regime could in many ways be justified. Compromises with the warlords had shortened the military phase of the revolution, and the new government desperately needed the expertise and experience in administration that the northern mandarins brought to Nanking.[15] The long-term effects of this compromise with the old-style political elements were, however, incalculable. Most directly, perhaps, these traditionalist elements brought with them to Nanking the values, attitudes, and methods of the warlord regimes. "Nanking," the *North China Herald* observed, "mirrored Peking not only in technique but in spirit."[16]

Even more serious may have been the fact that idealistic members of the party became profoundly disillusioned after seeing the old-style administrators promoted to the most desirable positions in the government and party. Ho Ying-ch'in's secretary, Liu Chien-ch'ün, for example, complained that warlords and bureaucrats with the right personal relationships were advanced to high party office, whereas a sincere revolutionary was simply a "weakling of society."[17] And Wang Cheng, in a doctoral dissertation at Stanford, recalled even more vividly his reactions at the time: "I, like many schoolmates, joined the Kuomintang out of the idealistic belief that the Kuomintang was the only agency capable of destroying warlordism." When the warlords were brought into the party and given prominent positions, however, "We were disillusioned with the Kuomintang and many of us virtually withdrew." "The inclusion of disloyal warlords," Wang concluded, "strained the faith in the party of otherwise loyal members."[18]

A second factor contributing to the new regime's lack of revolutionary momentum may have been the party purge. Begun as a means of forestalling a seizure of the revolutionary leadership by the communists, the purge quickly spread in ever-widening ripples that washed over persons of every political view. It was widely felt—with what justice is difficult to say—that most of the actual communists successfully escaped the purges, whereas thousands of persons who were not affiliated with the communists were being led out to slaughter. Indeed, even the venerated Ts'ai Yüan-p'ei, who at the time had contacts at the highest levels of the Kuomintang, proclaimed as early as December 1927 that the purges were senselessly destroying the youth of the nation.[19] There can indeed be no doubt that the purges had quickly ceased to be simply a weapon against the communists. All real, suspected, or potential opponents of the regime—from non-Kuomintang organizations like the China Youth Party, and individual critics like Hu Shih, to the Reorganization Clique of the Kuomintang associated with Wang Ching-wei—soon felt the terror of the purge.

How many persons were massacred during the purges is impossible to know. Estimates are utterly unreliable. A workers' organization, allegedly organized by the communists, put the number of dead during 1927 at 38,000. A communist historian has contended that 100,000 died during the first year of the purge. The *Ta-kung pao* ("L'Impartial") stated that "tens of thousands" had been killed by 1930.[20] Whatever the exact number, the Kuomintang revolution had been tempered in blood. Yet the communist movement survived.

The purge in its original conception may have been justifiable in terms of power politics. The communists, it is certain, would not have hesitated to employ equally bloody measures against the Kuomintang. Yet the advantages that the regime may have gained from the purge in the short-run were soon outweighed by the long-term disadvantages. For the purge cut off the Kuomintang from the wellsprings of its revolutionary dynamism.

During the revolutionary struggle before the Kuomintang acceded to power, the communists had become closely identified with the mass movement. "Because Kuomintang members were unwilling to do the real and lower-level work," Ho Ying-ch'in subsequently admitted, "the communists naturally took on this work to split our party from the peasants and workers."[21] Thus, a process of self-selection took place. Only the most idealistic and selflessly committed revolutionaries would be willing to undertake the hard and dangerous work of stirring up the masses at the fore of the revolutionary armies. And it was precisely these that became identified with the

Communist Party. The self-servers who joined the revolutionary movement during this surge of success avoided the perils and hardships of mass work. They were therefore untainted by the suspicion of being communists. And, as a result of the purge, these careerists remained safely in the party. As even the CC clique-related *Shih-tai kung-lun* (Contemporary forum) observed, the old-style and corrupt elements took on the guise of anti-communism, whereupon they became "loyal comrades."[22] The true revolutionaries, on the other hand, who had identified themselves with the mass movement or with radical reforms, were killed or repressed.

The contention here is not that there were no idealists or persons of true revolutionary fervor left in the Kuomintang. Yet the purge had manifestly changed the character of the Kuomintang. The advocacy of socio-economic revolutionary tactics had been equated with communism. Radicalism had thus been filtered out, leaving the advocates of reaction or the supporters of the status quo in control of the party. "The violent elements," Hu Shih wrote in 1929, "and even those who had a few innovative tendencies, have been expelled. The submerged conservative forces have become active, and have created the current counter-revolutionary situation."[23]

Not only did the purge filter out many of the most progressive activists. It also had a persisting effect in that it deterred the remaining Kuomintang members from advocating "radical" solutions for the nation's ills. Kuomintang leaders had been thoroughly frightened by the mass movement during the Northern Expedition. As a consequence, they distrusted mass initiative and felt that mass organizations and activity easily fell under communist domination. Tragically, then, the Kuomintang dissociated itself from the mass movement at the very time when surgent nationalism and modern communications were transforming the masses into a prime source of political power. The purge, moreover, alerted the surviving members of the Kuomintang that radical social and economic solutions were, ipso facto, suspected of being inspired by the communists. The Kuomintang therefore fitted itself into a programmatic straitjacket that prevented the regime from reaching out for solutions that would jolt the status quo.[24]

However one chooses to explain it—whether one stresses the influence of the purge, of the northern mandarins, or (as I shall do in the final chapter) of weakened political institutions and the political culture—the fact was that the Kuomintang had, in an astonishingly short time, demonstrated its incapacity to lay the foundation for an effective political system. Later, during the latter part of 1936 and 1937, surgent nationalism and improved economic conditions caused a sizable segment of the population to become reconciled to the government. Yet the fact remains that, throughout the Nanking decade, the Nationalist regime was marked by ineffective administration, corruption, political repression, and factionalism.

Ineffectual Administration

Ineffectual administration was perhaps the most debilitating feature of Kuomintang rule, for the revolutionaries of the Northern Expedition had quickly been transmogrified into the traditionalist bureaucrats of the Nanking period. Even as early as 1928 there was evidence of this transformation,[25] and by 1930 Chiang Kai-shek could be heard pleading for "a new spirit of zeal and enthusiasm" in government. "In all the Government offices," he complained, "there is no noticeable activity. Everybody is sitting about and doing nothing. Indeed, it is difficult to tell whether the offices are still functioning."[26] Most of the government offices were heavily overstaffed. The demands on upper-level officials to find positions for nepotistic appointments were ineluctable, and the bureaucracy became swollen with unneeded and often unqualified workers.[27]

With a surfeit of employees, the offices in Nanking took on the appearance of "gossip cafes." According to the *Ta-kung pao,* the usual preoccupation of the idle bureaucrats was "reading the papers, smoking, and chatting away the time." Only in the offices of the Ministry of the Interior, the paper said, were the bureaucrats seen to be busy, for there the energetic vice-minister, Kan Nai-kuang, had turned the entire ministry into a veritable school, assigning essays to be written by the bureaucrats in order to increase their knowledge and to provide a basis for judging their abilities.[28] Kan Nai-kuang's scheme was assuredly one way of occupying the time of the superfluous bureaucrats; it was not, however, an efficient means of putting the energies and abilities of the ministry to the service of national reconstruction.

It needs to be emphasized that many of the upper-level bureaucrats, in contrast to the mass of the officials, were prodigiously hard-working, because responsibility was inordinately concentrated in a few leading figures in the regime. Chiang Kai-shek, for example, at one time held twenty-one offices; Wang Ching-wei held twelve, Sun Fo held thirteen, and H. H. Kung held eleven. Another survey revealed that 176 members of the Central Executive Committee and the State Council held a total of 895 posts between them; an average of over five offices for each committeeman. The result was that a few officials were impossibly overburdened, having neither the time, the energy, nor the expertise to supervise effectively any of the operations with which they were involved.[29]

The most vaunted means of instilling efficiency into the bureaucracy was the system of selecting officials by means of examination. This scheme had been devised by Sun Yat-sen, and some Kuomintang theoreticians viewed the concept as the most important single idea in Sun's political schema.[30] The actual operation of the examination system did not live up to Sun Yat-sen's expectations. By 1935, for example, only 1,585 candidates had successfully completed the civil service examinations. Even if all these had been awarded official positions. they would have constituted an infinitesimal part of the total bureaucracy, probably less than 1 percent.[31] In fact, however, a substantial number of those 1,585 candidates never received official employment. To illustrate, a "higher-level" examination in 1931 qualified 101 persons for office. Three years later, only thirty-four of these had been appointed to official position—but ten of these had subsequently been dismissed and sixteen were still classed as trainees. Thus, only eight of the 101 successful examinees held substantive posts in 1934.[32]

Virtually the only way to attain government office was to win the backing of some powerful figure already in the bureaucracy, who could use his "connections" to find a place for the aspiring bureaucrat. So crucial were personal relationships that it was common for a new head of a ministry to dismiss all the old members of the ministry and replace them with his own adherents. Senior officials were frequently deluged with letters from friends requesting jobs for this or that person. To forestall the embarrassment of rejecting these requests, some officials would on occasion post an advertisement in the newspapers explaining that their offices were small and they could not, therefore, act on such recommendations.[33] The examination sys[...] moribund, and personal relat[...] means of access to the bureau[...] to office received little emphasi[...]

The chief defect of the system, however, was the work style of the officials. During the late dynastic period, Chinese government had been characterized by torpid officials and labyrinthine red tape. And neither revolutions nor exposure to the West had infused the bureaucratic administrators with a new spirit or purpose. "In China," Chiang Kai-shek remarked in 1932, "when something arrives at a government office, it is *yamenized*—all reform projects are handled lackadaisically, negligently, and inefficiently."[34] Scathingly he told the officials that they were ruining the nation with their refusal to *shih-kan*—that is, to act so that there are real results. "Our work," he declared, "consists almost solely of the passing back and forth of documents. Stated simply, the documents sound good, but they are written negligently without regard for the true facts of the situation. With regard to practical work, Chinese either do not know how, or—if they know—they are slow in the extreme. It is not simply a matter of not completing today's work, but of putting off this week's work until next week, and indeed often putting off this month's public affairs until next month, and even of not doing this year's work until next year. This matter of amassing and delaying documents in this way can procrastinatingly ruin everything, causing deadly suffering for the common people."[35]

Nanking was a Kafkaesque world of documents. Hsu Dau-lin, who knew the bureaucracy intimately from the inside, recalled that a document arriving at a provincial governmental office was transmitted through thirty-seven steps, each of which consumed from a few hours to a few days. As a consequence, Hsu wrote, "A reply after a half year's time was a surprise to no one. Not a few documents perished on their long and weary journey, buried alive in somebody's desk drawer. But just because of this lengthy processing procedure, mountains of documents were to be seen in every government agency."[36]

Perhaps the most characteristic aspect of yamenization was the tendency of the officials to produce documents of all kinds —plans, regulations, laws—that had little relation to reality and that had virtually no possibility of reaching the stage of implementation. The most telling indictment of this phenomenon appeared in one of Nanking's most partisan journals— the *Wen-hua chien-she* (Cultural reconstruction), which was managed by Chiang Kai-shek's intimate advisor, Ch'en Li-fu. "Government," read the inaugural editorial of the journal, "is simply the passing back and forth of bureaucratic jargon. If only a document reads smoothly, nothing else matters . . . The old eight-legged essay has been abolished, but a new eight-legged essay has now, in truth, become all the fashion. Frequently they go on for page after page, and one cannot tell what is being discussed. If one enquires into its practicality, one finds that it is nothing but the piling up of numerous technical phrases, making a game of words."[37]

The goverment's involvement with economic reconstruction offers apt illustration of this "game of words." The first systematic plan and budget for national economic development was drawn up in 1928 by Sun Fo in his capacity as minister of Railways. The next year, the Third Party Congress adopted its own plan, ''Definite Fixing of the Program and Budget for Material Reconstruction in the Period of Political Tutelage.'' Nothing having resulted from these plans, the Central Executive Committee of the party proposed in 1931 a new six-year Program for Material Reconstruction. Shortly afterwards, the newly instituted National Economic Council prepared its own three-year plan.

Besides these sundry schemes for nationwide development, other agencies independently prepared drafts for the development of specific sectors of the economy or areas of the nation. H. H. Kung had a ''Plan for Developing Basic Industries''; Ch'en Kung-po formulated a ''Four-Year Industrial Plan''; and Sun Fo returned to the bureaucratic arena with a new railroad plan. In addition, according to Gideon Chen (Ch'en Ch'i-t'ien), ''Practically every province has an economic plan, and very often more than one. Most of them are paper schemes and there is no co-ordination among the various provincial plans.''[38]

Most of these plans for the economic reconstruction of the nation were drawn up with little regard for questions of either administrative machinery or financial feasibility. Sun Fo's first plan, for example, called for an annual expenditure of ¥500 million—an amount equal almost exactly to the total annual budget of the government at that time.[39] T. V. Soong, seeing the proliferation of these rarified and impractical plans, remarked avuncularly, ''We have seen each department of the government proposing its own pet projects, all of them involving huge expenditures. Doubtless many of these projects are in themselves sound but they must be unrealizable because of the known lack of funds, and the fact that they are not coordinated with the projects of other departments.''[40]

Perhaps the classic example of the Kuomintang's administrative incompetence, however, was the New Life Movement. Initiated with enormous fanfare, the movement was viewed by the regime's leadership as a crucial means of attaining the nation's political, social, and economic regeneration. Despite the personal interest of the Generalissimo in the movement, it quickly degenerated into the bureaucratic "game of words." Three years after the movement had been inaugurated, Chiang Kai-shek pinpointed the administrative weaknesses of the movement:

This New Life Movement is a social movement, and cannot be accomplished with political methods—even less should one concern oneself only with writing bureaucratic essays and bureaucratic jargon (*teng-yin feng-tz'u*) to deal with the problems. We should know that changing [the nation's] customs cannot be accomplished with sheets of meaningless writing.

In our previous work, administration consisted of many slogans but little actual work, of many plans but little implementation; regarding the object of administration, attention was directed only to the upper strata of society, and it did not extend to the lower strata—attention was directed only to the thoroughfares and not to the sidestreets. Therefore, the result of three years of the New Life Movement has merely been a temporary and superficial renovation without attaining a fundamental reform.[41]

This assessment by Chiang Kai-shek of the New Life Movement reads like an epitaph for the Kuomintang and the Nationalist government.

Corruption

"The commonest conjugation in Chinese grammar," wrote Lin Yutang in 1935, "is that of the verb 'to squeeze': '*I squeeze, you squeeze, he squeezes, we squeeze, you squeeze, they squeeze.*' It is a regular verb."[42]

Squeeze, or corruption, may be roughly defined as the illegal appropriation of public resources for private purposes. Few Chinese of the Nanking period would have denied the existence of corruption in the Nationalist regime. But should corruption be viewed as a *negative* attribute of Kuomintang rule?

This is a real and difficult question. It is undoubtedly true that, during much of China's dynastic period, squeeze within not-easily-definable limits was accepted as a conventional perquisite of office. It can therefore be argued that to fault the Kuomintang for not eliminating official malfeasance is to apply Western standards of political conduct to a wholly different political tradition. Moreover, a revisionist school of political scientists has contended that corruption under certain conditions has positive benefits in modernizing societies. In capital-poor nations, corruption may facilitate capital formation that in turn is essential to economic growth; it may enable progressive-minded persons to cut through the thicket of red tape that impedes development in overly bureaucratized states; and it may help agents of modernization, such as members of the business community, to overcome discrimination by the bureaucrats.[43]

Despite these contentions, the following discussion premises that, as Gunnar Myrdal concluded in *Asian Drama,* corruption is "highly detrimental [to] the modernization ideals."[44] As even revisionist analysis of corruption concedes, malfeasance in office is a symptom of a lack of dedication by officials to the government and its ideals. And, when incorrupt officials see that corruption is not punished, there is an inexorable tendency for corruption to spread. In a society that places little moral stigma on corruption—as in traditional China—a moderate degree of corruption might have only mildly negative effects. Where a moral stigma does exist, however, the spread of corruption debilitates the administration, draining the bureaucracy of public spirit. In addition, corruption in such a society engenders popular cynicism toward and distrust of the government, thereby decreasing citizen cooperation with the government.

In Kuomintang China, the standards of political morality were changing, and at least some segments of society placed a high value on incorruptibility. Whatever economic or administrative benefits may have resulted from corruption tended, therefore, to be nullified by the political effects.

Hardly had the revolutionary government been established in Nanking before there were intimations that the new officials were beginning to enrich themselves by means of corruption.

As early as October 1927, for example, Ho Ying-ch'in stated, "Our party comrades still have a major weakness, which is that most harbor the thought of *sheng-kuan fa-ts'ai.*"[45]

It did not take long for these thoughts of *sheng-kuan fa-ts'ai* to be transformed into reality. George Sokolsky in November 1928 commented upon "the style of extravagance and luxury" that seemed to characterize the life style of party members. Officials, who had been virtually penniless before the revolution were soon wealthy enough to have beautiful residences erected for themselves in the capital city, and limousines bearing officials' children to school became a common sight. Most of the upper-level officials viewed Nanking as a cultural backwater, and they regularly fled the capital in favor of the amenities offered by Shanghai. Many of them built homes there in the foreign concessions and spent so much time in the city—"weekends" lasting from Friday to Tuesday were common—that people spoke of "government from Shanghai."[46]

Some of the officials became enormously wealthy. In 1932, it was reported that there were twenty-one depositors at the Shanghai K'uei-feng Bank with holdings of at least ¥20 million; of these, the great majority were officials or relatives of officials. Foreign banks also harbored the officials' richesse.[47] Many officials became major investors in industrial or other enterprises. They were, as H. D. Fong termed them, "the new Chinese capitalists." "Leaving moral questions aside," Fong stated with the pragmatic outlook of an economist, "without the horrible doings of these officials in many parts of China[,] capital probably would not have been accumulated to this day for any sort of industry going beyond the size of a small family workshop."[48]

High living and fat stock portfolios are, of course, only indirect evidences of corruption. Yet one may be forgiven if he agrees with Franklin Ho that, because "salaries of government and Party officials were not particularly high, one had to assume that inappropriate methods were employed to get money."[49] Corruption, by its very nature, is not susceptible of precise measurement, and it is possible that contemporaries exaggerated the extent of corruption during the decade. Without any question, corruption became infinitely greater during the 1940s. Yet, during the Nanking decade, corruption was already rampant. As one man, who has held secondary-level posts in the party for over forty years, remarked in 1969: "Corruption existed at all times, even in 1928 and 1929. This was natural . . . Among the revolutionaries only a small number were committed and incorrupt."[50]

Indeed, already in 1930 it was felt that corruption had become more extensive at all levels of government than it had been even under the warlord regimes in Peking.[51] And many observers thought that corruption was the single most corrosive feature in Nanking rule.[52] It was charged, for example, that the communist menace was in fact little more than a peasant reaction to the regime's corruption and maladministration. Rather than waging extermination campaigns to eliminate the communists, declared the *Ta-kung pao,* Nanking should: "Throughout the nation punish 10,000 [corrupt] civil and military officials."[53]

Few Chinese were more vocal in condemning the crippling effects of corruption than was Chiang Kai-shek. In 1930 he noted that corruption had already become pervasive. As a consequence, he said, "Most people regard us as a special class; nowhere do the masses regard us with good will."[54] In 1933 he returned to the theme, declaring that many officials "increase miscellaneous taxes without end, and corruption and extortion have become a common practice, causing the government to become rotten; the people cannot bear to live; and bandits naturally increase day by day."[55] Again, in 1934, Chiang spoke of the debilitating effects of the officials' striving for corruption: "Why is it that [the revolution] has not succeeded? The only reason is that our subjective conditions are imperfect . . . What is it that most people now call revolution? It is false! It is a pretense of revolution! These people are completely selfish, and what they call revolution is to *sheng-kuan fa-ts'ai!*"[56]

Official efforts to reduce the incidence of corruption had little or no effect. In almost every year of the decade, laws and regulations were issued that were designed to institutionalize restrictions on corruption.[57] These were often admirable expressions of intent, but—as in other areas of "paper government"—there was no administrative follow-through. Accounting offices were also instituted as a means of rationalizing and controlling the transmission of money within the bureaucracy. But Huang Shao-hung, who as provincial chairman established an accounting system in Chekiang in 1935–36, has testified that the system quickly became completely inoperable. It vastly increased the already excessive paper work in the province, it slowed down bureaucratic action even further, and the new system was itself not immune to corruption.[58]

The Control Yüan was constitutionally empowered to serve as the supreme watchdog of the bureaucracy, but it was equally ineffective in expunging corruption. Without real power, it had become a sinecure for ineffectual old men, ridiculed throughout the government as the "old-people's yüan" (*yang-lao yüan*).[59] From 1931, when it was established, through 1937, the Control Yüan was presented with cases of alleged corruption involving 69,500 officials. Of these, the Yüan returned indictments on only 1,800 persons.

This, however, was only half the story of the Control Yüan's efforts to fight corruption. For the Control Yüan served much the same function of a grand jury in the United States, and was not therefore empowered to punish those against whom it had brought indictments. It could only refer the cases of indictment to one of six organs that then placed the accused persons on trial.[60]

The road between indictment and punishment was therefore a long one, and there were innumerable opportunities for the cases to become sidetracked. As a consequence, of the 1,800 individuals indicted for corruption by the Control Yüan, only 268 were actually found guilty by the courts or other disciplinary agencies. And, of the 268 persons found guilty, 214 received no punishment whatsoever, and forty-one received merely a light punishment, such as a 10 percent reduction of salary. Only thirteen of the 268 guilty officials were actually dismissed from office.[61] Small wonder, therefore, that even the *Wen-hua chien-she* admitted that the government's efforts against corruption were a "paper tiger" and that no one feared them.[62]

Indeed, the entire system which was designed to impede and punish corruption was a laughing-stock, because it was felt that the only persons caught by it were the little men who did not have powerful friends. For example, nearly 70 percent of the officials indicted by the Control Yüan for whom there is information were hsien magistrates.[63] And, in the few instances when a high-ranking official was brought before the Control Yüan, it was regarded as a manifestation of a personal vendetta or a factional struggle. The most prominent case of this kind occurred in 1934 when the minister of Railways, Ku Meng-yü, was charged with misappropriation of funds. Although Ku may have been guilty, government insiders believed that the charges had been brought by Yü Yu-jen, head of the Control Yüan, as a means of attacking his bête noire, Wang Ching-wei. Wang proved to be too powerful, however, and the charges against Ku were dropped.[64]

Only when Chiang Kai-shek personally intervened, it seems, could stern measures be taken against corruption. In 1934, the Generalissimo ordered seven officials summarily shot for corruption. On another occasion, an official was brought to Chiang's Nanchang headquarters where he was charged with misappropriating funds from the "special tax"—a euphemism for the tax on opium which was allegedly Chiang Kai-shek's monopoly. The official was sentenced to die, but—as was customary in such cases—several divisional commanders interceded and seemingly dissuaded Chiang from carrying out the sentence. Shortly afterwards, however, just before he was leaving the headquarters for the front, Chiang signed the death warrant and had the official shot before his friends could again intervene.[65]

Yet Chiang's efforts to eliminate corruption were both spasmodic and selective. Indeed, he tolerated corruption among his most intimate advisers and even within his personal family. There is therefore cause to suspect that Chiang used his periodic crack-downs on corruption less as a means to eliminate it than as a device to control his subordinates. For the subordinates, most of whom were in some degree corrupt, had reason to fear that, if for any reason they lost the Generalissimo's goodwill, they were vulnerable to punishment for malfeasance in office. Even if Chiang's intentions were not so Machiavellian and if he was sincerely committed to wiping out corruption, he was bucking a huge and entrenched system. Broad-scale corruption therefore persisted throughout the Nanking period.

Political Repression

The rejoicing that the Chinese nation had felt at the Kuomintang victory in 1926–27 had turned into ashen disillusion by about mid-1929. By then, the revolutionary military victory was already a year old. The people could reasonably expect to discern some signs of recovery, of getting the nation back on its feet for the tasks of peaceful reconstruction. The revolutionary leadership had instead had a falling-out, fighting over their booty like a pack of thieves. And representatives of the regime—especially the *tang-pu,* or members of the party branches—confiscated properties, arbitrarily imprisoned opponents, and generally acted with the arrogance of conquerors. In the provinces, the *North China Herald* observed in February 1930, the "administration has brought unsparing odium on the Central Government. It would be difficult to exaggerate the harm which the Tang Pu have done to the cause of Nationalism among the people of China."[66] Chiang Kai-shek too remarked, "There are many places where *tang-pu* freely imprison persons, even to the point of ordering them to stand in wooden baskets . . . This is completely wrong!"[67]

For these and manifold other reasons, the signs of revolutionary failure—ineffectual administration, widespread corruption, and factional struggles—had been fully exposed by mid-1929. Thereafter, until at least 1934, public support for the Nanking rulers deteriorated even further. "Contrasted with the enthusiasm of less than eighteen months ago," the *North China Herald* wrote in May 1930, "the sense of hopelessness which one finds so commonly among all Chinese today is perhaps the worst feature of all."[68] And by mid-1933 a writer in the *Kuo-wen chou-pao* ("Kuo-wen Weekly") declared, "The masses unconcealedly dislike and detest the Kuomintang."[69] Indeed, Tsiang T'ing-fu (Chiang T'ing-fu) remarked in late-1935 that the prestige of the party had fallen so low that "the Kuomintang members are all embarrassed to admit publicly that they are party members."[70]

There was, perhaps, a degree of exaggeration in remarks such as these. Yet popular discontent had become so virulent that revolutionary sentiments were percolating against the regime. "The sound of dissatisfaction with party government," the *Ta-kung pao* editorialized in late 1933, "and the demand for revolution have in recent years filled the nation." "During the past five years . . . government and the economy have reached a dead end, and the people of the entire nation, above and below, frantically feel that they cannot live out the day . . . Now the people only hope for a true revolution to remove their sufferings."[71]

As a consequence of the Kuomintang's determination to hold on to power in the midst of popular resentment, political repression became a characteristic of Nanking's rule. Assassinations, midnight arrests, and summary executions became a common occurrence. In February 1931 twenty-three prisoners, alleged communists, were manacled and shot, some of them buried perhaps even before they died. Liu Yü-sheng, a newspaper editor, was imprisoned in mid-1932 and subsequently shot. The roll call of political prisoners mounted. Increasingly, the terror and the reportedly harsh treatment of prisoners stirred concern among the nation's intellectual elite. This concern crystallized in mid-December 1932, following the arrest of two prominent professors in Peiping, including the historian Hou Wai-lu, for alleged associations with the communists. During the ensuing month, the Chinese League for the Protection of Civil Rights was formed.[72]

The moving spirit and chairman of the league was Soong Ch'ing-ling, widow of Sun Yat-sen and an outspoken critic of her brother-in-law's, Chiang Kai-shek's, regime. Members in the league were drawn from a broad part of the political spectrum. Not only did avowed leftists like Lu Hsün, Harold Isaacs, and Agnes Smedley join, but Lin Yutang, Chiang Meng-lin, Li Chi, Tsou T'ao-fen, and the paladin of the liberals, Hu Shih, also became members. Ts'ai Yüan-p'ei, whom no one could suspect of communist sympathies, was chosen vice-chairman.

The league was particularly active in publicizing the treatment meted out to political prisoners. It published a letter from prisoners in Peiping that told of torturing by pouring petroleum and pepper into the prisoners' nostrils; by piercing the sexual organs with pig's bristles; or by suspending the prisoners by the hands—arms tied in back—from the ceiling.[73] Five prisoners implicated in sending this letter were shortly afterwards sentenced to death, and the *China Forum* claimed they were being executed for having exposed conditions in the prison. The accuracy of these reports of conditions in the prisons is uncertain. Hu Shih asserted that the charges were distorted—an assertion that led to bitter acrimony and ended in his being expelled from the league.[74]

In May 1933 the league's agitation came to full boil following the disappearance in Shanghai of the promising novelist Ting Ling and a companion, P'an Tzu-nien.[75] For weeks there was no word about the pair, and only gradually the rumor seeped out that P'an was in prison and that Ting Ling had been executed. (Actually, she had not been killed, but she remained under arrest—presumably without trial—for about two years.)

The activities of the league ended abruptly on a Sunday morning, June 18, 1933. Yang Ch'üan, secretary of the league, was leaving his office in the Academia Sinica to take his fourteen-year-old son for a ride. Hardly had he entered the car when four or five men in ambush let loose a fusillade of bullets. Yang, trying to shield his son, was killed. The chauffeur was seriously wounded, and the son was struck by a bullet in a leg. Yang had been marked as a target of the assassins, it was reported, because he had gathered information linking the Kuomintang Central Party Headquarters with the disappearance of Ting Ling.[76]

Soong Ch'ing-ling responded boldly to the situation. "These people and their hired murderers," she declared in a public statement, "think they can crush the slightest movement of struggle toward freedom by sheer force of violence, kidnapping, torture, murder—these are the weapons of their rule. They signalize and characterize the entire regime. The China League for Civil Rights represents one such movement and it was because of his activities in this organization that Yang was murdered in cold blood. But far from crushing us, the penalty he paid for his liberalism must mean renewed struggle and renewed efforts to carry on . . . Let the murderers of Yang Chuan realize that political crimes inevitably carry with them their own penalties."[77]

Soong Ch'ing-ling's words were overly optimistic, for force did crush the league. And, during the following years, the nation was exposed to political repression such as had not been seen since the bloody days of 1927. A few months after Yang's murder, Lu Hsün wrote that "the political atmosphere is still one of aimless terror." The following year, in 1934, Lu recorded that "the white terror in Shanghai gets worse day by day. Of many young people who are taken away there is no further word. I am still living at home. I don't know whether it is because they have no clue [where I am] or because they think I am too old and therefore don't want me."[78] Others were less fortunate, and the murders and arrests continued.

Schools and universities were especially hard hit. The regime, having witnessed the political potential of the student movement during the Manchurian crisis of 1931–32, and con-

vinced that communist activitists had served as agitators and
organizers of the movement, determined to bring the students
into line. Government informers permeated student bodies,
and the students were terrorized by the surprise searches,
sudden disappearances of fellow students, and mass arrests.
No one knows accurately how many students were imprisoned
during the 1930s, but the number surely ran to one, and
perhaps several, thousand.[79] The *Ta-kung pao,* usually moderate in its judgments, became so perturbed by the government's repression of the students that in December 1934 it
gave vent to impassioned rhetoric:

Now there are truly too many youth who are imprisoned because
of their thought and speech. (Oh pity! The thought of children! The
speech of children!) The authorities do not understand that fetters
and handcuffs and jail-life are not the means to reform the thought of
youth. The youth suspect that the government is no good, and you
then come with fetters and handcuffs, and prove that the government
is no good. The youth suspect that the law is no good, and you come
with military verdicts and confused evidence, and prove that the law
is really no good.[80]

The regime sought to control not only the actions but the
thought of the people. Censorship of the press, therefore,
became another prominent feature of political life during the
decade. Since the Enlightenment in Europe, freedom of the
press and freedom of expression have been shibboleths of the
liberals. In practice, however, every society has experienced a
felt need to impose some limitations on these freedoms—
whether to obstruct personal libel, to protect the minds of the
young from salacious literature, or to prevent the spread of
political doctrines and subversive criticisms that might en-
danger its existence. In China of the 1930s, the concept of
freedom of expression was a recent import from the West,
firmly held by a few and bandied about by many. It was,
however, a frail transplant, devoid of vitality; and the Nanking government's impulses to restrict the freedom of the
press were restrained by few real compunctions resulting
from that concept.

Censorship had begun during the purges of 1927, when the ruling Kuomintang clique sought not only to eradicate the communist organization but to eliminate the "vicious thoughts of communism, root and source."[81] The hand of the censor reached not only to communist writings but to all publications that diverged ideologically from, or that were critical of, the leadership in Nanking. Publications of the Reorganization Clique, which supported Wang Ching-wei, were particularly hard hit by Nanking's press censorship: in September 1928 the *Ko-ming p'ing-lun* (Revolutionary critic) was forced to cease publication, and it was soon followed by other pro-Wang journals such as the *Hsin-shih-tai yüeh-k'an* (New era monthly), the *Chien-t'ao* (Commentary) and the *Ko-ming chan-hsien* (Revolutionary front).[82] Even the British-owned *North China Daily News* felt the effects of the press censorship. The *Daily News* had reported that Nanking troops had suffered losses during fighting in north China. The government declared that this report was false, and that the paper was fabricating these rumors in order to create dissension and sabotage the revolutionary military advance. The *Daily News* was printed in a foreign concession, so that the government was unable to prevent the paper from being printed; it did, however, revoke the paper's postal privileges.[83]

Censorship prior to 1930 was relatively light-handed and sporadic. There was a variety of administrative orders and miscellaneous laws, such as the Regulations for Punishing Counter-Revolutionaries, that could be invoked to censor a publication. But the organization of censorship was haphazard. As a result, there was now a strong infusion of communist doctrinal and literary writings into China. "Translations from Russian authors," Lin Yutang recalled, "flooded the magazine and book market during these years, before Nanking rubbed its eyes and woke up to the situation."[84]

A comprehensive Press Law was not published until December 1930. This was a detailed document consisting of forty-four articles, yet it was so vague in some of its most critical provisions that the censors were provided an almost unlimited latitude of interpretation. Article Nineteen, for example, proscribed publications that attacked the Kuomintang or its principles, were inimical to the interests of the nation, endangered public peace and order, or were prejudicial to good morals.[85]

Armed with the authority of the Press Law, the censors mounted a full-scale assault on the nation's publishing industry. Between 1929 and 1936, 458 literary works were banned, usually under the charge that they advocated class struggle, slandered the authorities, or were "proletarian literature." Foreign authors on the banned list included John Dos Passos, Theodore Dreiser, Bertrand Russell, Gorki, and Upton Sinclair.[86] In 1936, the Central Publicity Bureau of the party listed 676 publications in the social sciences that had been proscribed.[87] Altogether, there were approximately 1,800 books and journals banned during the decade.[88]

There were, in addition, innumerable individual newspaper items that provoked the censors' displeasure. Examples of banned stories were the assassination attempt on T. V. Soong in 1931; the announcement that Salvador had extended diplomatic recognition to Manchukuo; and a factory strike in Shanghai. The main text of the economic report of the technical cooperation group of the League of Nations was also initially censored.[89] The *Min-sheng pao* (People's livelihood) of Nanking incurred official displeasure for publishing a news agency report that Chiang Kai-shek had attempted to mediate the dispute between Wang Ching-wei and Yü Yu-jen over the Control Yüan's impeachment of Ku Meng-yü. This report had passed one of the censoring organs and had also been published in several other newspapers. Despite this, the *Min-sheng pao* was suspended indefinitely and the editor was imprisoned.[90] In other instances, excessively cautious censors suppressed news emanating from the government itself. The classic case of this kind occurred in 1935. A censor banned a statement that had been issued by a government spokesman for the specific purpose of publicizing the Chinese explanation of Sino-Japanese clashes that had occurred in north China.[91]

Legally, the government imposed no restrictions on press exposés of government corruption or maladministration. Indeed, Chiang Kai-shek had even urged the press to do so.[92] Attempts by the press to take on the role of guardian of the public interest were, nevertheless, repeatedly rebuffed. To cite only one case, the *Shang-pao* (Commercial news) had charged that a judge had received bribes in a trial. For this, the editor of the paper was brought to court and charged with "hampering the conduct of public affairs."[93]

The limitations on the publishing world, so narrow as a result of domestic political concerns, were made even more stringent as a result of Japanese pressure. As Chinese enmity toward the Japanese mounted and as the Japanese became increasingly watchful, however, it was difficult for the press to avoid bruising Japanese sensitivities. In one prominent case, a writer for the *Hsin-sheng chou-k'an* (New life weekly) had stated that the emperor of Japan did not wield real power and that the actual rulers of Japan were the army and the capitalists. This seeming trifle proved to be terribly embarrassing to Nanking, because the offending article had passed through the censor, thereby enabling the Japanese to charge that the Nanking government had colluded in this monstrous slight on the Japanese imperial dignity. The episode became a *cause célèbre,* and was settled only after Nanking dismissed seven censors and the editor of *Hsin-sheng chou-k'an* was sentenced, without right of appeal, to fourteen months in prison.[94]

Foreign correspondents were also subjected to the censors' scrutiny, and they complained that restrictions on the press were far worse in China than in Japan. H. J. Timperley, correspondent for the *Christian Science Monitor,* noted that the Japanese had cut out less than 500 words from the dispatches of a leading United States news agency during the period 1932–1936; in China, by contrast, censors elided more than four times that number of words by that same agency during the far briefer period of the spring and early summer 1933. A foreign correspondent felt fortunate, Timperley said, if one out of three of his dispatches got past the censor. The most irritating and frustrating tactic of the Chinese censors was to rewrite the correspondents' articles, often completely changing the meaning. But the journalists would not learn of these alterations until several weeks later—long after the materials had been published.[95]

Paradoxically, the Chinese press is a principal source of criticism of censorship as well as of Kuomintang rule generally. There are several reasons for this paradox, the most notable perhaps being the fact that the Press Law could have no impact beyond the effective authority of Nanking. In north China, for example, the papers of Peiping and Tientsin—such as the *Ta-kung pao, Kuo-wen chou-pao,* and *Tu-li p'ing-lun* (Independent critic)—scourged Nanking with relative impunity. And the press of Canton, although careful not to run afoul of Ch'en Chi-t'ang, freely commented on the failings of Nanking.[96] No less important, Chinese authority could not, legally at least, reach into the foreign concessions. The umbrella of the unequal treaties consequently protected numerous newspapers and periodicals, although the censors could and frequently did revoke the postal privileges of these publications.

Administration of the censorship system also contributed to the uneven effect of the press laws. The Ministry of the Interior was formally charged with the responsibility for registration and censorship of publications and movies. In practice, however, supervision of the system rested with the Central Publicity Department of the party. Moreover, the actual administration was decentralized, and miscellaneous party, government, and military agencies shared the responsibilities.[97] The censors were seldom well qualified, sometimes being poorly educated and lacking either the knowledge or the sensitivity to judge the propriety of news reportage. And, being bureaucrats, the censors were more acutely attuned to the fear of approving a dispatch that might incur the displeasure of some superior than they were to the ideal of a responsibly free national press. As a consequence, it was remarked, "the average censor is rather inclined to suppress too much than too little."[98] The plight of the press in the hands of the censors was poignantly revealed in late 1934 when the leading newspapers and news agencies in north China petitioned the Kuomintang not to abolish censorship, but simply to adhere to the existing laws. The petition asked, in addition, that journalists and editors then in prison be brought to legal trial.[99]

Censorship resulted in a bewildering proliferation of periodical publications, some of them lasting two or three months, or perhaps only one or two weeks, before they were banned by the censors. In some cases, the publishers or editors were imprisoned, but in many instances they simply started a new journal under a different title. Tsou T'ao-fen, for example, founded three periodicals and one newspaper between November 1935 and December 1936, none of which survived more than three months.[100]

A less palpable but more serious consequence of censorship was the effect it had on the tone of the nation's political and intellectual life. Here we must guard against exaggeration. We should perhaps be skeptical of the charges, common in the press, that censorship was the chief reason that China did not have a developed public opinion and a politically concerned population. Yet one does sit up and take notice when the *Shih-tai kung-lun,* a periodical published at Nanking National University by a group of professors who were Kuomintang members and closely identified with the CC clique, ceased to publish on its own volition because of censorship. "There is no freedom of speech," the valedictory editoral read. "And we do not wish to speak out words we do not believe. Because we cannot discuss national affairs, we cannot find topics to write about, and are therefore stopping."[101]

The most trenchant comment on the effects of Nanking's censorship, however, came from the official organ of the party itself. In fact, the *Chung-yang jih-pao* (Central daily news) seldom printed editorials, but in November 1935 the editors had become so frustrated that they set aside a large space for an editorial denouncing the government's control of the press. "Such an irrational system of censorship is completely demoralizing," it declared, "and, if continued, the Chinese will become a nation of deaf and dumb people. How can a deaf and dumb nation organize a State and exist on earth?"[102]

Chapter 2 The Blue Shirts and Fascism

Factionalism is endemic in Chinese politics. Inevitably, therefore, the Kuomintang's quest for a political system was
marked by the rivalries and jealousies of cliques and factions.
Chiang Kai-shek was not wholly inimical to this form of
political competition. Indeed, like an emperor of old, he sometimes fostered these divisions. Under the dynasties, emperors
had frequently attempted to circumscribe the power of the
civil officials by establishing aristocrats, eunuchs, or some
other non-literati class to serve as a counterbalance to the
bureaucracy.[1] Whether or not Chiang Kai-shek was aware of
this precedent, it was the technique that he adopted after he
became aware that "the revolution has failed." For Chiang
turned to a group of young army officers, graduates of the
Whampoa Academy, in search of a force that could discipline
the civil administration and revitalize the party. This group
was the Blue Shirts.

The Blue Shirts became one of the most influential—and
feared—political movements in China during the 1930s. To
both contemporaries and historians, however, the Blue Shirt
movement has been a shadowy force, known mostly through
hearsay, with little solid information regarding its doctrine or

its activities. Now, on the basis of memoirs, interviews and especially Japanese intelligence reports of the 1930s, a rough picture of this secret organization can be pieced together. And the image that emerges is not simply a terroristic organization, but a political faction that reflected the concerns and ideals of many Chinese during the troubled Nanking decade.

Origins of the Movement

The origins of the Blue Shirts are found in the ill-fortuned months of the summer and autumn of 1931. Leadership of the regime was in unprecedented disarray. Chiang Kai-shek, chairman of the government and head of the Executive Yüan, had put the widely respected Hu Han-min under house arrest. And Wang Ching-wei, Sun Fo, and a host of other party notables had formed a separatist government in Canton. In five provinces along the Yangtze and Huai Rivers, devastating floods spread suffering and starvation, and Nanking proved to be incapable of organizing meaningful relief to the stricken people. On September 18 the Japanese began their occupation of Manchuria, meeting virtually no Chinese resistance.

Provoked by the seemingly hapless decline of the Kuomintang, Liu Chien-ch'ün—a thirty-year-old party member and secretary to General Ho Ying-ch'in—dashed off an eighty-seven-page essay entitled "A Few Ideas for Reform of the Kuomintang."[2] Liu's loyalties to Chiang Kai-shek were unquestioned—in contrast to opponents of Nanking who hoped to replace Chiang—and this fact added punch to his condemnation of the party that Chiang headed.

"Our party," Liu declared, "now seems to have dissipated the hopes of the masses! Not only has it become remote from the masses, but in many places it is simply hated by the masses!" Liu did not attribute this loss of popular support to the machinations of the communists nor to the oppression of the imperialists. The blame rested squarely on the Kuomintang. "We must admit," he stated, "that the complete lack of political and military solutions has resulted from the failure of the party." The Kuomintang was no longer a revolutionary organization; its members had ceased to struggle for the salvation of the nation or the well-being of the people; and there had been no meaningful achievements. "There is," he said, "only the name of the party, but one cannot see the work of the party."

In Liu's view, the Kuomintang was immobilized by capitalism and bureaucratism. The party was merely an arena where warlords and bureaucrats fought for power and the harvest of corruption.

What we now see between the leaders and party members [wrote Liu] is simply mutual utilization and indifference. The party leaders do not differentiate between those who are loyal and true party members and those who are not . . . And the members simply use the leaders in order to attain their personal goal of *sheng-kuan fa-ts'ai*. If only these members give voice support to the leaders' slogans, then they are regarded as loyal and true comrades. Even if the members do harm to society the leaders pay no attention . . . And, with regard to the relationships between party members, this even more causes one's teeth to turn cold. For the so-called comrades do not even love each other as much as do fellow-students or fellow-villagers.

Advancement within the ranks of the Kuomintang was not commensurate with one's loyalty to the revolution or to the principles of the party. Instead, he asserted—and one wonders to what extent this criticism was prompted by jealousy— the highest positions were occupied by powerful warlords and opportunistic politicians. "If you have not given attention to personal relationships (*jen-ch'ing*)—even though you have good ideas and actions—you will fall back in the ranks."

Liu rejected the view that the weaknesses of the Kuomintang were superficial, and that the regime could be regenerated merely by purging its corrupt members and by reorganizing the existing party. To the contrary, "We firmly believe that the turmoil of the party, the impotence of the party, the decadence of the party, are problems not of individuals, but problems of poor methods, an imperfect system, and of insubstantial content (*nei-jung pu ch'ung-shih*)."

Liu Chien-ch'ün wished that the existing party could be completely scrapped, and that in its place the true revolutionaries could create an entirely new organization. He recognized, however, that this would be impracticable: "For reasons of history and legitimacy, and because we do not want to provoke a great quarrel if at all avoidable, we advocate preserving the old shell of the party, but in addition organizing within the party a corps devoted to the common people of the nation that will give substance to the party and create the party's soul." Liu Chien-ch'ün would thus suffer the existence of the old Kuomintang but would deprive it of the substance of power. He proposed that at least two-thirds of the membership of the Central Executive Committee be composed of personnel of that special corps. And, of the ordinary Kuomintang members in the Central Executive Committee, one-half would be overseas Chinese. The old Kuomintang structure would not, then, be altered by the formation of the special corps, but the character of the organization would be transformed by placing effective power in the hands of a new revolutionary elite.

The special corps envisioned by Liu would consist of persons single-mindedly committed to the revolution. They would be men prepared to sacrifice everything for the nation and the masses; material well-being would hold no attraction for them. They would also discard such "feudal" relationships as that of the family, recognizing that "their relationship with their comrades superseded everything . . . and is many times deeper than the love for one's brothers or relatives."

The most important proposal in the essay, Liu told me in 1969, was to impose stringent limitations on the amount of personal property that could be owned by a member of the corps. Recruits to the elite organization would be required to give all their property in excess of a stipulated value to the corps; should they subsequently accumulate property beyond that value, they would be severely punished. At the same time, the financial needs of the corps member—the education of his children, medical treatment, care of his aged parents, and security in his own old age—would be met by the corps for the rest of his life. In this way, Liu declared, the member "absolutely cannot become rich (*fa-ts'ai*), nor can he ever go hungry." By precluding both the possibility and the motive for material enrichment, Liu thought that he had discovered the formula that would guarantee the unqualified revolutionary devotion of the elite, and that would prevent the reemergence of the old Kuomintang's most debilitating disease, corruption.

The unceasing factional strife within the Kuomintang after the death of Sun Yat-sen was another of Liu's primary concerns in proposing a reform of the party. Sounding like a Confucian expounding on the need for a sagely ruler, Liu declared, "If the leader is good, then the revolutionary enterprise that he leads will quickly progress; if the leader is not good, then the revolutionary enterprise that he leads can hardly avoid taking a wrong course." In China, no leader of preeminent spiritual qualities had yet won over the whole of the party or gained the trust of the masses, as had Gandhi in India or Mussolini in Italy. Liu was convinced, nevertheless, that China's long tradition of autocratic rulers and absence of social cohesion meant that a superior man must and would emerge to guide the revolutionary movement. The subsequent endeavors of the Blue Shirts to elevate Chiang Kai-shek to the role of dictator were a result of this conviction.

Chiang Kai-shek was in fundamental agreement with Liu's assessment of the Kuomintang. In November 1931 he admitted, "The revolution is in danger of failing, and the entire nation has gradually lost trust in this party."[3] But he was unable to act immediately on Liu's suggestion that an elite group band together to create a soul for the dispirited Kuomintang, because he was engulfed in a political crisis of major proportions. Following the Japanese attack on Manchuria, the separatist government in Canton had exploited the emotional popular demand for national unity in the face of Japanese aggression and declared that it would become reconciled with Nanking only on the condition that Chiang leave the government. Chiang finally bowed to these pressures, perhaps convinced that the regime could not long continue without his participation. He resigned his governmental posts on December 15, 1931.[4]

During the ensuing six weeks of enforced "retirement," Chiang laid the foundations of the Blue Shirts. At Hangchow he called together a small group of young army officers in whose loyalty he had absolute confidence. He ordered them to consult with Liu Chien-ch'ün and to form an organization similar to the special corps proposed in Liu's essay.[5] He stipulated, in addition, that the following principles guide the organizers of the new group: Chiang Kai-shek should be the permanent highest leader; graduates of the Whampoa Academy should serve as the leading cadre, with future expansion to form around that nucleus; and the Three People's Principles should be implemented, using "communist organizational methods" and adding the spirit of (as one source says) bushido or (according to another source) fascism.[6]

Chiang returned to Nanking on January 21, 1932, and became a member (and, shortly thereafter, chairman) of the newly formed military commission on the twenty-ninth—the day after the Japanese assault on Shanghai. Subsequently he held further meetings in Nanking with his disciples. And by March—or, at the very latest, April—the organization that became known as the Blue Shirts was formally, albeit secretly, instituted.[7]

The leading cadre of the new organization became known as the "Thirteen Princes" (*shih-san t'ai-pao*). This term has caused considerable confusion, for it has frequently been assumed that it referred to exactly thirteen persons. In the T'ang Dynasty, it is true, the appellation had applied to the thirteen favorites of an influential military commander, all of whom had been ennobled as *t'ai-pao*.[8] In the 1930s, the term referred loosely to the group of young and devoted followers of Chiang Kai-shek—numbering somewhere between nine and eighteen—who played leading roles in the new organization.[9]

Of the eighteen thus mentioned, all of them but one—Liu Chien-ch'ün—were graduates of Whampoa. And, of these, all but two—Tai Li and K'ang Tse (both of whom will appear prominently in the following pages)—had been cadets in the first two classes at the academy.

The large proportion of Whampoa graduates in the leadership of the Blue Shirts—a plurality that was maintained but that became less overwhelming as the organization grew—resulted from Chiang Kai-shek's long and intimate relationship with the Whampoa Military Academy. Sun Yat-sen had appointed him to be commandant of the new academy, which began instruction in May 1924. Chiang retained this post even after he became chairman of the national government; it was, however, with the first three classes, whose training he had personally directed, that he developed especially close ties.

The cadets of the academy developed the famous "Whampoa spirit"; they became known as fearless fighters and many of them gave up their lives in the revolutionary battles of the 1920s. Particularly famed for their dedication and selflessness were the first three classes. They had enrolled in the academy when military service with the Kuomintang offered not the prospect of comfortable careers but only the opportunity to fight and perhaps die for the revolution. The cadets in these early classes received the mere rudiments of military training, but those who survived the wars of the 1920s displayed an *esprit* and selflessness that won them the admiration of the nation.[10]

But the idyll of Whampoa was not complete. The academy was inevitably affected by the tensions and conflicts that buffeted the Kuomintang as a whole during these crucial years. During 1925, two groups were formed that tended to polarize the ideological differences within the academy. One group of cadets, using pro-communist publications (such as *The ABC of Communism, Hsiang-tao* [The guide], and *Hsin ch'ing-nien* [New youth]) as their ideological weather vane, first formed the Young Soldiers Association (Ch'ing-nien chün-jen lien-ho hui). In turn, a Sunist Study Association (Sun

Wen chu-i hsüeh-she) was organized by anti-communist cadets—Ho Chung-han being prominent among them—using the writings of Sun Yat-sen and the recently published expositions of Sun's thought by Tai Chi-t'ao to combat the propaganda of the leftist cadets. To impede the divisive tendencies among his students, Chiang in May 1926 ordered both these groups disbanded, and in their place he organized a single Whampoa Students Association (Huang-p'u t'ung-hsüeh hui).[11]

The ties between Chiang and many of the Whampoa cadets involved the deep personal commitment and mutual loyalty of a Chinese master and his disciples. Long after graduating from the academy they continued to refer to Chiang as *hsiao-chang* (head of the school) instead of as chairman (*wei-yüan chang*) or director-general (*tsung-ts'ai*) as did other officers or Kuomintang officials.[12] This signified the profound and unique relationship they maintained with Chiang. Even so, Chiang could not long maintain harmony among the cadets. Ch'en Kung-po wrote in 1929, "I still remember last year when Chiang addressed the Whampoa students saying that within five years, with the strength of Whampoa, he could unify China. Later several of these students came to see me in Shanghai and asked me my opinion about this. I replied that I was afraid this would not come to pass, for Chiang himself could not unify Whampoa!"[13] Many Whampoa graduates did "defect" to anti-Chiang forces during the following years, some (like Lin Piao) becoming prominent in the communist movement. The majority of them, however, remained loyal to Chiang.[14]

The Ideology of Chinese Fascism

It is impossible to comprehend the Blue Shirt phenomenon, or to fathom the motives of the movement's leaders, unless one realizes the depths of desperation and humiliation plumbed by politically alert Chinese in the 1930s. To them it seemed that their world was crumbling around them. So humiliated had China been during the past century, so abortive had been the repeated efforts to create an effective political system, that some intellectuals were wondering aloud if Chinese were as intelligent as other people.[15] This was a critical period in Chinese history, and many Chinese realized that uncommon measures were needed to rescue the nation and the race from obliteration.

To the Blue Shirts, fascism appeared to be the method that could preserve China. The Chinese officer corps had been richly exposed to fascist influences since late 1928, when a German military advisory mission was created in Nanking. Colonel Max Bauer, who led the mission from November 1928 to May 1929, had close ties with Hitler and the German Nazi movement, and many of his subordinates in the mission had been selected at least partially because they shared his political predilections. Bauer died in May 1929, but he was succeeded by an extraordinarily ardent Nazi, Lieutenant-Colonel Herman Kriebel. Kriebel had marched in the front rank with Hitler during the famed Beer Hall Putsch of 1923. And during his subsequent imprisonment, he had shared Hitler's prison cell. There is little information on precisely how Bauer, Kriebel, and other Nazis in the advisory mission propagated fascist ideas. Because they virtually dominated education in the military academies by 1929, however, they had unique opportunities to implant their political views among the army elite. Moreover, a sizable number of Chinese officers after 1928 went abroad to study (in 1930 alone, 176 went abroad); most of these went to Germany, while some of the others studied in Italy.[16] Hitler's rise to power gave a further impetus to the Chinese fascist movement. Not surprisingly, therefore, many Chinese after 1933 thought the world would soon be dominated by fascism, and translations of fascist writings now acquired a fresh fascination.[17]

Chiang Kai-shek, too, was intrigued by the fascist phenomenon. He had, no doubt, learned something about fascism from the German advisers and from the young officers who had studied in Europe. After the founding of the Blue Shirt organization, however, he sought to learn more. In August

1932 one of the military advisers wrote in these terms to a Nazi leader in Germany:

> His Excellency Chiang Kai-shek has shown great interest in the development of the national-socialist movement, and he tries to obtain material on the entire organization of our party through his agents. One point is especially important to him: how our party leadership succeeds to maintain such strict discipline among its followers and to take harsh measures against dissidents or opponents, and does all this with such success. The material he wants to have does not only deal with the SA but with the whole party.

Not long afterwards, Chiang secretly dispatched two officers to Germany to study Nazi methods of organization and operation, and to consult with high-level Nazi leaders.[18]

These contacts, together with the growing national power of Germany and Italy, made Chiang an enthusiastic admirer of fascism. Addressing a gathering of Blue Shirts in about 1935, he declared, "What China needs today is not an ism that discusses what kind of ideal future China will have, but a method that will save China at the present moment." "Fascism," he continued, "is a stimulant for a declining society . . . Can fascism save China? We answer: yes. Fascism is what China now most needs." Concluding this speech, Chiang proclaimed that "At the present stage of China's critical situation, fascism is a wonderful medicine exactly suited to China, and the only spirit that can save it."[19]

To many Chinese in the 1930s, fascism did not appear as a pernicious or retrogressive doctrine. On the contrary, it appeared to be at the very forefront of historical progress. Parliamentary government had been attempted in China since 1912, and with obviously tragic consequences. And, throughout the world, democracy and laissez-faireism were being rejected in favor of one-man or one-party dictatorships. To the Blue Shirts, it seemed idiotic to reject a system that had proven to be effective in Italy and Germany in favor of a governmental system that had manifestly outlived its historical utility. This attitude of the Blue Shirts was summed up by the *She-hui hsin-wen* ("The Society Mercury"), which editorialized that "Fascism is the only tool of self-salvation of nations on the brink of destruction . . . There is no solution [for China] other than imitating the fascist spirit of violent struggle as in Italy and Germany."[20] And Liu Chien-ch'ün, reminiscing in 1969, remarked that "Fascism is now thought to be backward (*lo-hou*). But then it seemed to be a very progressive means of resurrecting the nation."[21]

In the Blue Shirt ideology, this goal of resurrecting the nation was exalted above all other values. The Blue Shirt "program" (*kang-ling*) stipulated that "The nation is supreme and sacred, and the member's sole duty is to pledge himself to protect the national interest."[22] The appeal of fascism to the Blue Shirts was that it too glorified the nation and, moreover, seemingly provided a proven method of creating a strong and great nation. Fascism, remarked a correspondent to the *She-hui hsin-wen* "is the most positive, most courageous, most forceful, concrete manifestation of the national spirit."[23] And Ch'en Ch'iu-yün in the *Ch'ien-t'u* (Future) declared, "The organization of a strong nation and the establishment of a strong government: this is the first principle of fascism."[24]

The Blue Shirts' total exaltation of the nation was matched by their total abnegation of the individual. Ho Chung-han, who was perhaps the dominant figure in the Blue Shirt oligarchy beneath Chiang Kai-shek, called for the people to relinquish their freedom and even their lives so that the nation might be free. Only then, he said, could one speak of "true freedom."[25] The *She-hui hsin-wen* proclaimed it a "heavenly principle" for the individual to serve and sacrifice for the nation.[26] The Blue Shirt goal was the totalitarian one of the unqualified submission of the individual to the nation. He was to "perform his duties without speaking of his rights." Naturally, he would benefit if the nation became rich and strong. "But the individual definitely cannot impose conditions on society before serving."[27]

The fascist principle of obedience to a supreme leader was an integral part of the Blue Shirt ideology. The Blue Shirt "program" read: "Chiang Kai-shek is the Kuomintang's only supreme leader and also China's only great leader; therefore, members must absolutely support him, follow his orders only, and make his will their own."[28] And Ho Chung-han reportedly remarked, "Obedience to the leader is unconditional; one must live and die with him, sincerely, unwaveringly."[29]

The Blue Shirts' esteem of the leadership principle may be contrasted with their loathing for democracy. In their eyes, the political impotence of China since the Revolution of 1911 and the current disarray in the Kuomintang were largely consequences of attempts to implant democratic institutions and practices. "In the last several decades," Chiang Kai-shek complained, "we have in vain become drunk with democracy and the advocacy of free thought. And what has been the result? We have fallen into a chaotic and irretrievable situation."[30] And an article in the *She-hui hsin-wen* declared that "the inherited poison of democracy has produced the diffuse and powerless organization of the present Kuomintang."[31] Even the committee system, which was derived from the Soviet Russian model and then ostensibly employed within the Kuomintang, was unsatisfactory. "The greatest defect of the committee system," Liu Chien-ch'ün charged, "is that everyone makes excuses, and blames one another, and thereby dissipates the party's internal strength . . . In revolutionary reconstruction, no one acts . . . ; as soon as a meeting is called, there are disagreements. The number of civil wars is almost in direct ratio to the number of meetings."[32]

The Blue Shirt ideal was a society displaying perfect coordination between the will of the leader and the actions of the people; there were to be no inefficiencies, no hesitations, but only dedicated and thoughtless obedience. "Salvation for China today," Ch'en Ch'iu-yün stated in the *Ch'ien-t'u,* "can be attained only through selflessly organizing, obeying the leader, trusting the policies of the leader, and implementing the leader's orders. When the myriad masses are of one mind, their actions as one body . . . Truly besides this there is no other way."[33]

To attain this social and political ideal, there must be a leader possessed of saintly qualities—"a firm and glorious spirit, a pure and exalted person, a man with a thorough understanding of the military and the government."[34] The *She-hui hsin-wen* admitted that "the youth of China since May Fourth [1919] have developed anarchistic ideas and have emphasized individualism, considering veneration of an idol as backward. But this is wrong, because an idol serves the important function of strengthening the power of social organization, promotes the development of national culture, and unifies the trust of the mass spirit." Therefore, the editorial concluded, "the establishment of a central idol (*chung-hsin ou-hsiang*) is the important condition of a unified Kuomintang, and the first step toward resurrecting China. *We must not disguise that we demand China's Mussolini, demand China's Hitler, demand China's Stalin!*"[35]

What did Chiang Kai-shek, the man designated to become the "central idol" of the nation, think of this movement to enshrine one man as the omnipotent and supreme leader? In a speech delivered in September 1933 to a group of party cadre in Kiangsi, he asserted:

The most important point of fascism is absolute trust in a sagely, able leader. Aside from complete trust in one person, there is no other leader or ism. Therefore, within the organization, although there are cadre, council members, and executives, there is no conflict among them; there is only the trust in the one leader. The leader has final decision in all matters.

Now we in China do not have one leader. I believe that, unless everyone has absolute trust in one man, we cannot reconstruct the nation and we cannot complete the revolution . . .

Therefore, the leader will naturally be a great person and possess a revolutionary spirit, so that he serves as a model for all party members. Furthermore, each member must sacrifice everything, acting directly for the leader and the group, and indirectly for society, the nation, and the revolution. From the day we joined this revolutionary group we completely entrusted our rights, life, liberty, and happiness to the group, and pledged them to the leader . . . Thus for the first time we can truly be called Fascists.[36]

Publicly, Chiang was to deny that he held any ambitions to be dictator.[37] But these remarks clearly were not intended to forestall such an eventuality.

The ultimate cause of the failure of the Nationalist revolution, the Blue Shirts contended, had been the disintegration of the nation's culture. They believed, therefore, that cultural renovation would have to precede military or politial regeneration of the nation. Chang Yün-fu wrote in the *Ch'ien-t'u,* "The rise and fall of the nation is in direct ratio to the flourishing and decline of the culture. If we do not first establish a new national culture, then the restoration of the nation can hardly succeed."[38] And Ju Ch'un-p'u expressed the view that culture determines the character of all human behavior. "Cultural control," he asserted, "is the crux of social, political, educational, and indeed of all activity . . . It is the soul of national restoration. It has a mystical quality that causes everyone unknowingly to be under its control."[39]

Unlike Chinese conservatives of the nineteenth century, the Blue Shirts did not wish simply to reject Westernization in favor of the traditional culture. Indeed, Chang Yün-fu argued that the self-satisfaction, superstition, passivity, and individualism that had ripened under conditions in the rural areas were unsuited to the "scientific age." True, he admitted that the four traditional virtues of *li, i, lien,* and *ch'ih* (then serving as the moral basis of the New Life Movement) were eternally valid. However, "everything else in our traditional culture . . . must be changed, corrected, or reformed."[40]

Nevertheless, the Blue Shirts thought the pernicious influences of Western culture were the root cause of China's moral and cultural bankruptcy. They particularly execrated the concept of liberalism which had poisoned Chinese minds since the May Fourth Movement. Liberalism—literally, "freedomism" (*tzu-yu chu-i*)—carried a variety of connotations to different Chinese, but to the Blue Shirts it meant unrestrained

license. Liberalism meant political freedoms and hum
And liberalism meant—worst of all—individualism,
caused the people to yield to their personal whims and t
no heed to the overriding needs of society at large.

Everywhere the Blue Shirts discerned the baneful effec
Western liberalism. It filled the novels, plays, and newspa
with a decadent passivism. Literature was filled with a di
tionless romanticism and "humor-ism," and artists indul
in a solipsistic art-for-art's-sake. Among ordinary peop
liberalism was revealed in lives of decadent frivolity a
sybaritic consumption. Chang Yün-fu complained that st
dents in Shanghai spent their time in brothels and dance hal
rather than in the libraries, while the coeds majored in cos
metics and strange forms of dress. And Liu Ping-li, editor o
the *Ch'ien-t'u,* declaimed against young men in the city who
spent ¥3,000 in an evening courting their lovers. The money
they spent, he said, would support 30,000 peasants for a whole
day. Liberalism was a cultural disease, most pronounced in
the cities but which was now infecting the countryside as well.
"In short," concluded Chang Yün-fu, "the atmosphere of a
nation in ruins (*wang-kuo*) fills the world, and if this cultural
tendency is not quickly changed, not only the nation will be
destroyed but the race will be obliterated."[41]

To combat this cultural cancer, the Blue Shirts would replace the decadent, individualistic culture with a new "nation-
first-ism culture that is positive, progressive, and brave."
The work of transforming Chinese society was, on the one
hand, necessarily destructive. "Now," the *She-hui hsin-wen*
editorialized, "we must destroy without a trace the cultural
phenomena that harm the nation. Otherwise we cannot establish a new culture for the nation's new life and China cannot
be revived." In this holy cause of revitalizing the nation, the
Blue Shirts did not flinch at the use of violence. In a remarkable declaration, the *She-hui hsin-wen* proclaimed that "in
order to create a new culture, Lenin, Stalin, Mussolini, and
Hitler launched an unfeeling, cruel attack on the old culture,
replaying the drama of the First Emperor [of China, 221–210

B.C.], burning books and burying scholars alive. Naturally, this cannot but be done!''[42] The *Ch'ien-t'u* echoed this statement. Li Ping-jo wrote that, in the course of human history, actions cannot be judged as good or bad. The burning of the books and burying of the scholars, he declared, were necessary at that time, laid the basis for the greatness of the empire, and ''one need not feel ashamed of them.'' ''The successes of cultural control in the Ch'in period are precisely what we should emulate today.''[43]

These expressions of admiration for the First Emperor, who for nearly two thousand years had been cast as the arch villain of Chinese history, seem at first blush too fantastic to be believed. But they were consistent with the Blue Shirts' determination to employ any means necessary to obliterate the sources of national weakness. Chiang Kai-shek, for example, told the Blue Shirts that ''all the comrades must unite their thoughts and beliefs; and basic party members, with a strictly secret organization and within certain bounds, shall handle all matters in accordance with the principle of fighting violence with violence.''[44]

This determination to ''fight violence with violence'' (*i-pao chih-pao*) was voiced repeatedly by the Blue Shirts, and was justified by their conviction that, in the contemporary world, morality had been raped and power alone was the measure of success. Yü Wen-wei in the *Ch'ien-t'u* asserted: ''Where can one find truth and peace in the world? So-called truth and peace are nothing more than deceptions to cheat the people; at most they are nothing more than good-sounding words.''[45] And a writer in the *She-hui hsin-wen* similarly declared that ''in the current situation, truth has been entirely violated by force. Therefore, unless there is force, there can be no truth. If we cannot use violence to respond to force, then the slogans of liberty, equality, democracy, and liberation can never be realized. China today therefore has no other road to restoration than to use an absolutely revolutionary body as a violent force that supports the principle of nation-first-ism.''[46]

The Blue Shirts would direct this violence not only against

communists, Japanese, and political rivals; all persons who contributed to the moral and cultural decline were marked as targets. A *She-hui hsin-wen* editorial proclaimed, "There must be a determination to shed blood—that is, there must be a kind of unprecedented violence to eliminate all enemies of the people."[47] And the "Disciplinary Code" (*Chi-lü yao-kang*) of the Blue Shirts stated, "The decline of national strength is already extreme, and the sufferings of the people are beyond expression . . . At this time when the difficulties have become even greater . . . there are unthinking, unfeeling, heartless creatures whose nerves are numbed and who produce no emotions of loving the nation; there are traitorous merchants; there are betrayers. If we continue to use tolerant methods to deal with these rotten elements, we can never expect to exterminate them completely . . . Now we must punish them, killing them with 'extreme measures,' causing the masses to become so frightened that they . . . will not again transgress the laws."[48]

Violence would be aimed even against those persons in the party or government who did not measure up to the standards of the revolutionary elite. The Blue Shirt "program" proclaimed a "permanent purge" of corrupt bureaucrats.[49] And a *She-hui hsin-wen* editorial read: "To eliminate bureaucratic organization, we can only create a mass violence organization, that takes the people of the nation as its highest principle, that will on the one hand use direct methods to attack this corrupt group; and, on the other hand, with great force make this group which has forgotten their nation realize that, though the people are intellectually backward, they hate those corrupt bureaucrats who exploit them."[50]

Neither violence nor political repression, however, would suffice to forge a new national culture. And the Blue Shirts, in the constructive aspects of their cultural program, were unabashedly totalitarian. "All social phenomena, all activity," wrote Ju Ch'un-p'u, "can in theory be the subject of intervention by cultural control." This meant that they sought not merely to eradicate the old culture, but to engrain "the cultural patterns of a new collective life" into the instinctual behavior of the people. The people would then govern their own conduct in accordance with the new cultural patterns, and simultaneously they would control the minority whose conduct did not measure up to the accepted standards. The real force of cultural control, Ju concluded, comes only when "the masses control themselves."[51]

To attain their totalitarian goal, the fascists would put art and even religion into the service of the nation—the Buddhists, Taoists, Muslims, and Christians alike having to serve as instruments of national policy. For the same purposes, the publishing industry would ultimately be nationalized. Individual authors might continue to write, but publication of their writings would be subject to the approval of government authorities. At the same time, a national institute would be established to author and edit works, as a result of which "the citizens' consciousness will be easy to unify."[52]

The heart of the Blue Shirts' program of cultural transformation was education. Ho Chung-han proclaimed: "Today, China's greatest problem is education. The preponderant reason that China has been troubled within and without is the failure of education.[53] The Blue Shirt educational policy was epitomized by the slogan "Nationalize, Militarize, Productivize" (*kuo-chia hua, chün-shih hua, sheng-ch'an hua*). Nationalization of education meant that the nation and the state would, in every sense, become the center and *raison d'être* of the educational process. Administratively, all schools would be operated by the state, under the centralized direction of the Ministry of Education. Local autonomy of public schools would, of course, be eliminated, while missionary and private schools and colleges would be closed or taken over by the state. The curricula of the schools would also be "nationalized" by placing emphasis upon Chinese culture and Chinese problems.

The goal of this nationalized educational policy was to create students possessed of a single-minded love for, and a readiness to sacrifice even their lives for, the nation.[54] How radically this policy would break with Chinese tradition is seen in the words of Yü Wen-wei: "The children that we educate are the nation's children, *not children of the family or clan*. The ultimate goal of educational policies must be the nation."[55] Even pedagogical techniques would have to be revised to emphasize group activities, group cooperation, and group discussions. In this way the evils of individualism and familism would be uprooted, and students would learn to identify first with social groups and thence with the nation.[56]

"Militarization" of education would transform the educational system so that "future teachers will train students to be fighters in a great war." Schools would be organized like military regiments, and teachers and school administrators would receive compulsory military training and live the frugal, disciplined life of the army.[57] Military indoctrination of children would begin in the kindergartens. The youngsters would be given guns and warships for toys, and pictures of battle scenes would be placed on the walls, "so that from childhood they will develop an interest in military equipment and battle situations." From that time on, the children would be educated in a military environment. Middle-school students would be enrolled in the Boy Scouts which, like Hitler's Youth Movement, would have a strong military cast. Throughout the school years, heavy stress would be placed on physical training and group—not individual—sports competition. In this way, the frail and bookish (*wen-jo*) students of the past, so much despised by the Blue Shirts, would be replaced by warriors of the future.[58]

Formal military training for male students would begin in high school and continue into college; girls in these same grades would receive training as nurses. The content of academic courses would also be slanted toward this goal of militarization. Study in the humanities would be discouraged, whereas practical and scientific subjects, such as physics, chemistry, and engineering would be oriented toward their wartime applications. Classes in chemistry, for example, would stress the study of such things as poison gases and explosives.[59]

The educational goal of "Productivization" was a reaction against the traditional concept of education, which still prevailed in the 1930s. Students, the Blue Shirts thought, were not prepared through the educational process to assume productive and useful roles in the nation; instead, the invidious prejudices and habits of a decadent and parasitic elite were instilled and perpetuated. "When there is one more student in school," a *Ch'ien-t'u* author remarked, "society loses a producer; when there is one more graduate from school, society gains another unemployed."[60]

Under the Blue Shirt system of education, students would not be a privileged elite, wasting their time and lives poring over "dead books" (*ssu-shu*) in preparation to become officials. To the contrary, one-fourth of the courses for students in the lower grades, for example, would be devoted to training in some form of manual labor. And throughout the student years there would be a heavy emphasis upon on-the-job training. Before graduation, middle school and college students would be required to work for prescribed periods of time on farms, or in factories or businesses. Or students majoring in, say, engineering would work half of each day in a factory, and study the rest of the day in school. In this way, the intellectuals' traditional disdain for physical labor would be overcome, and everyone would serve as a useful, producing member of the nation.[61]

The Blue Shirts were acutely conscious of the need for economic reforms. And, in view of their totalitarian concept of society, and considering the fact that economic laissez-faireism was everywhere under attack in the 1930s, it is not surprising that they advocated an economy that would be completely planned and controlled by the state. They called their projected economic system "national socialism" (*kuo-chia she-hui chu-i*)—a term doubtless derived from Hitler's

Germany.[62] Under the system of national socialism, all productive activity would come under the purview of the government's planning apparatus, which would prepare output goals and detailed plans of development. The Blue Shirts did not attack the system of private enterprise per se. However, such critical areas of the economy as heavy industry, mining, large-scale transport, and foreign trade would be managed directly by the state. There was to be no proscription on private profit, but it was stipulated that private capital had to be used for the benefit of society as a whole. It is worth noting that the economic controls proposed by the Blue Shirts would apply solely to productive enterprises; the distributive sector of the economy would be left to the free functioning of the market.[63]

This Blue Shirt program for the modern sector of the economy shared certain obvious characteristics with Sun Yat-sen's plans of national reconstruction. There was, however, a difference in tone, for the Blue Shirts were keenly aware of economic schemes in Germany, Russia, and other Western countries. And they therefore thought in terms of a total control of the economy of which Sun probably had not even dreamed.

The Blue Shirts' thinking on agrarian reform is of particular interest. This is partially because there was a sharp divergence of views among the Blue Shirts, and partially because the more radical school of thought urged a program that would have revolutionized the countryside to an extent even greater than the communists were then proposing.

The moderate view enjoyed the imprimatur of the Blue Shirt "program." This stated simply, "We advocate the vigorous development of agriculture and improvement of agricultural technology."[64] This position was elaborated by the *She-hui hsin-wen* which admitted the existence of some "contradictions" within the existing system of land ownership. It specifically rejected, however, nationalization of land as a solution to the rural crisis, stating that the system of private landholding had resulted "from economic need and the evolution of history." To overthrow a system thus sanctified by history would simply exacerbate rural disorder. Instead of advocating changes in the system of land tenure or work organization, the *She-hui hsin-wen* proposed little more than a refurbishing of existing agricultural institutions. It urged, for example, a reduction in taxes and rents, elimination of corrupt and obstructive bureaucrats, and the improvement of transportation facilities in the countryside. It proposed also improved, scientific farm techniques, loan facilities for peasants, and extensive irrigation and flood prevention projects.[65]

The *Ch'ien-t'u* was one of the Blue Shirts' most distinguished and authoritative publications; frequently its prestige was enhanced by contributions from Chiang Kai-shek and such Blue Shirt luminaries as Ho Chung-han. It is puzzling and paradoxical, therefore, that the land policy advocated by this periodical differed fundamentally from the available version of the Blue Shirt "program."

The writers in *Ch'ien-t'u* demanded the nationalization of land and the organization of production by means of state-managed agricultural collectives. Like the Chinese communists of the late 1950s, these Blue Shirts sought to avoid the social and economic disadvantages not only of large-scale landlordism, but also of land ownership by "innumerable small and selfish" peasants. Simply redistributing the land to the farmers would merely perpetuate the cultural stains of economic individualism. By creating a system of large-scale, rationalized agricultural production on state-owned collectives, however, the introduction of improved farm technology would be facilitated, as would the accumulation and reinvestment of the farm surplus. The writers in *Ch'ien-t'u* also emphasized that the consolidation of the existing miniscule farm plots into great farms would permit the extensive use of farm machinery—or, as one termed it, "the industrialization of agriculture."[66]

In advocating nationalization of the land, these Blue Shirts were knowingly committing ideological heresy by challenging the teachings of Sun Yat-sen as they had hitherto been interpreted. Hsü T'ai-k'ung remarked that other members of the Kuomintang believed "that even a word about land nationalization violates the doctrines of Sun Yat-sen and adopts the communist heresy of violent expropriation of property."[67] To set these fears to rest, Hsü argued that Sun had never stated clearly whether the ultimate land system would be based upon private or national ownership. True, Sun had advocated a policy of "land to the tiller" (*keng-che yu ch'i t'ien*). But Hsü disposed of this objection—rather too facilely —by asserting that "this was merely a means of attaining equal land rights"—equal land rights (*p'ing-chün ti-ch'üan*) being the second of Sun's slogans regarding the rural economy. "We can definitely conclude," Hsü persisted, "that the real meaning of equal land rights is to replace the evils of the system of private landholding with land nationalization."[68]

Perhaps to obviate the charge of advocating a communist policy, the methods of nationalizing the land that was proposed by these Blue Shirts was neither violent nor revolutionary. Farm owners would be required to sell only those lands in excess of sixty *mou* (about nine acres), and they would receive government bonds in payment. Stimulus for the sale of all remaining lands would be provided by a progressive land tax starting at 1 percent of the total land value on the first twenty *mou,* 1.5 percent on the second twenty *mou,* and 2 percent on the third twenty *mou.*[69]

Despite the gradualism implicit in this proposal, these Blue Shirts were convinced that agriculture was in deep crisis. Liu Ping-li typified their sense of concern. Speaking of land reform he said, "If the Chinese revolution ignores this question, it will be the same as digging our own graves." And Sun Po-chien, another writer in *Ch'ien-t'u,* similarly concluded that "the question of the agricultural economy is the central question at the current stage of the Chinese revolution, and is the crux of the *min-sheng* (people's livelihood) revolution."[70]

The rather cavalier attitude of some authors in the *Ch'ien-t'u* toward Sun's agrarian advocacy adds piquancy to some tantalizing reports that the Blue Shirts actually jettisoned the Three People's Principles, bag and baggage, from their ideological program. According to a Japanese intelligence report, Chiang Kai-shek called a secret meeting of the leading Blue Shirt cadre in January 1934. The purpose of this gathering was to determine how to eliminate the liberalism that had spread within the Blue Shirts, strengthen fascism in order to bolster the attacks on the Japanese and the communists, and increase the terror against anti-Chiang groups. As a result of decisions made in this conference, the major programmatic documents of the Blue Shirts were revised so that fascism, rather than the Three People's Principles of Sun Yat-sen, became the guiding ideology of the Blue Shirts. Article Two in this version of the "program" was changed to read: "Abandon democracy and the Three People's Principles, proclaim fascism, and strive for the realization of dictatorship." Article Nine of the "Political Program" (*Cheng-kang*) read: "Eliminate the Three People's Principles education, and advocate productive education, and universalize commoners' education." And Article Eleven read: "Speedily promote the implementation of a new fascist society and nation." The disciplinary code changed "The members shall always have absolute belief in the Three People's Principles" to "The members shall always have absolute belief in fascism."[71]

What credence can be given to this Japanese report that the Blue Shirts had abandoned the Three People's Principles in favor of fascism? Without doubt, some Blue Shirts felt that Sun's Three People's Principles were an encumbrance. They were an embarrassment when they advocated land nationalization. And Sun's Principle of Democracy in particular caused consternation to these would-be totalitarians.[72]

Despite obvious misgivings about the Three People's Principles, some of the Blue Shirts vigorously protested their faithfulness to Sun's teachings. "We do not wish to replace the term Three People's Principles with that of fascism," Ch'en Ch'iu-yün said in the *Ch'ien-t'u,* because the two ideologies "have a common spirit." An article reprinted in the *She-hui hsin-wen* agreed, adding however that it would be necessary to combine the Three People's Principles with the "resolute, sacrificing, iron-and-blood spirit of fascism." Thus could "false democracy" be smashed and the Three People's Principles be realized.[73]

Did, then, the Blue Shirts replace Sun's teaching with fascism? A former Blue Shirt remarked recently that he could easily imagine that some members, more radical than others, had favored doing so.[74] And he added that if the Blue Shirts' ideological program had been changed he might not have known of the change, so great was the secrecy shrouding the organization (a statement which, if true, raises many questions regarding the ideological solidarity of the Blue Shirts). Liu Chien-ch'ün was very insistent, however, that the "program" was never revised, saying (unconvincingly, I thought) that because the organization had lasted only six years, *there had not been time* to make a revision.[75]

The fact, however, that some writers expounded the similarities of the two doctrines suggests that a debate about abandoning the Three People's Principles was in fact taking place. And where had the Japanese agents obtained the version of the "program" incorporating fascism? Was it an official document? Or only a version drafted by some of the fascist extremists? (It is unlikely that this version was a Japanese fabrication, for the agent's report was classified "secret" and hence was not intended for public eyes.) There is now no evidence to settle this problem conclusively. In any event, the "fascistization" of the Blue Shirts was an accomplished fact, whether or not the Three People's Principles continued to be its ideological bedmate.

The Organization and Its Names

The Blue Shirts were an elitist organization, and they probably never greatly exceeded the 10,000 membership that was recorded in late 1935.[76] One usually reliable source gives a membership of about 300,000 in 1937. This is implausible, although there is some indication that the author of this report may have included members of the Blue Shirts' satellite organizations in this count.[77] The selectivity of the membership procedures meant that a candidate for membership had to undergo an extraordinarily thorough background investigation. The recommendation of two Blue Shirts was also required—a guarantee not to be given lightly, for they were thereafter held accountable for the conduct of the recommendee.[78]

Once approved for membership, the candidate was initiated individually into the organization. Facing a portrait of Chiang Kai-shek, he vowed to obey the leader and preserve the secrets and discipline of the organization or suffer the penalty of death.[79] This ceremony completed, he had become a member of an organization so secret that he would never have more than the haziest notion of its organization, most of whose members he would never know, and which he theoretically could leave only upon death.[80]

Although the Blue Shirts were founded around a nucleus of Whampoa graduates, army officers who commanded troops were at first denied membership. The explanation given for this prohibition was that Chiang did not want military men involved with politics. This restriction, however, only lasted about a year-and-a-half.[81]

It has been extraordinarily difficult to gain something approaching a coherent picture of the organizational structure of the Blue Shirts. The secrecy enshrouding the movement has been one obstacle; another is that the organization of the movement was reportedly altered many times.[82] When one encounters conflicting evidence, therefore, it may be false or simply a temporal discrepancy. The fundamental structure that was erected in early 1933 seems, however, to have remained unchanged.

1. *The top-level administration.* At the apex of the Blue Shirt organization was the association chief (*hui-chang*), also

termed the leader (*ling-hsiu*). This post was held by Chiang Kai-shek. The actual management of the organization was delegated to a central executive committee (*chung-yang kan-shih hui*), which in effect acted in the name of the leader. This committee was formed of seventeen full members (*kan-shih*) and nine reserve members (*hou-pu kan-shih*).[83] The executive committee was ostensibly elected by a representative conference of the entire organizational membership, although it appears that in actual practice the committee was composed of Chiang's personal appointees.[84]

The real heart of the organization was doubtless the five-man standing committee of the executive committee (*ch'ang-wu kan-shih hui*), one of whom acted concurrently as the executive secretary (*shu-chi*, subsequently changed to *shu-chi chang*).[85] The executive secretary was also, of course, appointed by Chiang Kai-shek, and during the six-year life span of the Blue Shirts, five men in succession held this key post.[86] It was the responsibility of the executive secretary to oversee the administration of policies and operations determined by the leader and the executive committee. Assisting him in these duties were a secretariat (*shu-chi ch'u*) and approximately four departments or bureaus (*ch'u*) charged with specific functions, such as training, organization, propaganda, and intelligence and terror.[87] Similar departmental divisions directed operations at subordinate organizational levels.

2. *The mid-level administration.* The organizational network of the Blue Shirts was designed to cover the entire nation.[88] In 1935 there were about ten branch associations (*fen-hui*). Three of these were located in Nanking; others were in Wuchang, Hangchow, Peiping, Loyang, Lanchow, Chengtu, and Canton. These branch associations counted anywhere from 350 to 1,600 members, and were in turn divided into sub-branch associations (*ch'ü-fen hui*). In Nanking, for example, the first branch association numbered 1,582 members, and was organized into three sub-branch associations. The first sub-branch association consisted of 693 members,

most of whom were government officials; the second and third sub-branch associations, made up mostly of students, numbered 533 and 356 members respectively.

In some cases, sub-branch associations operated directly under the central leadership, without the intervention of a branch association. In Yunnan and Fukien, for example, special sub-branch associations (*t'e-pieh ch'ü-fen hui*) were established, presumably because the relatively small membership in these areas did not warrant classification as a branch association. Elsewhere, however, notably in Shanghai, the unique importance of operations resulted in the establishment of special sub-branch associations with direct administrative ties to the organization's central apparatus. Altogether, there were approximately forty sub-branch associations across the country. In some instances, a further administrative subdivision led to the creation of branch societies (*chih-she*), which often numbered thirty to forty members.

The administrative authority of the branch and sub-branch associations was vested in a system of executive committees and secretaries. Five full and three reserve members formed the executive committee of the branch associations. This group met once every two weeks; in the interim, a secretary appointed by the Blue Shirts' central executive committee directed operations. In the sub-branch associations, an executive committee of three full and one reserve member, together with a secretary, were in charge.

The activities of the Blue Shirts were not confined to China. There are no details of the operations conducted abroad, but it was reported that a number of branch societies and similar Blue Shirt units were located in such cities as Berlin (97 members), Rome (31), London (11), Paris (37), Washington (33), and Tokyo (57).

3. *The basic organization.* As in the Kuomintang itself—which had in turn been modeled after the Russian Communist Party—the small-group (*hsiao-tsu*) was the basic unit of organization and administration. The small-group, compris-

ing from three to nine members, held weekly meetings at which the members studied and discussed political and ideological questions, and undertook to evaluate their work as a group and as individuals. They also submitted reports containing information collected during the week that might have intelligence value.[89]

Parallel to the administrative structure of the Blue Shirts was a supervisory system that was responsible only to the leader. At the highest level was a general association supervisory committee (tsung-hui chien-ch'a hui), appointed by Chiang Kai-shek. This committee consisted of an unknown number of committee members, a four-man standing committee, and an executive secretary. Similar committees appointed by this top supervisory committee operated at the levels of the branch and sub-branch associations.

These committees had broad powers of overseeing the administrative work of the Blue Shirt organization, checking budgetary matters, and maintaining surveillance of the thoughts and actions of individual members of the organization. This supervisory arm of the Blue Shirts was also empowered to determine and carry out punishment for all violations of the Blue Shirts' stringent regulations.[90]

Although all Blue Shirts thought of themselves as an elite, some were more elite than others. The dominant leadership of the organization formed the exclusive Li-hsing-she (the "vigorously carry-out society")—a name reportedly derived from the determination to vigorously carry out the teachings of Sun Yat-sen and the commands of Chiang Kai-shek. Members of the central executive committee and secretaries of the branch associations belonged to this exalted group. Other select individuals might also be considered members of the Li-hsing-she, and one source states that by 1937 the membership of this exclusive club had grown to 528.[91]

A second stratum of the elite was known as the Revolutionary Youth Comrades Association (Ko-ming ch'ing-nien t'ung-chih hui). This was formed of the Blue Shirts' secondary level of leadership—administrative personnel in the branch and sub-branch associations, cadre involved with the Blue Shirts' "special service" operations, and personnel performing especially important functions, such as instructors in the military academy.[92]

A mark of the distinctiveness and prestige accorded to members of these elite groups is that they were not subject to the authority of the branch or sub-branch associations. Instead, members of the Li-hsing-she and the Revolutionary Youth Comrades Association were separated into administrative units responsible only to the central command of the organization. In Nanking, for example, there were forty-one "directly subordinate small-groups" (*chih-shu hsiao-tsu*) and two "directly subordinate branch societies" (*chih-shu chih-she*), outside the regular Blue Shirt administrative structure, which comprised members of either the Li-hsing-she or the Revolutionary Youth Comrades Association.[93]

All other members of the organization were included within the category of the Chung-hua fu-hsing-she (Chinese Revival Society). This was the lowest stratum of the elite, comprising all members who held no administrative responsibilities within the organization (leaders of the small-groups were included in this lesser category). Indeed, its members were never anything more than the foot soldiers of the Blue Shirts. As Kan Kuo-hsün, who was a member of the Li-hsing-she, has observed, "The Fu-hsing-she from top to bottom had no independent organization or administrative personnel."[94]

Iwai Eiichi contends that no name was ever officially adopted for the so-called Blue Shirts. The first representative conference of the organization, which was convoked early in 1933, had considered a number of names: Revival Society (Fu-hsing-she), Blue Shirt Corps (Lan-i t'uan), Chinese Kuomintang Vanguard Society (Chung-kuo Kuo-min-tang ch'ien-wei-she), and Chinese Kuomintang Iron-and-Blood Corps

(Chung-kuo kuo-min-tang t'ieh-hsüeh t'uan). Iwai concludes, however, that the conference decided to continue the operations of this elite society simply using the name of the Kuomintang.[95]

Iwai's report is generally the most reliable of the available accounts on the Blue Shirts. There is, however, contradictory evidence. A new recruit to the organization was informed that the name Chung-hua fu-hsing-she was the real name of what outsiders called the Blue Shirts.[96] Iwai, too, records that communications within the organization did occasionally use the terms Fu-hsing-she, Revolutionary Youth Comrades Association, and Li-hsing-she to designate the separate strata of the group. And two of the secondary accounts assert that the name adopted, after several changes, was either Fu-hsing-she or Chung-hua fu-hsing-she.[97] I have concluded tentatively that the designation of Chung-hua fu-hsing-she, the Revolutionary Youth Comrades Association, and Li-hsing-she were commonly used, and did refer to real stratifications within the organization. These names, however, had no official status.

One thing is certain: the term Blue Shirt Society (Lan-i-she) was not an official designation. Less certain, however, is the provenance of this term which became common coinage not only among the Chinese public but even among Blue Shirt members (former high-ranking Blue Shirts, whom I interviewed in 1969, still readily used the term Lan-i-she when referring to the organization). One common theory—accepted by most Chinese and some Japanese—is that Liu Chien-ch'ün had used the term in his essay of late 1931. In available editions of the essay, however, Liu suggested the term *pu-i-t'uan* (cotton-cloth corps), and the name Lan-i-she appears nowhere in its pages. Liu himself insisted—and I am inclined to believe him—that the term Blue Shirt had been used first by the Japanese to slander the movement by equating it to Mussolini's Black Shirts. Thereafter, the term Blue Shirts won general usage by the Chinese themselves.[98]

Within the organizational structure just described, Blue Shirt members were expected to measure their conduct against the most demanding revolutionary criteria. The leadership principle was the first fundamental organizational tenet. Obedience to the leadership was to be absolute and unquestioning. Accordingly, opposition to the leader, rejection of the organization's doctrines, or the false transmission of commands were crimes punishable by death.[99] Because of the cardinal importance of the leadership principle, democracy was not a strong feature of the movement, although lower-level cadre (for example, in the small-groups and the sub-branch associations) were theoretically selected by election. The results of all elections could, however, be voided by the corps leadership. And one long-time member of considerable prominence in the movement, insists that there were no elections in the movement at any level of organization, all secretaries and small-group leaders being assigned by the higher authorities.[100]

Secrecy was a second organizational principle. The first article of the disciplinary code read: "The basic character of corps members is always the strict maintenance of secrecy," and death was the penalty for revealing secrets of the organization.[101] As a consequence, the general public knew of the Blue Shirts only through vague and fearsome rumors. And even members of the corps itself had but a limited knowledge of the organization. Corps members were to have contacts with other members only when this was required by their work. Thus, as one former member remarked, two members could "bump noses" without knowing they both belonged to the Blue Shirts.[102]

This statement was corroborated by a former Blue Shirt who had been inducted into the organization while still in middle school. Although he thought there were other Blue Shirt members among his fellow students, the only member he knew outside his own small-group was the liaison man, a college student, who attended each of the meetings of his small-group.[103] Another former member, who had been a member of a branch association executive committee, responded to questions about the existence of the Revolutionary Youth Comrades Association stating, "It could very well be, but members themselves did not know much about the organization."[104] Perhaps he was being less than candid. It is clear, however, that only members of the Li-hsing-she, and perhaps only the Thirteen Princes (aside from Chiang Kai-shek, of course) really possessed clear knowledge of the corps' organization or the scope of its activities.

A final organizational principle was that the members were to be committed single-mindedly to the corps and to the revolution. "The member," read the Blue Shirts' disciplinary code, "must maintain a spirit of dedication, restraining improper lusts and desires, concerned only to become a nameless hero so as to implement the doctrines and policies of the organization and to transform society into a place of happiness."[105] Liu Chien-ch'ün's urgent suggestion in 1931 that a limitation be imposed upon the property of the members was never incorporated into the regulations of the organization. Nevertheless, Blue Shirt members were to be models of frugality. When traveling, they were not permitted to take first-class accommodations; and dancing, gambling, and whoring were strictly forbidden.[106] To enable the members to direct their efforts to the revolution instead of toward material enrichment, the corps provided money for weddings, the education of the elder son, and stipends would be given to members who were unemployed or were ill. A relief fund also provided aid to survivors of members who were killed when on duty.[107]

The selfless commitment of Blue Shirt members was to be manifested in their relations with their comrades in the corps. In place of the cliquism and absence of *esprit de corps* among members of the old Kuomintang, there was an "absolute need of intimate friendship" among the members of the corps. Not only was there to be a "spirit of cooperation" in their work, but members were also enjoined to give material and financial assistance to comrades who were in pressing need. And if a comrade died, the others were to feel that "a savior of the world has been lost."[108]

Blue Shirt Activities

The Blue Shirts never realized the original goal of capturing control of the Kuomintang so that they might instill a soul, or a new revolutionary spirit, into the old party. Yet its influence both within the Kuomintang and in society as a whole was enormous, albeit incalculable. The Blue Shirts almost completely dominated political training and the party organization within the army. After February 1933 political training throughout the nation—not only in the army but in the government and the schools—also in effect fell under the purview of the Blue Shirts when Ho Chung-han became head of the central political training offices. Blue Shirt control also permeated many of Chiang Kai-shek's sprawling public security organizations, such as the Nanking police, the Central Military Police (Chung-yang hsien-ping), the Public Security Office (Kung-an chü), and the Peace Preservation Corps (Pao-an tui). And the director of the Central Press Censorship Bureau established in 1936 was, again, Ho Chung-han.[109]

In 1934, the National Military Training Commission (Kuo-min chün-shih hsün-lien wei-yüan-hui) was instituted with the aim of creating a people's militia of twelve million men, and with the ancillary goal of "militarizing" much of the Chinese population. Only six of the thirteen executive directors of the commission were Blue Shirts. The overwhelming majority of the middle and lower-ranking cadre in the commission, however, were members of the secret organization. As a result, stated Iwai Eiichi, "the actual authority of the training commission is entirely in the hands of the Blue Shirts."[110] Under the direction of the commission, military training was made compulsory for two years in both high schools and universities. Special summer training camps were also established at Loyang, Hankow, and Nanking where the students received an additional three weeks to a month of military training.[111] These summer camps were also used as a source of recruits to the Blue Shirts. One former Blue Shirt, now in the United States, related that he attended one of these camps in 1937 as a sixteen-year-old middle-school student. At the end of the training period, he was called into the office of the political training officer, and *told* that he had been selected to be a member of the Blue Shirts. The officer said that he would be contacted after he returned to his school. Shortly afterwards he was enrolled in a small-group.[112]

Middle-school and university students were not the only targets of Blue Shirt organizational activity. Government officials and even farmers were designated by the military training commission to be organized into army reserve units. The Boy Scouts was another area of Blue Shirt activity, and chairman of the National Boy Scouts Association was Kuei Yung-ch'ing, one of the Thirteen Princes. With a momentum imparted by the Blue Shirts, the Boy Scouts expanded dramatically during the 1930s, membership being required of all junior middle-school students. Thus were tens of thousands of Chinese youth introduced to the rudiments of military training and discipline.[113]

By 1934 Blue Shirt efforts to create a "militarized society" were bearing fruit. "Fascism," it was observed, "has definitely taken root in Central China," and "a new military spirit was abroad in the country." Youth of the country were being fitted into uniforms, and even children in elementary school were encouraged to construct war-like toys, such as tanks and airplanes. And the schools revealed an unwonted cleanliness and regimentation. "One would think," remarked an American missionary in 1935, "a Fascist utopia had been let down from heaven upon the spot. It's all very neat and wonderful but gives me a slightly shaky feeling inside." An executive secretary of the YMCA expressed the same misgivings. "This 'militarization of the mind of China,'" he speculated, "might well prove to be the decade's most significant development."[114]

Political indoctrination and military training were but two areas of Blue Shirt concern. It is impossible with the limited information available to provide a description of all Blue

Shirt undertakings. The following pages, therefore, will focus on but three kinds of activities that are illustrative of the scope and ramifications of the Blue Shirt movement.

The New Life Movement. The New Life Movement has sometimes been regarded as a futile and somewhat comic effort to regenerate the nation by reviving the morality of Confucianism and by prescribing quaint rules of personal conduct. To many observers, this movement seemed to prove that the Kuomintang was hopelessly out of touch with the needs of the nation, and that Chiang Kai-shek was simply an "old-fashioned Confucian." The New Life Movement has been described, however, as "the masterpiece of the Blue Shirts."[115] This is a dimension of the New Life Movement that has customarily been overlooked—a dimension that should encourage a reevaluation of both the New Life Movement and Chiang Kai-shek.

It is uncertain who provided the initial inspiration for the New Life Movement. Some sources credit Chiang himself or Madame Chiang with the idea,[116] and it is incontestable that Chiang had for many years been preachifying the Confucian-flavored, mind-over-matter philosophy that characterized much of the New Life Movement. Iwai Eiichi stated that the movement was "created" by the Chinese Culture Study Association (Chung-kuo wen-hua hsüeh-hui), which was a Blue Shirt front organization.[117] And many Chinese sources state that Yang Yung-t'ai, Chiang's chief private secretary, inspired the movement—which would be highly ironical, if true, for Yang and the Blue Shirts were deadly enemies.[118]

Regardless of who conceived the original idea, the New Life Movement as it took form meshed precisely with the spirit and program of the Blue Shirts. Chiang Kai-shek was himself keenly aware of the relationship. Speaking to a conference of Blue Shirt leaders in late 1933 or early 1934—that is, probably shortly before the New Life Movement was formally inaugurated—Chiang recited the weaknesses of the Chinese people. They were, he said, selfish, undisciplined, and dissolute. If the Chinese revolution was to be revived, he told the Blue Shirts, "it is necessary to spread our revolutionary spirit to the masses of the entire nation, and to cause them to have faith in our group."[119]

The New Life Movement was one of the means that Chiang Kai-shek and the Blue Shirts would use to implant this spirit —this fascist spirit—among the Chinese people. But it was a means that disguised the goal, for Chiang Kai-shek would use Confucianism, and even Christianity, in realizing his desired transformation of the nation. It was an attenuated Confucianism that Chiang Kai-shek brought to the New Life Movement. It was a Confucianism for the masses, devoid of philosophical subtleties, stripped to its ethical essentials. It was a sloganized Confucianism, encapsulated for popular consumption in four vague virtues: *li-i-lien-ch'ih* (rendered loosely as "propriety, justice, honesty, and sense of self-respect").

Observance of *li-i-lien-ch'ih* was made easier for the people by spelling out in detail ninety-five rules governing the individual's daily behavior. The Chinese were now instructed to be prompt, button their clothes, stand straight, and not eat noisily.[120] These rules were not incidental to the goals of the New Life Movement; they were, in fact, very close to its heart. "If we are to have a new life that accords with *li-i-lien-ch'ih,*" Chiang asserted, "then we must start by not spitting heedlessly." "If we are to restore the nation and gain revenge for our humiliations, then we need not talk about guns and cannon, but must first talk about washing our faces in cold water."[121]

Such statements can always evoke a hearty and condescending chuckle. It was ludicrous, we think, that Chiang should even conceive that China could resist the Japanese once all the people regularly plunged their faces into buckets of cold water, or urinated only in a *tz'u-so*. Chiang, however, had no illusions that *li-i-lien-ch'ih* or the ninety-five rules of conduct were ends in themselves. He did believe that the strict observance of these standards of behavior would result in a change in the "inner man." And if all the people could be thus transformed, then society and the nation would likewise be created anew.

Chiang found the models for his ideal society in the specifically militaristic aspects of Japan and Europe. He recalled his student days in a Japanese military academy, convinced that the moral fiber of the cadets had been strengthened by the rigorous observance of barracks discipline. "They did not speak about *li-i-lien-ch'ih*," Chiang said of academy life, "but the spirit of all conduct, whether with regard to eating, clothing, housing, or walking, was in every respect in accordance with *li-i-lien-ch'ih*."[122]

The fascism of Germany and Italy likewise provided Chiang with an image of the future society. "In fascism," he declared, "the organization, the spirit, and the activities must all be militarized . . . In the home, the factory, and the government office, everyone's activities must be the same as in the army . . . In other words, there must be obedience, sacrifice, strictness, cleanliness, accuracy, diligence, secrecy . . . And everyone together must firmly and bravely sacrifice for the group and for the nation."[123] This image of fascist society was incorporated essentially unchanged into the New Life Movement. "What is the New Life Movement that I now propose?" Chiang enquired rhetorically. "Stated simply, it is to thoroughly militarize the lives of the citizens of the entire nation so that they can cultivate courage and swiftness, the endurance of suffering and a tolerance for hard work, and especially the habit and ability of unified action, so that they will at any time sacrifice for the nation."[124]

Militarization of the nation was also one of the chief goals of the fascistic Blue Shirts, and Chiang was more than casually aware of this basic similarity between fascism and the New Life Movement. In September 1933 he had explained that the militarization of society was one of the three basic elements in fascism (the other two elements, Chiang said, were a sense of national superiority and faith in the leader).[125] Five months later, the New Life Movement was inaugurated, with Chiang explicitly declaring that the militarization of society was the chief goal of the movement. There can be no doubt that Chiang Kai-shek was very clear in his own mind regarding the correspondence between the New Life Movement and fascism.

The Blue Shirts assumed a leading role in the New Life Movement. The movement was administered by a national system of New Life Movement promotional associations (Hsin-sheng-huo yün-tung ts'u-chin hui), and a former high-ranking Blue Shirt has stated that "most" of the cadre in these associations were Blue Shirts.[126] A recent article in Taiwan has also proudly claimed that the Blue Shirts were the *chung-hsin*—the nucleus, or the heart—of the New Life Movement.[127]

The testimony of Westerners in China corroborate these claims that Blue Shirt influence was preponderant in the movement. George Shepherd, a Protestant missionary who in 1935 became one of the directors of the New Life Movement, complained in 1936 that the movement was dominated by military officers (who would presumably have been Blue Shirt members in most instances).[128] And in April 1936 at least some of the secretaries of the YMCA were concerned that the New Life Movement was "really a blue-shirt movement, looking forward to the regimentation of the country under a sort of Fascist regime."[129] There was, in addition, ample indirect evidence that the New Life Movement was developing in directions that could only have pleased the Blue Shirts. In accordance with plans of the New Life Movement promotional associations, government officials, teachers, and students began wearing uniforms and received military training.[130] In Wuhan, the New Life Movement reportedly "set in motion forces that would organize the man in the street and the literati each in a separate organization, but with fascist ideals as the foundation."[131]

The New Life Movement also displayed the Blue Shirt antipathy to Western-inspired dissipation. One effect of the

New Life Movement in Wuhan, for instance, was to force all cabarets to close at midnight, Chinese were not permitted to dance, and the music was to be "of a classical nature."[132] This anti-modernist strain in the New Life Movement was expressed violently by small groups of fanatics who burst into dance halls and movie theaters throughout the country, pouring acid over persons dressed in Western clothing. These ruffians were often identified as Blue Shirts.[133] Whether or not they were in fact members of the corps their actions were perfectly consonant with the attitudes of those critics of decadent Westernization who wrote in the pages of *Ch'ien-t'u*.

However influential the Blue Shirts may have been in the New Life Movement, their control of the movement was never complete. If it had been, it is inconceivable that Ch'en Li-fu would have supported it as strongly as he did.[134] Moreover, YMCA and Christian elements were conspicuous in the movement. But all these ingredients mixed poorly. After the missionary George Shepherd became one of several directors in the movement, for example, he disparaged the martial salutes and the goose-step, and he worked to deemphasize the military-style discipline that characterized the "new life." "Thus the battle is drawn," observed a United States diplomat, "between the Anglo-American-Christian democrats and the German-Italian totalitarians."[135] Such conflicts among the leadership, and disparities of goals contributed to the movement's dwindling dynamism.

The Pieh-tung-tui. The number of actual Blue Shirt members was not large. The influence of the corps was multiplied many times, however, because its members acted as the leading cadre of satellite or front organizations and bent these to the Blue Shirts' will. Some of the numerous front groups among the students were, for example, the Hangchow Youth Vanguard Corps, the Peiping Restoration Society, and the Nanking Right-Customs Society. Workers' groups were similarly penetrated by Blue Shirt activists. Most members of these organizations would have had no intimation that they were doing the bidding of the Blue Shirts. But the most active of them were frequently recruited into the mother organization itself.[136] The Pieh-tung-tui, or Special Movement Corps, was not really typical of the many Blue Shirt-related organizations, but it was probably the most consequential. In 1933 Chiang Kai-shek's fourth major campaign to annihilate the communist force in Kiangsi had failed. After reassessing the campaign, Chiang proclaimed a new strategy to wipe out the Reds: "Seven parts political; three parts military." Chiang's primary vehicle for this political operation against communism was the Pieh-tung-tui.[137]

K'ang Tse, one of the four or five most influential men in the Blue Shirts and a trusted adviser of Chiang, was selected to command the new corps. K'ang had been a cadet in the fourth class of Whampoa, but like many Whampoa graduates he never commanded troops in the field. Instead, he had first gone to Moscow to study at Sun Yat-sen University—at one point, he became a communist only to leave the party about 1928—and after his return to China held various organizational or training posts. In mid-1933, when Chiang picked him to take charge of the new organization, he was serving in Nanchang as director of a summer training institute for army officers.[138]

The Pieh-tung-tui was organized into a headquarters corps (*tsung-tui-pu*) and three large-corps (*ta-tui;* subsequently expanded to five, and then seven or eight large-corps); at its peak in 1936, the organization comprised somewhere between 10,000 and 20,000 men.[139] The upper command levels of this structure (that is, heads and political commissars of medium-corps and above) were filled almost entirely by Blue Shirts, although Blue Shirt members also held positions of lesser importance. Although the remainder of the organization was formed largely of ordinary personnel of the regular army, K'ang Tse imposed the same principles of rigid discipline and unconditional obedience that were demanded of the Blue Shirts themselves. Pieh-tung-tui members could marry, for example, only with the approval of the corps headquarters. And, to dramatize the life-long and absolute dedication expected of his subordinates, K'ang Tse frequently remarked that they "Enter alive, depart dead."[140]

During the initial period, 1933–1935, when its operations centered in Kiangsi, the corps endeavored to control and win over the masses in the former communist areas and to enforce the blockade of the communists. As soon as a team of corps cadre entered an area recently recovered from the communists, they organized the entire population into a *pao-chia* (mutual responsibility) system and launched a "social survey" (*she-hui tiao-ch'a*) as a means of weeding out communists and other undesirable elements.[141]

The team then organized a Communist-Annihilation Volunteer Militia which became an extension of the Pieh-tung-tui itself. The militiamen were given rigorous training for three months—said to be as thorough as that given regular troops. Armed only with spears and swords, the militia performed guard duty, and rounded up communists, bandits, or deserters from the Nationalist army. A vital task for the militia was that of strengthening the blockade of the communists, the militiamen patrolling to prevent the movement of goods and men to or from the communist areas.[142]

Following Chiang Kai-shek's formula of stressing political methods to fight communism, the Pieh-tung-tui endeavored to improve the welfare of the masses in Kiangsi. In characteristic Kuomintang fashion, this meant emphasis on education. All children between the ages of seven and fifteen were required to attend school—reputedly the first instance of *enforced* compulsory education in Chinese history[143]—and adults were encouraged to attend schools. Illiteracy was one target of the educational movement, and the Pieh-tung-tui applied the methods of the "Little Teacher" movement to teach 600 to 1,000 of the most common characters.

Political indoctrination was doubtless at the heart of this educational effort. As one observer remarked, "Emphasis is placed on good citizenship, health and sanitation, courtesy and good behaviour generally.'"[144] The Pieh-tung-tui was also the chief agency for promoting the New Life Movement in Kiangsi, forcing on the long-suffering Kiangsi farmers a radically different social ideal than had been pumped into them by the communist cadre.

Free medical treatment was another part of the Pieh-tung-tui's program of attracting the masses away from the communists. Probably the most welcome measure of the Pieh-tung-tui, however, was to end the abuse of the masses by the Nationalist government's own officials. The corps undertook to expose malfeasance by Nanking's civil administrators and mistreatment of the commoners by the local gentry.[145] During the first two months of Pieh-tung-tui operations, "1,200 major cases, and innumerable minor cases" of corruption were reportedly investigated and judged.[146] The corps also attempted to uphold standards of discipline among the regular army.[147]

One potential area of reform was neglected by the Pieh-tung-tui. Although the corps did instruct the farmers in improved farming techniques,[148] it did nothing to meliorate the problems of land tenancy. In 1933 three agricultural experts representing the League of Nations visited Kiangsi and had concluded that the system of land ownership was the crux of the agrarian crisis and mass discontent. But the Pieh-tung-tui not only did not address itself to this problem; in all probability, it actually took lands that had been redistributed by the communists and restored them to the original landlords.[149]

The Pieh-tung-tui's operations in Kiangsi were, in some respects, singularly successful. The blockade of the communists, resulting in severe shortages of salt and other necessities, forced the Reds to break through the encircling Nationalist armies and to start on what became the Long March. The corps may also have been successful in winning over the masses. A *North China Herald* correspondent concluded that "Though it is greatly feared by evil doers, the Pih

Tung Tui . . . is generally welcomed by the people."[150] However, other reports from former communist areas—without specifically mentioning the Pieh-tung-tui—indicate that the masses suffered at least as much under Nationalist rule as they did under the communists.[151]

Generalissimo and Madame Chiang were, in any case, pleased with K'ang Tse's works. Madame Chiang, in spreading the gospel of the New Life Movement, declared that the Pieh-tung-tui had "put an end to military oppression of the people" in Kiangsi; and she urged that the same methods be adopted in Honan.[152]

After the communists erupted from the Nationalist blockade, the Pieh-tung-tui continued its work in Kiangsi, but the focus of its operations shifted to Szechuan. This large and potentially rich province in remote western China had maintained an obdurate independence of Nanking. But, using the pretext of pursuing the retreating communists, Chiang moved his armies into the province, and it was soon converted into one of the Nationalist government's relatively firm strongholds. The Pieh-tung-tui was instrumental in this political transformation and was a dominant force in the province until the corps was disbanded in 1938.[153]

Tai Li and "Special Services." The aspect of Blue Shirt activities that instilled almost universal fear and hatred in China was called *t'e-wu,* or Special Services—a euphemism for intelligence and terroristic operations. The guiding genius of the Blue Shirts' Special Services was Tai Li, who until his death in an airplane crash in 1946 was one of Chiang Kai-shek's most trusted lieutenants and one of China's most powerful and shadowy political personalities. Tai Li's early career is largely shrouded in mystery. He, like Chiang Kai-shek, was born and reared in Chekiang. A turning point in his life was 1926, when a former schoolmate returned to Chekiang and told him that the real heart of the national revolution was in the Whampoa Military Academy. Tai, at the age of thirty *sui,* went to Canton and within the year was accepted into the academy's sixth class. While a cadet, Tai began gathering information on communists in his class. And when the Kuomintang's purge of the communists began in April 1927, Tai informed on over twenty of his fellow cadets. Chiang Kai-shek learned of Tai's "merit" and immediately began employing Tai in intelligence work. Thus, Tai's unique career had begun. He never finished the formal course work at Whampoa—a fact some envious Whampoa graduates could never forgive him— but he was granted a diploma by special dispensation.

When the Blue Shirts were organized, Tai became chief of the Special Services Department (T'e-wu chü). In the same year, 1932, Chiang Kai-shek appointed him to head the Second Section (that is, the special service section) of the military commission's Bureau of Investigation and Statistics.[154] Thus Tai directed one of China's largest special service networks and seemingly deserved the title—which unfriendly writers awarded him—of "China's Himmler."

Tai Li's operations haunted the Chinese political world; his agents were suspected of being everywhere, and each assassination and abduction was readily attributed to his fearsome organization. In one sense, this gave Tai too much credit, for other political groups—such as the CC clique, and also anti-Nanking groups—had their own special service organizations.[155] Yet Tai's organization was just about what the popular imagination feared.

Tai provided a glimpse into the character and methods of his organization in a fascinating book called *Political Spying,* which he prepared as a textbook for his fledgling secret service agents.[156] In China, he wrote, where the nation's leader bore complete responsibility, it was essential that he be provided with "ears and eyes" so that he would be protected from deception and harm. These "ears and eyes," that is, political spies, should be planted at every level of society. And "they do not adhere too closely to the nation's civil and penal laws."[157]

In one section of this work, Tai listed the duties of the

political spy. The order in which the duties are listed, with those relating to the leader placed first, may or may not be suggestive of the relative priorities in Tai's own mind:

1. Insure the leader's security. The safety or danger of the leader is the same as the safety or danger of the nation. We must therefore determine always and everywhere to guard the leader's security.

2. Punish corruption. Corruption is the worm in the revolutionary struggle. Unless this task is carried out completely, it will be impossible to build a pure and honest government.

3. Destroy all counter-revolutionary forces. This includes control and investigation of assemblies, societies, and publishing. Political spies and counter-revolutionary elements cannot coexist, either in terms of action or of thought.

4. Assist national reconstruction. Just as the farmer must eliminate the weeds before his seeds can bear fruit, so the path of national reconstruction must be cleared of obstacles.

5. Defend against international spies and traitors. The political spy is the sentinel of national defense. When a country is at war, the success of its main fighting force is often decided by the success of its spies fighting behind the scenes.[158]

The book further detailed the methods that the agents should employ in fulfilling these duties. Most political spy work, Tai wrote, involved the gathering of intelligence. And he instructed his operatives how to examine letters secretly, how to employ disguises, and how to report their findings quickly and secretly using codes or invisible writing. Political and social disruption, and sabotage, were other forms of political spy work that Tai discussed.[159]

It is interesting, in view of the reputation of Tai's operations, that the textbook devoted little attention to the work of assassination. Here is the single paragraph in the book on the subject:

The methods of secret arrest and assassinations are all extremely simple. There must, of course, be no mistake about the road [where the subject is to be accosted]. In addition, regarding the job itself, the assignment of tasks is of paramount importance: who will serve as lookout, who will carry out [the murder], who will handle the means of transportation—everyone must be suited for his task. Aside from this, one must check the weapon, and everyone must be at the appointed place at the appointed time. If everything can be done in this way, then there will not be one failure out of ten.[160]

It is clear that Tai glossed over political murder, not out of moral compunction, but because it posed no technical problems.

To what extent were the duties of Tai Li's special services actually fulfilled? The fact that Tai's Second Department grew in size from 145 operatives in 1932 to over 1,700 in 1935 is some indication of its growing role. (By the end of World War II, it had ballooned to forty or fifty thousand!)[161] By the very nature of the work, however, it is impossible to determine the exact scope of Tai's special services. The first of Tai's political assassinations was allegedly that in February 1933 of Chang Ching-yao, an old-style militarist who had been cooperating with the Japanese.[162] Thereafter, virtually every assassination—and there were many of them in the 1930s—was at some time or other attributed to Tai Li's agents. In June 1933 Yang Ch'üan was gunned down in the French Concession in Shanghai, allegedly in retribution for his leading role in the Chinese League for the Protection of Civil Rights. This murder came off so smoothly that, it has been said, it was subsequently used as a model in the training of future Blue Shirt assassins.[163] In November 1934 Shih Liang-ts'ai, who was the editor of Shanghai's leading newspaper, *Shen-pao,* was stopped on the road between Hangchow and Shanghai and murdered by six assassins wearing black gowns and helmets. The attempted murder of Wang Ching-wei and the liberal journalist Lo Lung-chi have also been laid to the Blue Shirts. Raids and bombings of newspaper offices, such as the *I-shih pao, Ch'en-pao,* and *Min-hsing pao* in Tientsin, were also blamed on Tai's secret services.[164]

Although Nanking and Shanghai bore the brunt, Tai Li's operations extended from Canton to Manchuria. "The Blue Shirts," it was reported in late 1933, "have Canton all a-twitter and also all a-jitter."[165] Hu Han-min wrote vehement denunciations of them from Hong Kong;[166] and Ch'en

Chi-t'ang, the warlord of Canton, arrested seventy-four suspected Blue Shirts and executed nine of them. The *North China Herald* observed: "Communism has not been dealt with [here in Kwangtung] in more drastic fashion."[167] When the Fukien rebellion broke out in November 1933, one of the prominent slogans was "Overthrow the Blue Shirt Party,"[168] and a prominent participant in that uprising has remarked that "a most important cause of discontent [leading to the revolution] was the rise of the fascist movement."[169] Japanese sources also remarked on how the Blue Shirts were making the domestic situation "unprecedentedly tense."[170]

No one, however, was more disturbed by the Blue Shirts than were the Japanese. In 1934 an intelligence report warned Tokyo, "Chiang Kai-shek uses the Blue Shirt Society as the core of his anti-Manchukuo, Resist-Japan Policy."[171] The Blue Shirts, it was reported, dispatched bands of assassins to kill high-level Japanese and Manchukuo officials and Chinese traitors; they organized anti-Japanese militia in Manchukuo, and they led boycotts against Japanese goods. These actions were, as Iwai phrased it, part of the Blue Shirts' strategy of "long-term resistance."[172] And, to prove the anti-Japanese attitude of the Blue Shirts, Iwai quoted from their "program": "Japanese imperialism is the mortal enemy of the Chinese people, and we absolutely deny the possibility of a compromise peace. If this party does not overthrow Japanese imperialism, Japanese imperalism will destroy China. Therefore, we resolutely maintain an attitude of absolute enmity toward Japan, and the work of resisting Japan is this party's most important and most holy task."[173]

There can be no doubt that the Blue Shirts were profoundly anti-Japanese. But this fact poses some intriguing questions because this was precisely the same period when Chiang's government was harshly repressing the activities of students and other anti-Japanese groups. There are at least three possibilities. First, was Chiang purposefully conducting a policy of covert resistance to Japan, even while he mollified the Japanese with overt concessions? Second, did Chiang, against his real desires, sanction the Blue Shirts' anti-Japanese measures in order to maintain their loyalty? For, although the Blue Shirts were fiercely loyal to Chiang and under strict discipline, would not their loyalties be attenuated if he did not allow them to vent their anti-Japanese spleen? Or, third, were the Blue Shirts indeed becoming so anti-Japanese that they were acting in defiance of Chiang Kai-shek's wishes? The British journalist James Bertram has suggested this vaguely and without corroborative evidence, stating in this connection that the Blue Shirts were "getting rather out of hand."[174] Certainly it is intriguing that the central authorities of the communists in August 1935—while in the same breath castigating Chiang Kai-shek—proposed joining hands in an anti-Japanese coalition with " 'Blue Shirt' organizations who are nationally-minded."[175] It is impossible, with the materials now available, to answer these questions definitively. They do, however, suggest the complexity of relationships within Chiang's political family.

The Blue Shirt organization was disbanded in the spring of 1938. According to an unsubstantiated report, Chiang Kai-shek was released at Sian only after he made a number of concessions, one of which was that Blue Shirt activities would be halted.[176] In fact, it has never been proven that Chiang made any commitments to his captors at Sian.[177] In any event, after Chiang did determine to resist the Japanese, the continued existence of such known clandestine anti-communist and terrorist organizations as the Blue Shirts and the Pieh-tung-tui would have obstructed a rapprochement with the communists.

The spirit of the Blue Shirts did, however, survive the dissolution of the organization. In March 1938 the Three People's Principles Youth Corps (San-min chu-i ch'ing-nien-t'uan) was instituted as a means of uniting the diverse political elements of the nation during the war with Japan. Thus, the CC clique, the Blue Shirts, and the Reorganizationist clique of Wang Ching-wei were brought together even with non-Kuomintang groups like the China Youth Party and the

National Socialist Party. On the executive committee of the Youth Corps, five were of the Thirteen Princes of the Blue Shirts—including Ho Chung-han and K'ang Tse.[178] During the first years of the Youth Corps, the old Blue Shirt element did not exercise complete control, but by the end of World War II their power had become preponderant.[179]

The term "fascism" is one of the most ambiguous and emotion-laden words in the political-science lexicon. Too often the term has been used simply to slander rather than to shed light upon a political phenomenon. In view of this, can we still maintain that the Blue Shirts were a fascist movement? There is no single form or simple definition of fascism. As S. J. Woolf observed, almost in despair, "The varieties of fascism are notorious."[180] Some scholars have questioned that the Nazi movement could, strictly speaking, be counted as fascist; and recently a serious student of fascism has suggested that even "Italy under fascism was not a fascist state."[181]

Marxists have defined fascism as the highest and last stage of monopoly capitalism, but the realization that there can be "peasant" and "proletarian" forms of fascism[182] as well as bourgeois forms has forced the realization that fascism is not easily defined in either sociological or economic terms. Fascism, rather, is a political ideology that has historically proven to be attractive to widely disparate social groups in widely diverse societies. The participants in the various fascist movements have, however, shared a sense of political desperation, that often stemmed from threatened or real economic impoverishment, national humiliation, or a sensed loss of cultural roots. Whatever the stimuli of the fascist movements, they generally displayed the following ideological traits:

1. Exaltation of the state and advocacy of totalitarian controls.
2. One-party rule and glorification of the leader. A corollary to this was the rejection of democracy.
3. Nationalism, which often invoked the restoration of traditional

cultural values, as exemplified in the classicism of Mussolini and Hitler (and in the attenuated Confucianism of the New Life Movement).

4. The goal of creating a new fascist man, who would subordinate his individual will and aspirations to the collective will. As George L. Mosse wrote: "All fascism believed that, in the last resort, the spiritual unity of the nation would solve all problems.[183]

5. The glorification of violence and terror.[184]

All these traits were shared by the Blue Shirts.

Rascism was not a part of the Blue Shirt ideology, but it is doubtful that all recognizably fascist movements have stressed this aspect.[185] A more significant departure of the Blue Shirt ideology from the "ideal model" of fascism was the advocacy that the land be nationalized and collective farming be instituted. J. Solé-Tura, for example, has asserted that "No fascist movement recommends the abolition of private ownership of the means of production."[186] Yet that is precisely what the Blue Shirts writing in the *Ch'ien-t'u* did recommend. This does not, I would suggest, prove that the Blue Shirts were not fascist. To the contrary, it demonstrates again the multifarious forms that fascism assumed in different national settings.

In studying the Blue Shirts, one is inevitably struck by the fact that many of the movement's goals and policies were similar to those that have appeared in Chinese communism. The Blue Shirts' glorification of the leader, for example, has a counterpart in the communist exaltation of Mao; the Blue Shirts' desire to create a new fascist man who subordinated his personal will and welfare to that of society at large is mirrored in the communist effort to remold social behavior; the Blue Shirts' determination to transform all citizens into productive members of society has largely been put into practice by Mao's program of eliminating distinctions between those who work with their hands and those who work with their minds. And there are, of course, also the shared stress on nationalism, the common goal of totalitarian controls, the mutual repugnance for capitalism and its cultural accouterments, and the similar effort to minimize the family as the locus of social relationships.

It appears significant that two movements, as fundamentally different as were the Blue Shirts and the communists, should have propounded so many essentially similar policies. The explanation, I would suggest, is that both were responding in pragmatic fashion to Chinese conditions and behavioral traits that had defeated earlier political movements. Glorification of the leader, for example, may have resulted from the insight that a nation as large and diverse as China could not easily coalesce and hold shared political values without the force of a dominant and charismatic personality. The goal of making everyone a producer in society was no doubt a reaction to the long-gown tradition, wherein the elite disdained the masses, and the bureaucrats acted without regard for the needs of the people. Both movements rejected liberalism, for they perceived that the masses would rather be well governed than have freedom. And both would abnegate individualism, for this concept was not only alien to the traditional subordination of the individual to the social group but had been a primary symptom of cultural and national dissolution in the modern period.

Despite these resemblances, the Blue Shirts and the communists differed fundamentally, not merely in ideological terms but because they held very different conceptions of the sources of political power. Mao Tse-tung had learned that the masses could be used to create political power. The Blue Shirts, too, perceived the usefulness of mass organizations and mass support, but they seemed to believe that the masses were simply objects to be manipulated. They had not transcended, as had Mao, the traditional concept of elitist rule over a politically passive population.

The Blue Shirts should not, perhaps, be blamed for failing to comprehend the dynamics of mass politics. Indeed, only a few Chinese in the 1930s had gained the insight that mass initiative could be used to create political power. The fact that the Blue Shirts remained essentially elitist in their concept of political power may, however, have been of decisive consequence for the movement. In the first place, it raises doubts that the Blue Shirts would have been any more resolute about putting their socioeconomic program into practice than was the Nationalist bureaucracy. This is because political principles have no momentum of their own; they are borne by men, by a party, by a political movement. And if this political movement has no social base, no political constituency outside itself, it lacks a keel to keep it committed to those principles. Without a social base, the struggle for power soon becomes an end in itself, and programmatic statements cease to have meaning except as a political weapon with which to attack factional rivals.[187]

That the Blue Shirts held an elitist concept of power also helps explain why the movement did not attain the goals of reigniting the revolutionary spirit within the Kuomintang and of winning the dominant leadership of the Nanking government. Lacking a social basis for political power, the Blue Shirts became heavily dependent on the person of Chiang Kai-shek. But Chiang was only qualifiedly committed to the Blue Shirts. Thus, when in 1934 tensions between the Blue Shirts and the CC clique became so sharp that fighting nearly erupted,[188] he merely arranged for a division of labor between the two competing factions: the CC clique was to concentrate its work within the Kuomintang, while the Blue Shirts would work within the military. This jurisdictional demarcation was effective for a brief time only. The rivalry between the two factions continued, and Liu Chien-ch'ün contended that the CC clique's opposition contributed decisively to the Blue Shirts' failure[189]

Chiang Kai-shek did not wholly disapprove of these factional struggles among his supporters, for they enabled him to avoid becoming the captive of any one faction. Moreover, he vacillated in his relationship to fascist doctrines. These were doubtless attractive to him. Yet he was capable of beguiling foreign missionaries with his protestations of his Christian belief. And he even convinced some persons of his commitment to democracy. Chiang, in other words, had a multifarious constituency, and he did not conceive it to be in his interests for the Blue Shirts to gain unchallenged dominance over all other factions. The Blue Shirts had discerned some of the fundamental ills of Chinese society. Without a new concept of political power, however, fascism in China became a victim of the same factionalism, empty rhetoric and petty politicking that afflicted the Kuomintang throughout its tenure as the government of China.

Chapter 3 **The Fukien Rebellion**

The breakdown of the traditional political system had been most clearly manifested in the weakened grip of the central government upon the provinces. It was an article of faith, unquestioned by the Nationalists, that in reconstituting a viable political system they would have to destroy warlordism and make the provinces amenable to the will of the central regime.

Regionalism, however, persisted. Warlords viewed the centralizing tendencies of Nanking with distrust—not simply because they were jealous of personal power but also because Nanking's legitimacy as a national government and Chiang Kai-shek's credentials as the paramount leader remained in doubt. Furthermore, Chiang Kai-shek's rivals for dominance within the Kuomintang—men like Wang Ching-wei and Hu Han-min—losing the contest for power in the arena at Nanking, tried to recoup their political fortunes by allying with one or several of the regional autocrats. Factionalism was therefore exacerbated by regionalism, and regionalism thrived on factionalism. And Nanking never wholly succeeded in eliminating either of these centrifugal forces.

During the Nanking decade there were no fewer than twenty-seven revolts and perhaps scores of lesser uprisings that do not merit count.[1] Many of the characteristics of these revolts—the complex mixture of personal ambition, selfish regionalism, and political idealism—were highlighted in the Fukien rebellion of 1933–34.

The Fukien rebellion is known to most students of modern China primarily as a result of Mao Tse-tung's remark to Edgar Snow that "In this period [of the Fifth Extermination Campaign] we made two important errors. The first was the failure to unite with Ts'ai T'ing-k'ai's army in 1933 during the Fukien Rebellion."[2] In the end, the Fukien rebellion proved to be a minor episode during the Nanking period; in some ways it was—as several Chinese writers have put it— merely a *pa-hsi,* a sideshow or farce. The almost laughable lack of preparation and the lightening-like collapse prevented it from significantly changing the course of the nation's history. Yet, for a brief moment, the lines of strain in the Chinese political structure emerged with unusual clarity, revealing the complex and often tenuous linkages of Nanking to the provinces.

Ch'en Ming-shu and the Nineteenth Route Army

It has, perhaps, never been adequately stressed that Chinese armies, like other Chinese social institutions, tended to be bound together by close personal relations. Weberian concepts of a rationalized, universalistic structure held little sway here; and the loyalties among fellow officers customarily transcended their loyalties to the president or the national government. The Kwangsi army, commanded by Li Tsung-jen and Pai Ch'ung-hsi, is a particularly interesting example of this phenomenon; and Chiang Kai-shek doubtless cultivated his relationship with the cadets of the Whampoa Academy for the specific purpose of building up that network of personal loyalties so essential to a cohesive and obedient military force. Not all Chinese military commanders were equally successful in winning the personal loyalties of their subordinates. The armies of Feng Yü-hsiang and Ch'en Chi-t'ang, for example, both revealed fissiparous tendencies that ultimately contributed to the downfall of their commanders.

The ties that bound the Nineteenth Route Army were unusually strong, and the close relationship between Ch'en Ming-shu and the officers of that army was a critical factor in the Fukien Rebellion. The Nineteenth Route Army was formally created in the summer of 1931. The personal bonds among its leading officers had, however, been formed almost a decade earlier.[3] The first ancestor of the Nineteenth Route Army, the Fourth Regiment of the Kwangtung Army's First Division, had been formed in 1921 during the period of collaboration between Sun Yat-sen and Ch'en Chiung-ming in Canton. Ch'en Ming-shu had been commander of this Fourth Regiment, and his immediate subordinates included Chiang Kuang-nai, Ts'ai T'ing-k'ai, Tai Chi, and Ch'en Chi-t'ang. The Fourth Regiment was subsequently reorganized, renamed, and expanded several times during the revolutionary struggles of the 1920s, but these officers maintained close personal and professional ties. During the Northern Expedition in 1926, for example, Ch'en Ming-shu commanded the Eleventh Army; under him, Chiang Kuang-nai and Tai Chi were divisional commanders, and Ts'ai T'ing-k'ai was an assistant divisional commander.[4] With the notable exception of Ch'en Chi-t'ang, all these officers of the old Fourth Regiment were leaders in the Fukien rebellion.

Throughout the revolutionary campaigns of the 1920s, these comrades of the former Fourth Regiment had fought loyally and seemingly selflessly for the Kuomintang cause. By about 1929 or 1930, however, Ch'en Ming-shu began to nurse a grievance against the dominant leadership of the party. The reasons for this change of heart are unclear. A Japanese writer has suggested that Ch'en had been distressed by the Kuomintang's oppression of the people, and had begun to doubt its capacity or willingness to cope with the nation's economic problems.[5] Another event may have been of even greater gravity. During 1928 Ch'en's star had been rising. He was appointed chairman of the provincial government in

Kwangtung, and early the next year he was named to the Central Executive Committee of the Kuomintang. But then Nanking selected Ch'en Chi-t'ang to be supreme military authority in Kwangtung, thus promoting him over the head of Ch'en Ming-shu. Ch'en Ming-shu might very naturally have felt resentment at Nanking; and his relations with Ch'en Chi-t'ang were thereafter always strained.

If this is true, it would plausibly explain several of Ch'en Ming-shu's subsequent actions. For example, when Ch'en Chi-t'ang, Sun Fo, and Wang Ching-wei organized a separatist government in Canton in May 1931, Ch'en Ming-shu abandoned the provincial chairmanship and refused to support the rebels. Chiang Kai-shek was delighted and interpreted Ch'en's actions as loyalty to Nanking. It is more probable, however, that Ch'en acted out of hatred for Ch'en Chi-t'ang—for his loyalties to Chiang Kai-shek were, it is now clear, already extremely tenuous.

That Ch'en Ming-shu's loyalties to Chiang had been weakened is evidenced by the fact that he had already in 1930 acquired a controlling interest in the Shen-chou kuo-kuang-she.[6] This was a small publishing firm that since 1903 had specialized in books on art. Under Ch'en's control, however, it began to publish books on socialism. In early 1931 it also began to publish a journal, the *Tu-shu tsa-chih* ("The Research Monthly"). There is no proof that this venture into publishing was prompted by political considerations. In fact, the inaugural issue of the *Tu-shu tsa-chih* proclaimed strict political neutrality.[7] Subsequent developments at the Shen-chou kuo-kuang-she nevertheless raise suspicions that Ch'en's interest in publishing was not merely, as the editor claimed, to provide a forum for creative writing and intellectual controversy.

After Ch'en gave up the provincial chairmanship in Kwangtung in May 1931, Nanking appointed him area commander of the anti-communist forces in Kiangsi. This returned him to formal command of his old comrades of the

Fourth Regiment, who had been transferred to Kiangsi in late 1930.

Ch'en was only in Kiangsi from June through September 1931. During this short period, he formed a relationship that was to be crucial in the events leading to the Fukien rebellion. For, in Kiangsi, he came into contact with the A.B. Corps, which soon became, in Ch'en's coterie of followers, the civilian counterpart of the Nineteenth Route Army. The A.B. Corps—an abbreviation for Anti-Bolshevik Corps—had been organized in 1926 by young Kuomintang members who were opposed to the increasing communist influences within the party.[8] By mid-1931, its political coloration had changed. Wang Li-hsi, now the leader of the movement, had become disillusioned with the Kuomintang, and he was reportedly searching for a way to create a political movement with a broader appeal than mere anti-communism.[9] Whatever his motives, he and Ch'en Ming-shu, meeting in Kiangsi, quickly sensed an identity of interests. And in September 1931, no doubt through Ch'en's influence, he became editor of the *Tu-shu tsa-chih*.

As editor of the *Tu-shu tsa-chih,* Wang Li-hsi maintained a pose of political impartiality. And most of the journal's readership was, in all probability, attracted by the lively, if prolix, controversy on the essentially innocuous question of the nature of Chinese society that was carried on in its successive issues. From the time Wang joined the *Tu-shu tsa-chih,* however, Ch'en Ming-shu and the Shen-chou kuo-kuang-she were steadily sucked into the maelstrom of Chinese politics.

Wang had barely arrived at the publishing house when it began to publish journals—first the *Wen-hua tsa-chih* (Cultural magazine), soon followed by the *Wen-hua p'ing-lun* (Cultural critic)—both of which were manifestly political in orientation. Involved with the editorship of these journals was the fiery Hu Ch'iu-yüan, a former member of the Communist Youth Corps, reportedly a member of the A.B. Corps, and an inveterate activist.[10]

Soon, the Shen-chou kuo-kuang-she became a magnet for political malcontents. The Trotskyites in particular rallied around the *Tu-shu tsa-chih*. They were, perhaps, attracted by the substantial rates that *Tu-shu tsa-chih* could pay its contributors as a result of Ch'en Ming-shu's generous financial support. There was also, however, an ideological congeniality between the A.B. Corps and the Trotskyites, both of whom shared a distaste for the Communist Party as well as for the Kuomintang.[11] This group reportedly became the nucleus of a new political organization, the Social Democratic Party, headed by Ch'en Ming-shu.

The facts surrounding the alleged formation of the Social Democratic Party are obscure. It is known that Ch'en Ming-shu and the Nineteenth Route Army were transferred to Shanghai during October and November 1931. Subsequently, following Chiang Kai-shek's resignation from government on December 15, Ch'en became vice-premier of the Nationalist Government, a post that he held for only a month. Sometime during January 1932 Ch'en convoked a conference at his residence in Shanghai. Some forty persons attended, and a Social Democratic Party was reportedly organized. Ch'en Ming-shu was elected director-general (*tsung-li*), and a political program was drawn up. Members in the new party were drawn from the A.B. Corps, officers of the Nineteenth Route Army, many of the Trotskyites, and the adherents of Eugene Ch'en (who had previously formed their own Social Democratic Party under the nominal leadership of Kao Ch'eng-yüan). Some members of the reorganization clique, like T'ao Hsi-sheng, were also reported to be members of the new movement. Sun Fo, who served as premier of the central government during Chiang Kai-shek's retirement, was also said to have contributed money to it.[12]

Despite these reports, the Social Democratic Party was probably never formally instituted. What probably occurred is that the organizational progress of the new party was aborted by the outbreak of fighting in Shanghai on January 28, 1932.[13] The Shanghai Incident had a profound impact upon the officers of the Nineteenth Route Army—analogous, perhaps, to the Long March in the lives of the communist leaders. It has been remarked, for example, that the personality of Ts'ai T'ing-k'ai changed after the incident,[14] and it seems certain that their subsequent political thinking was colored by the afterglow of that legendary encounter. Had there been no Shanghai Incident, there probably would have been no Fukien rebellion.

The events of the Shanghai Incident are complex and deserving of a detailed study—there is a wealth of material on the subject.[15] The impression received by the Chinese public, however, was fairly straightforward. The Japanese, after launching their invasion of Manchuria in September 1931, struck a diversionary blow at Shanghai late in the night of January 28, 1932. To the surprise of the Japanese, and to the unrestrained satisfaction of the Chinese people, the Nineteenth Route Army fought off the attack. And then, contrary to the wishes of Nanking and without supplies or support, they held out for thirty-three bloody days, withdrawing only in the face of massive new Japanese reinforcements.

What actually occurred in the Shanghai Incident is considerably more controversial than this brief sketch would lead one to believe. Some have argued, for example, that Chiang Kai-shek actually supported the resistance against Japan, but that he posed as an advocate of appeasement in order to avert a full-scale war with Japan. And it is also contended that it was not the Nineteenth Route Army, but the central government's Fifth Army, that bore the brunt of the fighting.

Whatever the historical facts, the Nineteenth Route Army became national heroes as a result of the Shanghai Incident. The Chinese people, who had been gagging on never-ending humiliations and pusillanimous compromises, took the Nineteenth Route Army to their hearts. The names of Ts'ai T'ing-k'ai and Chiang Kuang-nai resounded through the nation. Such was their popularity that they overnight became legends. "Someday," a Chinese wrote, "when historians are busy compiling the world's history of wars, they will have grave difficulties in deciding who are the greatest two among the heroes, Washington and Nelson in the past, or Tsai Ting-kai and Chiang Kwang-nai of the present Nineteenth Route Army.''[16] The name Ts'ai T'ing-k'ai even appeared, like the name of a movie idol, as a brand name on cigarettes and other goods. And Chinese everywhere, in China and abroad, contributed money—approximately ¥40 million—to support the fight.[17] The Nineteenth Route Army had become a national symbol of selfless patriotism and courage.

The Shanghai Incident served, however, to exacerbate the strained relations between the officers of the Nineteenth Route Army and Chiang Kai-shek. During the fighting, a small newspaper was printed for the men of the Nineteenth Route Army, and it was allegedly even more acrimonious toward Nanking than toward the Japanese. And, immediately after the cease-fire, the commanders of the Nineteenth Route Army issued an open letter to the nation complaining that the government had not supported them during the Shanghai war.[18]

Chiang Kai-shek was therefore displeased with the heroes of Shanghai. Moreover, he doubtless sensed that any military unit enjoying such popularity represented a threat to his power. He therefore transferred them to Fukien barely a month after the ceasefire agreement with the Japanese on May 5, 1932. It has been alleged, with what truth is uncertain, that Chiang hoped that the Nineteenth Route Army, sent to Fukien to fight the communists, would be chewed up and destroyed in the fighting there. The Nineteenth Route Army, remarked a knowledgeable foreigner in July 1932, ''are marked men.''[19]

The government, at the same time, tried to dampen public adulation of the Nineteenth Route Army. In August a movie entitled ''A Soldier of the Nineteenth Route Army'' was banned on the grounds that it was ''undesirable for political reasons.'' The *North China Herald* assumed that the proscription resulted from a fear of antagonizing the Japanese, though it was puzzled, for it found little in the film that would excite hatred for the Japanese. ''It is nothing,'' the *North*

China Herald observed, "but the very proper praising of an ardent young soldier, a member of an army which had endeared itself to the nation."[20] It was, of course, precisely that praise that made the film politically undesirable from Nanking's point of view.

Ch'en Ming-shu, meanwhile, had broken openly with Chiang Kai-shek. After resigning as vice-premier in January he had taken up the post of minister of Communications. There he soon came under a political cloud. No doubt he was too blatantly critical of the government's handling of the resistance at Shanghai. At the same time, doubts were cast on his morality after his close associate and vice-minister of Communications, Ch'en Fu-mu, absconded to Hongkong with some ¥700,000 in government funds.[21]

Ch'en Ming-shu might have weathered this storm, for, after his resignation from his ministerial post on March 3, 1932, Chiang Kai-shek offered him the post of Army chief-of-staff. He flatly rejected this conciliatory offer, however, and he soon departed for Paris.[22] He did not return to China until the eve of the Fukien rebellion.

The Third Party

Several anti-Kuomintang groups, like the Trotskyites and the China Youth Party, participated with Ch'en Ming-shu and the Nineteenth Route Army in the Fukien rebellion. The role of the Third Party, however, was crucial. During the nascent stages of the rebellion, Ch'en Ming-shu was surrounded by and seemed to be dominated by the Third Party leaders; indeed, the revolutionary program of the rebels was in large part derived from the tenets of the Third Party. The Third Party had sprouted from the ruins of the first united front between the Kuomintang and the Chinese Communist Party. Its founders had all held positions of consequence in the left-dominated Wuhan government in 1926–27. Teng Yen-ta had held the key position of director of the general political department; T'an P'ing-shan had been minister of Agriculture; Hsü Ch'ien (George Hsü) had been on the executive committees of both the political and military councils; and Chang Po-chün served as head of the propaganda department in the general political department. Soong Ch'ing-ling, the widely respected widow of Sun Yat-sen and a member of the State Council at Wuhan, was also reputed to be a leader of the Third Party, although there is no firm evidence that she was directly involved with the Third Party after 1927.

The events of the summer of 1927 had left a deep impression on this group of revolutionaries. They all felt revulsion toward the seemingly counter-revolutionary policies and toward the military dictatorship of the Kuomintang dominated by Chiang Kai-shek. At the same time, they had been appalled by the violence then favored by the Communist Party. After the collapse of the leftist Wuhan government in July 1927, therefore, this group had no political home. Many of them, like Teng Yen-ta, Soong Ch'ing-ling, and Eugene Ch'en, had taken refuge in Russia or Europe after leaving Wuhan. There they decided to reform their revolutionary ranks and called on their former comrades still in China to form a new party—a third party—that would perpetuate the ideals of Sun Yat-sen, combat the reactionary regime in Nanking, and avoid the revolutionary excesses of the communists. In about December 1927 this third party was formally organized as the Chinese Revolutionary Party (Chung-hua ko-ming-tang). This had been the name of Sun Yat-sen's organization from 1914–1919 and had been adopted at the urging of Soong Ch'ing-ling, who felt that it commemorated the revolutionary spirit of her husband. But the term "The Third Party" (Ti-san-tang) always had greater popular currency than the formal name.[23]

The new party was plagued with chronic factionalism. Initially, the moderate faction looked to Teng Yen-ta as their leader. Teng did not return from Europe until mid-1930, however, and so his position was represented by Chi Fang and Huang Ch'i-hsiang.[24] Their rival for domination of the Third Party was the so-called "communist faction" led by T'an P'ing-shan. T'an had quit the Communist Party in about September 1927, and he had soon molded a following composed for the most part of ex-communists. They opposed the violent excesses of the Communist Party but nevertheless advocated relatively radical measures. T'an P'ing-shan, in addition, persistently toyed with the idea of allying with the Chinese Communist Party.[25]

These intra-party tensions blew up into a crisis in 1930 when Teng Yen-ta informed his adherents in China that he had, on his own initiative, established an alliance between the Third Party and the social-democratic Second Communist International.[26] T'an P'ing-shan was enraged by this turn of events. He resented the fact that Teng—who had remained in Europe throughout the organizational phase of the party— treated the party as a personal possession. Moreover, T'an disapproved of the moderate reformism of social democracy. To resolve the conflict, a representative conference of the Third Party was convoked in Shanghai on September 1, 1930. There, Teng Yen-ta's faction carried the day. T'an was either expelled from the party or he simply became inactive—it is not clear which. And a party program incorporating Teng's advocacy of state capitalism and workers' democracy was adopted.[27]

During the ensuing year, under the guidance of Teng Yen-ta, the Third Party attained the height of its influence. From headquarters in Shanghai, the party leadership directed regional councils in eleven provinces—the one in Fukien becoming the largest and most active. Membership of the party had reached nearly 4,000 in April 1930, and although it expanded rapidly during 1930 and 1931, the Third Party never became very significant in terms of the number of its members.[28] Nevertheless, the activities of the Third Party worried Nanking, and Chiang Kai-shek is quoted as saying, "If this group does not die, the nation will never be at peace."[29]

Chiang obviously meant this statement to be taken literally, for Teng Yen-ta was arrested in the International Settlement at Shanghai in August 1931, turned over to Nanking, and quickly executed for treason.[30]

Teng, a man of awesome abilities and an engaging public

speaker, was one of the most highly regarded men in Chinese politics.[31] And his death dealt a near fatal blow to the Third Party. Deprived of his commanding leadership, factional enmities burst uncontrollably to the surface. (Perhaps it was merely a rumor generated by the intra-party hatreds, but suspicions were voiced that Teng had been arrested only after the communist faction of the party had betrayed him to the Kuomintang.[32])

The chief competitors for leadership of the Third Party after Teng's arrest were Hsü Ch'ien, Chang Po-chün, and Huang Ch'i-hsiang. In November a conference of the party was held in Shanghai to select Teng's successor, but after three days of meetings, still no decision had been made. Whereupon Chang Po-chün—who had succeeded T'an P'ing-shan as head of the communist faction—delivered a speech declaring that the principles of social democracy were non-revolutionary and were unsuited to China's circumstances. He demanded in conclusion that the party adopt a truly revolutionary program. This speech threw the meeting into an uproar. And the participants, fearing that the tumult would draw the police, fled the meeting without coming to any conclusion regarding who would lead the party.[33]

Reports of the intra-party struggles during 1932 and 1933 are notoriously unreliable. Seemingly, the chief factions were a military clique headed by Huang Ch'i-hsiang, and a civilian (and pro-communist) clique headed by Lo Ch'un-i.[34] During the year preceding the Fukien rebellion, this latter group focused its activities in western Fukien. Elsewhere, however, the Third Party was in shambles.

Reform in Fukien

The Nineteenth Route Army arrived in Fukien, unit by unit, during July 1932. They were received ecstatically. The local population, it was reported, "welcomed them madly, and respected them as gods."[35] A foreigner remarked, "It is rather pathetic to see how all the people who have been suffering from official and unofficial oppression are looking forward to the righting of their wrongs by the new leaders.''[36]

The task of the Nineteenth Route Army was to fight the communists in western Fukien and in neighboring Kiangsi. And, for a few desultory battles, it did engage in the "extermination" campaigns. Soon, however, the energies of the army commanders were absorbed by other problems. Perhaps it was the warm welcome they had received from the local people; in any case, they had concluded that operations against the communists would be ineffectual as long as the social and economic problems in the province remained unsolved.

Fukien is one of China's most scenic provinces. For centuries, poets and painters had been inspired by its sheer, pine-draped mountains. But the people of Fukien suffered chronic impoverishment. Tillable land was scant; even fishing the cragged bays, the predominant occupation of the province, could not feed the dense population.[37] In recent years, warlord politics had engulfed the province. It was fragmented politically on a small scale much as the nation as a whole had been divided by large, regional potentates. Nominally, the province was governed by an appointee of Nanking. Much of the real power, however, was held by independent military forces. The naval clique had been a dominant force in the area of Foochow since the nineteenth century. And, in the interior, a variety of "provincial defense armies" reigned supreme. They had acquired a stamp of legitimacy from the provincial government. But they were widely regarded as "local bandits" (*t'u-fei*) who taxed and oppressed the inhabitants unmercifully.[38]

The Nineteenth Route Army's decision to remedy these problems quickly plunged it into a struggle for power with the existing authorities. The army posted slogans, "Abolish all exploitative taxes, disband bandit-like provincial defense forces"; the provincial police tore them down. The army commanders convoked meetings to plan provincial improvements; but the provincial authorities refused to attend. The dispute was coming to a head in September 1932 when charges were made against the provincial chairman that he planted and smoked opium, and that he had publicly referred to Sun Yat-sen as a bandit chieftain. The charges may have been trumped up, but they worked. In late October the entire provincial government resigned, and a month later Nanking appointed General Chiang Kuang-nai to serve as provincial chairman. Ts'ai T'ing-k'ai succeeded General Chiang as commander of the Nineteenth Route Army and simultaneously assumed the post of pacification commander. The *North China Herald* observed that "these new appointments make the Fukien Government practically a 19th Route Army affair."[39]

The Nineteenth Route Army eliminated the armed bands in the interior of the province with equal efficiency. Employing treachery worthy of Ts'ao Ts'ao, the most prominent commander of a "provincial defense army," Ch'en Kuo-hui, was invited to Foochow. There he was quickly arrested and placed on "trial." He had, it was charged, imposed a "reign of terror . . . creating miseries to the people, and . . . had killed numerous persons that displeased him." He was executed in December 1932. Despite some further fighting in the interior, the remaining provincial armies for the most part quickly fell into line and accepted the hegemony of the Nineteenth Route Army.[40]

The reform efforts of the Nineteenth Route Army were directed largely to improving communications, abolishing the miscellaneous and arbitrary tax assessments on the peasants, and protecting the common citizen from general political oppression and harassment. The most intensive and significant of these reforms were instituted in the western districts of the province, in an experimental project administered by the Western Fukien Reconstruction Council (Min-hsi shan-hou wei-yüan-hui). Subsequently, during the Fukien rebellion, the political and economic programs of the rebel regime were modeled on the measures introduced by this Reconstruction Council.

Western Fukien had long been a focus of reform and revolutionary activity. As early as 1928, Teng Yen-ta had sent a party organizer to Fukien, and the western and southern parts of the province became the stronghold of Third Party activity. Even after the communists occupied the area in 1929, Third Party members continued their work there, infiltrating the Communist Party organization and participating in the communists' land revolution.[41]

The Nineteenth Route Army became involved with these reform activities in western Fukien through the person of Hsü Ming-hung. Hsü was a long-time director of the Nineteenth Route Army's secretariat and was himself a member of the Third Party. After the Nineteenth Route Army had recovered the area around Lung-yen in western Fukien from the communists in October 1932, Hsü took the initiative in establishing the Reconstruction Council. Hsü had also been cultivating Ts'ai T'ing-k'ai's political awareness, encouraging him to read Marxist theory and the writings of Teng Yen-ta. Ts'ai therefore enthusiastically supported the undertaking, and accepted the title of chairman of the Reconstruction Council. While others in the Kuomintang spent their time fighting for control of the party, he remarked, they in Fukien were actively realizing the revolutionary spirit.[42]

Although the Western Fukien Reconstruction Council was actively supported by the Nineteenth Route Army, it was essentially a Third Party undertaking: the reforms adopted were derived from Third Party ideology, and a sizable part of the remaining Third Party membership came to participate in the reforms.[43] The heart of the Reconstruction Council's work in western Fukien was the Third Party's land reform program, sloganized as *chi-k'ou shou-t'ien* (per capita land distribution). According to the *chi-k'ou shou-t'ien* formula, all land was to be nationalized and would in turn be distributed equitably for the use of all elements of the population. Twenty percent of the harvest from the lands thus distributed would be turned over to the government. This, at the time, was viewed as a radical reform program, for, in contrast to Sun

Yat-sen's proposal of "land to the tiller" (*keng-che yu ch'i t'ien*), it would abolish private possession of land. It also differed from the communist program, because the government would retain title to the land, and the lands would be distributed without regard to the prior economic status of the farmers.[44]

The reforms of the Nineteenth Route Army in Fukien during the sixteen months prior to the outbreak of the rebellion are difficult to assess. In nearby Kiangsi, the communists were sharply critical. They asserted, for example, that the real purpose of *chi-k'ou shou-t'ien* was to preserve the privileges of the exploiting classes by mollifying the poorer peasants. The virulence of the communists' criticism suggests that the programs of the Reconstruction Council were a success. As a communist writer commented in 1934, these programs "were extremely dangerous for us."[45]

Other sources also support a favorable judgment of the Nineteenth Route Army's reconstruction efforts. A foreigner who returned to Amoy after an absence of two years found the roads and communications greatly improved. And he concluded, "There is at least change, and a spirit of progress." A tour of Amoy University students to western Fukien obtained a generally favorable impression of the work of the Reconstruction Council. The students' shock at some of the primitive aspects of life there demonstrates, however, that the reformers still had not solved some of the province's basic problems.[46]

Other reports indicate that the troops of the Nineteenth Route Army displayed a discipline seldom seen in China at that time. Said one journalist: "The people of Foochow . . . concede that [men of the Nineteenth Route Army] were the best behaved soldiers Foochow had seen in many a day. They always paid ready money for their purchases, and even during the recent days of fighting [during the rebellion], we haven't heard of a single instance of looting or hooliganism."[47]

Despite these favorable observations, the common people of

the province had become restive under the rule of the Nineteenth Route Army. A journal published by the Nineteenth Route Army acknowledged that costs of road construction had necessitated the imposition of compulsory public loans in each district. This had provoked much public discontent, and the writer sadly noted, "This certainly was not the original intention of the Nineteenth Route Army when it came here." Another official publication recorded that labor service had been required of the people, and it admitted that "the work of the masses had been [adversely] affected."[48] A less friendly source observed that the army officers displayed no respect for the people, the administrators had become corrupt, and the officers' lack of administrative experience had resulted in a constant revision of government policies which in turn created hardships for the people.[49]

It was traditional in China for political sentiment to receive expression in verse or song. One such folk song, addressed to the Nineteenth Route Army, read:

> When we heard you were coming to Fukien,
>   We rejoiced in Heaven and felt pleasure in Earth,
> After you arrived in Fukien,
>   You overturned Heaven and upset Earth;
> If now you should leave Fukien,
>   We would thank Heaven and thank Earth.[50]

However noble the intentions of the Nineteenth Route Army commanders might have been, they had failed to retain the popular support of the Fukienese. Plagued by financial shortages, it had proven impractical to lessen the people's tax burden. And the army's domination of the provincial government had had two adverse effects. First, numerous native Fukienese had been put out of work, and this had a seriously depressing effect on the economy, particularly in Foochow. Second, the Nineteenth Route Army was composed overwhelmingly of Cantonese, and—because regional prejudices in China are often intense—much popular dissatisfaction was engendered by the Fukienese distaste for being ruled by "outsiders."[51] For whatever reasons, public opinion had turned against the Nineteenth Route Army. And, as a consequence, there was no mass uprising in its support when the revolutionary movement faced military defeat.

Preparations for Revolution

The outbreak of the Fukien rebellion caught no one by surprise. The movements of the *dramatis personae* were regularly reported in the press, and Chiang Kai-shek knew of the final decision to revolt almost as soon as did Ch'en Ming-shu.

After Ch'en Ming-shu resigned as minister of Communications in March 1932, he resided in Shanghai. Already he was suspected of political intrigue, and the very secrecy of his movements drew attention to him and prompted comment. In October 1932 he suddenly departed for Hong Kong, where he dropped out of sight for ten days. Again this was reported in the press, and there were conjectures that he was planning to use the Nineteenth Route Army in some political adventure. He had, one observer remarked, "a hero's plans" (*hsiung-t'u*). And from Hong Kong he left for Europe, where his every move and every act were—or so he complained—reported back to Nanking.[52]

Ch'en returned from Europe, after a six-month sojourn, in May 1933. It is uncertain whether or not he had formulated any plan of revolutionary action at that time. According to one report, he returned at the instance of Hu Han-min, who was now plotting his own anti-Chiang revolt and who was tempting Ch'en to join the revolt by offering him his former post of Kwangtung provincial chairman. Some support for this view is provided by the fact that, when Ch'en arrived at Hong Kong, he was met at the dock by an imposing delegation of Kwangtung dignitaries, including Tsou Lu, Lin Yün-kai, and Hu Han-min himself.[53]

Ch'en, however, did not linger in Hong Kong, but went directly to Fukien. There, at the end of May, a huge reception was staged for him, and he was greeted with banners hailing him as a "national hero" (*min-tsu ying-hsiung*). In a lengthy speech to the gathering, Ch'en denounced Nanking's foreign policy, and demanded greater freedoms for the people. In this public address, he denied that he had any political ambitions or that he planned to form a new political party. He had come to Fukien, he said, simply to read, be with old friends, and help out if his services were needed.[54]

Ch'en's real motives were not so innocent, and in private conversations he said that they must launch a revolution if the nation were to be preserved. Chiang Kuang-nai from the outset supported Ch'en's view. But Ts'ai T'ing-k'ai demurred. Despite his vexation with Nanking and Chiang Kai-shek for inadequate support during the Shanghai fighting and now for niggardly supplies to the army in Fukien, he still professed loyalty to the central authorities. Moreover, for military and financial reasons Ts'ai felt it would be foolhardy to revolt against Nanking. The Nineteenth Route Army was no match for the whole of the Nanking army. And Fukien was not financially self-sustaining. The army barely subsisted on monthly allotments from Nanking and Kwangtung—financial support that would vanish when a revolt began.[55]

Confronted with Ts'ai's objections, Ch'en—having stayed only six days in Fukien—returned to Hong Kong to work out an alliance with Hu Han-min's anti-Chiang movement in Kwangtung and Kwangsi. Ch'en was doubtlessly optimistic, because he had learned that the Kwangtung and Kwangsi authorities had set October 10, the Chinese national holiday, as the date for the establishment of a new, anti-Chiang military government. Entirely counter to expectations, however, Ch'en Chi-t'ang, the military lord of Kwangtung, adamantly refused to participate in the undertaking. Thus, in June 1933, the revolutionary project stalled.[56]

Four months later, there was a swirl of new activity, inspired in all probability by the belief that Kwangtung–Kwangsi would now participate in a revolt against Chiang. On October 6 Ch'en Ming-shu secretly flew to Fukien for a week of meetings with the provincial authorities and members of the Third Party. Shortly afterwards, several Fukien leaders, including Chiang Kuang-nai and Hsü Ming-hung, went to Hong Kong where further discussions with Kwang-tung–Kwangsi and Third Party leaders were held. By mid-October, the revolutionary forces were coalescing. Less than four weeks later, Fukien declared its independence, and the rebellion began.

A swarm of would-be revolutionaries descended on Foo-chow during mid-November. Ch'en Ming-shu and Huang Ch'i-hsiang flew from Hong Kong on November 10. During the next ten days scores of others followed, including Li Chi-shen, Fang Chen-wu (acting, it was reported, as Feng Yü-hsiang's representative), and Eugene Ch'en, who arrived on November 20.[57]

With each arrival, the composition of the revolutionaries became more complex. In addition to the relatively non-doctrinaire members of the Nineteenth Route Army and to the left-leaning Third Party, there were now Trotskyites, members of the right-wing China Youth Party, and intellectuals like Hu Ch'iu-yüan and Mei Kung-pin, who claimed no party affiliation.

Nanking had, of course, been watching the peregrinations of the conspirators with exceeding interest. It was not until November 10, however, that it obtained information that a revolution was definitely to be attempted. To dissuade the revolutionaries, Nanking sent Lin Sen, the venerable chairman of the Nationalist Government, to Foochow. Lin arrived in Foochow on November 13, declaring to the press that he had returned to his native province to pay respects at his mother's grave. He met repeatedly with Ch'en Ming-shu and other rebel leaders, but without effect. He returned to Nanking stating, "All is quiet in Fukien."[58] Even on the eve of the revolution Nanking still hoped to avoid the conflict.

To forestall the planned uprising, Nanking still had one card to play. This card was the person of Ts'ai T'ing-k'ai. Ts'ai's support of the uprising was crucial, for most of the troops of the Nineteenth Route Army were loyal to him, and they probably would not participate in any engagement without his command. Ts'ai may even have informed Chiang Kai-shek several times during the planning stages that he did not wish to participate in a rebellion.[59] Chiang therefore had reason to hope that Ts'ai, a key to the whole plot, would declare his loyalty to Nanking. Acting on that hope, Chiang on November 19 sent an airplane to bring Ts'ai back to Nan-chang where they might negotiate a settlement.[60]

This maneuver failed, and the pilot of the airplane, an American, was arrested by the Fukien revolutionaries. For Ts'ai had finally determined to support the revolutionary attempt. The sheer momentum of events, it seems, had over-taken him. Still convinced that the revolution could not suc-ceed, yet firmly loyal to his friends, he declared his support of the enterprise. "O.K.," he said, "this army was originally created in the cause of truth; now, if it is to be destroyed, it might as well be destroyed in the cause of truth."[61]

The Rebel Government and Its Ideology

The rebellion was not formally started until November 20, but it moved into low gear two days earlier. On November 18, Ts'ai T'ing-k'ai's Pacification Commission quietly assumed control of the Foochow and Amoy branches of the Central Bank and of the Maritime Customs Offices.[62] The following day the province was declared to be under martial law.

The rebels sent two important telegrams. In one, Ch'en Ming-shu wrote personally to Chiang Kai-shek, searingly criticizing his policies and suggesting that he resign. In the other, Ch'en Ming-shu, Li Chi-shen, Chiang Kuang-nai, and Ts'ai T'ing-k'ai jointly appealed to the authorities of Kwang-tung and Kwangsi to join forces in overthrowing Chiang Kai-shek. "Chiang Kai-shek's dictatorship and destruction of the nation," they declared, "have lasted for six years, and the people of the whole world hate his perverse and unrighteous actions."[63]

The next morning, November 20, soldiers, workers, peas-ants, businessmen, teachers, students, and a few curiosity seekers gathered at the Foochow Public Gymnasium to attend the Chinese All-Nation People's Provisional Representative

Assembly.[64] Estimates of the crowd went as high as twenty and even thirty thousand—though the official account stated that 100,000 had attended the mass meeting. Over 100 of those present were official delegates, representing twenty-seven of China's twenty-eight provinces. Some of these had come to Foochow specifically to participate in the rebellion; most of them, however, were natives of other provinces now residing in Fukien.

Enthusiasm, according to some sources, ran high. The spontaneity of the revolutionary fervor has, however, been questioned. Many of the "masses" who attended the assembly had allegedly either been hired or compelled to participate. And an American foreign service officer reported that the revolution was opposed by practically the entire population of Fukien. "For once," the report read, "not even the students show any enthusiasm."[65]

The leadership of the revolution was undaunted. At least seventeen of the leaders delivered impassioned speeches. A proposal to establish a new revolutionary government was unanimously adopted by a show of hands. And then two major revolutionary documents, the Political Program (*Cheng-kang*) and the Declaration of People's Rights. (*Jen-min ch'üan-li hsüan-yen*) were approved. Slogans, reflecting the goals and discontents of the revolutionaries, reverberated through the gymnasium:

Protect People's Rights!
Liberate the Peasants and Workers!
Establish a Government of the Producing People!
Abrogate all Traitorous Secret Treaties!
Overthrow Imperialism!
Overthrow Chiang Kai-shek!
Destroy Chiang Kai-shek's Running Dogs, the Blue Shirts!
Overthrow Japanese Imperialism, Restore the Lost Territories of Manchuria!
Oppose Conciliation with Japan, Abolish the Tangku Truce![66]

In the midst of the excitement, the flag of the Nationalist government was torn down, and a new one unfurled. The same day, orders went out to remove the picture and revolutionary testament of Sun Yat-sen from all public buildings.[67] A new calendar was also introduced, beginning—like that of a new dynasty—with the Year One.

These were symbolic acts that had a profound impact on public opinion throughout the nation. This was the first uprising since the Nationalist government was established, that had the effrontery to rebel not just against the government— for which most people sensed little affection—but against Sun Yat-sen and the Kuomintang! It would surely be an exaggeration to suggest that these acts in themselves determined the outcome of the revolution. Most Chinese at that time had, however, learned to venerate Sun Yat-sen as *kuo-fu,* the father of the country, and the rejection of him and his teachings seemed to be a radical excess that puzzled and shocked the people. At the very least, it provided important potential allies (like Kwangtung and Kwangsi) with a convenient pretext to remain neutral. At the mass meeting, however, these thoughts did not becloud the revolutionaries' fervor, and they paraded through the streets of Foochow, shouting slogans, until late in the afternoon.

During the two days after the mass meeting of November 20, the structure and policies of the People's Revolutionary Government took form. The Representative Assembly had approved a temporary seventeen-member council of directors (headed by Huang Ch'i-hsiang); this body in turn appointed an eleven-man Revolutionary Government Council (Ko-ming cheng-fu wei-yüan-hui), which was to be the highest policy-formulating organ.[68] Beneath this council, a complete administrative bureaucracy was established. This included a Ministry of the Interior headed by Ch'en Ming-shu; Foreign Affairs, headed by Eugene Ch'en; and an economic commission directed by Chiang Kuang-nai.[69]

Chairman of the new government was Li Chi-shen, a veteran revolutionary who was once described as "stocky and goggle-eyed . . . He entertained no doubts that he was called on to play a leading role on the political arena."[70] Li was, in fact, pretty much of a figurehead. The real prime mover of the revolutionary movement was Ch'en Ming-shu, although he shunned the top post in the government thinking that a man of wider reputation was needed in order to win international recognition. He had hoped to entice someone like Hu Han-min or Ts'ai Yüan-p'ei to the position, but, failing these, settled for Li Chi-shen.[71]

On the evening of November 22 inaugural ceremonies for the new officials were held in the auditorium of the Fukien Provincial Government. The People's Revolutionary Government was now officially established. The establishment of the new government had been accompanied by a shower of declarations, which spelled out the motives, goals, and general policies of the revolutionaries. The immediate target of the revolution was, of course, Chiang Kai-shek and his supporters in the Nanking government. Chiang, it was charged, had done nothing to improve the livelihood of the people, democracy was a meaningless slogan, he recklessly provoked civil wars, and his administration was corrupt and ineffective. The Nanking government's "sole task has been to exploit and repress the producing masses of the nation."[72]

While the revolutionaries thus expressed anger about domestic conditions, they fulminated even more against Chiang Kai-shek's failure to fight the Japanese:

Now Chiang has completely adopted a pro-Japanese policy. And if this policy is not stopped, the whole of China will fall before Japan's system of aggression . . . If we permit Chiang Kai-shek and his regime to continue running the government so that they carry out their policies of disregarding the will of the nation and betraying the race, then the Chinese people will become the slaves of Japan."[73]

Intemperate words! Yet they were good politics. For, especially after the Tangku Truce of May 1933, Chinese everywhere were deeply resentful that their government had been forced repeatedly to yield to Japanese arrogance and aggression. The urban and intellectual classes particularly were distraught by Chiang Kai-shek's policy toward Japan, and this statement now made a bid for their support.

The anti-Japanese orientation of the revolutionaries did not imply, as a corollary, reliance on the Western powers. In a vitriolic declaration to the outside world, the new government condemned the Westerners for reneging on their treaty commitments under the Nine-Power Agreement at the Washington Conference and the Kellogg-Briand Peace Pact. It even rejected international technical cooperation, stating that reliance on the League of Nations or on a single nation, like the United States, would simply place China under international controls. This, the revolutionary government asserted, would have even more invidious consequences than the results of Chiang's pro-Japanese policy.

The foreign policy goal of the new government was to attain complete national independence. Existing treaties would be renegotiated on the basis of national equality. Foreign loans inimical to Chinese interests would be disavowed. And foreign enterprises in China would be either expropriated or subject to Chinese controls.[74] These, again, were propositions that had a strong appeal to nationalistic sentiments.

The economic programs of the revolutionary government were for the most part modeled after those of the Western Fukien Reconstruction Council. The system of *chi-k'ou shou-t'ien* was adopted. Forests, mines, and waterways were also to be nationalized. And even commercial enterprises that affected the daily needs of the people were to be managed by the state.[75]

This was a radical program that was substantially the same as the Third Party platform that Teng Yen-ta had written in 1930. Here in Fukien, however, it had been hammered out only after heated quarrels among the several disparate political groups that had been drawn to Fukien by the smell of revolution.

The first indication of partisan conflict among the Fukien revolutionaries occurred even before the declaration of independence. On the evening of November 17 the leaders of the several parties had met in the home of Chiang Kuang-nai to lay the foundations for the new government. There a debate erupted, so acrimonious that—to use the words of a reporter —"the air smoked and the bricks shook."[76] Indeed, the conflict was so serious that it threatened to destroy the revolutionary movement. To prevent this, the leaders of the several parties held a second meeting, late the same night. And they finally accepted Hsü Ch'ien's suggestion that all groups participating in the revolution cease independent partisan activity. Instead, an umbrella organization called the People's Revolutionary Alliance (Jen-min ko-ming ta-t'ung-meng) should be formed to coordinate all political activities.[77]

For the moment, the ideological fissures were papered over. And Ch'en Ming-shu enthusiastically greeted the solution, saying that henceforth "We will not talk about right-wing or left-wing, but will join hands and advance."[78] Ch'en's optimism soon proved to be misplaced. Control of the revolution was at stake, and the struggle could not be dissipated by ad hoc organizational innovations. This became clear during the mass meeting of November 20, when the proceedings were marred by the Third Party members. Some of these passed among the crowd handing out Third Party propaganda sheets. And a Third Party member, giving a speech, proclaimed the slogans: "Teng Yen-ta's spirit has not died!" and "Long Live the Third Party."[79]

Ch'en Ming-shu had been ill and had not been present at the meeting. But Ts'ai T'ing-k'ai was furious at this show of partisanship which so manifestly violated the recent agreement banning independent party activity. After the mass meeting, Ts'ai called Huang Ch'i-hsiang and other Third Party leaders together and demanded that their party be abolished forthwith. Huang Ch'i-hsiang initially asked for three days to decide. But the next day he announced that he was leaving the Third Party. And on December 11 the Third Party declared its dissolution. The announcement stated that, since the Third Party was in complete agreement with the principles of the revolutionary movement, there was no need for them to cling to their separate party affiliation.[80]

The disbanding of the Third Party was the final act in a sharp struggle for control of the revolution. In the first days of revolutionary preparation, the Third Party had largely dominated events. As Hu Ch'iu-yüan recalled, "Among the parties and factions on the eve of the rebellion, the Worker–Peasant Party [that is, the Third Party] was the most powerful. Everything was decided by them."[81] This preponderant influence did not result simply from their numerical size, although it is true that the Third Party was the largest single political party involved in the revolutionary preparations. Rather, the Third Party in Fukien was better organized and possessed a more coherent ideology than the other parties. Consequently it was able to exert an influence out of proportion to its size.[82] There had, for example, been strong opposition to the Third Party's policy of *chi-k'ou shou-t'ien*. As one opponent of the Third Party remarked, with considerable understatement, "We thought the land policy had been overemphasized."[83] Yet the Third Party had been able to overcome this opposition, and the *chi-k'ou shou-t'ien* solution to the agrarian problem was incorporated prominently into the revolutionary program.

This influence of the Third Party in the rebel forces quickly waned. Ch'en Ming-shu had become distrustful of the Third Party and of Huang Ch'i-hsiang in particular, thinking that they were only using him and the Nineteenth Route Army for their own partisan purposes.[84] As a consequence, the Third Party was ultimately "pushed outside the inner circle, and they could only look on from the sidelines."[85] Deprived of real power, the leaders of the Third Party had nevertheless been mollified with nominally prominent posts in the new government: Huang Ch'i-hsiang was head of the General Staff Department, Hsü Ch'ien was judge of the Supreme Court, and Chang Po-chün was director of the educational commission.[86]

This encounter with the organized machinations of the Third Party had convinced Ch'en Ming-shu's group that they themselves needed a more tightly disciplined political party. As a consequence, they formed the Sheng-ch'an-tang (Producers' Party), the core of which was the old *Tu-shu tsa-chih* group—notably, Wang Li-hsi, Hu Ch'iu-yüan and Mei Kung-pin. A problem that I have been unable to resolve is *when* the Sheng-ch'an-tang was formed. Chiang Kai-shek, in a telegram dated November 23, stated that Ch'en had already organized the Sheng-ch'an-tang—although other reports as late as December 30 stated that the Sheng-ch'an-tang had still not been formally organized.[87] Obviously, further research is needed to clarify this point.

The Race for Allies

It has become customary to speak of the "nominal" unification of China after 1927. But the political condition of China at the provincial and sub-provincial levels has not been systematically studied. It has, as a consequence, been difficult to visualize how really delicate was the balance of power between the Nanking Government and the numerous regional powers, and among the regional powers themselves. The Fukien rebellion momentarily shook that balance of power, forcing all elements in the Chinese political world to shift, or threaten to shift, their positions in order to maintain themselves in the new political equilibrium.

The fundamental strategic assumption of Ch'en Ming-shu and his fellow conspirators had been that much of the nation would join the revolution against Nanking as soon as Fukien declared its independence. This assumption was based partially on a reading of popular sentiment toward the Nanking regime. But, far more important, the revolutionaries had already negotiated with many of China's regional powers, and had obtained more or less firm promises of support. Huang Ch'i-hsiang had visited Yen Hsi-shan, Feng Yü-hsiang, Han Fu-chü, and other prominent leaders in north China and had returned satisfied that at least some of them had agreed to aid the revolution.[88] Soong Ch'ing-ling, whose voice was still influential, was said to have promised to declare her support for the revolution if and when the revolutionary armies captured Hangchow.[89] And there were even some officials in

Nanking—the names of T. V. Soong and Sun Fo have been mentioned in this regard—who vowed support for the revolutionary undertaking.[90]

However, the factor which could be decisive for the success or failure of the revolution, as both Fukien and Nanking recognized, was the attitude of Kwangtung and Kwangsi. The virtual autonomy of these two provinces vis-à-vis Nanking had been formalized at the end of 1931 with the creation of the Southwest Political Council and the Southwest Headquarters of the Kuomintang Central Executive Committee.[91]

Despite this apparatus that administratively linked Kwangtung and Kwangsi, the governing authorities in these so-called "Southwest" provinces each pursued essentially independent policies. In Kwangsi, Li Tsung-jen and Pai Ch'ung-hsi were relatively enlightened militarists whose reforms in this poor and backward province were attaining impressive results. But their political interests and ambitions were national. There was a good prospect, therefore, that they could be tempted to declare support for the revolution.

The warlord of Kwangtung, Ch'en Chi-t'ang, was a different kind of political animal. He was the most powerful force, militarily and financially, in south China. But his commitment was to his province, and he displayed no aspirations to extend his power beyond the provincial borders.

Complicating the arrangement of political forces in south China was the presence of the venerable party elder, Hu Han-min. After Chiang Kai-shek released him from house arrest in October 1931, Hu came to south China where Ch'en Chi-t'ang received him warmly. Ch'en apparently sensed the advantages of ridding himself of a warlord image by associating with the Kuomintang's leading theoretician. He therefore provided sumptuously for Hu, giving him a large house in Hong Kong, a retinue of servants, and a sizable monthly stipend. But he carefully prevented Hu from gaining any real political power. Ch'en, it was said, "respects Hu like a Buddha, but defends against him like a bandit."[92]

Hu Han-min was important in Ch'en Ming-shu's strategic

planning, because Hu was also actively plotting to remove Chiang Kai-shek from power. As early as 1932, he and his supporters, in concert with Li Tsung-jen and Pai Ch'ung-hsi, had formed a covert "New" Kuomintang in preparation for their return to the national political arena. It had possibly been in conjunction with these New Kuomintang plans that Ch'en Ming-shu had returned from Europe in May 1933.

Ch'en Chi-t'ang had strongly opposed this endeavor. He had recently inaugurated a three-year plan of economic development and was loath to divert funds to a military adventure that, in his eyes, offered faint prospects of success. Indeed, for a time, the New Kuomintang conducted an "Overthrow Ch'en, Welcome Hu" campaign, designed to remove Ch'en Chi-t'ang and place Hu Han-min in control of Kwangtung's modern army and rich resources. Ch'en responded ruthlessly to this challenge, executing two of the New Kuomintang propagandists. By July 1933, nevertheless, the leaders of the New Kuomintang felt that they had won Ch'en Chi-t'ang to their cause, and they had therefore proceeded with their plans to launch an expedition against Chiang Kai-shek.[93]

The New Kuomintang's scheme to overthrow the Nanking regime in October 1933 was never tested, for Ch'en Chi-t'ang had finally refused to participate. Nevertheless, Ch'en Ming-shu had been confident of support from Kwangtung and Kwangsi when he launched his own anti-Chiang rebellion on November 20. Why? Ch'en Ming-shu may have reasoned that he could invoke the provisions of the "Kwangtung–Kwangsi–Fukien Alliance Agreement." This was a mutual defense pact, ostensibly directed against Japan and the communists, that the three provinces had concluded in January 1933. In fact, the pact had been designed so that the three provinces would form a united front in the face of Chiang Kai-shek's threatened encroachments—a threat more real to these southern provinces than either the communists or Japanese. The agreement provided, for example, that if one province "encounters external aggression," the other two provinces would come to its aid and protection. And, if two of the provinces agreed on a matter of common benefit, the third province would be obliged to participate.[94]

When the rebellion did occur, this pact proved to be useless. For the authorities of Kwangtung and Kwangsi claimed that the agreement had been invalidated when Fukien abandoned the Three People's Principles.[95] Despite its impotence, the agreement provides fascinating demonstration of the diplomatic relationships that existed between the various warlord regions during the Nanking period.

It is, moreover, doubtful that Ch'en Ming-shu was so politically naive as to expect that the pact would of itself induce Kwangtung and Kwangsi to participate in the rebellion. What Ch'en probably planned was to *force* Kwangtung to join. Several months earlier, he had conceived the idea that the Nineteenth Route Army in conjunction with the forces of Kwangsi could frighten Ch'en Chi-t'ang into aiding a revolutionary undertaking.[96] And, when the rebellion did erupt, the Fukien leaders did in fact ponder the alternative of attacking Kwangtung before turning their guns against Nanking.

Even if Ch'en Ming-shu thought that Ch'en Chi-t'ang could be pressured to join the revolution—in itself a questionable premise—he was foolish and reckless to launch the revolution when he did, for it was improbable that even Kwangsi would support the undertaking. On November 5, two weeks before the outbreak of the revolution, Li Tsung-jen and Pai Ch'ung-hsi had proposed to Kwangtung that they join Fukien in forming a revolutionary government. At the same time, however, Li and Pai sent a telegram warning the Fukien leaders that Fukien should not carry out an agrarian revolution. The Kwangsi leaders also remarked that there were rumors of an alliance between Fukien and the communists. And they therefore cautioned Fukien against seeking assistance from their revolutionary neighbors in Kiangsi.[97] Since an agreement with the communists had already been signed,[98] the Fukien conspirators had had fair warning that Kwangsi was opposed to some of their most basic policies.

After the rebellion erupted, the Fukien leaders courted

Kwangtung and Kwangsi even more assiduously than previously. They sent telegrams urging the Southwest authorities
to join the revolution against Chiang. And personal emissaries soon followed the telegrams.[99]

Kwangsi was tempted. As soon as the Fukien leaders had
proclaimed their revolution, Li Tsung-jen—who customarily
resided in Canton as a representative to the Southwest Political Council—had rushed back to his native province. Relations between Kwangsi and Kwangtung were so tenuous that
Ch'en Chi-t'ang feared that Li's departure might mean that
Kwangsi was planning to attack Kwangtung. Repeatedly he
entreated Li to return to Canton. Instead of returning, however, Li sent a telegram to Ch'en declaring that Fukien had
been forced into rebellion by the perfidy of Nanking, and that
Kwangtung and Kwangsi should now come to Fukien's aid by
unitedly proclaiming their opposition to Chiang.[100]

Ultimately, however, Li Tsung-jen and Pai Ch'ung-hsi decided against participating in Fukien's revolutionary effort.
They had sent observers to Fukien, and these had sent back
extremely pessimistic reports about the situation there and
about the probable outcome of the rebellion.[101] And, finally,
the Kwangsi leaders feared that if they declared their support
for Fukien, one of their neighbors would seize the opportunity
to attack Kwangsi. Huang Hsü-ch'u recalls that "the Kwangtung authorities were not resolute in opposing Chiang, and the
Hunan authorities [Ho Chien was the governor of that partially autonomous province] were not dependable . . .
Kwangsi was squeezed between Hunan and Kwangtung; it
was weak; and it could not be adventuresome and lightly take
risky actions."[102] Perhaps the most succinct characterization
of Kwangsi's attitude toward the revolution was made with
specific reference to Li Tsung-jen: he "had the will but not the
strength" (*yu-hsin, wu-li*).[103]

The situation in Kwangtung was different. There, Ch'en
Chi-t'ang had the strength to join the revolution and perhaps
to be a decisive factor in its outcome. It was less certain,
however, that he had the will. Ch'en had in the past assumed a

public posture of recalcitrance toward Nanking and had many times signed his name to declarations criticizing its policies. But Ch'en was anxious not to inflame Chiang Kai-shek's antagonism toward Kwangtung. Virtually every time the Southwest authorities sent a joint telegram criticizing Nanking rule, therefore, Ch'en would secretly send a private telegram assuring Chiang Kai-shek that he had been constrained to sign the public telegram.[104]

It is doubtful that Chiang Kai-shek had taken seriously Ch'en Chi-t'ang's professions of loyalty. Wth the outbreak of the Fukien rebellion, therefore, Chiang took extreme pains to prevent Ch'en from joining the rebel forces. He wired Ch'en immediately upon the outbreak of the rebellion urging that Nanking and Kwangtung launch a coordinated attack on Fukien. Chiang is also alleged to have proposed that Ch'en should assume command of Fukien after suppression of the uprising. And, with the rebellion three days old, Chiang flew from his Nanchang headquarters to a meeting in southern Kiangsi to talk with Ch'en personally. It was widely reported at the time that Ch'en received ¥15 million as a bribe to support Nanking, ostensibly as a loan to aid Kwangtung's provincial reconstruction.[105]

Ch'en was nevertheless in a dilemma regarding which side to support. His own military staff was of divided counsel. He was also frightened, and perhaps justifiably, that his old rival, Ch'en Ming-shu, would strike against Kwangtung. The leaders of the revolution, it was reported by an American observer, "apparently had as their primary objective their return to power in Canton."[106]

In the end, Ch'en Chi-t'ang only partially resolved the dilemma. On about November 26 he sent a telegram to Chiang Kai-shek declaring his support for the central government. He also massed some of his best troops on the border facing Fukien, but these remained in strictly defensive positions. At the same time, however, he continued to send Kwangtung's monthly financial aid to Fukien. One payment arrived November 23, and other sums arrived later.[107]

Although Chiang Kai-shek largely succeeded in neutralizing Ch'en Chi-t'ang, similar efforts with Hu Han-min were less rewarding. One of Chiang's first acts after the beginning of the rebellion was to schedule a plenary session of the Central Executive Committee. On the agenda of this meeting were such questions as the rebellion, reorganization of the government, and greater political democracy. By holding out the lure of official positions and broader democracy, Chiang hoped that such party luminaries as Hu Han-min, Tsou Lu, and other Southwest leaders would come to the plenary meeting in Nanking and thereby give public expression of support for the central government.

Hu and the other central committeemen in Canton rejected the invitations. Chiang therefore sent a high-ranking delegation, headed by Chang Chi, to south China to discuss the crisis and, if possible, to persuade the leading party figures there to attend the Nanking meetings.[108] The delegation on December 11 arrived in Hong Kong, where they paid a visit to Hu Han-min. Hu minced no words during the interview:

Chang Chi to Hu Han-min: You are a Kuomintang comrade and should come to Nanking for the sake of party unity.

Hu: You gentlemen come urging me to go to the capital; I in turn urge that you gentlemen leave Nanking. If you say that we are all Kuomintang comrades, I reply that the Kuomintang represents the search for democracy and for the people's freedom of speech and of the press. China today does not plan for the realization of democracy, but is the China of warlordism . . . I cannot recognize that you are Kuomintang comrades.

Chang Chi: But now Fukien revolts and leaves the Kuomintang.

Hu: Nanking opposes the Kuomintang, and its crime is even greater than that of the Fukien rebels who leave the Kuomintang. For none of Nanking's actions is in accordance with Kuomintang principles, but it hangs out the signboard of the Kuomintang—so all of its actions desecrate the Kuomintang . . . Fukien revolts against the party, but its actions do not befoul it.

Chang Chi: What method then do you propose?

Hu (angrily): The solution is simple. My idea is to ask the authorities in Nanking to kill themselves as a means of vindicating themselves before the people.[109]

Hu Han-min's detestation of Chiang Kai-shek was complete. If the Fukien revolutionaries had not renounced the principles of Sun Yat-sen, he would probably have supported a joint Fukien–Kwangtung–Kwangsi expedition against Nanking.[110]

The situation in north China was nearly as volatile as in the south. Prior to the rebellion, the Fukien conspirators thought they had elicited firm promises of support for the revolution. They were so convinced that Feng Yü-hsiang would come to Fukien that they had named him to the Revolutionary Government Council. Feng was in fact very sympathetic with the revolutionaries—he subsequently praised them as being pure and incorrupt and as being motivated by anti-Japanese convictions. But he was powerless. Only three months previously, his own revolt in Chahar had collapsed. And now, with virtually no troops at his command, he professed to be devoting all his attention to study and calligraphy.[111]

Other regional authorities in north China probably had made less firm promises to the conspirators. In the end, however, they posed a more real challenge to Nanking than did Feng Yü-hsiang. Nanking's sway in the north had never been unchallenged. And recently, with Nanking's declining prestige and increasing financial problems (Nanking's supply of funds for the troops in the north had recently been delayed), the loyalties of many commanders for the central government—if one dare speak of warlord "loyalties"—had been particularly strained.[112] So, when Nanking on November 30 was constrained to transfer some of its loyal forces southward to cope with the Fukien rebellion, the regional authorities in the north were presented with a host of new political opportunities.

Yen Hsi-shan, for example, who had once pronounced his support for Nanking in opposition to Fukien, now sent a representative to contact the Fukien leaders. At the same time he approached Feng Yü-hsiang, Han Fu-chü, and other leaders in the north proposing a concerted move against Chiang Kai-shek. In Hopei, the provincial governor, Yü Hsüeh-chung, wavered and contacted Chang Hsüeh-liang, whose sudden return from Europe added impetus to the centrifugal forces at the time.[113] The situation in Shantung was particularly ticklish. The governor, Han Fu-chü, was an old-style warlord whose career was besmirched with numerous perfidious betrayals. He was, it was said, "loyal to the Nationalist government only when the government was careful not to interfere in local affairs." He was now leaning toward Fukien and had even begun preparations for a military attack on Nanking.[114]

In the end, all this ferment came to nothing. Nanking's chief political and military representatives in north China, Huang Fu and Ho Ying-ch'in, had scurried from one regional lord to another, dissuading them from declaring their support for Fukien.[115] If Nanking was now overthrown, they argued, Japan might seize the opportunity to expand its control in China; the communists might also grow in power and influence.

These arguments may have been less than persuasive, for some of the local authorities replied that they would support Huang as ruler of an independent north China if he would join the anti-Chiang movement. The authorities in Shantung were exceptionally recalcitrant, and Huang spent several days closeted in negotiations before he was able to persuade them to disavow support for Fukien. In all probability, Huang's most persuasive argument in these negotiations was money, one of Chiang Kai-shek's most effective military weapons.[116]

Ultimately, only one force actually raised the flag of revolt in response to Fukien's initiatives. Sun Tien-ying, an army commander in Ning-hsia, revolted on January 10, 1934. By that time, however, the fate of Fukien was sealed.[117] Once again Chiang picked off his challengers, one by one.

The Fukien Revolutionaries and the Kiangsi Communists

Even before the outbreak of the Fukien rebellion, rumors had spread through the nation that the Fukien authorities were planning a rapprochement with the communists in Kiangsi. And a "Preliminary Agreement" had in fact been concluded between the two forces on October 26, 1933. How word of the agreement had spread is unclear, for it had been such a tightly kept secret that some of the leading personalities in the Fukien movement did not know certainly of the agreement until after the revolution had collapsed.[118] Nevertheless, one of Nanking's most telling arguments to potential supporters of the Fukien movement was the alleged alliance with the communists. Furthermore, because the revolutionaries derived little benefit—and considerable damage—from the agreement, it proved in the final analysis to have been a grievous miscalculation.

The signing of the pact between the Fukien and the Soviet governments came like a bolt out of the blue, for, until it was concluded, there was every indication that the two were mortal enemies. There had been the customary recriminations and name calling. More significant, the communists had attacked the Nineteenth Route Army in August after an undeclared truce of almost a year, and bloody fighting lasted for a month.[119]

The communists, however, had been seeking precisely this kind of agreement. Almost a year earlier, in January 1933, they had proclaimed their willingness to agree to a ceasefire with any hostile force, on the condition that that force grant civil liberties and permit the formation of people's militia. Several times the communists had repeated this offer: in April to Chiang Kai-shek, and again in May to the military authorities of both Fukien and Kwangtung.[120]

Why should Ch'en Ming-shu have been attracted by an alliance with the communists? He could have known that the leaders of Kwangtung and Kwangsi would be opposed to it. And he could not even be certain that the officers and men of the Nineteenth Route Army would take kindly to such an alliance. The answer, in all probability, is that Ch'en was now under the influence of the generally pro-communist Third Party. Moreover, Ch'en himself would not have been averse to the suggestion, for he had—according to his close friend and associate, Huang Ch'iang—become "drunk with the French Popular-Front Policy" during his recent stay in Europe.[121]

And, with regard to the probable opposition of Kwangtung and Kwangsi to a communist alliance, Ch'en may have thought to keep them ignorant of it, for the communists did consent to hold the agreement in secrecy.

There are numerous conflicting reports regarding how and where the agreement was negotiated. It is probable that Hsü Ming-hung (who was the Grey Eminence throughout the early stages of the rebellion) went to the Kiangsi Soviet in early October with a letter from Ch'en Ming-shu proposing "fundamental cooperation" with the Red Army.[122] The communist leadership, recounts Kung Ch'u, was sharply divided over how it should reply to Ch'en's letter. Chou En-lai argued that this was an opportunity for close cooperation with another anti-Chiang armed force. The Soviet, Chou argued, should manifest its serious intentions by sending a high-ranking representative to negotiate terms of the alliance. Mao Tse-tung, however, had little confidence in the revolutionary potential of the Fukien group, and he proposed sending only a lesser official to Foochow. According to Kung's account, Mao's view prevailed, and a relative unknown, P'an Han-nien (vice-minister of foreign affairs in the Soviet government) returned with Hsü to Foochow, where they signed the "Anti-Japanese, Anti-Chiang Preliminary Agreement" on October 26, 1933.[123]

The Preliminary Agreement provided for the cessation of all hostile military operations between the two signatories and for the resumption of trade between the Soviet area and Fukien. It also stipulated that Fukien was to release all political prisoners, permit all forms of revolutionary organization (such as mass organizations and the people's militia), and guarantee freedoms of speech, assembly, and labor strikes.

The agreement did not—as Ch'en Ming-shu had proposed in his initial letter—provide for immediate military cooperation between the two parties. It stipulated only that a "concrete military agreement" would be signed after Fukien had begun preparations for an anti-Japanese, anti-Chiang campaign, and after all other provisions of the Preliminary Agreement had been fulfilled. A supplementary agreement did stipulate, however, which areas were to be occupied and held by the respective armies.[124] This agreement on military jurisdictions was to be of crucial importance for the fate of the Fukien revolution.

Historical assessments of this agreement have come to diametrically opposite conclusions. William Dorrill suggests that it was "obviously one-sided" in favor of Fukien; Wang Chien-min, to the contrary, calls it "a kind of unequal treaty" favoring the communists.[125] In fact, both Fukien and the communists were justified in thinking that the agreement improved their respective positions. The Fukien group secured their western flank against attack so that they could concentrate their military force against the armies of Nanking in the north. This was an extremely important strategic gain, and it just does not make sense to dismiss it, as does Wang Chien-min, as of no value to the Fukien revolutionaries.

The communists also derived advantage from the agreement. For the agreement punctured the Nationalists' siege during the Fifth Extermination Campaign by opening a supply line to the world beyond the blockaded area. And, in fact, critically needed supplies did flow into the Soviet area via Fukien during the Fukien uprising. The communists could also derive satisfaction that the agreement provided them greater freedom to agitate and engage in organizational work in Fukien. And, finally, the communists benefited just from the occurrence of the rebellion, for it forced Nanking to ease its military pressures on the Soviet area.[126]

Despite the manifest advantages derived by both sides, neither party long remained satisfied. The military truce remained in force, but in all other respects the agreement became virtually a dead letter. Which side was initially responsible is still uncertain. The communists quickly if not immediately adopted a disdainful attitude toward their new ally, and regarded the agreement as a license to subvert the Fukien revolutionary movement and to communize Fukien.

"We should," wrote a communist, "grasp the People's Revolutionary Government's every deceit, wavering, superficiality, betrayal, and sell-out, and prove to the masses that the government cheats them . . . and prove that the People's Revolutionary Government is neither the 'people's' nor 'revolutionary.' We should increase class divisions and class struggle within the united front. We should lead the masses to resolutely oppose the People's Revolutionary Government and all counter-revolutionary factional revolts so that they come under our leadership."[127]

Communists in Fukien did in fact act on the assumptions in this statement. And the Fukien authorities, regarding the resulting disruptive activities as unfriendly, took measures to restrict communist activities in Fukien.[128]

Other Fukien policies convinced the communists that the new government was not truly revolutionary. Fukien did fulfill its commitment to release all political prisoners.[129] But on November 19—on the very eve of the uprising—it declared the province under martial law. The effect was to invalidate its previous promise to protect popular freedoms. And finally, rather than permit the masses to organize local militia, the Fukien authorities actually disbanded the units of militia that had been formed prior to the rebellion.[130] These measures, so patently in violation of the agreement with the communists, may have resulted partially from a distrust of the communists' agitational activities. The ouster of the Third Party from the leadership of the revolution, however, was also no doubt a factor in the progressive deradicalization of the revolutionary movement in Fukien.

Fukien's refusal to pursue a more revolutionary course provoked an irate response from the communist authorities in Kiangsi. Commencing with a declaration from the Central Committee of the Chinese Communist Party on December 5 and continuing even after the collapse of the rebellion, the communists vehemently criticized the "counter-revolutionary reformists in Fukien."[131]

The People's Revolutionary Government, the communists

declared repeatedly, "is neither the people's nor is it revolutionary." True, the Fukien group shouted slogans opposing imperialism, warlords, landlords, and corrupt bureaucrats. But such slogans were merely a deception "with the aim not of overthrowing imperialism and the landlord-capitalist classes, but of maintaining their own rule in order to prevent the masses from becoming revolutionary and from advancing on the Soviet path." "We do not believe," sneered the communist leadership, "that verbal proclamations make a real revolution."[132]

These vicious denunciations did not mean that the Soviet authorities had utterly abandoned hope of closer cooperation with the Fukien movement. On December 20, Mao Tse-tung and Chu Teh sent a telegram to Fukien vowing that the Soviet government and the Red Army would ally militarily with Fukien as soon as it took decisive action against Chiang, armed the masses and formed a true people's revolutionary army, and gave the people real freedoms in order to start the mass struggle against Japan and Chiang Kai-shek.[133] Any other measures than these were counter-revolutionary. "There is no middle path," entoned the communist Central Committee, "and all elements that think they can take a third path between revolution and counter-revolution will inevitably meet with savage defeat and become a helping hand of the counter-revolutionary attack on the revolution."[134]

Following the collapse of the Fukien rebellion, the communist leadership betrayed no trace of regret. To the contrary, it seemed to gloat with satisfaction both with having negotiated the Preliminary Agreement and with the defeat of their former ally. The agreement, declared the Central Committee, had broken the economic blockade of the Soviet areas and had diverted Nanking's fifth encirclement campaign.

Equally important, the experience during the rebellion had proven the ideological correctness of the Soviet leadership. First, it had demonstrated that the Soviet's reliance on the masses was the only correct revolutionary policy. It proves, declared the communist leadership, that a political movement can defeat imperialism and the Kuomintang "only if the masses themselves rise up and, under the guidance of the proletarian class and its vanguard, rely on the masses' own independent revolutionary action." And second, it had shown that the policy of accepting alliances with true anti-Japanese, anti-Chiang elements could strengthen the revolutionary movement. For, during the Fukien rebellion, they had been able to exploit contradictions among the enemy: they had developed an independent leadership in the people's militia and had encouraged soldiers of the Nineteenth Route Army to join the Red forces.[135]

"These measures," Po Ku, general secretary of the Communist Party, declared in a final burst of self-approbation, "had proved that the party's basic line was correct, expanded the influence of the Party and of the Soviet, caused the masses to understand the real character of the third path, and had *caused it quickly to become bankrupt.*"[136] Po Ku, in other words, was boasting that the communists had contributed directly to the defeat of the Fukien rebels!

Only two years after the Fukien rebellion—after the communists had themselves been crushed by Chiang Kai-shek in Kiangsi and had been forced to retreat on the legendary but costly Long March—Mao Tse-tung asserted that the communists' failure to provide full military and political support to Fukien had been a serious error.[137] Mao's reassessment was probably motivated primarily by the desire to denigrate his political opponents (such as Po Ku) and to establish the infallibility of his own judgment. Yet, Mao's motives aside, his post hoc analysis was correct. For, in all probability, more sincere cooperation by the Soviet with the Fukien rebels would have prolonged the life of the rebellion and would thereby have seriously challenged Nanking's rule.

During the uprising, however, the communists had adopted a "wrecker" policy toward Fukien, and they consequently contributed directly and substantially to the rapid demise of the rebellion. As Kung Ch'u, a former communist who had been in Kiangsi during the rebellion, remarked: "The causes of the Fukien defeat are many, but the procrastinations and negligence of the Chinese communists are surely one of the most important.''[138]

Fukien and the Japanese

One of the more vexing problems encountered in this study has been the nature of the relationship between the Fukien rebels and Japan. This, at first glance, would not appear to be a problem at all, for the Nineteenth Route Army was seemingly the incarnation of Chinese hatred of the Japanese. Moreover, the rebel regime had repeatedly and in most emphatic terms proclaimed its opposition to Japan. Their primary grievance against Chiang Kai-shek, they declared, was that he had not resisted Japanese encroachments. Yet, even before the revolution had been proclaimed, rumors had been bruited that the Fukien authorities were acting in collusion with Japan. And, immediately upon the outbreak of the rebellion, not only Nanking but the Southwest authorities had issued formal statements charging that Fukien was pursuing a pro-Japanese policy.[139]

The nation's press took up this refrain, reporting that the rebels had been silent about the Japanese, and produced alleged evidence of complicity with Japan. It was, for example, reported that the Nineteenth Route Army was employing Japanese military advisers.[140] On December 9 a news item recorded that Fukien had concluded a sugar loan with Japan for ¥10 million. And Japanese merchant ships, escorted by Japanese naval vessels, allegedly flouted Nanking's naval blockade to bring equipment to the revolutionaries.[141] A score of other examples could be mentioned.

Most of the allegations were probably without foundation. It is true, however, that the rebels had been offered an opportunity to form an alliance with Japan if they had desired to do so. The incident occurred at a time when the outlook for the revolution had already turned bleak, probably in late December or early January. A Japanese warship sailed up the Min River to Foochow harbor, and a Japanese admiral disembarked, asking for a meeting with Eugene Ch'en, the foreign minister of the revolutionary government. Ch'en was apprehensive, suspecting that the Japanese was delivering an unpleasant threat or demand. Instead, the admiral said: "Japan wishes, within twelve hours, first to aid Fukien with its air force by eliminating the danger of Nanking's air raids. Later, it will respond to the needs of the People's Government by supplying weapons and money whenever needed."[142]

According to a participant in the rebellion, this offer of assistance was made without any conditions attached. Nevertheless, the Fukien leaders were never tempted by the offer and were unanimous in rejecting it.[143]

Lei Hsiao-ts'en relates a different version of the incident. After making the offer of aid, the admiral added: "Japan has only one request: that after [the successful outcome of] the affair, the two nations will cooperate to establish an East Asian New Order and expel the Western powers. This accords with Sun Yat-sen's policy of Greater East Asianism."

Lei contends that the offer sorely tested the revolutionaries' anti-Japanese convictions, for without this proffered aid the revolution was predictably doomed. According to Lei, Chang Po-chün and several others present urged that the Japanese offer be accepted so that the revolutionary base might be preserved. But Wang Li-hsi and Mei Kung-pin retorted heroically that it would be better to be defeated with their honor intact than to be victorious with their honor sullied. Lei—whose study is basically unsympathetic to the Fukien movement—suggests that Ch'en Ming-shu and the other top leaders had initially intended to accept the Japanese offer. After this moving declaration, however, they dared not speak out, and as a consequence Japanese assistance was declined.[144]

Lei Hsiao-ts'en may be right that the rebel leadership was tempted by the Japanese offer. Significantly, however, he nowhere suggests that they actually accepted the Japanese offer of aid.

A Japanese government declaration should have given the quietus to all these rumors: "The new Fukien government

implements an anti-Japanese policy, and we therefore resolutely refuse to recognize it.''[145] But the most conclusive
evidence that the Fukien revolutionaries were not in league
with the Japanese is provided by the communists. During the
uprising, the communists criticized the rebel leadership for
every conceivable sin and shortcoming. Never, however, did
they even hint that Fukien had abandoned their basic anti-
Japanese position. Instead, the communists spoke of ''our
mutual enemies, Japan and Chiang''; and charged that
Chiang—not Fukien—had formed an alliance with Japanese
imperialism.[146] If there had been any shred of evidence of a
rapprochement between the People's Government and Japan,
the communists would surely have seized upon it as further
justification for not having rendered greater support to the
rebel movement.

But why, since these rumors had no basis in fact, had they
originated and continued so persistently? My guess is that the
rumors were sheer fabrications, possibly originating in the
propaganda mills of Nanking. This need occasion no surprise.
Charges that one's enemies were in partnership with the
Japanese were made in practically all political struggles during this period. The Fukien revolutionaries were themselves
masters of this game, and they many times charged that
Chiang Kai-shek was working hand-in-glove with the Japanese.

Having established that the Fukien leadership was innocent
of collaborating with Japan, it is intriguing that a number of
them who were caught in Foochow during the collapse of the
movement escaped on Japanese ships. Ch'iu Kuo-chen recounts how the Japanese consulate-general arranged for him
and two other officers to take passage to Taiwan. They were
treated with great courtesy and consideration. In fact, while
they were waiting in Taipei for a ship to Hong Kong, the
Japanese authorities even entertained them in Pei-t'ou—a
mountainside resort outside Taipei, then as now renowned
for its hot springs and friendly hostesses. Among other
revolutionaries who escaped by Japanese ship were Li Chi-

shen, Huang Ch'i-hsiang, and Hu Ch'iu-yüan. These latter escapees apparently did not receive the Japanese red-carpet treatment. Hu Ch'iu-yüan, for example, had to buy his own boat ticket.[147] And there is no information that any of them were treated to an evening in Pei-t'ou. The fact, however, that these men escaped with the assistance of the Japanese does not demonstrate complicity of the rebel leaders with the national enemy. It merely proves that they would rather accept Japanese hospitality than possibly die at the hands of compatriots.

The Course and Collapse of the Rebellion

The rebellion had begun not with a bang but with a fizzle. There were no climactic coups, no dramatic battles. Government and party officials in the provincial regime prior to November 20 had for the most part either quietly abandoned their posts or joined the rebellion. Actual skirmishes between the rebel armies and those of Nanking were a month away. For most people, little had been changed by the outbreak of the "revolution."[148]

The revolutionary leadership soon sensed, however, that they had made a serious miscalculation. A fundamental strategic assumption had been that other anti-Chiang forces in the country would revolt in response to Fukien's initiative. Yet, even a month after the revolution had been declared, Fukien had only the uncertain alliance with the communists.

Acting on the assumption that potential allies had been forestalled from joining the revolution by the radicalism of their program, the Fukien leadership on December 22 issued a second declaration to the nation. All anti-Chiang forces were again urged to join the revolution. Now, however, allies were invited to participate within the framework of federalism. China was composed, declared the Fukien leadership, of many independent political and economic regions, each with unique circumstances and problems. The unification of the nation could therefore be attained only if each of these regions was permitted to determine its own policies and administrative forms. The only restriction would be that the policies of the various regional political entities must be consonant with the one supreme principle of political power for the producing masses.[149]

This declaration represented a huge ideological retreat. It meant that the programs prepared by the Fukien revolutionaries were to be applicable only to Fukien. Regional authorities elsewhere would be free to adhere to virtually any political or economic system, however retrogressive. It meant, for example, that the authorities of Kwangsi, who had balked at the *chi-k'ou shou-t'ien* policy, would not be constrained to adopt what to them seemed a dangerously radical agrarian solution. Above all, the declaration signified that the Fukien rebels had become so desperate for allies that they willingly scuttled the ideological heart of their revolution. What remained was a military-political uprising against Chiang Kai-shek, with no concrete program of social and economic melioration for the Chinese people.

The military phase of the rebellion developed slowly, but ended with dramatic swiftness. When the uprising began, the bulk of the Nineteenth Route Army had been encamped in southern and western Fukien. The leaders were utterly undecided what to do with the army now that they had proclaimed the revolution. They felt no immediate threat from Nanking, thinking that Chiang Kai-shek could not soon organize a significant force to strike in the north.[150] They thus hesitated between alternatives.

There exists no reliable source material that can provide an insight to the strategic thinking of the rebel leadership. There was apparently some sentiment in favor of either threatening or attacking Kwangtung. This maneuver might have succeeded in forcing Ch'en Chi-t'ang into the revolutionary ranks. And if Ch'en did not join the revolution, then the occupation of Kwangtung by the Nineteenth Route Army would give the revolution the rich base that Fukien province so obviously could not provide.[151]

It was finally decided, however, to strike against Nanking and not Canton. Conceivably this decision resulted from negotiations and a financial settlement with Ch'en Chi-t'ang.[152] In any event, the revolutionaries had now to transfer their army to the northern part of the province. From there they would gamble all on a thrust through Chekiang to Shanghai and, catching the Nationalist forces unprepared, seize Nanking.[153] This decision was followed by the painful and slow task of moving the army from one end of the province to the other—a distance of approximately three hundred miles over some of the most rugged mountain roads in China. The shift of troops and equipment required over twenty days, leaving both men and horses exhausted.[154]

Then the strategy was changed again. Perhaps it was because the army was now too debilitated to launch the campaign initially envisioned. Or perhaps it was because Chiang Kai-shek's armies were mobilizing more rapidly than the Fukien leaders had anticipated. Whatever the reason, the army was now ordered to take up defensive positions in order to protect the political heart of the revolution.[155]

Nanking experienced none of these indecisions or difficulties. Only recently a network of roads and railroads had been built—most notably the Hangchow—Yü-shan line, which was rushed to completion just in time to counter the uprising. Chiang Kai-shek, as a result, was able to shift men and equipment to the border of Fukien with a speed that caught the Fukien commanders badly off balance. By mid-December, Chiang (who had flown from his headquarters at Nanchang to direct the military operations personally) had concentrated approximately eleven divisions on the Fukien border.[156]

First blood in the fighting was drawn by Chiang's air force whose total strength in the Fukien campaign was about thirty planes. On December 1 small raids hit several towns in the northern and central parts of the province. Similar attacks were made the following two days.[157] Damage in these attacks was light, and since the raids did not continue, the pace of civilian life in Fukien changed little.

The mood became one of utter panic, however, when for three days, December 23–25, the bombings were renewed. Foochow was now also hit, leaving about twenty dead; thirty were killed and one hundred wounded in Chang-chou. The revolutionary forces were practically defenseless against these attacks. They had ten or more airplanes, but all these were trainers and of no use for combat. And their scattering of anti-aircraft guns did not prevent the attacking planes from coming in virtually at will.[158]

The actual destruction wrought by the air raids was not heavy. But the attacking planes—this was a new experience for most Chinese—induced a fear out of all proportion to their destructive powers. In an attempt to stop the bombings, a group of Foochow residents dispatched an emotional appeal to Nanking. "In the last three days," the telegram read, "over ten planes have come dropping over one hundred bombs, strafing with machine guns and using poison gas. The dead exceed a thousand. That which Chiang Kai-shek hates is the Nineteenth Route Army, but those he kills are the Fukienese people."[159] (There were repeated reports that the Nationalist forces were using poison gas—with what veracity is uncertain.[160])

Ultimately, however, it was ground operations that defeated the Fukien armies. The first preliminary skirmishes with Nanking forces occurred on December 16. Nanking did not launch a concerted offensive until about January 1, 1934. Even then, the fighting was light, for the rebel troops retreated quickly, only occasionally taking a stand to fight back. On January 12 Nanking forces took Ku-t'ien after a battle, and thereafter everything was anti-climactic. Foochow was spared a destructive siege, because the Chinese navy—which had been straddling the political fence throughout the rebellion—arranged a peaceful transfer of the city from the revolutionaries to the government forces.[161] On January 16 the tail end of the Nineteenth Route Army left Foochow, and the main body of the army retreated southward to Chang-chou, where they hoped to regroup the army and even turn the tide of battle. As late as about January 19 the retreating revolutionaries issued a proclamation that they were determined to liberate China, fight imperialism, and oppose Chiang Kai-shek and fascism. Boldly they vowed that "As long as one man remains alive, this determination will not flag."[162]

Perhaps the spirit was willing, but the flesh was weak. For now most of the rebel army vanished, the result of an appalling rash of defections. Of the five army commanders, four of them—with most of their troops—defected to the government side. Ch'en Ming-shu and Ts'ai T'ing-k'ai therefore had virtually no forces left to hold the last redoubts in southern Fukien. Chang-chou fell on January 21 and the Kuomintang flag was lifted over Ch'üan-chou on January 22. The revolution was over. It had lasted just two months.

The rout of the Nineteenth Route Army, the heroic defenders of Shanghai, startled and amazed the nation, for it had the reputation of being the most fierce fighting force in the nation.[163] In fact, the army in January 1934 was considerably different from what it had been two years previously. It had lost about nine thousand men in the Shanghai fighting; many of the new recruits were still green, and financial stringencies had prevented adequate replacements of weapons.[164]

The soldiers, moreover, did not have their hearts in this battle as they had had in the Shanghai fighting. From divisional commanders down to the lowest trooper, morale was at a minimum. Ts'ai T'ing-k'ai recalled that the ranking officers in the army had raised no objections when he informed them that they were to be part of a revolution against Nanking, but "in their hearts they were dissatisfied." And some of the soldiers, when they were shown the new flag that was to replace that of the Kuomintang, actually wept.[165]

A further explanation for the precipitate defeat of the rebel army might be the lack of preparation and the indecisive leadership. Ts'ai T'ing-k'ai subsequently complained that everyone had a different idea regarding what strategy should be adopted.[166] Because most of the revolutionary leaders were or had been military commanders, it is probable that this was a classic case of too many cooks spoiling the stew.

Finally, treachery was a further cause of the defeat. For Nanking had a spy who was in a position to relay to Chiang Kai-shek every plan and stratagem of the revolutionary military command. Prior to the outbreak of the revolution, the Fukien authorities had arrested or dismissed officers who were suspected of being agents of Nanking.[167] Nevertheless, during the fighting Chiang Kai-shek displayed impossible prescience regarding Fukien's military plans. On one occasion, for example, the revolutionary army hoped to catch the central government forces off balance by suddenly launching an offensive from their own basically defensive posture. When the attacking forces reached their objective, however, Chiang's forces had already evacuated the area.[168]

Only after the rebellion was it learned that Chiang's source of information was General Fan Han-chieh, assistant chief-of-staff of the Fukien forces. Fan was, of course, fully informed of all the army's plans, and he used a radio hidden in his home to convey his information to the central government forces. Fan had long been associated with both Ch'en Ming-shu and the Nineteenth Route Army. Thus, although the revolutionary leaders had suspected an intelligence leak, he had remained above suspicion.[169]

A second instance of treachery was attributable to the rebels' ally, the communists. In accordance with the military supplement to the Preliminary Agreement, the communists and the Fukien authorities had each agreed that they would take possession of certain areas. Because the supplementary agreement has never been made public, one cannot be certain what the provisions of the document were. Did the signatories, for example, contract to hold and defend the areas thus assigned to them? Whatever the precise terms of the agreement, the Fukien authorities had plotted their defense against Nanking on the assumption that the Red Army would obstruct Nanking's access to Fukien by way of the town of Li-ch'üan in eastern Kiangsi. With the approach of Chiang's army, however, the communists—without informing Fukien—abruptly withdrew their forces from Li-ch'üan. This opened the dikes. Chiang's Fifth Route Army, commanded by Wei Li-huang, poured down the valley of the Min River toward Foochow, and the revolution was doomed.[170]

It is probable that the Nineteenth Route Army, with all its internal weaknesses, could not long have resisted the armies of Chiang. But these betrayals, both within and without the revolutionary forces, contributed signally to the precipitate collapse. Following the defeat, only one man received direct punishment. That was Hsü Ming-hung, who was executed after his capture on the orders of Ch'en Chi-t'ang.[171] As for the rest of the revolutionaries, some six thousand men from the Nineteenth Route Army were incorporated into the Kwangtung army, a few joined the communists, and some became small independent armies or bandits. The majority of them, however, the twenty thousand or so that had defected or surrendered to the Nanking side, were reincorporated into the Nationalist Army with the new name of the Seventh Route Army. Commander and deputy commander of this new force were Mao Wei-shou and Chang Yen, two of the rebel commanders who had defected in the waning days of the movement. (The other two commanders who defected, apparently for whom no suitably honorific posts could immediately be found, were each given ¥50,000 for a trip abroad.)[172]

Many of the rebel leaders took refuge in Hong Kong, where the inundation of refugees briefly created a crush on the local hotels. But soon they scattered. Li Chi-shen for a time concentrated on the study of Tang dynasty poetry. Ts'ai T'ing-k'ai went on a widely heralded trip around the world, later writing a book on his impressions of Europe and the United States. And Ch'en Ming-shu went to Europe, appearing briefly in Moscow in 1935.[173]

Political activity, however, had become part of their lives. As early as March 1934 the Chinese press sparked reader interest with recurrent reports that Ch'en Ming-shu was plotting a new revolt.[174] And in August 1935 the former Fukien leaders actually did form the Chinese People's Revolutionary Alliance (Chung-hua min-tsu ko-ming ta-t'ung-meng). Li Chi-shen was again chosen chairman of the group, and prominent members included not only Ch'en Ming-shu, Chiang Kuang-nai, and Ts'ai T'ing-k'ai, but also Feng Yü-hsiang, Hsü Ch'ien, and Eugene Ch'en. (The *North China Herald* remarked about Eugene Ch'en—with more than a dash of sarcasm: "He has now become the chief exponent of the part of the temporary Minister for Foreign Affairs—a part filled by him at short notice, perfect satisfaction guaranteed, communiques a specialty. It seems, however, to be highly irritating that he should be encouraged to give this performance so frequently. It is seldom justified by the box office returns."[175])

And, as shall be seen in Chapter 6, the old Fukien crowd was again prominently on hand during the revolt of Kwangsi in 1936. Only after the beginning of the war with Japan and after the warrants for their arrests were rescinded, did these revolutionaries make amends with Chiang, many of them assuming official positions in the Nationalist Government during the war.

The Fukien revolutionaries had acted on the conviction that dissatisfaction with Kuomintang rule was so pervasive that the Chinese people and the regional militarists would rise in arms against Nanking at a signal from Foochow. This strategic assumption was not wholly groundless. Since 1927 the popularity of the Nanking regime had fallen sharply. And at no time was it held in lower repute than at the outbreak of the Fukien uprising. As Charles E. Gauss, then American Counselor of Legation, observed on December 5, 1933, "The Kuomintang, which has been repudiated by the rebels, has reached the lowest ebb so far recorded."[176]

Nor had the Fukien leaders completely miscalculated the response of the public to their revolutionary undertaking. There had indeed been indications of popular support, outside of Fukien, for the demands to abolish party rule and for greater civil liberties. And some of the intellectuals, albeit not the merchant class, expressed approval of the revolutionary economic program. "The really serious factor in the situation," observed the *North China Herald,* "is the sympathy which, however academic in essence, is being generated for the opposition to General Chiang Kai-shek."[177]

Yet support of neither the "masses" nor the regional warlords materialized. If we look into the reasons, it is possible to discern some of the forces that held the Republic together during the troubled years of Nanking rule. China, even seven years after the revolutionary conquest by the Kuomintang, was like an ill-fitting jig-saw puzzle: most of the pieces seemed almost to fit, but they did not really interlock. The regional rulers—militarists like Lung Yün, Han Fu-chü, Liu Hsiang, and Ho Chien—were constantly straining against Nanking's authority, jealous of Chiang Kai-shek's growing power, fearful of his pretensions to centralized rule, and ready at a propitious moment to sunder their ties with Nanking.

It still appears miraculous that Chiang retained and even enhanced his powers vis-à-vis the warlord interests. Displaying remarkable intuition, he knew when to bribe, when to threaten, and when to fight to maintain the advantage in this delicate balance of political forces.

But Chiang Kai-shek's survival was attributable only in part to his own peculiar talents. For his rivals displayed truly uncanny ineptitude, failing almost completely to coordinate their efforts to overthrow their mutual bête noire. Why was it, for example, that the leaders of Kwangtung and Kwangsi had, only months before and after the Fukien uprising, importuned the Fukien leaders to join a rebellion against Nanking—but they refused to assist Fukien when the uprising did occur? Why was it that Feng Yü-hsiang, Yen Hsi-shan, and Li Tsung-jen, among others, had revolted one after the other during the period 1929–1931, but had not gone to each other's support while Chiang picked them off one-by-one?

The regional militarists' perverse refusal to aid their beleaguered peers has no simple explanation. One of the reasons may have been that each aspired to preeminence, realizing that, should they join a rebellion instigated by another, they would have no claim to the number one position in a new regime. Also, of course, these regional satraps had acquired a healthy respect for Chiang Kai-shek's abilities to maneuver in the maze of warlord politics. They were therefore loath to commit themselves to a revolt against Chiang until they were assured of its success. And, by not committing themselves, they assured that it would not succeed.

The political tone of the period is also indicated by the failure of the populace to rise in support of the rebellion. Despite the disgust and antipathy that many felt for the Kuomintang, they were utterly weary of civil strife. For about two decades Chinese had been killing Chinese, all seemingly without purpose or positive effect. The Chinese people had therefore become skeptical of the utility of all such political ventures, whatever the rebels' ideology and whatever the seeming justice of their criticism of the existing authorities.[178] They had also become cynical of the rebels' motives. Too many times they had heard revolutionary slogans which, although admirable in themselves, merely veiled a struggle for power within the ruling clique.

Another factor that contributed to the survival of the Nanking regime was that, while the Chinese disliked the Kuomintang, they hated the Japanese more. All recognized that a new period of revolutionary upheaval would serve as an invitation to further Japanese aggression. Even most of the warlords acted with some regard for the national survival. In a paradoxical way, therefore, the Japanese threat may have been a significant reason why Chiang Kai-shek's regime survived the period 1931–1934, the most precarious years of the entire decade.[179]

Chapter 4 Democracy and Dictatorship: Competing Models of Government

In their search for a political form, the Chinese of the Nanking period were possessed of an ambiguous legacy. First, China's own political traditions were essentially authoritarian, but the dominant strand of Chinese political thinking in the early twentieth century had been democratic. Second, Sun Yat-sen had initially evinced a strong faith in democracy, but during the last decade of his life he had in both thought and action become increasingly dictatorial. And, finally, the democratic enthusiasm that had characterized the Western political world for the half century or so prior to World War I was seemingly being displaced by the conviction that the democratic system would collapse in the face of the crises engendered in a modern, industrialized society.

The Kuomintang had embraced both strands of this legacy. Drawing upon the formulations of Sun Yat-sen, the regime in October 1928 officially proclaimed that the ultimate goal, to be attained by 1935, was constitutional democracy. Until that time, however, until the masses had been adequately trained for their responsibilities in a democratic republic, the Kuomintang would rule by means of a party dictatorship.[1] By the early 1930s, as discontent with the Nanking regime mounted, this political formula came under attack, and there began a search for a new model or at least a new emphasis in government. But which values of the ambiguous legacy were to be embraced in devising an alternative political structure?

The ensuing struggle between democracy and dictatorship was fought in two separate arenas. In the newspapers and journals of the period, intellectuals debated the relative merits of the two systems of government. Although the debate was academic, its implications were real, because the debate revealed the concerns and values of the nation's intellectuals. Thus, the fact that the proponents of libertarian values fared badly in the debate meant that the Nationalist leadership, in creating a new political structure, was working in an environment favorable to authoritarian solutions.

The second arena for the contest between democracy and dictatorship was within the councils of the regime itself, where the party leaders were preparing the draft of a permanent constitution. Here, the participants in the debate were concerned less with values than with power. Kuomintang leaders therefore took sides on the question of, say, the autonomy of the legislative organs, not primarily on the basis of the relative advantages to the electorate, but on the basis of whose power within the government would thereby be enhanced. The constitution, in other words, had become a vehicle in the struggle for power.

Democracy under Attack

The debate among intellectuals was mundane, a trifle stodgy. For the most part it was college professors who participated. Gone now was the intellectual effervescence of the May Fourth period; gone was the excitement of an infinitude of possibilities. By the 1930s the political alternatives had narrowed, and the intellectuals seemed sobered by the political failures of the preceding generation. During the debate there emerged no genius of political philosophy, nor political theories that were new or lasting. Yet there were certain themes in the political literature of the decade that stood out clearly, themes that reveal the preeminent political concerns and values of the nation's intellectuals.

China's intellectuals were in touch with the dominant strands of political thinking throughout the world. Their criticisms of liberal democracy, for example, had also been made by the guild socialists, the fascists, and the Marxists of the West. The matrix for their criticisms, nevertheless, was undeniably the political traditions and experiences of China itself.

Disillusionment with Democracy. One theme that suffused the political dialogue of the 1930s was the disillusionment that all Chinese intellectuals sensed as a result of the nation's experience with democratic institutions since 1912. After the revolutionary overthrow of the Ch'ing dynasty, the new republic had been outfitted with a full complement of democratic machinery: a constitution, a representative assembly, popular elections, and a Montesquieuan separation of governmental powers. These had proved to be a mockery of their Western models. Elections had evoked little popular response, and the results were often rigged. Members of the representative assembly were more responsive to the dollars of a Yüan Shih-k'ai or Ts'ao K'un than they were to the will and needs of the people. The fact, too, that there had been five official constitutions or draft constitutions during the period 1912–1926 did little to fortify public confidence in democratic institutions.

What were the causes of this progressive political decay after the Revolution of 1911? Even today, students of Chinese history are baffled by the flow of events after the revolution, certain only that the factors and forces involved were potent and complex. To many during the Nanking decade, however, the answer was clear: China had attempted to institute democratic government before the Chinese people had been prepared for the responsibilities of democracy. As Yang Yu-chiung, a Kuomintang theoretician, wrote in 1928, "In the past seventeen years, the greatest obstruction in politics resulted from hanging out the specious sign-board of democracy."[2]

Sun Yat-sen had recognized that democratic institutions

could function effectively in China only after the people had received experience with the concepts and techniques of self-government. He had, as a result, ordained that constitutional government should begin only after representative assemblies and self-government had been effectively established in at least half the hsien of the nation. Sun had not stated how long this period of "political tutelage" should last. The Kuomintang leadership in 1929 had decreed, however, that after a six-year period of tutelage the Chinese people would be ready to assume the responsibilities of constitutional rule.[3]

Many Chinese, both inside and outside the Kuomintang, soon repented this sanguine promise that the period of constitutionalism would be inaugurated in 1935. Like the cultural iconoclasts of the May Fourth period, they realized that democratic constitutions could survive only if sustained, in some profound way, by society itself. This contention could, of course, serve as a convenient pretext for self-serving Kuomintang partisans to maintain party rule. But even non-partisan intellectuals, some of whom (like the famous philosopher and reformer, Liang Shu-ming) were outspokenly critical of the government, warned that the inauguration of democratic rule now would further weaken the nation and worsen the conditions of instability. And Wu Ching-ch'ao, a prominent sociologist at Tsinghua University, further cautioned that another premature and disastrous experiment with democratic institutions, like that after 1912, would provoke such a popular reaction that it would be difficult in the future—when cultural conditions had improved—to institute democracy.[4]

This mood of disillusionment with democratic experiments led directly to a second theme in the dialogue of the period, the advocacy of dictatorship. This theme is exemplified by Tsiang T'ing-fu, a leading intellectual and future diplomat, then teaching at Tsinghua University. Tsiang, like Liang Shu-ming, contended that a viable democratic system is rooted deeply in the culture of a nation. Democratic institutions had not functioned after 1912, he suggested, because Chinese had no sense of social or national community. People outside government took no interest in national affairs, and men in power sought the benefit not of the nation but of themselves. Before China could institute democracy, said Tsiang, it must become a nation, politically unified and emotionally bound together by the citizens' loyalty to the state.

Thus far, Tsiang's argument was unexceptional. But he drew an extraordinary conclusion from his premises. Nostrums such as universal literacy or an extensive communications system, he argued, would not suffice to fuse China into a nation. His conclusion was that China could be transformed into a modern nation only by means of "personal despotism." Tsiang, a historian, argued that the despotism of the Tudor dynasty had spiritually and materially transformed England into a national entity. Similarly the Bourbons and the Romanovs had produced the consciousness of national oneness in France and Russia, that had enabled these countries to become strong and wealthy modern nations. Now China had to go through the same historical process of being fused into a national unit.

China had already experienced a long period of autocratic rule, of course, but Tsiang was not embarrassed by this historical irony. Autocracy in China, he stated, had not, as a result of "special circumstances," fulfilled its historical function of creating the basis for a modern nation. He did not explain what those special circumstances were. But, because history had once failed China, China now again had to traverse the historical stage of government by a personal despot. He even admitted, "I do not demand that this government be enlightened, although the more enlightened it is the better." His only demand of a personal despot was that he maintain stability and peace in the nation. For even if the unified government did not seek progress, he wrote, "progressive leaders outside the government would accomplish the desired advances in education, transportation, and commerce."[5]

Tsiang T'ing-fu's historical analysis was embarrassingly superficial, and Hu Shih made mincemeat of his argument that despotism was a necessary preparatory stage of nationhood.[6] What makes Tsiang's analysis so interesting is certainly not the profundity of his thinking. Rather it is fascinating because Tsiang, highly intelligent and Western-educated, had become so disillusioned by China's experiences with democracy, that he had resigned himself to any form of government, however despotic, if only it would restore domestic tranquility, national strength, and racial pride. "We are tired," Tsiang wrote, "of revolution, of war, of lost hopes."[7]

Tsiang T'ing-fu's political weariness and despair were characteristic of virtually all Chinese intellectuals. Few of them, however, were prepared to acquiesce in a tyrannical despotism. For most, the ideal dictator would be a national leader who stood above class strife, above economic interests, and would strive for the welfare of the entire nation. He would, as many writers of the decade phrased it, be a "new-style" dictator. Chang Hung, a former student of Hu Shih, for example, explained that the despotism he envisioned "must not be a barbaric despotism, lawless despotism . . . a stop-freedom-of-speech despotism, but an enlightened despotism, a meaningful despotism, a put-public-welfare-first despotism."[8] And Ch'ien Tuan-sheng wrote, "What I call a totalitarian state must have a dictator . . . who has ideals, who plans for the real benefit of the people."[9]

What the Chinese advocates of dictatorship sought, in other words, was an effective system of government. They despaired of the inefficiencies of democracy, partially because of China's recent experience with democratic institutions and partially because of political trends in the world at large. Since the military triumph of the democratic allies in World War I, democracy as a system of government had everywhere come under attack for its seeming inability to cope with the mounting economic and political crises. In Italy, Mussolini's dictatorship had transformed a weak and humiliated nation into one that was an international power. The achievements of Stalin, Ataturk, and more recently Hitler equally left a deep impression on Chinese political thinking. Chinese were aware of ideological differences between Stalin and Hitler, but they believed that both dictators were employing fundamentally similar political methods to restore hope and pride to their nations.

Events in the United States and Britain strengthened the Chinese trend away from democracy. For even these proto-types of the democratic experience seemed to be jettisoning democracy as their countries lay in the grips of the economic depression. Franklin D. Roosevelt, for example, was thought to be creating an economic dictatorship (some Republicans in the United States agreed). And the all-party coalition cabinet under Ramsay MacDonald in Great Britain was likewise seen as a step in the direction of dictatorship. If even these wealthy nations, with a democratic tradition, were abandoning democracy, Chinese reasoned, then surely it was inopportune to perpetuate the experiment in China.[10]

Ch'ien Tuan-sheng, a Harvard-trained political scientist, may be taken as an example of Chinese intellectuals whose original sympathies for democracy had been weakened by the world-wide advances of dictatorial rule. As recently as 1930 he had written in defense of democracy, claiming that democratic governments were relatively beneficial to the people, and that dictatorship was a fundamentally unstable form of government. "Therefore," he concluded, "we . . . have limitless hopes for democracy, and assert that dictatorial governments that violate democracy will ultimately fail.'"[11]

By 1934 Ch'ien had changed his mind. In an article that attracted much attention among China's intellectuals at the time, he proclaimed his conviction that a "totalitarian state" was China's only means of national salvation. Explaining why he had shifted positions, Ch'ien wrote: "I now still have limitless hope for governments that take the common people as their primary concern, and have not in the least lessened my detestation for dictatorships that ignore the welfare of the common people. But I cannot ignore a governmental form that is organized, idealistic, and that can plan for the benefit of the masses—even if it is a dictatorship.'"[12]

In Ch'ien's view, democratic government had been adequate

when the sole task of government had been to act as policeman for society. The development of modern economic systems had, however, transformed the responsibilities of government. Now economic production must be planned and rationalized. And, according to Ch'ien, only a totalitarian system of rule could coordinate the complex operations of a modern economy. "Democracy" he proclaimed, "is not suited to a controlled economy, and therefore the decline of democracy is inevitable." Italy and Russia, on the other hand, had discovered the system of government that could "correct the [economic] dislocations of the democratic era."[13]

For Ch'ien Tuan-sheng the implications for China were manifest. China's economy was backward, and it was threatened by a foreign aggressor. An industrial economy, particularly in the coastal provinces, must be rapidly developed. And agriculture would have to be rationalized and controlled so that it would contribute to the task of industrialization. To accomplish this, he concluded, "it is absolutely essential to have a totalitarian nation."[14] Ch'ien's assumptions regarding the superiority of a planned and controlled economy were broadly shared by the intellectual community.[15] Chang Chin-chien, for example, a political scientist trained at Stanford University, attributed the world economic crisis to the laissez-faire policies of capitalism. In reaction to the current depression, he said, "The people inevitably rise together and cry for 'controls' and 'planning.'" Dictatorships, he continued, "sweep aside yesterday's planless, unorganized, anarchic conditions, and implant social, economic, and political controls that are organized and planned."[16]

But economic planning required administrative efficiency and farsightedness—qualities, most Chinese agreed, that democracy did not possess. Chang Chin-chien spoke of "superfluous-words, mass-stupidity democracy," which he contrasted with "efficient, forceful, decisive dictatorial national movements." Dictators, he added, "can act quickly by just issuing one command; this is why dictators can in a minimum period of time perform awesome achievements."[17]

Chang Chin-chien was a Kuomintang member, but his outlook was broadly shared even by those who did not share his partisan loyalties. Ch'en Chih-mai, for instance, a Columbia Ph.D. and at the time a frequently bitter critic of the Kuomintang, shared Chang's admiration for the capacity of dictators to act quickly. "China's current situation," he wrote, "absolutely does not allow us time for old-fashioned Western thought. We should immediately abandon superstitions about democracy . . . We need a government with centralized powers that can produce the best talent that is efficient and competent."[18]

The Individual and the State. The focal concern of political writers in the 1930s was how to "save the nation" (*chiu-kuo*). This problem inevitably involved such central questions as governmental structure, economic strategies, and foreign policy. Ultimately, however, the Chinese had also to confront the problem of the relationship between the individual citizen and the nation they sought to save. This question has been central to political thinking throughout all of history, East and West; it is a question that has defied permanently satisfactory solution. In all probability, the inherent contradictions between individual aspirations and the constraints of society can never be permanently resolved.

Western Europeans and North Americans, particularly since the eighteenth century, have generally adopted the theoretical position that the individual is the starting point of social organization, and that society is a means for the fulfillment of the individuals constituting that society. John Locke and Voltaire both argued that man is possessed of certain natural rights that society may not transgress. And John Stuart Mill brilliantly articulated the Anglo-American faith that individual freedoms are inalienable, and that governments are to be judged by the extent to which they protect and foster individual liberties. True, there were alternative ideals, such as those expressed by Rousseau and Pope Pius IX. And even John Stuart Mill in the later years of his life had reasserted the rights of society as a whole as against the untrammeled freedoms of individuals. Yet even in this social-ist tradition, nowhere better exemplified than by Karl Marx, the full realization of man's potentialities *as individuals* was the base concern.

Chinese writers of the 1930s were not, like Karl Marx, products of the Judeo-Christian tradition, but rather of China's so-called Confucian tradition.[19] This Chinese intellec-tual tradition was, like the European tradition, richly varied. In the realm of political thought, however, it generally sup-ported the claims of society and of the state as against the claims of the individual. Thus the intellectuals of the 1930s easily drew upon a tradition of authoritarian and statist thinking.

At least partially as a consequence of this historical and cultural background, the third theme in the political writings of the 1930s was that most analyses began from the stand-point of society; the freedom of individuals was viewed as a dependent variable, entirely determined by the needs of so-ciety. Ch'ien Tuan-sheng, for example, stated that "since dictatorship is really able to advance the welfare of the ma-jority (which is almost all the people), then one cannot, because of the suppression of the freedoms of the minority, insist on maintaining a democracy which is not the equal of dictatorship in planning benefits."[20] Ch'en Chih-mai shared Ch'ien's view. "The protection of freedom," he wrote, "is not the only goal of government." Ch'en opposed any dictator who engaged in "useless oppression." And he argued that the strongest form of government was one that, rather than sup-pressing opposition, could enlist the cooperation of its citi-zens. He concluded, however, that in the final analysis people desired a government that effectively worked for the benefit and prosperity of society. "And if it attains those goals, people do not begrudge sacrificing their own freedoms."[21]

Within the Kuomintang, this principle that a political mi-nority had no claim to civil liberties had been developed into an article of faith. In a lengthy and influential analysis in 1928, Chou Fo-hai wrote that human freedoms are not inalienable but are granted and may be taken away by society. The concept of "the natural rights of the individual" (*t'ien-fu jen-ch'üan*) had been concocted in the West when new economic groups were struggling for social and political change. Chou declared that this theory, which had at the time been suitable in Europe, "does not now fit China." Instead, he wrote, the Kuomintang advocated the doctrine of "people's revolutionary rights" (*ko-ming min-ch'üan*), which guaranteed liberties and political rights only to supporters of the revolution. If China were to accept the interpretation that human beings are possessed of inalienable rights, he argued, then those persons who are servitors of the warlords and the imperialists could use their freedoms and political power to destroy the revolution.[22] Sa Meng-wu, who was closely associated with Ch'en Li-fu, echoed Chou Fo-hai, declaring that "only the Three People's Principles can now save China. So only the supporters of the Three People's Principles should have rights."[23]

Not only the proponents of authoritarian rule, but most of the more "liberal" elements in the Kuomintang, too, accepted the view that individual freedom must be secondary to and relative to national needs. Sun Fo (Sun K'o), for example, stated, "We can definitely say that the constitution we need is not one that takes individualism as the starting point of society and government."[24] And Wu Ching-hsiung, a chief architect of the Nanking government's first and most liberal constitutional draft, wrote, "Westerners, in struggling for freedom, started from the individual. Now we, in struggling for freedom, start from the group . . . We wish to save the nation and the race, and so we cannot but demand that each individual sacrifice his own freedom in order to preserve the freedom of the group."[25]

Sun Fo and Wu Ching-hsiung reflected the ideological predispositions of the Kuomintang. Their suspicions of individualism were nevertheless broadly shared by non-party intellectuals. Chang Fo-ch'üan, a graduate of Johns Hopkins University of teaching at Peking University, was typical. Chang, who was an opponent of dictatorship, asserted that

John Stuart Mill's concept of liberty "is harmful and of no benefit, especially to Chinese," because it predicated that the individual existed independently of society. Such a concept of the "isolation of the self" might be valid in philosophy, he declared, but in society and government it was a concept that must be destroyed. For Chang, there could be no areas of an individual's existence that are inviolate. "Freedom," he said, "is public, not private," and concerns the needs of society fully as much as of the individual.[26] Another avowed supporter of the democratic ideal declared that the evils of individualism and laissez-faireism "cannot be denied." "The result of the criticism of democracy during the past ten years," he concluded, "is that most people now suspect extreme individualism."[27]

These criticisms of Western-style democracy did not imply an unqualified rejection of democracy. Indeed, democracy had become one of the "good" words in the Chinese political lexicon. Even many outspoken advocates of dictatorship therefore affirmed that democracy was their ultimate ideal and that dictatorship was merely a means of attaining democracy.

When these writers spoke of democracy as an ultimate goal, however, they usually meant a democracy that would be based on economic equality. It would be a democracy of the whole people, and not just of a class or party. And, because candidates for office would be initially screened by means of the examination system, it would be a democracy run by men of ability. China's future democracy, in other words, would be a "real," or "improved," or "new-style" democracy.[28]

Democracy's Faltering Defense. Democracy of the old style did not want for defenders. Indeed, it is possible, as a leading sociologist, Wu Ching-ch'ao, remarked, that a majority of the intellectuals were "inclined toward" democracy.[29] Yet they defended democracy poorly. The advocates of democracy seldom articulated a comprehensive defense of their position and instead sniped at the shortcomings of the Kuomintang's system of party rule. Abolish party rule, they demanded, and "return government to the people." Then, they said in the parlance of the day, China could "get back on the tracks."

Perhaps these advocates of "return government to the people" (*huan-cheng yü min*) were correct; perhaps the patent ineffectuality and inequities of the Nanking regime would have been eliminated by a liberalization of the political process. Infrequently, however, did they explain why. And, when they did, they sometimes revealed a remarkably unsophisticated understanding of the true character of liberal democracy. P'eng Hsüeh-p'ei, for example, who was at this time a critic of the government, extolled the advantages of democracy. Governments are like kitchens, he asserted, and unless they are cleaned out once in a while, they became messy. Under a democratic form of government, the people supervise and control the government and periodically accomplish this necessary governmental housecleaning. He concluded, however, that his ideal of government was one that was "efficient as a great sword, fast as lightning."[30]

Chang Fo-ch'üan similarly argued the desirability of democracy in China. He also contended, however, that the primary task of government in China at that time was to create *power*. The democracy that he envisioned would, therefore, be one with strong centralized authority. Chang at least sensed the ambiguity of his proposal, admitting that in China, at least in the near future, democracy would "inevitably carry a bit of the flavor of elitist rule (*kua-t'ou cheng-chih*)."[31]

Both P'eng and Chang gave evidence of impatience with the slowness, the divided authority, the muddling-through that is apt to characterize the democratic process. This was an infirm foundation for democracy. As J. L. Talmon has suggested, liberal democracy "assumes politics to be a matter of trial and error, and regards political systems as pragmatic contrivances of human ingenuity and spontaneity."[32] Most Chinese intellectuals, however, were intolerant of trial-and-error methods; they believed that the means of attaining clearly enunciated goals could and must be rationally planned and efficiently implemented. They felt that there existed objective truths in politics and that government should be empowered to act swiftly to realize those truths. In Talmon's view, this attitude is incompatible with the attainment of the liberal ideals.

Chinese intellectuals, therefore, were attracted to democracy less because it provided guarantees of individual freedoms than because they were disillusioned with the ineffectiveness of Kuomintang authoritarian rule. The democrats' opposition to dictatorship stemmed, in other words, from discontent with the Kuomintang rather than from deep convictions in democratic values. This, indeed, was expressed explicitly in the liberal newspaper, *I-shih pao* ("Social Welfare"). "If party-rule in China," it editorialized, "were as successful as it is in Turkey, Russia, and Italy, then even if the Kuomintang proposed abolishing it, the Chinese people would probably in unison plead to have it continued."[33]

In another instance of democracy's faltering defense, Hu Tao-wei attempted to refute the argument that the Chinese people were not yet prepared for democracy. Hu, who held a doctorate from Princeton, contended that widespread illiteracy had indeed been an obstacle to the implementation of democracy in the nineteenth century. In the twentieth century, however, there existed electrical voting machines that used colors to represent the candidates. With such scientifically advanced machines, he said, pervasive illiteracy among the masses could no longer be considered an obstacle to democracy.[34] This was, of course, an inane retort to the critics who perceived democracy not merely as a question of casting ballots but as a political practice inseparable from the whole cultural environment.

Occasionally, but only occasionally, a Chinese writer did reveal a highly sophisticated appreciation of the basic values of democracy. One article, for example, by a pseudonymous Ming Hsia, argued compellingly that only a democracy could claim moral authority, for it was the only form of government based on the consent of the governed. In a democratic government, Ming Hsia wrote, the individual is the goal of government. Any limitations on the freedom of the individual were accepted freely, for the citizen was imbued with the citizen's morality of accepting the decisions of his elected representatives.[35]

Reading this essay, the Western reader suddenly feels a bond of intellectual community with the author, for Ming Hsia was expressing the shibboleths of the Anglo-American democracies. One wonders, however, who Ming Hsia was. The essay makes no attempt to relate the theory of democracy to Chinese circumstances. It reads like the essay of a returned-student who got *A's* in his classes in political science in an American university, but who had utterly lost touch with the realities of government and society in China. It is doubtful that Ming Hsia's views won many supporters among even China's Western-educated intellectuals.

Hu Shih was the nationally recognized leader of Chinese liberalism, a scholar who drew serious attention as a result of his incisive mind, cogent literary style, and a publicist's flair for the dramatic. Despite his voluminous literary output, he was seldom dull; he was the inaugurator of, or a participant in, virtually every intellectual debate of the period. People often did not agree with him, but they could seldom ignore him. His intellectual presence was so pervasive that he had become a political force in his own right.

In contrast to Ming Hsia, Hu Shih was sensitive to the frustrations that the experiments with democracy had instilled in his fellow countrymen. He also recognized that China was not possessed of a literate and politically sophisticated population, which was customarily thought to be a prerequisite for democracy. Hu Shih, however, tried to turn this situation to his advantage, contending that China's backwardness was precisely the reason China should abstain from a dictatorial form of government and should adopt constitutional democracy. Constitutional democracy, he argued, is a "childish political system." "The strong point of democracy is that it does not greatly require outstanding talents . . . Democracy is a government of common sense, whereas enlightened despotism is a government of heroes . . . Constitutional democracy is the most childish of all political schools, and is therefore most suitable for our childish dumb-bells.''[36]

Dictatorship, Hu continued, is an enormously complicated form of rule which requires that the leaders be possessed of truly outstanding ability and knowledge. Dictatorship is a government of specialists, whereas democracy merely requires that the masses be possessed of a modicum of common sense, which could be acquired through practical experience.[37] Hu therefore, in a curious, involuted way, accepted the concept of political tutelage. In his view, however, political tutelage was necessary to prepare China not for democracy but for dictatorship. ''After we have carefully and continually undergone thirty to fifty years' training with constitutional democracy,'' he wrote, ''then perhaps we will have the opportunity to zealously implement an enlightened despotism.''[38]

The contention that democracy is a kindergarten of politics was a novel argument, and Hu Shih himself called it a ''crazy idea.'' Yet it was not just a momentary whim or aberration. He had formulated other arguments against dictatorship—he had said that there was no individual, party, or class in China that was capable of leading a dictatorship, and there was no vital, emotional issue—not even opposition to Japan—that could galvanize the entire nation so that the people would accept the authority of a dictator.[39] Even three years later, he still contended that his idea of democracy as kindergarten government was, of all his reasons, the most important. And he fumed when Tsiang T'ing-fu and Ting Wen-chiang—his personal friends, but intellectual antagonists—refused to take him seriously enough even to dispute the idea. They have been ''blinded by the textbooks,'' he wrote, ''so they feel that this explanation of mine is something interesting and laughable, but need not be rebutted.''[40]

Hu Shih also tried to refute the prevalent argument that only dictatorial domination of the economy would bring about democracy in China. Economic reforms that are pushed through by a centralized authority, he insisted, will be superficial, and in the long-run will not benefit the nation. Effective and permanent modernization, he contended, could be accomplished only through "diffused permeation"—Hu's infelicitous phrase meaning individual experimentation and gradual achievement. He admitted that economic development by means of diffused permeation would necessarily be "slow, sporadic, and often wasteful." In contrast to the forced changes that can be accomplished by authoritarian controls, those implanted through diffused permeation will have deep and strong roots, for they will be sustained by social, intellectual, and political forces that will develop functionally with the economy.[41]

Hu Shih's arguments in defense of democracy may have been provocative and challenging, but they won few converts to democracy. He may even have been *theoretically* correct in contending that economic growth will be fragile unless it be "slow, sporadic, and often wasteful." But surely he was *psychologically* wrong. For the Chinese people were in no mood for "slow, sporadic, and often wasteful" solutions. They were impatient for results. Hu's advocacy of kindergarten government also revealed how badly he had misread the national temper. For, by depicting dictatorship as a more advanced system of rule than democracy, he was telling the people to accept an old, second-hand brand at a time when they could aspire to the most recent, streamlined model. His argument was, in fact, acutely embarrassing to other partisans of democracy, because it was so vulnerable to attack, and because it implied that democracy was not an ideal form of government toward which China should strive. In disgust, Chang Hsi-jo complained that Hu Shih's crazy idea "is not merely no help, but is also damaging" to the cause of democracy.[42]

Chinese had first become familiar with the precepts of democracy during the waning days of the Ch'ing dynasty. Literati had then sensed humiliation at the weakness of China in the face of the Western powers. In their search for a way to restore a strong and wealthy nation, they attempted to plumb the wellsprings of Western strength. Britain in particular, France and the United States in lesser degree, then seemed the most powerful states of the West. And each of these had a democratic form of government. The conclusion of the Chinese who sought to reinvigorate China was logical, albeit probably fallacious : if China would be strong, then it too must become a democracy.

Initially the Chinese had viewed democracy formalistically —as a package of institutions that would strengthen the nation. Gradually, however, they realized that democratic political institutions remained viable only if they were supported by a liberal society and liberal values. Thus Sun Yat-sen had adopted the concept of political tutelage, and the radical intellectuals of the May Fourth period had proclaimed that Confucianism and traditional social institutions must be wholly discarded. Yet even the more sophisticated proponents of democracy, like Liang Ch'i-chao and Yen Fu, seem to have embraced liberal values less because they contributed to the fulfillment of individuals than because they presumably contributed to a more vigorous society and in turn to a stronger nation.[43]

Liberal democracy therefore had shallow roots in China. When it was perceived that Russia, Italy, and Germany had devised apparently more effective methods of strengthening the nation—means that were more compatible with the traditions of China—democracy had little to sustain it. Moreover, many Chinese intellectuals in the mid-1930s were becoming reluctantly reconciled to the Nationalist regime. Chiang Kai-shek seemed now to be securely in power. And most intellectuals, salaried and living in the cities, were materially better off than they had been for years. Thus, seeing that the movement toward some kind of Nationalist dictatorship was inexorable, they realistically concentrated on trying to enlighten that dictatorship. The considerable number of non-partisan

intellectuals who joined the Nationalist government after 1935
—for example, Tsiang T'ing-fu, Wong Wen-hao, and Wu
Ching-ch'ao—bespeaks their political mood at the time.

The movement favoring dictatorship was also fostered by
the pervasive mood of cultural despair. It is difficult for
Westerners to fathom the despair and humiliation that Chinese felt in the early 1930s. For a century the nation had been
in political decline. The Chinese had been a proud people, sure
of their culture, confident of their superiority. And, in the
1930s, they were a proud people still. But now this pride was
bittersweet, for, despite the continuing sense of superiority,
they were filled with doubts and jealousies. They were per-
plexed that everything they tried—war, reform, revolution—
seemed only to accelerate the decline. By the early 1930s, it
had become manifest that the latest attempt to arrest the
decline, the Nationalist Revolution, had in its turn failed.
Why? Some Chinese blamed imperialism. But more felt there
was something basically and radically wrong with the Chinese
people. The 1930s was, in consequence, a period of painful,
remorseless national self-flagellation.

"In China," a writer bemoaned, "everything is more backward than in Western Europe." Others charged that the
Chinese people were indolent, they feared difficulties, they
lacked any progressive spirit, they assumed no responsibility
but waited for others to act for them, they had no concern for
the collective welfare, they lacked human-heartedness. Another remarked that Chinese not only lacked creative power;
they "do not even have very strong powers of imitation."[44]
And Hu Shih observed that the Chinese had become "a spine-
less, worthless people," who had failed to meet the challenges
of the modern period because "our rottenness is so deep."[45]

The self-doubt became so extreme that some writers questioned that Chinese were either the physical or intellectual
equals of other peoples in the world. A scholar named Shen
T'ung, for example, believed that the quality of the Chinese
people had declined just as had that of the early Greeks and
Romans. As a result of pervasive famines, use of opium and

heroin, and the spread of venereal disease, the supreme qualities of their ancestors were being laid waste and Chinese were becoming an "inferior race" (*lieh-teng min-tsu*). This decline in the quality of the race could not be quantified, he said, as could the loss of Chinese territory; it was, however, of far graver concern. For, convinced of the universal truth of social Darwinism, Shen declared that "inferior races will inevitably be destroyed in the struggle for survival."[46]

Yet another writer asked: "Is the intelligence of the Chinese people up to that of other people?"[47] Comparing the IQ tests of various races, he concluded that the Chinese were as intelligent as white Americans, and—apparently accepting the racist theories of the day—they were more intelligent than American blacks and Indians. Although this conclusion salved his nationalistic fears, the fact that he seriously undertook the study was indicative of the despair and self-doubt that assailed all Chinese during the Nanking period.

Cultural despair is highly favorable to the development of dictatorship. In pre-Hitlerean Germany, for example, there was a pervasive malaise. Society under the Weimar Republic was fragmented; old beliefs and privileges were under attack; the former certitudes and faiths had crumbled. In this milieu, the Germans longed for a leader who would compel unity, and who would create a new spiritually unified community.[48] In a similar way, most Chinese derived no confidence from the democratic alternative, characterized as it was by Hu Shih as "slow, sporadic, and often wasteful." But dictatorship seemed to provide the sure, easy answers desired by a people who felt threatened and despised.

Power Politics in Constitution-Drafting

The Nationalist regime was plunged into unprecedented crisis by the events of late 1931 and early 1932. Kwangtung, under the leadership of Sun Fo, Wang Ching-wei, and Ch'en Chi-t'ang, was in revolt. The Yangtze River flooded. And the Japanese attacked first Manchuria and then Shanghai. Nanking, in the face of these challenges, proved to be impotent.

The popular mood, already dark because of resentment at the Kuomintang's ineffectiveness and self-seeking, now turned ugly and mean. "Some people," observed a leading political commentator, "say that the major catastrophes afflicting China today are the spread of Japanese aggression and the violence of the communists. But I say no, China's greatest catastrophes are still the foul governmental organization and the lack of cooperation among the national leaders."[49]

Popular animus focused on the Kuomintang's system of one-party rule. "Party rule," proclaimed the *I-shih pao*, "has become the political institution most hated by the people."[50] Party rule was blamed for the nation's social, moral, and economic decline. It was turning the youth of the nation to communism. It was the cause of civil wars and foreign aggression.[51] As even the level-headed geologist, Ting Wen-chiang, warned: "If [the demand to end party rule] is not granted . . . revolution is absolutely unavoidable . . . Our demand is absolute and unconditional."[52] Chiang Kai-shek had two stock responses when popular dissatisfaction appeared to be getting out of hand: he held out the prospect of sharing power with his critics, or he threatened them with violence. This time he chose the former alternative and convoked a National Emergency Conference.

The National Emergency Conference. The decision to convoke a National Emergency Conference (Kuo-nan hui-i) was made formally at the Fourth Party Congress of the Kuomintang on November 22, 1931. Ts'ai Yüan-p'ei, who presented the proposal on behalf of the Nanking leadership, stated that there were many men of ability and experience who were currently excluded from the party and the government. He observed that opposition parties in Europe frequently formed coalitions during periods of national crisis. It seemed appropriate, therefore, that a National Emergency Conference be convened as a means of enlisting the support and expertise of these outstanding non-party men. The proposal was approved, and the conference was scheduled to be held the following month.[53] Twice the conference was postponed. The political crisis leading to Chiang Kai-shek's retirement, and then the fighting at Shanghai, prevented the assembly of the conference until April 7, 1932.

In November and December 1931, when the National Emergency Conference was being organized, the leadership of the regime had been in a state of near panic. It had therefore given a broad-ranging mandate to the conference, including the right to adopt resolutions with regard to foreign policy, financial administration, military affairs, "and all matters relating to the national emergency." In addition, the Executive Yüan of Sun Fo's interim government had named to the conference 189 delegates, representing a broad spectrum of China's elite, over 80 percent of whom did not belong to the Kuomintang.[54]

Many of these delegates were confirmed critics of the Kuomintang, and they viewed the National Emergency Conference as an opportunity to dismantle the hated Kuomintang's one-party system. Not only did they plan to recommend "an immediate end of the monopolistic system of party government"; they sought also the immediate formation of a non-partisan coalition government and the termination of all governmental subsidies to the Kuomintang party apparatus.[55] These recommendations, or rather demands, threatened not only the power but the financial viability of the Kuomintang.

The government, headed since late January 1932 by the duumvirate of Chiang Kai-shek and Wang Ching-wei, might have forestalled the confrontation with its critics by again postponing the conference. Instead, they packed the conference with 200 additional delegates—nearly all of whom were Kuomintang members.[56] Wang Ching-wei furthermore stipulated that discussions in the conference were to be restricted to three specific problems: foreign aggression, flood relief, and suppression of the communists. All other matters, he declared, lay outside the jurisdiction of the conference.[57]

The regime's attempt to turn the National Emergency Conference into a meaningless facade of popular participation infuriated the non-party delegates. They retorted that political questions lay at the root of the national crisis, and that they would be betraying the nation if they restricted the discussions to the topics specified by Wang Ching-wei. A delegate from Shanghai declared: "We doubt the sincerity of the government in convening such a conference, when its scope has been limited to certain problems. We are neither flood specialists nor military men who can tackle such problems . . . What concerns us the most are those problems relating to the reformations which the government should follow in speedily forming a constitutional government, so that henceforth the government will not be dominated by one single party and the people will have a voice in it."[58] Approximately one hundred of the delegates publicly declared that they would not attend the conference unless they were assured complete freedom to discuss all questions relating to the national emergency.[59]

When the National Emergency Conference did finally convene in Loyang, where the capital was temporarily located after the Japanese attack on Shanghai, only about one-third of all the delegates were in attendance, and most of these were Kuomintang members.[60] Despite this boycott by the regime's most obdurate critics, the conference proved to be anything but placid. In defiance of Wang Ching-wei's restriction on the scope of the discussions, a group of the delegates proposed the formation of a coalition government. This motion threw the conference into an uproar.[61] Following colorful if unseemly dispute among the badly factionalized delegates, the proposal was rejected. Yet discontent with the political situation was so deep, even among these presumably "safe" delegates, that the conference did adopt a resolution calling for the establishment of a National Representative Congress (Kuo-min tai-piao ta-hui). This body would—until the beginning of constitutional rule—have authority in matters of the budget, national debts, and important treaties. The final declaration of the National Emergency Conference also urged upon the government the necessity of safeguarding basic civil liberties in order to foster democracy and to prepare for constitutional rule.[62]

Despite all the precautions of the regime's leadership, therefore, the National Emergency Conference had ventured to discuss political questions. By doing so, it had revealed the depth of disillusionment with the system of one-party rule and demonstrated that democratic rule was still an effective rallying cry in national politics. "Since the National Emergency Conference," the *Kuo-wen chou-pao* reported, "the sound of the people's demand for constitutional government increases daily."[63]

Sun Fo and the Demand for a Constitution. The Nationalist leadership was unsympathetic to this rising chorus of demands for representative government. Wang Ching-wei, for example, declared himself in favor of constitutionalism "in principle." "What concerns us, however," he added—making reference to Ts'ao K'un's subornation of the parliament—"is that we do not want to return to the situation of 1923."[64] Yet popular emotions were running high, and it would have been impolitic for the government wholly to ignore the demand.

The Executive Yüan therefore announced that the government would—following Sun Yat-sen's formula for political tutelage—create popularly elected advisory assemblies at the local level. This would be done gradually. Experimental assemblies would be instituted first in six of the major cities of the country. Subsequently, similar assemblies would be formed first at the hsien level and ultimately at the provincial level.[65]

This scheme was an old one that had been gathering dust in the Kuomintang's closet for years. It was dusted off now only to appease the brewing public displeasure with party rule. And in fact the government even now did not act on its promise to institute the system of local assemblies. The Kuomintang leadership would not broaden the scope of political participation impetuously.

One prominent member of the Kuomintang, by contrast, viewed the constitutional demands not as a threat but as an opportunity. This was Sun Fo. Sun Fo was a long-standing rival of Chiang Kai-shek, but his political fortunes had recently declined cruelly. In January 1932 he had been squeezed out of the premiership, which he had occupied for only one month. At much the same time, his sole military backing, the naval and air forces in Kwangtung, had suddenly rejected his leadership and had defected to Ch'en Chi-t'ang.[66]

Yet Sun still had hope. As "the Prince" (*t'ai-tzu*), the son of Sun Yat-sen, he savored a political prominence that he could not have won by dint of his talents alone. It was still considered dangerous to leave him outside government, where he would be free to scheme and agitate and organize. Thus the government of Chiang Kai-shek and Wang Ching-wei in March 1932 offered him the presidency of the Legislative Yüan.[67]

Sun Fo was too experienced in Kuomintang politics to accept a prestigious appointment without assuring himself of some political leverage. He therefore refused to assume the office until he had repaired his political fortunes. The widespread clamor for constitutional government suited his purposes. Previously, in 1929, when he had enjoyed some power in the government, he had dismissed proposals for constitutional government, saying that a constitution would be just so much waste paper, because the masses had not been trained to exercise their political rights.[68] Now, however, his political position within the regime was weak. And the ripe, exploitable issue of constitutionalism could be used to loosen Chiang Kai-shek's control of the regime. Less than two weeks after the close of the National Emergency Conference, therefore, Sun Fo became the champion of constitutionalism.

Sun during 1932 was doyen of a small coterie of political malcontents, the so-called "Shanghai Committeemen" (*hu-wei*)—members of the Kuomintang's Central Executive Committee who, at odds with the Nanking authorities, rusticated themselves in Shanghai. All told, they numbered only about thirty. Some of them adhered to the cliques of Hu Han-min, Li Tsung-jen, Yen Hsi-shan, or Feng Yü-hsiang. The largest single group, comprising eight or nine, were Sun Fo's men. But all shared a political pique that was directed at the regime of Chiang and Wang, and all more or less gravitated around Sun Fo.

After the National Emergency Conference, and in consultation with the Shanghai Committeemen, Sun wrote a "Draft Program of National Salvation." This document was to serve as the spearhead of his political comeback. Made public on April 24, 1932, it called for the inauguration of constitutional rule "in the shortest possible time." Subsequently it was widely reprinted, Sun hoping to win a broad following, both among the populace at large and among the diverse and fragmented opponents of Chiang Kai-shek who wielded political or military power.[69]

By autumn 1932 Sun Fo's political stock had sharply improved. He met in late September with Chiang Kai-shek at Lushan, Chiang's airy retreat in Kiangsi. The meeting went well. Chiang accepted Sun's demand to convoke a plenary session of the Central Executive Committee in order to discuss the question of a constitution. And Sun, in turn, expressed his readiness to assume the presidency of the Legislative Yüan.[70]

For the promised plenary session, Sun Fo prepared a resolution calling for extensive political reforms and for the drafting of a constitution. In the current crisis, he wrote, the nation could be saved only if the people would unite to resist foreign aggression. And the only means of attaining national unity, he asserted, was to adopt a constitutional form of government.[71]

He astutely anticipated one of the Central Executive Committee's chief objections to a constitution: that members of the party would be thrown out of work if the Kuomintang's one-party rule was ended. Such fears were unfounded, Sun assured them, for the Kuomintang would naturally retain governmental power after the promulgation of a constitution. In explaining this paradoxical conclusion, Sun prophesied that, if the Kuomintang would implement constitutional rule, the people would as never before rally to the party's support. As a consequence, he declared, "the governing powers of the

Kuomintang will definitely be even more secure than previously.''[72]

When the plenary session convened on December 15, 1932, there was nevertheless spirited opposition to Sun Fo's resolution.[73] But Chiang Kai-shek had promised to support Sun's demand for a constitution; and Chiang's faction controlled the Central Executive Committee. Therefore, after some revisions, Sun's resolution was adopted. The Legislative Yüan was thereby empowered to prepare a constitutional draft, which was to be submitted to a National Constituent Assembly (Kuo-min ta-hui) in March 1935.[74] Satisfied of his political leverage on Chiang Kai-shek, and believing that the party was committed to constitutionalism, Sun Fo on December 18 accepted the appointment as head of the Legislative Yüan that had been first offered him nine months previously.[75]

A Kuomintang leader had a responsibility to provide for the livelihood of his followers. During his negotiations before agreeing to join the government, Sun Fo had asked that the Ministries of Communications and of Railroads be assigned to his appointees. These offices would have provided a rich source of squeeze for his supporters. But Sun still lacked the clout to win such rich political plums. He was instead permitted to make his own appointments to the Legislative Yüan. This he now did with gusto. He raised the membership of the Yüan from its previous figure of forty-nine to ninety—an increase that forced a new budgetary allotment for the Yüan.[76] Sun had, however, proved his ability to provide for his supporters. On January 16, 1933, the new members of the Legislative Yüan took the oath of office. Immediately thereafter, the Yüan began preparing a constitutional draft.

Preparation of the Constitutional Draft. The Legislative Yüan began work on the constitutional draft in January 1933; the final draft was not promulgated by the government until May 5, 1936. During the intervening three years, variable political forces buffeted the constitutional draft, but the force that prevailed was unmistakably authoritarianism. The Legislative Yüan began with a relatively liberal document in 1933.

By 1936 most of the democratic features of the earlier drafts had been removed and had been replaced by provisions designed to sustain Chiang Kai-shek's growing powers.

Sun Fo and his associates in the Legislative Yüan approached their task with two guiding principles. First, the future constitutional government should be structured in accordance with the model depicted in the writings of Sun Yat-sen. And second, the locus of power should be the legislative organs of government, preventing thereby the authoritarian control of a military dictator.

Adherence to the first principle proved to be more difficult than anticipated. Sun Yat-sen had decreed, for example, that the government should consist of a National Assembly, the "Five-Power Constitution" (that is, that there were to be the five branches of government—the Executive, Legislative, Judicial, Examination, and Control Yüan), and that the powers of the central and local governments should be so defined that there would be a tendency toward neither centralization nor decentralization of authority. At first glance, these instructions appeared only slightly ambiguous.[77]

Close examination of Sun's doctrinal legacy invariably raised knotty if not insoluble questions. Sun had never been pestered by the bugaboo of consistency, and the relationship between the several organs of government therefore acquired unclear if not mystical qualities. Even during Sun's lifetime, the "profundity" of his thinking had made it difficult for him to convey his concept of government to others. He himself told of his attempt to instruct a Japanese about the Five-Power Constitution. But the Japanese, who had a doctorate in law, was incapable of comprehending Sun's meaning until Sun had explicated it for two or three months.

Sun also related that he once spent two weeks instructing a Chinese scholar—it was probably Wang Ch'ung-hui—about the system of the five yüan before the concept became clear. Later, after the scholar had obtained an advanced degree in law at Yale and had subsequently studied further in England, France, and Germany, he again did not understand Sun's concept of the Five-Power Constitution. "I am afraid," Sun remarked, "that the more I explain the more obscure it will become." "It is true," he added, "that no one at present has fully understood it."[78]

Despite the formidable problems of interpreting Sun Yat-sen's vision of the future government, the Legislative Yüan by July 1934 had produced not only a concrete and clear document, but one that would have been generally supportive of popular democracy.[79] One of the most notable features of this "Revised Preliminary Draft" was that the president of the Republic would have been a figurehead, endowed with little more than symbolic powers. Executive and administrative powers of government were to repose in a cabinet, to be composed of the premier (head of the Executive Yüan) and of the heads of ministries subordinate to that Yüan.

The really noteworthy feature of the Revised Preliminary Draft, however, was the considerable powers that were vested in the two "legislative" organs of the government. The Legislative Yüan, for example, would have the authority to "discuss and decide" matters of laws, the budget, martial law, declarations of war and peace, and "other important matters relating to foreign affairs." It would, moreover, have the right of interpolation in the conduct of affairs in each of the other four yüan of government. The National Assembly, a representative body elected indirectly by the people, would also have broad-ranging authority. It was to elect most of the top-level members of the government, including the president, heads of the yüan (except the head of the Executive Yüan, who would be appointed by the president), and the members of the Legislative and Control Yüan. The National Assembly would also have the right of final decision in all matters of legislation, budget, peace and war, and so on. And, if dissatisfied with either the policies or the administration of the government, it could interpolate and—if still unsatisfied—impeach the president.[80]

The National Assembly would ordinarily be in session but one month every two years. It would, however, elect from its membership a standing committee, which would be empowered to perform the duties of the National Assembly when the Assembly was itself not in session. This standing committee might, in other words, maintain a close and effective control of the day-to-day conduct of the government's administration.

In general, then, the executive authority of the government would, as envisioned by the Revised Preliminary Draft, have been relatively weak. Power would have been decentralized, with an exceedingly large measure of authority residing in the National Assembly and the Legislative Yüan.

Despite the essentially anti-authoritarian bias of the Revised Preliminary Draft, the document did contain two provisions that revealed the limitations on the liberalism of Sun Fo and his colleagues in the Legislative Yüan. Moreover, these provisions were so congenial to the entire Kuomintang hierarchy that, despite changes in all the other articles of the various drafts, they remained virtually untouched throughout the drafting process.

Article One of the Revised Preliminary Draft read: "China is a Three-People's-Principles Republic."[81] This simple statement was pregnant with the most far-reaching consequences. It would have forced all governmental policies within the channels of Sun Yat-senism. Possibly this in itself would have had no serious practical effects, for Sunist ideology had already proven sufficiently vague and elastic that extremists of both the political right and left could simultaneously claim its sanction. More serious for the future of democracy in China, was the implied proscription of political activities that were incompatible with the Three People's Principles. Since those principles were subject to diverse interpretations, this provision could be used by those in power to suppress non-Kuomintang parties and persons and even to outlaw factions of the Kuomintang that were at odds with the ruling elite. Potentially, therefore, this article subverted whatever democratic provisions were contained in the remainder of the document.

The second illiberal feature of the Revised Preliminary Draft was in the section on People's Rights.[82] This section was similar to the American Bill of Rights in guaranteeing citizens the enjoyment of the various freedoms. All these freedoms were restricted, however, with the clause that they "shall not be limited except in accordance with the law." For example, the article on religious freedom read: "Every citizen shall have the freedom of religious belief; such freedom shall not be limited except in accordance with the law."

Within the Legislative Yüan this provision had been a major source of controversy. Chang Chih-pen, assistant chairman of the first drafting committee, criticized the tendency of the committee to emphasize the needs and the rights of the state rather than of the citizens. He therefore opposed the phrase, "except in accordance with the law," stating that "the constitution's spirit of protection is lost, and having a constitution will be the same as not having a constitution."[83]

Neither Sun Fo, nor the majority of the Legislative Yüan's drafting committee shared Chang's concern. For them, the transcendent purpose of a constitution (other than to limit Chiang Kai-shek's power) was to facilitate the salvation and development of the nation. "Freedom," explained Sun Fo, "is a tool for the development of individuality so that [the individual] may strive for society. This is the new meaning of freedom. It goes without saying that it should be subject to many forms of restriction."[84] This "new meaning of freedom," in which the individual was subordinated to society, was incorporated in all official constitutional drafts published during the 1930s.

Three times during this initial phase of constitutional drafting, the Legislative Yüan had published successive versions of the constitutional draft in order to elicit public discussion and criticism. Initially, the publication of the drafts had provoked a great deal of public comment. In June 1933, for example, following publication of the so-called Wu Draft (named for Wu Ching-hsiung), the Legislative Yüan received over 200 letters containing suggestions for revisions, and the press printed numerous articles criticizing various features of the draft.[85] When the Revised Preliminary Draft was published on July 9, 1934, by contrast, few criticisms were voiced. The absence of criticism, Sun Fo exclaimed, proves "that the contents of the draft have gradually become one with the views of society. Oh, great contentment!"[86]

Sun Fo's jubilation proved to be short-lived. He thought the constitutional draft had attained perfection, and that the work of preparing the constitution was therefore finished. Yet by mid-October the draft was to be completely revised and infused with a fundamentally different philosophy of government. Thus the Legislative Yüan's work of the previous year-and-a-half was undone in a few brief weeks.

The new changes were incorporated in the Constitutional Draft of October 16, 1934. According to this newest revision, the president would be the dominant power in government, possessed of strong centralized powers and unfettered by the National Assembly. Moreover, the premier and heads of the ministries were to be appointed by the president, responsible to him personally and removable at his pleasure. This was a presidential form of government—the form of government that Sun Fo had hitherto sought to avoid by vesting preponderant power in the Legislative Yüan and the National Assembly.

The embarrassing task of explaining why the constitutional draft had been so precipitately rewritten went to Sun Fo. Sun stated that, in mid-September, China's outstanding legal scholar, Wang Ch'ung-hui, had returned to China on vacation from his judgeship on the Permanent Court of International Justice at The Hague. According to Sun Fo, he had visited Wang Ch'ung-hui in Shanghai, and learned that Wang's interpretation of Sun Yat-sen's governmental model differed sharply from that which had thus far guided the deliberations of the Legislative Yüan. In Wang's view, Sun Yat-sen had intended that the people should be sovereign but that they should not interfere with the actual governance of the nation. The draft constitution in its current form, he said, bestowed

excessive powers on the National Assembly and thereby obfuscated the separation, desired by Sun Yat-sen, between the
sovereign powers of the people (*cheng-ch'üan*) and the governing powers of the government (*chih-ch'üan*).[87]

Sun Fo elaborated, remarking that his father had "long ago
distinguished very clearly" between the sovereign powers of
the people and the governing powers of the government. The
Legislative Yüan, however, "did not consider this point
clearly." "This," Sun Fo admitted, "was truly a mistake."[88]
Sun Fo's explanation was surely disingenuous. True, the
ambiguities in Sun Yat-sen's writings could be used to justify
the newest revision with regard to the role of the National
Assembly. By the same token, the earlier drafts were not as
incompatible with Sunism as Sun Fo now claimed.[89]

The actual explanation must be that Sun Fo and the Legislative Yüan had been subjected to strong external political
pressures. As Ch'ien Tuan-sheng wrote, "The self-denial of
the Legislative Yüan in willingly curtailing its own substantial powers was of course a purely compulsory act."[90] What
kind of compulsion was employed is uncertain, but the reasons
are clear. Powerful elements of the regime had now determined to formalize the dictatorial powers of Chiang Kai-shek.
And a constitution such as the Legislative Yüan had contem-
plated, which would have narrowly circumscribed the powers
of the presidency, was contrary to their wishes.

The Movement to Establish a Dictatorship. The movement
to install Chiang Kai-shek as dictator coalesced during 1934.
The Blue Shirt organization had now matured, and its influence was spreading by means of the schools, political training,
and control of the press. During 1934 the New Life Movement
began (see Chapter 2). And, early in the year, twenty of the
provincial and municipal party headquarters in north China
had formally urged Chiang Kai-shek to assume the position of
tsung-li, or director-general, of the Kuomintang.[91] The title
of tsung-li had been adopted by Sun Yat-sen in 1924 when he
assumed dictatorial powers over the party. Since his death,
the position of tsung-li had been forever reserved for him.

The proposal that Chiang be named tsung-li was a euphemistic way of suggesting that Chiang should now also become dictator of the party—and hence of the nation. Chang Chi, a powerful figure in the party and an intimate of Chiang, expressed the idea even more directly: "Support Chiang Kai-shek as China's Hitler."[92]

The stream of articles in the national press favoring dictatorship reached full flood in 1934. One of these articles even remarked that Chiang Kai-shek was fully as capable as Sun Yat-sen and might therefore properly assume the post of tsung-li.[93] To compare anyone else with Sun Yat-sen would have been blasphemous, for Sun had now been exalted into a virtual deity. Yet truly heroic qualities were now also being ascribed to Chiang.

Chiang publicly denied aspiring to become dictator. It was ridiculous, he said, that he or the Kuomintang should be accused of wishing to establish a dictatorship, for it was the spirit and not the structure of a political movement that determined success or failure.[94] If the opponents of dictatorship had been mollified by these denials in March, their fears were revived in August. For then the Central Executive Committee of the party announced the agenda for the Fifth Party Congress, which was scheduled for November. To a neophyte, this agenda appeared innocuous; to Chiang Kai-shek's opponents, however, the agenda signaled that Chiang planned to use the party congress to formalize his dictatorial powers in both the party and the government:

Agenda of the Fifth Party Congress announced by the Central Executive Committee[95]	Interpretation by Chiang Kai-shek's opponents[96]
Convene a National Constituent Assembly	Authorize the presidential system of government by means of adopting a constitution, and elect Chiang Kai-shek to that position

Revise the party statutes	Install Chiang in the new position of tsung-li of the party
Promote party affairs	Enable the Blue Shirts to usurp control of the party in order to fascistize the Kuomintang
Determine administrative policies	Determine policies that will implement the dictatorship of Chiang Kai-shek and eliminate all domestic opposition

Convinced that Chiang Kai-shek planned to use the Fifth Party Congress to formalize his political dominance, the opponents of Chiang, led by the Kwangtung-Kwangsi clique, now did everything in their power to obstruct the convening of the congress. On September 8, 1934, Hu Han-min, Ch'en Chi-t'ang, Li Tsung-jen and others sent an impassioned telegram to the Central Executive Committee in Nanking. If a party congress is to be convoked, the telegram stated, it must punish the authorities who were responsible for "losing power and humiliating the nation." Previously, the telegram read, the Central Executive Committee had resolved that no national territories were to be surrendered and that Chiang Kai-shek should quickly go to north China to direct the resistance against Japan. But Chiang Kai-shek had not gone to the north, and he had, moreover, adopted a policy of abject appeasement.

The Southwest leaders declared in addition that the Fifth Party Congress must punish the leaders of the Blue Shirts who "misuse their authority, arbitrarily murder people, and create terror in society." If these and other demands regarding national defense and economic reconstruction were not met, the leaders of Kwangtung and Kwangsi would refuse to attend the party congress.[97]

This telegram, by itself, would have had little effect on Chiang Kai-shek's plans. But the Southwest leaders were simultaneously constructing a broad united front against Chiang's assumption of dictatorial powers. In north China, a coalition consisting of Feng Yü-hsiang's clique, the China Youth Party, a Social-Democratic Party, and the North China National Salvation Society (Hua-pei chiu-wang hui) had been formed and was in contact with the provincial leaders in the south.[98] Hu Han-min and company also appealed—only eight months after Kwangtung and Kwangsi had refused to support the Fukien rebellion—to Ch'en Ming-shu, Li Chi-shen, and other Fukien leaders to join the new movement opposing Nanking.[99]

A group that covertly lent support to this movement was sometimes referred to as the European-American Clique (O-Mei p'ai). This clique—including such prominent figures as T. V. Soong, Sun Fo, C. T. Wang (Wang Cheng-t'ing) and Wellington Koo (Ku Wei-chün)—similarly wished to obstruct Chiang's absolute control of the party and government. In contrast to the growing movement for dictatorship, they advocated the formation of a coalition government comprising all Kuomintang factions and advocated arbitration of the differences with the Southwest forces.[100]

Confronted with imminent rebellion, Chiang Kai-shek began to tack. On October 9 he dispatched Wang Ch'ung-hui to Canton to arbitrate the conflict.[101] At the same time, he issued yet another denial that he planned to establish a dictatorship. In one of his then rare interviews with the press, Chiang "laughingly said that these [rumors] were lies. There was no need for dictatorship." As the interview continued, however, it became clear that he did indeed aspire to highly concentrated executive powers. As the interviewer recorded the conversation, "General Chiang said that, although there is no need for a dictator in China, he believes that there should be more action . . . At the present time, there is too much overlapping in the official bureaux and there are conferences without end. Little has been achieved through these weighty discussions, the results of which, in many cases, could not be enforced and, in any case, were not enforced, with the result that they were only empty talk. 'There is nobody to assume responsibility for the carrying out of the decisions,' he declared, 'and therefore nothing is accomplished.' Of course, he admitted, the principals of the government should confer but, he added, 'It is a waste of time to hold too many conferences.' "

Chiang then reportedly added—presumably with tongue in cheek—that "As he has been assigned a number of posts in the Government, it is only natural that, at times, he should express his opinions, but the mere fact that he expressed his opinions and that these were sometimes carried out by the National Government could not signify that he was proposing to make himself a dictator."[102]

Such transparent denials did not convince Chiang's opponents, and the threat of rebellion grew. Recognizing that he faced a formidable and determined coalition, Chiang on October 25 ordered the Fifth Party Congress postponed.[103]

The May Fifth Draft Constitution. In forcing postponement of the Fifth Party Congress, Chiang Kai-shek's opponents had won a battle; they had not won the war. Chiang had been forced to defer his assumption of the powers of tsung-li. He continued, nevertheless, to attempt to create a powerful presidential office by influencing the drafting of the constitution.

Subsequent to the Legislative Yüan's formal approval of the Revised Draft Constitution on October 16, 1934, the draft was transmitted to the Central Executive Committee of the party. Soon it became apparent that the party leadership was still not satisfied with the provisions of the new draft. For a full year, the Central Executive Committee brooded on the draft. Finally, on October 17, 1935, it sent the draft back to the Legislative Yüan, instructing that the draft be rewritten. "Governmental organization," the Central Executive Committee declared, "should consider actual political experience in order to create a practical, efficient system that can concentrate national strength. The executive authority should not be limited by inflexible regulations."[104] Paraphrased, the Central Executive Committee was actually saying: "You have been overly idealistic in preparing the constitutional draft. Go back now, rewrite it, and see that all authority is concentrated in the hands of the Supreme Leader. Do not place silly restrictions on his power!"

There is no record of Sun Fo's response to these instructions. It had become obvious, however, that the Legislative Yüan was powerless to resist the forces favoring dictatorship and that the substance of the permanent constitution would be determined by Chiang Kai-shek. During the ensuing months, the Legislative Yüan twice more revised the constitutional draft and twice more sent it to the Central Executive Committee. Finally, on May 1, 1936, the party applied its stamp of approval. And on May 5, the government formally promulgated the Draft Constitution of the Republic of China, better known in history as "the May Fifth Draft."[105] After approval by a National Constituent Assembly, this draft would become the law of the land.

The May Fifth Draft was satisfactory to practically no one, for it provided simply for a strong presidency, but not for a dictatorship. For illustration let us look at the president's powers to decree legislation. These powers are the very essence of a dictatorship. According to the May Fifth Draft, the president would be empowered to issue legislation following the declaration of an emergency by the "Executive Council"—a body comprising the head of the Executive Yüan and the governmental ministers. Since all members of this Executive Council would be appointed and removed by the president, such a limitation on the presidential powers would have been little more than a formality. This extraordinary presidential power was limited, however, by a provision that all presidential decrees, to remain in effect, required the ratification of the Legislative Yüan within three months of being issued. Because the May Fifth Draft contained several such provisions counterbalancing the otherwise strong executive powers of the president, the draft did little to cheer the advocates of dictatorship. It was, perhaps, for that reason that the May Fifth Draft was never presented to a National Constituent Assembly, and for that reason was never put into effect.

Chiang Kai-shek did ultimately realize his ambition of being named director-general of the Kuomintang. In March 1938, during the war with Japan when nationalistic fervor disposed most Chinese to accept greater concentrations of executive power, the party finally bestowed on him the title of tsung-ts'ai. The title was not tsung-li, but this was a distinction without a difference.[106]

For complex, historical reasons, the term democracy had acquired a strongly positive connotation to most educated Chinese, and it had become a shibboleth in the political discourse of the 1930s. But most Chinese, politicians and intellectuals alike, were weakly committed to the content of democracy, to the core values of liberalism. When many of the political leaders used the term democracy, therefore, they did so cynically and opportunistically. Sun Fo and Wang Ching-wei, for example, had advocated democracy when they were excluded from power. But each, when in power, had resisted the expansion of democratic procedures—Wang, for instance, declaring in 1932 that the proponents of constitutionalism used democracy merely as a disguise for their efforts to overthrow the Kuomintang.[107] Thus, democracy was a weapon of the "outs," used to bludgeon the "ins."

Chiang Kai-shek, even when in power, also used democracy as a weapon. Indeed, whenever political opposition threatened his regime, he promised that the regime would adhere to the rule-of-law or would broaden political participation. He had, therefore, ordered preparation of a *Yüeh-fa* (provisional constitution) in 1931; he convoked the National Emergency Conference in 1932; and, during the Fukien rebellion, he announced the convening of a plenary session of the Central Executive Committee in order to discuss ways of "opening-up political power."[108] So often did the Nanking authorities hold out this political carrot, without actually giving the public a nibble of democracy, that the *I-shih pao* remarked that no one any longer believed the government when it said it would abolish party rule.[109]

Chiang Kai-shek's support of Sun Fo's demand for a constitution in 1932 had not, therefore, demonstrated his commitment to constitutionalism, to the rule of law, nor to the protection of human freedoms. His support of the constitution was rather a political act necessitated by the political exigencies of 1932–33. Even if a liberal constitution had been promulgated, it probably would have had little effect on the conduct of government. In China, personalities much more than political machinery or laws determined the allocation of power. As a high-ranking Chinese observed in 1933, "the attention being given to the drafting of a Constitution is so much window display and . . . everybody knows that constitutions are of no importance in actual political developments in China."[110]

The career of Chiang Kai-shek provides clear evidence that persons rather than law were preponderant factors in the political process in Kuomintang China. During much of the Nanking decade, Chiang held no formal title or office that bestowed on him the great powers that he actually wielded. His had been the dominant voice in the civilian administration even after he relinquished the chairmanship of the government in 1931, and not until the end of 1935 did he assume the title of premier. And, within the party, he was only one of nine ostensibly equal members of the Standing Committee of the Central Executive Committee. Yet, during his extended stays in his Nanchang military headquarters, the Nanking administration ceased to rule in all but the most perfunctory manner. All significant problems had to await his personal decisions. The promulgation of a democratic constitution would not, therefore, have deprived Chiang of power. It might, however, have been an inconvenience.

Because of the nature of Chinese society and of its political traditions, it is perhaps one of China's tragedies during the twentieth century that, in the quest for a viable political system, attempts had been made to erect democratic institutions. In a profound sense, Anglo-American democracy was not suited to China. This, I think, is not a value judgment. Democracy is still evolving, and neither its permanence nor ultimate preferability to other systems of governance is yet assured, even in the countries of the West where it has developed. In China, an authoritarian system of rule is perhaps better able to produce the "greatest happiness of the greatest number."

In the Nanking period, most Chinese would have agreed with the remark that "We oppose a dictatorship that is for private benefit, but approve of a dictatorship that is for the public welfare."[111] Most Chinese were also convinced, however, that the Kuomintang dictatorship did not act for the public welfare.

Chapter 5 **Nanking and the Economy**

Agriculture was the soul of the Chinese economy and way of life. Most Chinese were farmers or in some way derived their major income from occupations directly related to farming. Agriculture contributed approximately 65 percent of the gross national product; modern industrial manufacturing, by contrast, contributed only about 2.2 percent of the national income in the mid-1930s.[1] Here was Chinese life at its essence; here the political, economic, and social ills were most exigent. If, therefore, we are to acquire some sense of the Nationalist regime's impact on the life of the ordinary Chinese and of the character of the political system being created, we must shift our gaze from the central government and the political leaders to the villages and the farmers.

Since the latter years of the eighteenth century, the Chinese farmer, even in "normal" times, had lived a precarious and uncertain existence. Living on or near the subsistence level, the average farmer was buffeted by the vagaries of weather and the whims of the tax collector. Good fortune brought adequate food and perhaps sufficient savings to buy a farm plot; ill fortune meant hunger and perhaps death.

China's population had increased dramatically during the Ch'ing dynasty. From 1650 until 1850, for example, the population had more than doubled. Cultivable land during approximately the same span of time, however, had increased only about 63 percent.[2] Thus, the average amount of land per capita during this period had declined roughly from one acre to less than one-half acre per person. In the mid-nineteenth century, the Chinese farm population existed very close to that society's Malthusian limits.

For the period since the mid-nineteenth century, data on demographic trends are sparse and often contradictory. Most recent estimates see an annual increase of about 0.7 percent since 1850.[3] This, by recent standards, was a relatively low rate of increase, attributable not so much to a low birth rate as to a high death rate. The population of China would nevertheless have increased by about one-third during the half century prior to the 1930s, raising the population very close to the 500 million level. Cultivable land, during the same period, had expanded only about 20 percent. Inexorably, then, the rural population was subsisting on ever-dwindling plots of land, perhaps only one-third the size of the farms tilled by their ancestors in 1650.[4]

Despite the shrinkage of the farms, the standard-of-living of the villagers probably remained fairly constant during the decades prior to the Nanking period. Dwight Perkins' study of long-term agricultural trends has shown that modest improvements of farm technology, including new crops, changed cropping patterns, and increased use of fertilizers had caused farm production to keep pace with population increases. Cultivation of special crops for the market, such as cotton; handicraft production; and increased opportunities for non-farm employment also enabled the farmer to supplement his basic farm earnings.[5] John Lossing Buck's classic survey buttresses Perkins' findings. Buck and his co-workers found that nine-tenths of their informants felt that their living conditions were at least as good in about 1930 as they had been in previous years. Only 11 percent of the localities surveyed felt that conditions had worsened, whereas over 80 percent sensed that their standard of living had improved.[6]

Whether the average farmer was just holding his own or was actually improving his economic condition, his living standard at the beginning of the Nanking decade is not in serious dispute. He lived in grinding poverty. His labor was less expensive than that of an ox. Often in the winter he would, like an animal, sleep as much as possible to conserve energy and food. Statistically speaking, the food he ate normally provided the requisite calories, but hunger, disease, and death were his constant companions.[7]

John Lossing Buck's investigations revealed a death rate in China of 27.1 per 1,000 persons—although Buck also speculated that the actual death rate probably exceeded 30 per 1,000 inhabitants. Even at the lower figure, however, the death rate was far higher than in Japan (18.2/1,000) or the leading Western countries (England and Wales: 12.3/1,000; France: 16.3/1,000; United States: 11.3/1,000). Only British India had a death rate (24.9/1,000) remotely approaching that of China.[8]

R. H. Tawney's study, *Land and Labour in China,* written in 1931, serves as something of a benchmark for my own description of the agrarian scene under Nationalist rule. "Exaggeration is easy," said Tawney. "Privation is one thing, poverty to the point of wretchedness—*la misère*—another. A sturdy and self-reliant stock may grow in a stony soil. But, when due allowance has been made for the inevitable misconceptions, it is difficult to resist the conclusion that a large proportion of Chinese peasants are constantly on the brink of actual destitution."[9] During the five years after Tawney wrote these words, China's farmers fell into even more straitened circumstances.

Agrarian Depression, 1931–1935

The principal cause of China's intensified agrarian crisis was the rapid decline of farm prices after 1931. Economic data for the period are frighteningly unreliable, and the data disagree regarding how abruptly after 1931 the decline occurred.[10] It is not in general dispute, however, that farm prices struck their nadir in 1934, when the index of prices received by farmers had dropped from 118 in 1931 (computed with 1926 as the base year) to 49 in 1934—a decline of 58 percent.

The precise effect of this price decline upon the livelihood of the farmers is not easily calculated. An important consideration is that the prices paid by the farmers for daily necessities dropped neither as rapidly nor as far as did the prices received by the farmer for his produce. Table 1 indicates that the ratio of prices received to prices paid—which is to say the purchasing power of the farmers—dropped approximately 31 percent between 1931 and 1934. The effect of this reduced purchasing power would have hit various segments of the rural population in very different ways. Some farmers raised nothing but cash crops (such as tea, silk, or tobacco) and were therefore sharply affected by fluctuations in the marketplace. Most of them, however, were only par-

Table 1. Index Numbers of Prices Received and Prices Paid by Farmers, 1926–1935

Year	Prices received	Prices paid	Ratio of prices received to prices paid
1926	100	100	100
1927	93	104	89.4
1928	93	113	82.3
1929	122	135	90.3
1930	126	142	88.7
1931	118	152	77.6
1932	117	154	75.9
1933	57	108	52.7
1934	49	106	47.2
1935	79	121	65.3

Source: Yang Sueh-Chang, p. 162. Indices of prices for the period are seldom in agreement. For a different set of index numbers (for the period through 1933) that reveals the same general—but not such a drastic—decline, see Chi-ming Hou, *Foreign Investment and Economic Development in China, 1840–1937* (Cambridge, Mass., Harvard University Press, 1965), p. 266.

tially dependent on the market for their sustenance. In Ting hsien in north China, for example, an average farmer consumed 76 percent of his own farm produce. Market exchange therefore had a significant, but not decisive, effect on the livelihood of most farmers. Commodity purchases, however, were not the farmer's only need for currency, for he had frequently to pay taxes or rents, and to repay loans, in money. As is always the case in a condition of deflationary pressures, it is the debtor and the non-salaried persons on non-fixed incomes that suffer most drastically. The farmers were therefore hard-hit; professors and officials by contrast fared much better.

This deflationary trend doubtless resulted from a complex interaction of numerous forces—such as the relative supply and demand of commodities, and the amount of silver in the Chinese currency. The most decisive factor affecting Chinese prices in the 1930s, however, was the changing demand for silver.

China during this period was the only large nation in the world whose currency was backed by silver. This had been a godsend for the Chinese economy during the first three years of the world depression, for the world price of silver (relative to gold) fell off sharply after the stock-market crash of 1929. The result was that China, in contrast to most other countries, entered a period of commercial and manufacturing boom.

The fact that China's currency had depreciated meant that foreign commodities sold at prohibitively high prices. The result was that China's commercial and manufacturing interests suddenly met little competition from foreign competitors. Simultaneously, the depreciated currency made investments by foreign holders of silver highly attractive, so that silver poured into the country.[11] One result of this influx of silver was that the banks, now holding large reserves of silver, were able to lend money at low rates of interest, and this contributed to the expansion of China's commercial and manufacturing enterprises.[12] Another consequence was that considerable quantities of this cheap silver were diffused through the countryside, thereby bringing down interest rates, pushing prices upward, and generally contributing to a mood of optimism that encouraged the farm population to borrow money, buy land, or acquire other forms of property and goods.

During the winter of 1931–32, this short period of relative prosperity came to an abrupt end. The Japanese attacks on Manchuria in September 1931 and on Shanghai in January 1932 deprived Chinese producers of one of their largest markets, and deeply shook investor confidence.[13] Even more important was the fact that the world depression had finally caught up with China by 1932. Both Great Britain and Japan in late 1931 abandoned the gold standard in order to make their goods more competitive on the world markets. This had the effect almost immediately of depriving Chinese producers of the shelter of a depreciated currency and placed China again in direct and debilitating rivalry with Japanese and British entrepreneurs. Simultaneously, China lost its attractiveness as an area of investment; the flow of silver into the country slowed; interest rates rose; prices fell.

The American government soon exacerbated these deflationary trends in China. In 1933 the United States followed Japan and Britain in devaluing its currency. And in June 1934 Congress passed the Silver Purchase Act, which made the United States government a big purchaser of silver at artificially inflated rates. Chinese interests, both governmental and private, had tried to dissuade Washington, warning that the measure would result in a drain on China's silver reserves, force it off the silver standard, and have dire consequences on the entire national economy. But the silver-producing states in the United States were convinced that a higher price of silver would ease their own economic difficulties, and these had more political clout in Washington than did even the most carefully reasoned appeals of the Chinese.[14]

American silver policies drove the Chinese economy into a second and deeper phase of depression.[15] Silver, which had been merely trickling out of China since 1932, cascaded out of the country after the Americans' silver-purchasing policy went into effect. Silver reserves had mounted to a high of ¥602 million in April 1934, but these dropped by September of the same year to ¥461 million. Nanking tried to staunch this drain of her fiscal blood in October 1934 by imposing both a higher export duty and an equalization charge (intended to eliminate disparities between foreign and Chinese prices of silver). These measures retarded the outflow through legal channels, but they had the effect also of encouraging smuggling operations through the Japanese-dominated areas in north China. And the country's silver reserves had dwindled to a mere ¥288 million—approximately one-third its holdings in April 1934—when China finally switched from a silver-based to a managed currency in November 1935.[16]

China's urban economy was severely depressed during the years after 1931. Many business and industrial undertakings had overextended themselves during the boom period of 1929-1931. With inadequate capitalization, relying on low-interest loans for operating expenses, and often with inferior management and technology, these ventures crumbled in the new environment of tight money and foreign competition. In Shanghai during 1934, twenty-four modern-style banks and fifteen native banks were closed. Uncounted numbers of factories and shops went out of business or were forced to curtail operations. The Shanghai municipal government reported in 1935 that the period since 1931 was one of "disastrous business depression" and observed that over 82 percent of the families in the city were earning insufficient wages to cover their living expenses.[17]

The cities, however, were partially shielded from the full brunt of the depression. Employee wages, for example, declined less sharply than did commodity prices. As a result, the real wages of Shanghai workers between 1930 and 1934 had not declined but had actually increased by 14 percent. (It is unlikely, however, that the rise of real wages resulted in an improvement of the workers' standard-of-living, for shortened working hours, lay-offs, and fewer bonuses reduced the laborers' total take-home pay.)[18] Modern manufacturing industries, both Chinese and foreign, continued to expand throughout the depression in terms both of the quantity of production and gross value-added.[19] Moreover, Shanghai avoided the full deflationary effects of the outflow of silver from China, because—as a result of a decline of commerce in the rural regions and because of the political and social instability there—silver left the countryside for the greater security of the city banks. As a consequence, Lin Wei-ying remarked, "the deflationary processes have gone much farther in the interior with more serious consequences."[20]

Contributing to the distress of the farmers was the series of droughts and floods that afflicted many of the farming areas during these years of depression in the 1930s. It is tempting to argue that these climatic difficulties were one of the causes of the deepened agrarian crisis. Yet China is so vast and diverse, and the statistical data so incomplete and unreliable, that generalizations about crops and productivity during the decade are fraught with difficulties.

There can be no doubt that some areas of China encountered the nation's worst weather within memory. The flood of the Yangtze River in 1931 attracted worldwide attention at the time; torrential summer rainstorms raised the crest of the river to a previously unrecorded fifteen feet above its normal level at that time of year. The river dikes had been grossly neglected—administration of the Hunan Dike tax was, according to an American state department official, "notoriously scandalous"—but, with the waters at a level of fifty-three feet seven inches, even solid dikes probably could not have held back the river currents. The devastation was enormous. An area the size of New York state was covered by water to an average depth over the fields of nine feet when the waters peaked. And over twenty-five million people—a population approximately equivalent to the entire farm population of the United States—were displaced and suffered losses from the flood.[21]

Even the Yangtze flood, catastrophic though its effects were, probably affected the economy in but a peripheral way.

Only 5 percent of China's total farm area was hit by the flood; losses amounted to only about 6.8 percent of the total farm income for 1931; and crop production in the country as a whole declined by a serious, but not catastrophic, 10 percent. In the judgment of Yang Sueh-Chang, therefore, the Yangtze flood might have accelerated the depression and business contraction after 1931 but could not have been a primary cause.[22]

The years 1932 and 1933 produced "normal" harvests,[23] but in 1934 and 1935, when the monetary depression was at its depth, peasants in many sectors of the country were again struck by ruinous weather conditions. A drought in 1934 struck most of the provinces, turning rice paddies particularly in Kiangsu and Anhwei into cracked cakes of dried mud, and resulting in the loss in those provinces of an estimated one-half the customary rice crop. Losses the same year in other parts of the country from wind, hail, and other natural calamities amounted to "not less than" ¥1,300 million. The following year, in 1935, various parts of the nation were again struck by either floods or droughts. Rains inundated both the Yangtze and Yellow River valleys and the resulting floods in eight provinces affected over twenty million people. At the same time, thirteen provinces suffered drought conditions.[24]

What were the effects of these climatic conditions? Chang P'ei-kang, an agricultural specialist at the Academia Sinica, computed that the productivity of all major crops in 1934 fell over 24 percent from the average of the previous five years. Even as compared with the relatively poor harvests of 1931, rice production in 1934 (according to Chang's data) was down 34 percent; wheat was down 7 percent, millet and kaoliang were down over 19 percent, and soya beans down almost 36 percent. The cotton crop on the other hand, exceeded the 1931 figure by over 14 percent.[25]

Chang P'ei-kang's data may have exaggerated the decline of crop production during the depression. Data published by the official National Agricultural Research Bureau's *Crop Reports* (*Nung-ch'ing pao-kao*) during the years 1931–1936, for example, show that total crop production in the worst year

(1934) was only 11 percent less than that of the best year (1932).[26] This figure, while markedly less than Chang P'ei-kang's, still represented—when taken as a national average—a large if not disastrous decline in farming conditions. And, when taken in conjunction with the decline of farm prices, did contribute to a severe and ruinous crisis in agriculture.

It is again necessary to raise a caveat against placing reliance upon statistical data for the period. Nevertheless, Liu Ta-chung's computations of the gross national product during this period may provide some rough indication of the vicissitudes of the rural population. Liu estimated that the value-added by agriculture dropped from ¥24.43 billion in 1931 to ¥13.07 billion (in current prices) in 1934. This was a drop of 47 percent.[27] And for the many millions of peasants who paid taxes, owed debts, or were committed to fixed money rents, the consequences could be, and often were, ruinous.

The worsening conditions in the villages were reflected in the considerable flight of farmers from the villages—similar, no doubt, to Dakota farmers who abandoned farming during America's own depression of the 1930s. According to an extensive official survey of emigration from the rural areas, almost 5 percent of the Chinese peasantry left the countryside during the three-year period 1934–1936.[28] Statistical averages, again, conceal the extent of rural emigration in the most afflicted parts of the country. Cheng-ting hsien in Hopei, for example, lost one-third of its farming population between 1931 and 1934.[29] And the sharp increase of emigration from Ting hsien is strikingly revealed in Table 2.

Eye-witness accounts corroborate the impression derived from the statistical data that the Chinese countryside was in a deep crisis during much of the 1930s. It became something of a fad for city-dwelling intellectuals, after visiting their native villages, to write articles recording their impressions of life in the rural areas. As a consequence, nearly all the major periodicals of the day devoted numerous pages and even regular sections to "the village problem." These articles were sometimes excessively impressionistic and emotional and they may

Table 2. Emigration from Ting hsien, Hopei

Year	Number of people	Index number (1931 = 100)
1924	1,563	112
1925	732	54
1926	781	57
1927	767	56
1928	532	39
1929	774	57
1930	443	32
1931	1,368	100
1932	3,367	246
1933	7,849	574
1934 (January to March)	15,084	1,103

Source: Chang Yu-i, ed., *Chung-kuo chin-tai nung-yeh shih tzu-liao,* III (Peking, 1957), 882. See also Fang Hsien-t'ing, ed., *Chung-kuo ching-chi yen-chiu* (Changsha, 1938), pp. 178–187.

at times have been colored by political bias. Taken together, however, they add up to a picture of deep and worsening bankruptcy throughout the nation.

In 1934, for example, a young scholar wrote after a year-long visit to his native Kweichow: "Six years ago, when I was in my native village, 70–80 percent of the families had enough food to eat. Now, however, I learned that only 3–5 of the 400–500 families could barely get by. None of the others had enough to eat, living from hand to mouth, and not knowing where tomorrow's meal is coming from. I went to their homes, where they had only a few badly broken things, their clothes were in rags, their children were naked, and their faces had a cadaverous look." "Poverty, poverty, poverty! Everywhere is poverty! Everyone is in poverty!"[30]

This story was repeated countless times. One writer, originally from a customarily well-to-do silk-raising hsien in Kiangsu, reported that early in the depression the price of cocoons had fallen from ¥70–80 a picul to less than ¥30. And mulberry leaves, which had marketed for ¥10 a picul, were often left to spoil for want of a purchaser. By 1935, therefore, many farmers had cleared away the mulberry bushes and restored the land to rice paddies. But the sale of rice that year brought only ¥30–40 instead of ¥60–70 per picul. As a result the once prosperous farmers, after paying their debts and rents, were left almost penniless. Many deserted the old village for the cities, where they hoped to find livelihood as manual laborers.[31]

In a report from northeastern Hopei in 1934, the prices of the main crops, millet and wheat, had tumbled from ¥1.55 to ¥0.60 a picul. Many farmers, pressed by debts or taxes, were forced to sell land to clear their financial obligations. But the price of land had also fallen: fields that had been valued at ¥990 an acre sold for ¥264, and land previously valued at ¥660 an acre sold for only ¥132. As a consequence, "countless numbers of families, even families that had been well-off but who had owed debts, were bankrupted and left propertyless.[32]

Southern Kiangsu had long been one of the most lush farming areas in China. "Above, there is heaven," went a popular saying; "below, there is Soochow and Hangchow." But now, a native of this area reported, Soochow and Hangchow were more like hell than heaven. There had been a bumper rice crop in 1933, but the prices had been so low that the savings of many farmers had been wiped out by the end of the winter. That spring, weather killed off their production of silkworms. And then drought spoiled the summer rice crop. As a result, the desperate farmers sought relief by ransacking the homes of the rich and the rice shops for what food they could find. These "rice riots" became a common occurrence in Chekiang and Kiangsu during this period, but government troops successfully suppressed the "bandits."[33]

Even landlords felt the squeeze of the depression. The Fei clan, which has been studied in detail by Muramatsu Yuji, may serve as an example. The fortunes of this clan, which had been one of the richest and most influential families in the

Soochow region since the eighteenth century, declined rapidly after the Kuomintang acceded to power.

After the revolution of 1927 [Muramatsu writes] it would appear that the financial prosperity of the landlord enterprises of the Fei clan rapidly deteriorated. This was partly the result of the increasing independence of their tenants, and partly the result of the development programme initiated by the new Nationalist Government . . . which suddenly aggravated the tax burdens on their lands. This situation became still more grave with the onset of the general economic depression after 1931. According to a history of the Fei family compiled by Chang Chung-jen, 600 *mou* of their hereditary lands . . . in the neighborhood of Su-chou suffered bad harvests in successive years, and even though the Feis sold some of these lands to pay off their tax arrears, this was still insufficient. Fei Chung-shen in desperation petitioned the government to have all the family lands confiscated in settlement of their outstanding tax debts, but naturally his request was rejected. He could not press his poverty-stricken peasants to pay rent, and so in 1935 he addressed another long and extremely moving letter to the government. But before this could be sent he fell sick and died.[34]

The decline of the Fei clan is especially noteworthy, because of the original wealth and influence of the family. The experience was not, however, unique. A writer from Chekiang, for example, complained that landlords in Chekiang were on the verge of bankruptcy because the tax rates had been maintained at a high rate even though the prices of farm products had fallen. During the drought of 1934, he reported, the government had indeed ordered that taxes be decreased by 20 or 30 percent. But the tenants had such poor harvests that they were unable to pay their rents—the landlords were nevertheless still compelled to pay the taxes. The result, he said, was that even the richest landlords were reduced to selling their family collections of paintings and books, while the lesser landlords were going bankrupt. Some landlords, he contended, even tried to give their lands to the tenants, but the tenants refused to accept them because they feared the harassments of the tax collectors.[35]

Another landlord wrote that he had moved to the city to

escape the extortions of local bandits in his native village. His neighbors in the city were a water peddlar, a yamen runner, and a ricksha puller. To this landlord's chagrin, he found that his annual income from thirteen acres of land, after paying taxes, was less even than that of his low-status neighbors.[36] These testimonies from complaining landlords provoked numerous responses from readers, who displayed little sympathy for the landlords' contention that they had become simply "non-profit brokers" for the tax collectors.[37] Yet it does appear that a substantial part of the landlord class did experience economic deprivation during this period. This fact testifies to the depths of economic distress throughout the rural areas. It also helps explain why, despite the sharp decline in land prices, there was no general increase in the incidence of landlordism during the depression.[38]

Readers may have inferred that this description of worsening conditions in the rural areas conflicts with Ramon H. Myers' interpretation of the village economy.[39] The conflict may be more apparent than real. Myers was largely concerned with long-term trends during the period 1890–1949 rather than with short-term vicissitudes. He contended no more than that *"where normal conditions prevailed* living standards did not decline,'' and he recognized that civil war, social disorder, marauding troops, poor harvests, and so on, were sometimes causes of a deterioration in farmers' living standards. Because Myers gave minimal attention to the depression of the 1930s—which he regarded as an abnormal period—his general picture does not reflect, nor is it intended to reflect, the conditions described in this study. By contrast with Myers, however, I suspect that the political, economic, and social fabric of rural society was weakened by such "abnormal" conditions as the depression of 1931–1935.

The Land Taxes

The monetary deflation and unfavorable weather conditions no doubt contributed in large degree to the agrarian crisis after 1931. During this period, however, the rural population was also in the grips of an exploitative sociopolitical system that had matured under the dynasties, been given new flourishes by the warlords, and been perpetuated with only minor changes by the Nanking regime. The excessive taxation, usurious interest rates, and inequitable system of land tenure were not the *cause* of the agrarian crisis. They were, however, factors that became more onerous during the period of Nationalist rule.

Taxation, often extortionate and seldom expended on projects that palpably benefited the farmers, was one of the harshest of the burdens. Actually, as is to be expected in an underdeveloped economy, taxation was not high when compared with the rates in modern industrialized societies. Middle-income farmers in a Hopei village, for example, paid only about 10 percent of their total income in taxes.[40] But, because these farmers customarily existed on the very edge of the subsistence level, a tax exaction of even as little as ¥20 during a year could mean the difference between full rice bowls and a trip to the pawnshop.

Virtually every item of property and every business transaction was subject to a tax which, if not levied by the central government, was exacted by agencies of the provincial government, by the hsien government, or by one of the innumerable tax farmers. There was nothing novel in this system of tax collection—most of the institutions and practices had been inherited from the warlord period. Yet, under Kuomintang auspices, the farmers' total tax burden increased substantially.

The land tax had traditionally been the principal tax in the rural areas. In the late 1890s, for example, a hsien in north China derived 90 percent of its total tax revenue from the land tax.[41] Since the fall of the dynasty, new sources of tax revenue had been increasingly exploited, so that by 1935 the land tax and its related surtaxes accounted for only about two-thirds of the revenue of the average hsien in China proper.[42] Nevertheless, land-related taxes continued to take the biggest single tax bite out of the land-owning farmer's income, and an examination of the system of land taxes provides our initial access to the relationship between the farmer and the government. (Nanking in 1928 had decreed that land taxes were to be administered, and the revenues retained, by the provincial governments. That the Kuomintang approved of the land-tax system as it developed during the 1930s is demonstrated by the fact that the system as it evolved in Chekiang and Kiangsu, which were closely controlled by Nanking, did not differ in any essential respects from the system in areas under warlord-type governors.)

The main land tax (*cheng-shui*) was levied on the basis of tax assessments that had been made during the Ch'ing dynasty, sometimes as long ago as 1713 when the K'ang-hsi emperor had decreed that the rate of the land tax should never be increased. Since that time, despite changes in land fertility and values, the basic tax rate on most pieces of land had changed but slightly. This had, for the most part, worked to the advantage of the landowning peasant, because the almost steady inflation of the currency since the late nineteenth century meant that the peasant would customarily have a larger income with which to pay the relatively unchanging land tax.[43]

The basic assessment, however, was only a part—and sometimes only a small part—of the total tax on the land. Even during the Ch'ing period, the emperors had circumvented K'ang-hsi's proscription against increasing the land tax by imposing a variety of surtaxes (*fu-shui*). The warlords subsequently found the surtaxes to be a profitable device, and during the early Republican period the ratio of surtaxes to the basic land tax had grown steadily.[44] During the Nanking period the practice of imposing surtaxes on the land tax not only continued but reached unprecedented proportions.

Chekiang had been unusual among China's provinces in that there had been relatively few surtaxes there prior to the Kuomintang's consolidation of political control.[45] In 1928, however, the Kuomintang authorities had authorized a "Military Reorganization Surcharge" to finance the Northern Expedition. This had ostensibly been merely a temporary assessment. But after the conclusion of the fighting in north China, the surtax remained, although it was now called a "Reconstruction Surcharge." During the next few years, one surtax after the other was added, including the following:

Special Surcharge for Reconstruction
Surcharge for Water Conservancy
Surcharge for Self-Government
Surcharge for Education
Surcharge for Hsien Education
Surcharge for Police
Hsien Surcharge
Anti-Insect Surcharge
Surcharge for Capital of Farmers' Bank
Surcharge for Poor Relief
Surcharge for Ch'ü (sub-district) Education
Surcharge for Public Fund Collection
Surcharge for the Purchase of Airplanes by the Peasants
Surcharge for Peace Preservation Army
Surcharge for Land Tax Assessment Schedule
Surcharge for Road Construction
Surcharge for Welfare Work
Surcharge for Free Education
Surcharge for Land Survey

By 1933 there were between twenty and thirty surtaxes in every hsien of the province.[46]

As a result of the proliferation of surtaxes, these soon became an even more important source of revenue than the main tax. In Kiangsu, the surtaxes in 1933 provided almost eight times as much revenue as the main tax.[47] Other provinces, more or less directly under Nationalist control, similarly derived more income from surtaxes than from the main land tax (see Table 3).

The impact of the land tax system on the individual farmer varied greatly from area to area and from taxpayer to taxpayer. Surtaxes were customarily levied with utter disregard for the ability of the farmers to pay. When a provincial government imposed a new surtax, the quotas for each hsien were assigned on the basis of population.[48] This method

Table 3.   Provincial Revenue from the Main Land Tax
and Surtaxes, 1931–1935

(in millions of yüan)

Province	Main tax	Surtax	Surtax in excess of main tax (percent)
Chekiang	10,416	13,842	133
Anhwei	5,239	6,133	117
Hupei	2,860	6,631	232
Hunan	3,598	11,560	320
Honan	7,152	11,496	161

Source: Hung-mao Harold Tien, "Political Development in China, 1927–1937" (Ph.D. diss., University of Wisconsin, 1969), p. 318.

ignored the fact that some hsien were richer than others. In Chekiang, for example, the surtaxes in five of the wealthier hsien amounted to only 25 percent of the main tax, whereas in some of the poorest hsien, the surtaxes were three-and-a-half times the main tax.[49]

The disparities in the incidence of surtaxes were even greater in Kiangsu than in Chekiang. The part of Kiangsu to the south of the Yangtze River, Chiang-nan (Kiangnan), was notably richer than the part to the north, Chiang-pei. The basic tax in Chiang-nan was high, and according to an official report, the surtaxes exceeded the basic tax by two to three times. The surtaxes in Chiang-pei, by contrast, were eight to ten times the basic tax. Indeed, in several hsien, the surcharges were fifteen times the basic assessment; and in one hsien, Hai-men hsien, the surtaxes were twenty-five times the basic rate.[50] "It is usually the case" concluded Franklin Ho, "that in a poor hsien the burden of surcharges is much heavier than that in a relatively rich hsien."[51] Ramon Myers supports this general conclusion, stating with regard to north China that "the land tax varied greatly from county to county [hsien] and bore little relationship to the value and productivity of the land."[52]

During the greater part of the Nanking period, there was a persistent tendency for the total tax assessments on the land

Table 4.   Index Numbers of Land Taxes (Main and Surtaxes Combined) in Selected Provinces

(1931 = 100)

Province	1932	1933	1934	1935	1936
Anhwei	107	106	111	101	106
Chekiang	113	106	104	108	104
Fukien	103	103	89	82	81
Honan	102	107	92	88	86
Hopei	98	93	93	87	88
Hunan	102	108	111	93	109
Hupei	110	114	116	103	103
Kiangsi	111	115	113	110	106
Kiangsu	116	123	117	109	103
Kwangsi	117	116	126	122	124
Kwangtung	105	108	123	118	114
Szechuan	120	123	130	112	107
National average	107	108	108	101	101

Source: Chang Yu-i, ed., *Chung-kuo chin-tai nung-yeh shih tzu-liao,* III (Peking, 1957), 9. See also ibid., pp. 24–31; and John Lossing Buck, *Land Utilization in China* (New York, 1964), p. 316, table 3.

—that is, the main tax and the surtaxes combined—to rise. This tendency was already apparent before 1931.[53] More significant, however, the increases continued even as the depression swept over the villages, having risen in 1934 by a national average of 8 percent. It should be noted in Table 4 that, in the provinces most directly controlled by Nanking— Kiangsu, Anhwei, and Chekiang, the taxes tended to be higher than the national average.

Eight percent, in absolute terms represented a modest tax increase. This increase was contemporaneous, however, with a precipitous decline in farm prices. The increase of taxes relative to farm prices by 1934 and 1935—which would be the true tax increase as far as the farmer was concerned—was therefore in the neighborhood of 30 to 50 percent above the year 1931.

Corroboration of this increased rate of taxation is provided by T'ao Chi-k'an. In a broad-ranging survey, T'ao compared

Table 5.   Index of Farm Prices

Year	Yang Sueh-Chang's data	Liu Ta-chung's data
1931	100	100
1932	86	72
1933	74	61
1934	59	56
1935	86	57
1936	99	60

Source: Yang Sueh-Chang, p. 150; Liu Ta-chung, p. 11. In yet a third series of data, wholesale food prices in north China since 1931 showed a decline of 29 percent in 1934 and 17 percent in 1935. See "Economic Indices," *Nankai Social and Economic Quarterly* 10.1:134 (April 1937). Obviously, statistical exactness is impossible.

increasing taxes with decreasing land values. In these terms, the tax increase between 1931 and 1934 was:[54]

Rice-paddy land	47%
Dry fields	40
Hilly land	36

Land taxes did not continue to increase after 1934. Indeed, as shown in Table 4, the land taxes in 1935–36 declined by a national average of 7 percent. The customary explanation for this tax reduction has been that many of the surtaxes were abolished after 1934. The system of surtaxes had, in fact, become so manifestly inequitable that the Second National Finance Conference in May 1934 had decreed that no new surtaxes were to be levied, and the amount of the surtaxes was not to exceed the basic land tax. The result was one of Nanking's most vaunted measures of rural reconstruction. According to official information, a total of 5,200 surtaxes were abolished during the year following the order, resulting in a reduction of tax revenue of ¥49 million.[55]

The actual efficacy of the attempt to reduce the burden of the surtaxes is difficult to assess. Y. C. Wang has expressed doubts that the number of surtaxes abolished was anywhere close to the figures announced, for Nanking's information had been based entirely on the reports of local authorities.[56] Actually, it is probable that many of the surtaxes were revoked just as the government claimed. At the same time, however, the local governments replaced the surtaxes with the system of taxes known as *t'an-k'uan* (special assessments). T'an-k'uan were taxes customarily assessed by local officials to make up budgetary deficits that were not covered by regular sources of revenue.[57] This system of tax collection had begun presumably during the period of the Taiping rebellion as a military exaction levied primarily upon businessmen. Subsequently, the system of t'an-k'uan expanded, taking root particularly in the northwest.

After the government's decision in 1934 to limit the surtaxes, local governments were faced with the necessity of making up the loss of income. And the system of t'an-k'uan lay ready-made for this purpose. During the Nanking period, therefore, the assessment of t'an-k'uan became more pervasive, striking the farmers even more than the businessmen, and tending to exceed even the surtaxes that had been abolished.

The methods of collecting t'an-k'uan were extremely diverse, differing from place to place, and even within the same place. Occasionally, for example, the levy would be on the number of houses in an area, or proportionate to the population. Usually, however, the assessment was computed on the basis of the taxpayer's land tax or the amount of land that he possessed.

What made the system of t'an-k'uan particularly onerous for the villagers was that the higher authorities at the provincial level were virtually powerless to supervise or limit these tax collections. About 85 percent of t'an-k'uan was collected, on their own authority, by the ch'ü and even the village officials. Moreover, t'an-k'uan could be assessed at any time of the year, without prior warning. The taxpayers were therefore unable to anticipate either the time or the amount of the next tax levy. Small wonder therefore that, as Ramon Myers observed, "The tax [the farmers] dreaded most was the *t'an-k'uan.*"[58]

Whatever the form—whether it was in the shape of t'an-k'uan, surtaxes, or the basic tax itself—the entire system of land taxes was extortionate and inequitable. The taxpayer had to pay, for example, a collection fee to the tax collector. This fee had been officially set at 10 percent of the main tax in 1928, although in actual practice it sometimes approached the full amount of the main tax.[59] The collection fee was essentially a legitimate exaction; many other exactions were not.

The key personnel in land-tax collection were the unsalaried quasi-official keepers of the tax rolls—known variously as *ts'e-shu, chuang-shu, li-shu,* and so on—who bridged the gap between the governmental structure and the landowner. In most cases, the hsien was too large for the officials themselves to conduct tax collections, and they relied on this large corps of persons—bequeathed them by the Manchu and warlord regimes—to keep the tax records and to collect the taxes. In Chiang-ning hsien near Nanking, for example, approximately 3,000 persons lived on the collection of land taxes. Because these men were given no salaries and were often entirely dependent on the tax-collecting process for their livelihood, and moreover because they alone had complete access to the records of landholdings, there was inevitably a great deal of peculation that crept into the system.

These tax collectors were possessed of an enviable ingenuity, and their methods of milking the system were too multifarious to be listed here.[60] The result, in any case, was that the average landowner was saddled with a substantial financial burden in addition to the legal tax assessments. The extent of these irregularities varied enormously from place to place. Franklin Ho observed in Chekiang, for example, that "in some of the worst cases" the illegal assessment was 20 to 50 percent more than the legal tax.[61] And Sidney D. Gamble estimated that the unofficial tax collectors in Ting hsien took 75 percent over and above the legal assessment.[62]

The most invidious aspect of the whole land-tax system was that its burden rested unequally upon different taxpayers, because some landlords evaded paying taxes, thus shifting the tax burden to less powerful landowners. Some, for example, registered their lands under numerous or fictitious names. (Franklin Ho reported from Chekiang, ''It is usually the case that a large piece of property has titles under ten to twenty different names.'') Or they lived in different hsien from their landholdings and thus avoided the tax collector. Or they simply bribed the tax collector. So successful were they in avoiding tax payment in Chekiang that only 74 percent of the assessed tax in 1928–29 was actually collected. But by 1930–31 only 62 percent, and by 1931–32 a mere 52 percent of the assessed taxes reached the government coffers. Forty-eight percent of the total assessed tax, in other words, was not forwarded to the government.[63]

A favorite expedient of evading the payment of the land tax was simply to arrange to have the land expunged from the tax records. In a 1932 survey of five villages in Hopei, for example, large amounts of unreported and untaxed lands were discovered (see Table 6). The Nationalist government never successfully remedied this leakage of land from the tax records. The eminent economist H. D. Fong contended at the end of the decade that the government's inability to impose a levy on all lands was still the most critical problem of the land-tax system.[64] And John Lossing Buck estimates that approxi-

Table 6.   Untaxed Lands in Five Villages, Hopei, 1932

Village	Land on the tax records	Actual landholdings	Percentage of untaxed land
A	335 acres	544 acres	38
B	306	352	13
C	125	243	49
D	310	561	45
E	152	322	53

Source: Fang Hsien-t'ing, ed., *Chung-kuo ching-chi yen-chiu,* p. 1116.

mately one-third of the taxable land was still not on the tax records in 1937.[65]

It was not generally the little farmer who escaped the tax collector but the landlord with wealth and influence. The bulk of the tax burden, as a consequence, rested on the small landowner, who barely eked out a living and could little afford the tax collectors' exactions.[66] What was the actual burden of the land tax on the individual landowner? This question, which seems so important and obvious, received little attention from contemporaries despite the fact that they focused a great deal of concern and study on the problem of the land tax generally. The reason for this neglect may be that the question was nearly impossible to answer in any generalized terms. Not only did the tax burden vary greatly among individuals as a result of this or that form of tax evasion but also as a result of the vast discrepancy of tax rates from one hsien to the next. In Shantung, farmers in one hsien where the land taxes amounted to ¥2.97 per acre, paid only 7.5 percent of their harvest for land taxes; in other hsien, the tax rate was ¥19.93–25.54 per acre and cost the farmers an average of 35–40 percent of the harvest. And, in Anhwei, the tax rate covered the whole range from ¥1.19 per acre in T'ung-ch'eng hsien to ¥60.06 per acre in T'ien-ch'ang hsien.[67] In addition, an uncertain amount of the tax revenue collected by local authorities was never reported upwards, and the illegal exactions imposed by the tax collectors varied enormously. Generalizations about the burden of the land tax must therefore be approached with caution.

If the land tax system had been administered more efficiently and less corruptly, the government could simultaneously have decreased its assessments on the poor landowners and increased its total tax revenues. The authorities were aware of this fact, but they felt that the task was beyond their powers. The only way to reform the system, it was argued, was to undertake a cadastral survey of the entire country—a task, it was estimated, that would require thirty to forty years to complete.[68]

It is doubtful that an elaborate and expensive cadastral survey would have been required to eradicate much of the corruption associated with the land tax. In all probability, an efficient and dedicated local government could easily and quickly have restored a measure of rationalization to the system. This is evidenced by the fact that, when the Japanese took over the administration of Chang-li hsien (Hopei), they increased in just two years the taxable land from 47,000 to 285,000 acres—an increase of over 500 percent![69] It was, of course, infinitely easier for the conquering Japanese to accomplish this task than it would have been for a non-communist, Chinese administration, because the Japanese could almost entirely disregard the mass of vested interests and the outcries of the politically and economically influential elements. Yet one cannot skirt the fact that reforms which would have measurably ameliorated the lives of the majority of farmers could have been accomplished by the Nationalist government without undertaking such radical structural changes as land redistribution.

Indirect Taxes

The land tax was the only tax that was assessed directly upon the farmers. There was, however, a bewildering variety of indirect taxes, imposed by all levels of the governmental apparatus, which had ultimately to be borne by the individual citizen. The central government collected the salt tax, the tobacco and wine taxes, and the consolidated taxes, which were indirect levies imposed at the point of manufacture on some fifteen items, including rolled tobacco, cotton yarn, flour, matches, and cement. Nanking also collected a stamp tax, which was an assessment on documents, such as receipts, invoices, account books, loan agreements, and permits.[70]

At the local levels, the provincial, hsien, and ch'ü administrations imposed an incredible number and variety of miscellaneous taxes, which varied greatly from one area to the next. There were sales taxes on pig bristles, cloth, grains, animals, oil cake, animal hides and bones; there were taxes assessed on mills that pressed peanut oil, taxes when a pig or chicken was slaughtered; taxes on mortgages and land sales, taxes for night watchmen and local police.[71]

Of the central government's various revenue-raising schemes, the sale and taxation of salt was one of the most important. To modern Westerners, salt seems a relatively insignificant commodity in one's daily life. A Chinese declared, however, that "the thing that now causes the greatest distress in the villages is the question of eating salt."[72] Perhaps this was exaggeration. Yet salt was a sheer necessity in the Chinese diet. Subsisting on an essentially meatless diet, Chinese without a supplementary salt intake became weak, lethargic, and sometimes wracked by agonizing muscle cramps. Chinese rulers had traditionally capitalized on this need, and salt either as a state monopoly or as a source of taxation had long been one of the government's principal sources of income.

The salt administration that the Nationalist regime inherited was ramshackle and inefficient.[73] The country was divided into eleven salt-producing and consumption areas, within which merchants who had purchased the privilege exercised a monopoly over the transportation or sale of the product. This system had produced grave inequities. Within the mutually exclusive salt districts, the monopoly merchants arbitrarily imposed high prices on the salt, and there had been no effective attempts to coordinate either prices or tax rates among the several districts. Obviously the temptations to smuggle salt from a low-priced to a high-priced district were irresistible, and the entire salt administration had as a result been thoroughly corrupted.

T. V. Soong, as minister of Finance, had recognized the inefficiencies of the system, and by 1931 he promulgated a new law on salt, banning monopolies and paving the way for a uniform and fixed tax. Like the Kuomintang's Land Law and Marriage Law, however, the Salt Law was merely a declaration of intentions, and the invidious effects of the system persisted or worsened during the Nanking period. The basic price of salt, for example, increased between 10 percent and 26 percent between 1931 and 1934, and was costing the consumer thirty to seventy times the cost of production.[74] And the salt tax, which the regime also increased, ranged in 1934 from less than ¥1.00 per picul in some areas to ¥12.00 per picul in others. Over one-third of the salt consumed was taxed at the rate of from ¥3.00 to ¥6.00; but nearly 13 percent was taxed in the top range of ¥9.00 to ¥12.00. These assessments reportedly included a surtax, a provincial government surtax, and a foreign-loan surtax on the basic salt tax. Surcharges attached by hsien and ch'ü governments, however, were not included in these figures.[75]

A family of five persons might have to spend ¥4.00–7.50 a year for salt. This expenditure appears small to a Westerner's eyes. But for the poorer of the farm families in China—where annual household income in 1934 averaged about ¥290, and where the averages in sixteen provinces ranged between ¥163 and ¥480—this represented one of their largest cash outlays for food.[76] An expense of that size could cause considerable hardship. It was common, therefore, for farmers to try to avoid paying the unreasonable prices and taxes for salt. Smuggling became common, although the government heavily punished those who were arrested. In north China, when many farmers reportedly could not afford salt, quotas were imposed on villages so that the inhabitants were forced to buy salt.[77]

Even in Ting hsien, one of the relatively well-to-do hsien in north China, peasants could not afford salt at the official rate of ¥1.00 for eight catties. They therefore soaked the soil to obtain *hsiao-yen*—sometimes called "earth salt"—as a substitute for salt. Government troops stopped this practice, claiming that the peasants were obtaining salt illegally.[78]

Much further study is necessary before we can draw firm conclusions about how much the tax burden of the farmers increased during the Nanking period. But that it did increase, and increased significantly, is clear. Chiang Kai-shek, for example, complained, "Government expenditures grow steadily higher. Whenever a program is begun, new taxes arise. Surtax charges are often attached to the regular taxes as needed, and miscellaneous taxes are also created. Occasionally, [the local authorities] collect unspecified taxes from house to house according to their wishes. As a result tax items are numerous. The people have suffered immensely under this heavy tax burden.'"[79] Ramon Myers has also remarked that the regime's growing involvement with control and administration in the villages resulted in markedly increased costs that had to be met with increased tax revenues.[80] The extent of the increased taxes, however, is still in question and will remain so until some future scholar finds a key to the pattern of unrecorded tax levies and misleading official statistics that becloud the actual situation.

An increased tax burden as such, was not necessarily injurious to the interests of the farmers, for if the government were to accomplish reforms, it would need money. As will be demonstrated in the following pages, however, the added tax burden was generally not put to uses that would ameliorate the farmers' lives. Military expenditures and corruption took a sizable share of the revenue. And a further share of the increased taxes was used simply to expand the local bureaucracy—so that the bureaucracy could collect taxes, in order to support an expanded bureaucracy.[81]

Ad Hoc Impositions and Conscription

Peasants were subject not only to the more or less regular exactions of the tax collectors. They had also to meet the unpredictable demands of both the army and the government for supplies, labor, and land.

Nanking armies, like those of many warlords, were generally poorly disciplined, inadequately paid, and without sufficient supplies. When troops moved through an area, therefore, they were like a pestilence upon the land: seizing possession of homes and property, and arbitrarily requisitioning food, animals, carts, and manpower. So harassed were people in some areas that, remarked a writer in the *Tu-li p'ing-lun,* many "hoped for liberation by the communists."[82] Especially persons living near the communist-occupied areas found themselves caught, as though on a millstone, between the Nationalist armies on the one hand and the communists on the other. In Szechuan in 1934, for example, a farmer stated, "When the bandits [communists] were here they held meetings every day, and every day levied taxes. Those who disobeyed even a little were killed. Now the bandits are gone, and only the old and the weak are left behind with only a few buried beans and a couple pints of rice. But the government troops again come, brandishing knives, and steal even those away."[83]

The troops requisitioned not only food. Carts, horses, and other forms of movable property were also appropriated until, said one writer, the cost to the peasant was "forty times more than the regular taxes."[84] The rhetorical flourish in this remark is obvious, but it did contain the essential truth that the requisitioning and looting of the soldiers could indeed reduce the peasants to destitution with a suddenness and completeness that even the tax collector could not claim.

Even the labor of the peasants was requisitioned, and it became a common form of self-defense for the men to flee their homes when they learned that government troops were approaching their village.[85] "If there is anything that the country farmer hates worse than to have his home looted by bandits," wrote a correspondent of the *North China Herald,* "it is to be herded up by the army and be forced to serve as an army transport mule . . . The army gives these forced carriers food so long as they are with the army itself, but it takes them many days journey away from home and then turns them loose with absolutely no payment for themselves. They are left to starve or else to beg their way home."[86] When such labor conscription came at planting or harvesting time, the peasants' losses could be substantial.

Comparable to the scourge of the government armies in their effects on the peasants were the governmental impositions related to road and railway construction. There was perhaps no area of development during the decade that caused Kuomintang partisans more pride than the spread of the transportation network. And, indeed, the regime's achievements in this sphere were notable. Between 1927 and late 1938 railway construction in the country was approximately doubled, with the addition of 6,592 kilometers of new track. And, as compared with the approximately 28,000 kilometers of highway which had been built during six years of warlord rule, 1921–1927 (from 1,185 kilometers to 29,170 kilometers), more than 82,000 kilometers were added to the road system during the Nanking decade.[87]

But at what cost were these railways and highways built? Much of the labor for the construction was provided by peasants who were conscripted, often forcefully, into labor gangs. No pay was given for their work. Moreover, the government simply seized, or gave grossly inadequate compensation for, the land appropriated for the roadways. Hsiung Shih-li, one of China's most prominent contemporary philosophers, reported after a visit to his native village in Hupei that:

Wherever the road extends, all the land is expropriated and nationalized without giving even a bit of compensation. When those bitterly poor people who survive on just a tip of land encounter this kind of calamity, there is nothing for them to do but die. But wealthy officials, who have a lot of land, have the route of the road changed so that they can appropriate the property of the poor. Furthermore, when they construct the roads, they force the people to build them; and if the people arrive for work somewhat tardily, they are often shot on the spot by the troops supervising the work . . . Today the only reconstruction that one sees in the countryside is the roads . . . but the implementation of the policy of road construction actually deprives the people of their property and robs them of their energy.[88]

The general truth of Hsiung Shih-li's critical comments regarding the effects of forced labor was attested by scores of other writers, both Chinese and foreign.[89] Chiang Kai-shek, however, encouraged even greater use of labor conscription, for he viewed it as a means of reconstructing the nation without making large outlays of scarce government revenue.[90]

There was nothing inherently wrong with the policy of forced labor, and some developmental economists today regard labor conscription as a rational means of promoting economic construction in capital-poor countries. What made forced labor invidious was that it weighed inequitably upon the poorest elements in society, and most of the building projects brought the conscripted workers few palpable benefits. The new roadways, for example, were constructed primarily for military and not for economic purposes. Many of the new roads simply duplicated or paralleled existing transport lines—waterways or cart paths—that were generally adequate for the economy at that stage of development but which were too slow for Chiang's modernizing armies. Furthermore, there was no coherent plan of using highways as feeders to railroads, which could best serve as major trunklines of transportation. The roadways therefore brought little or no immediate advantage to the farmers. As a League of Nations adviser observed in 1934, "If we exclude the public value of military use, which we cannot assess, it must be confessed that the roads do not at present give any economic benefit commensurate with their real cost in cash and confiscation."[91] After Franklin Ho joined the Nanking government, he told Chiang Kai-shek that the economy of the country was not being aided by the building of transportation lines, because there was no coordination between the roads, railways, and water system. Chiang, Ho recalls, "was really surprised."[92]

In many cases, moreover, the farmers were not even permitted to use the new roads. If their carts had no rubber tires, for example, they would usually be banned from the roadways. And because truck transport was still exorbitantly expensive, the roads were seldom used to haul civilian commodities.[93] A report of the British commercial counsellor serves as a fitting summary and conclusion to this section:

Military and strategic, rather than economic, reasons have prompted most of this (roads) development . . . Undertaken often with the assistance of forced labour (the corvée system has been instituted in sixteen provinces), built on land which has been in many cases confiscated from the peasant owners without compensation, and along routes already served by railways or waterways, their use forbidden, in some cases, to barrows and carts carrying produce, and allowed only to motor-bus companies which have purchased a monopoly, there is no doubt that the immediate result of their construction has been to place further burdens on local industry and agriculture.[94]

The Cooperative Movement

The government's relation to rural society was evidenced again in the cooperative societies that shot up throughout the country during the 1930s. The cooperative movement in China had originated in 1918, but growth of the movement before the Kuomintang assumed power had been slow. As late as 1928, there were still only 584 cooperatives in the country—most of them in Hopei, where the China International Famine Relief Commission had actively promoted and supported the movement. After 1928 several of the provincial governments promoted the cooperatives. And, at the depth of the depression, in 1934, the central government began actively promoting the cooperative movement. Thereafter the cooperatives grew with exploding force. From 3,978 cooperative associations in 1932, the movement grew to 9,948 in 1934; 26,224 in 1935; and 46,983 in 1937. The movement encompassed over one and a half million persons in 1936, each cooperative comprising an average of forty-four persons.[95]

Most cooperatives were established to supply credit.[96] The need was real enough, for the stringency and high cost of credit were among the major causes of rural distress. Probably half the nation's farm families were in debt.[97] No doubt an even higher percentage of them would have borrowed money, but the insecurity of loans—resulting from rural instability, the fact that few farmers held clear titles to their lands to offer as collateral, and the absence of adequate legal resort when a debtor defaulted—forced the moneylenders to exercise caution.[98]

Interest rates reflected the shortage of capital and insecurity of loans. The average annual interest on loans in 1931 was 28 percent in the rice-growing regions and 38 percent in the wheat-growing sections. Nearly 13 percent of all loans, however, bore interest rates of more than 50 percent a year. A hypothetically "average" peasant in north China (who borrowed ¥80, at 38 percent interest, for a period of nine months) would therefore expend ¥23 a year—perhaps 8 percent of his total income—in interest. In China, non-productive expenditures of this magnitude could easily make the difference between a year of plenty and months of hunger.[99]

Despite roseate descriptions by Kuomintang propagandists, the cooperative movement by 1937 had failed to ease the farmers' financial needs. Indeed, it worked to the advantage not so much of the village poor as of the rural elite. The cooperatives did not, for example, change the basic pattern of borrowing in the countryside. Probably less than 3 percent—some sources say only about 1 percent—of the credit extended even at the height of the cooperative movement was provided by the cooperative societies. For the rest, borrowers had to resort to the traditional sources of loans—rich farmers and landlords, merchants and pawnshops—who continued to charge the customary usurious rates of interest.[100]

Cooperative associations did provide loans at lower rates of interest than did the traditional moneylenders. But the benefits from these lower interest rates seldom filtered down to the most needy farmers. The cooperatives were theoretically able to let loans at annual interest rates of between 13 and 18 percent.[101] Customarily, however, members of the rural elite—landlords, rich peasants, and merchants—controlled the cooperatives, and they decided who would receive loans and at what rates of interest.[102] It was a common practice, therefore, that the officers of the cooperatives let loans to other members of the rural elite at the low, basic interest rate. Common farmers, however, were regarded as security risks, and the interest rate to them was often doubled. This practice was defended by a provincial chairman, who insisted that lending money was, after all, a business matter, and that cooperatives were not charitable institutions.[103]

Elite dominance of the cooperatives, at the expense of the common peasants, is revealed strikingly in Table 7. The more

Table 7.   Recipients of Cooperative Credit, 1933–1935

	Landowners	Part owners	Tenants
Average amount of credit obtained from cooperatives (yüan)	16.10	11.20	7.30
Percentage of total credit obtained	52	35	13

Source: Tamagna, p. 195.

well-to-do in the villages therefore not only obtained preferential interest charges, but they received a majority of the total money loaned.

Moreover, the elite used the cooperatives to enhance their already favored financial position. In some cases, cooperatives loaned money to the local elite at the low rate of interest, only to have the borrowers loan the money in turn to poor farmers at the traditional rates of interest.[104] Cooperatives also provided an additional source of corruption for the officials and local elite. There was no adequate system of audit, so that two yüan were frequently absorbed by the cooperative committees for every yüan that reached a borrower.[105]

With the encouragement of the central government, the number of cooperatives approximately doubled between 1935 and 1937. This proliferation of cooperative societies had not resulted from popular enthusiam for the movement. It was rather a typical product of unsustained bureaucratic enthusiasm. In a great many cases, people had—for reasons that can only be imagined—joined the cooperative societies when they were first formed by buying a share for ¥2.00. Thereafter they contributed nothing further to maintain their memberships.[106]

The bureaucratic impetus behind the cooperative movement is evidenced further by the case of a new hsien director of cooperatives. After assuming his post, he discovered that one of the cooperatives within his jurisdiction consisted of a lodge at a scenic spot in the hsien. Having investigated the seeming inanity of locating a cooperative there, he concluded that it "was initiated by the district magistrate for the double purpose of providing a guest house for all official visitors who might not be able to find modern conveniences in the existing hotels, and also as a gesture to show that they were promoting the cooperative movement." The over one hundred members of this cooperative had bought shares in it because they were beholden to the chief bureaucrat in the hsien. This same director of cooperatives found that other so-called cooperatives in his area of jurisdiction registered only one member, whereas others that were on record were completely nonexistent. The explanation, he learned, was that his predecessor as director of cooperatives had simply falsified the records, reporting the non-existent cooperatives (as the predecessor finally admitted) "in order to satisfy the Provincial Bureau of Reconstruction. I did this because I was well aware that the high officials would not look into the matter anyway."[107]

It is impossible to know how many of the nearly 47,000 cooperative associations in 1937 were nothing more than the creation of some minor bureaucrat's pen. Yet even Chang Yüan-shan (Y. S. Djang), the national director of the Department of Cooperatives admitted that "qualitative" control of the movement was a real and persisting problem.[108]

The cooperative movement is a particularly revealing case of the Nanking regime's incursion into rural life. It illustrates how officially inspired movements were superimposed on village life, and the bureaucrats' sensed need of reporting quantitative development disguised the fact that the movement was having few beneficial effects in the stricken rural communities. The movement also demonstrated that the Kuomintang chose not to alter the sociopolitical relationships in the villages. As a consequence, the old local elite—sometimes called the "gentry"—retained a dominating and often exploitative position over the common farmers throughout the Nanking period.

Accomplishments in Rural Reconstruction

This concern not to depose the rural elite was evidenced also in the government's actions regarding problems of land tenure. Sun Yat-sen had enshrined the goal of the equalization of landholding at the heart of his principles of economic reform. And the Nanking government had accordingly promulgated a detailed Land Law in 1930 that was designed, inter alia, to decrease the rents on land and to put an end to absentee landlordism (by enabling tenants who had tilled land belonging to an absentee owner for more than ten years to have the legal right to buy that land).

Despite these programmatic commitments, and despite the fact that nearly half of the farmers rented all or part of their land at rents that rose in some instances to as much as 60 percent or even 70 percent of the harvest,[109] Nanking failed even to begin putting the land law into effect. The Kuomintang did, of course, continue to pay lipservice to the principle of land equalization. But it upheld landlord rights with perverse persistence.

After Nationalist armies recovered areas where the communists had carried out their program of land redistribution, for example, it was customary for the lands to be wrested from the farmers and restored to the original landlords. In many cases, this was a difficult task, for the communists had sometimes held these areas for six years or more, and most of the deeds of ownership had been destroyed.[110] This policy of resurrecting the landlord system in the former communist areas was scathingly criticized by Tsiang T'ing-fu. He wrote that Kuomintang forces used landlords as guides when they moved into an area, restored their lands, and allowed the landlords to use the Kuomintang to work revenge on their enemies. These practices, Tsiang charged, not only gave substance to communist propaganda that the Kuomintang was fighting a class war of landlords against the peasants; they also violated the Kuomintang's own ideological commitment to give land to the tiller.[111]

It is probable that more popular and scholarly attention was given to the problems of tenancy and the evils of land-lordism than to any other single problem of agriculture during the 1930s. The leading League of Nations' agricultural specialist, for example, observed that "Of the economic and social factors [contributing to the rural crisis], perhaps the system of tenancy is the most disquieting."[112] Many persons, specialist and non-specialist, similarly felt that redistribution of the land was the only means of alleviating rural discontent.

The Kuomintang leadership rejected the alternative of land redistribution. "If we wanted to adopt [this] policy," Chiang Kai-shek declared, "we would have to discard our party principles and adopt a new name for our party like the Fukien insurgents." Chiang explained that China had more than enough land. He anticipated that, through the peaceful and gradual means of cooperative societies and collective farming, land tenancy would cease to plague the farmers.[113] Another consideration, not expressed by Chiang but undoubtedly foremost in his thinking, was articulated by George Taylor in 1936: "It is difficult to conceive of any method of radically improving the land-tenure system that would not involve considerable social upheaval."[114] The Nationalist leadership therefore chose not to attack head-on the problems of land-lordism but rather to alleviate agrarian distress by means of technological improvements. And all that China needed—or so it seemed to the Nationalist leadership—was a green revolution, the weapons of which are high-yield seeds, pesticides, fertilizers, and a sure supply of water. In fact, countries that in the 1960s have experienced the green revolution, such as the Philippines, India, and West Pakistan, have discovered that technological improvements, without changes in the system of land tenure and without new political institutions, tend to exacerbate existing economic inequities and political instability.[115] The Nationalists, of course, could not foresee these problems. But it mattered not, for the Nationalist policy of emphasizing technological reforms proved to be virtually fruitless.

Of the sixty-two agencies of the central government that in 1934 were involved in agricultural matters, two of them—the Ministry of Industries and the National Economic Council— emerged as the dominant policy and administrative agencies. In 1931 the functions of a Ministry of Agriculture and Mining were assumed by the newly created Ministry of Industry then headed by H. H. Kung. This ministry, through its Departments of Agriculture, of Forestry and Land Reclamation Administration, and of Fisheries and Animal Husbandry, was thereafter charged with the routine administration of agricultural matters. Through the National Agricultural Research Bureau, the ministry also engaged in agricultural research and extension work.[116]

The National Economic Council was instituted in 1931 at the suggestion of a League of Nations' official, Sir Arthur Salter, who envisioned the council as a means of attaining planned economic development within a capitalist framework.[117] Salter's suggestion had been accepted enthusiastically by the Nanking government. Chiang Kai-shek himself assumed the council chairmanship. And, in its original conception, the council would have wielded broad powers of planning and execution. In Chiang Kai-shek's words: "The archives of all the Ministries abound in schemes and proposals of all kinds. It will be the first task of the National Economic Council to translate into definite projects such of the schemes as will be selected as being the most urgent, to correlate them with one another, to establish an order of priority, and, in essence, to elaborate as rapidly as possible a co-ordinated plan of development."[118] In pursuit of these goals, the National Economic Council was assisted by a long train of distinguished League of Nations' advisers, among them Ludwig Rajchman, Sir Arthur Salter, and Carlo Dragoni.

The effectiveness of the council was, from the beginning,

restricted by the fact that it formally possessed only consultative powers. Thus, the projects devised by the Chinese and League of Nations' specialists in the council were dependent upon the favor and cooperation of the various ministries and bureau heads. The chief of the League of Nations' advisers, Ludwig Rajchman, felt as a consequence that the government placed many obstacles in the path of the council. Its agricultural competence, for example, was limited to Kiangsi and Shansi. And even in Kiangsi the council had to work through the provincial commissioner of reconstruction, who so frustrated the council's efforts that Rajchman recommended that the League of Nations' technical adviser there resign in protest.[119]

Some of the most successful work of the National Economic Council lay in improving the production of silk, cotton, and tea, which had fallen into near ruin by the 1930s. Numerous silk farmers, for example, had rooted out their mulberry trees and replaced them with other crops after both their trees and silkworms had been decimated by disease. The council distributed new disease-resistant trees, introduced new scientific methods of silkworm cultivation, and organized new and more profitable avenues of marketing.[120]

Floods and droughts were traditionally major causes of agricultural distress, and some of the most consequential work of the National Economic Council was in the field of water conservancy. By 1937 the council had participated in the completion of sixteen separate irrigation projects that brought water to about six thousand square miles of land. The council also supervised dredging and dike-construction work on the Yangtze, Yellow, and Hwai Rivers, and at other troublesome sources of flooding.[121]

Such, at any rate, are claims that were made for the National Economic Council. There was frequently, however, a broad gap between Nanking's declarations of accomplishment and the reality.

After Nanking published a bulletin boasting of achievements in water control, for example, a League of Nations' specialist cautioned privately that the situation was less praiseworthy than the bulletin reported. And a French expert with the League observed (in the paraphrase of Cheryl Payer) that "the reports submitted to Geneva by the secretary-general of the N.E.C. bore little relationship to reality, and that virtually nothing practical was being done to carry out the expensive and infeasible projects that were published from time to time."[122]

Chinese claims that the health services of the country had been vastly improved by the work of the National Economic Council were similarly deceiving. A central hospital and central field station were indeed established in Nanking, and health services were reportedly instituted in many of the major cities in the provinces. As late as July 1936, however, a League health expert, with six years experience in China, reported disgustedly, "To drift on as we are now doing makes our work here extremely difficult, and, in my opinion, useless."[123]

With reference to agricultural reform generally, some of the best work was done in the areas of education, research, and experimentation. Some of the experiments with seeds, fertilizers, soils, and disease control, for example, may indeed have had important implications for future development.[124] But virtually nothing was done in the area of agricultural extension—that is, in disseminating the results of research and experimentation to the farmer. "In agricultural extension," Franklin Ho concluded, "nothing went beyond the planning stage at the national level during the period from 1927 to 1937."[125] Ho's statement doubtlessly oversimplifies a complex situation. But, aside from the limited impact of the National Economic Council, the achievements in extension work do indeed appear to have been less than modest.

The principal obstructions to rural reconstruction were inadequate funding and the persistence of yamenization. The shortage of money for programs of economic reform resulted from a conscious decision by the Kuomintang leadership that the military and political unification of the nation was of greater importance than other areas of national reconstruction. This I think, and as I shall argue in Chapter 6, was a mistaken ordering of national priorities. But it does explain, at least in part, why attainments in the field of economic reconstruction were so limited.

During the 1930s, Nanking each year spent approximately 60 to 80 percent of its revenue on the military and on the servicing of loans—both essentially non-productive expenditures. In addition, 7–12 percent of the budget was devoted to the administration of tax-collecting agencies. Only 8–13 percent of the total budget was therefore left for maintenance of the bureaucracy and for productive undertakings.[126] Table 8 reveals just how miniscule were the sums allotted for development of the economy down to 1935 (there are no reliable budgetary figures after that year).

The striking feature in Table 8 is the sharp increase in the budgetary appropriations for reconstruction in 1934 and 1935. It would, however, be a mistake to conclude from this data that Nanking had in 1934 significantly shifted its priorities to reconstruction projects. It may or may not be true that the government had begun to channel more revenues to reconstruction activities; but these official statistics seriously dis-

Table 8. Government Allocations for Economic
Reconstruction (*chien-she*)

Year	Amount (in 1,000 yüan)	Percentage of total government expenditures
1931	13,630	1.52
1932	19,149	2.42
1933	10,033	1.21
1934	95,642	10.41
1935	106,665	11.14

Source: Yin Po-tuan, "Chien-she yün-tung yü ching-fei lai-yüan" (The reconstruction movement and sources of revenue), *KWCP* 13.27 : articles pp. 4–5 (Aug. 13, 1936).

torted the picture of actual expenditures. Fourteen million yüan in the 1935 budget, for example, had originally, in the preliminary draft, been designated for "military construction." To minimize the appearance of excessive expenditures on the military, this item in the final budget appeared under the rubric of "reconstruction" and was in fact expended for military purposes. Another large portion of the money listed under "reconstruction" was devoted to the construction of highways, which were designed primarily for military purposes. And, again, a budgetary allocation of ￥15 million was in fact for "military education."[127] Because of the limited amounts of revenue available for productive reconstruction, Hsu Dau-lin has remarked, "We will not marvel at how little was accomplished in economic and community development (like land survey, irrigation, factories, and hospitals) under the Nationalist Government."[128]

Even when money was available for rural reconstruction, much of it was dissipated in the purely administrative and planning aspects of the work. "The year before last," Kao T'ing-tzu, a Kuomintang partisan, wrote of the water conservancy programs, "the work was to survey such-and-such a place; last year the work was also to survey such-and-such an area; this year the work is still simply to survey, gather statistics, draw maps, and hold conferences. But, because the appropriations have been expended, the actual engineering work cannot be carried out." Kao saw some improvement in the administration of the water conservancy program by 1937. He admitted, however, that "in fact, the money and the administration have not been employed most rationally or effectively."[129] Huang Shao-hung, one of Nanking's most energetic administrators, came to the same conclusion. His memoirs, where he recounts his experiences as minister of the Interior (May 1932–December 1934), are a woeful tale of paper shuffling, jurisdictional rivalries, nepotism, and non-achievement. It is perhaps symbolic of the regime's failure in rural reconstruction that Huang boasted of no accomplishments in the fields of health and sanitation, water control, land reform or local self-government—all tasks within the purview of his ministry—but of the publication of an administrative yearbook.[130]

Despite the bureaucratic boondoggling and budgetary constrictions that afflicted the government's programs of reconstruction, the rural economy had largely recovered from the depression by 1936 and 1937. The factors affecting this recovery appear to be precisely the ones that had dropped the country into the depression in 1931–32: prices and weather.

The decisive turning point in farm prices was the currency reform of November 3, 1935. During 1935, as silver flooded out of the country, the monetary system of the country moved inexorably toward collapse. Banks were closing; public confidence in the system disappeared; the redemption of paper notes with silver was suspended. As long as the United States maintained its artificially inflated price on silver, the question for China was not whether to abandon the silver standard, but when? On the weekend of November 3, 1935, China switched to a managed currency.

The reason this measure affected farm prices was that it made possible a large expansion in the volume of currency in the economy—the quantity of notes in circulation tripling in less than a year-and-a-half (see Table 9). This increase in the

Table 9. Notes in Circulation
(in millions of yüan)

Date	Amount
November 1935	453
December 1935	673
June 1936	948
December 1936	1,331
June 1937	1,477

Source: Chiang Kia-ngau, "Toward Modernization of China's Currency and Banking, 1927–1937," *Strenuous Decade,* p. 160. Only about one-half of this increase was issued in return for silver turned in to the government.

volume of liquid capital had an immediate inflationary effect. Farm prices quickly moved upward. By mid-1937, prices had regained the level of 1931 before the depression began. At Shanghai, for example, wholesale prices increased about 30 percent in the eighteen months since the currency reform.[131] The greater quantity of capital also increased the availability of credit, and interest rates fell.

Simultaneously with these monetary developments, the farmers reaped a bumper harvest. Except in Kwangtung and Szechuan where drought destroyed the rice crops, 1936 saw the best crops in nearly twenty years.[132] The happy combination of good harvests and high prices revivified the villages. Indeed, the Bank of China estimated that the value of the main crops in 1936—due both to the greater quantity of the crops and higher prices—was nearly 45 percent above the average of 1933–1935.[133] The value of those crops in 1937 was probably even higher.

The irony of this spectacular recovery from the depression was that the rise in prices, that had triggered the recovery, was unplanned, unanticipated, and actually contrary to the wishes of Nanking's monetary experts. For H. H. Kung and his advisers in the Ministry of Finance were not Keynesian economists. They had never conceived of a controlled inflationary trend as a solution to the depression, and they were in fact determined to avoid inflation.[134] Despite these convictions, prices did rise, because Nanking found it impossible to resist the temptation of running money off the printing press now that the yüan was no longer pegged to silver.

Surveying the rural economy as a whole during the Nanking period, the most striking feature was the depression of 1932–1935. Even before the depression began, China's villages were in the grips of an economic illness that reduced the ordinary farmer to debilitating poverty. The depression brought that illness to a critical stage, driving millions of farmers from their homes and inflicting awful suffering on millions more. There was probably little that the Nanking government could have done to prevent this economic disaster. China was now part of the international system, and if anyone deserved to be castigated for having caused the most extreme suffering of the period it was the responsible leaders of the United States government. Nanking can be blamed, however, for exacerbating a bad situation with its inequitable systems of taxes and onerous practices of ad hoc conscriptions and expropriations.

Some observers have argued that the regime had to tax if it were to bring reforms to the villages, and it had to conscript if it were to bring peace to the provinces. This argument would be irrefutable if the tax monies and the labor service had been employed constructively. Seldom, however, did the farmer derive benefits from his contributions. The rural reconstruction policies of the government had been essentially barren of results. There had been some achievements in water control, seed improvement, and marketing, but these had done no more than offer "promise" of future improvement. As even an apologist for the government admitted in 1936, "The direct benefits to the people [from the government reconstruction measures] were very small," because "the Government was not seeking to give immediate and direct help to the people by drastic changes, but preferred to follow a slow and gradual policy that would avoid too great a disturbance in the country."[135]

Perhaps the Nanking government could have done nothing more than adopt "a slow and gradual policy" in agriculture. China is, after all, an immense nation; and the administrative and fiscal resources that would have been required to significantly transform the village scene would have been enormous. Yet Nanking in the 1930s had only begun to create an administrative system, and its finances were being diverted—in part justifiably—to the tasks of national unity and defense.

Nanking ought not therefore be blamed for having failed to reconstruct agriculture. It can, however, be faulted for having added unnecessarily and fruitlessly to the burdens of the villagers. The local bureaucracy, the police force, the militia, and the tax collectors did not improve their services, but they greatly expanded in size and salaries.[136] So burdensome and ineffectual was the government that Hu Shih pleaded with Nanking to stop the rural reform projects and reduce the numbers of officials and soldiers. This, he said, was a time for *wu-wei* government—for government that undertook no positive measures—because the more the government attempted to do, the greater was the suffering of the farmers.[137]

By 1937 the village economy was seemingly back where it had been in 1931. But had not the suffering, the growing tax burden, the administrative ineptitude, and the regime's basic insouciance about the villages during the 1930s taken a toll? It may at least be speculated that the condition of the villages was politically, if not economically, more fragile in 1937 than it had been when Kuomintang rule began. This judgment is subjective and perhaps overly pessimistic. But, even if the political and economic disintegration had not worsened, objective conditions in the countryside at the end of the Nanking period were at a critical stage. As Paul Linebarger, a scholar noted for his sympathies for the Kuomintang, acknowledged: ''Today, if one judges by past experience, rebellion or reform seems long overdue.''[138]

The Urban Economy

The focus of this chapter has been on the impact of the Nanking regime upon the rural areas. The government itself, however, was more oriented to the cities, and it is fitting that we devote some attention to the government's relationship to the urban sector of the economy.

It is a matter of record that several significant accomplishments in the modern sector of the economy were performed under the aegis of the Kuomintang regime. First, the almost perverse economic fragmentation of the past was increasingly being superseded by the mechanics of a unified national economy. This was an accomplishment on a par, perhaps, with the creation of the Zollverein in Germany. The tariff on the movement of goods within the country, the likin, was abolished by 1931. And the practice of placing a duty on rice and wheat when shipped from one Chinese port to another was ended two years later. An attempt was also made to standardize the weights and measures throughout the nation. Since time immemorial each region, and even different trades within a city, had employed variant standards of measurement, so that interregional trading was constantly hampered by impossible discrepancies. As a remedy, the government in 1930 formally adopted the metric system, and this was actually put into effect in the tax and customs agencies.[139]

A signal achievement was unification of the national currency. Previously the usual measure of accounting had been the tael, which represented a quantity of silver that varied markedly in weight and fineness from one place to the next. In addition, Chinese and foreign banks, private and government, issued banknotes, the values of which fluctuated with the vagaries of both economics and politics. In 1933 the central government effectively abolished the tael. Two years later, with the currency reform of November 3, 1935, the issuance of paper notes was legally limited to four major banks controlled by the national government. For the first time in the nation's history, China's economic community could hope to operate within a uniform currency system.[140]

A second area of progress was in that small corner of the economy, modern industry, which in 1933 accounted for 2.2 percent of the net domestic product.[141] Despite the welter of obstacles—monetary deflation, collapse of the domestic market due to rural decline, and warfare—modern industrial production (exclusive of the lost provinces in Manchuria) increased about 6 percent annually during the Nanking decade.[142] Thus, while the contribution of agriculture and other non-modern occupations (professional services, home industries, trade, and so on) to the gross national product tended to decline during most of the 1930s, the contribution of modern manufacturing industries steadily grew:[143]

Year	Billion yüan (in 1931 prices)
1931	1.65
1932	1.71
1933	1.89
1934	1.98
1935	2.24
1936	2.39

These achievements have lead John K. Chang, a careful economist now working with the World Bank, to conclude: "On the basis of this record of active government participation in economic planning and of actual achievements, it seems reasonable to claim that the foundation for modern economic transformation was being built during the decade concerned."[144] If we peer beneath the surface, however, we find that the record of the Kuomintang in even the urban economy was considerably more splotchy than Chang has indicated.

The basic defect of the Nationalist government, so far as the urban economy was concerned, was that the regime's leadership placed its highest priority upon the military and political unification of the nation. The regime therefore valued the urban economy, but as a source of revenue; it devoted little attention to the problems of economic development. The fundamental attitude of the regime toward the financial and business groups was revealed with clarity during the first years after the Northern Expedition. In early 1927 these groups had been among the most ardent supporters of Chiang Kai-shek and the anti-communist wing of the Kuomintang. They had felt desperation and panic during the Northern Expedition when the striking workers, presumably under the leadership of the communists, struck for higher wages and even assumed control of factories.[145] When the moneyed classes of Shanghai in early April 1927 contributed a reported ¥10 million to Chiang Kai-shek in return for repression of the communist elements in the city, it appeared that an alliance between China's capitalist class and Chiang Kai-shek had been consummated.[146]

Chiang's military conquest of north and central China had only begun, however, and the ¥10 million that the Shanghai capitalists had contributed merely whetted the new regime's financial appetite. In May, just weeks after the purges had begun, Nanking asked the Shanghai business community to subscribe to a ¥30 million loan. Government agents went from shop to shop and factory to factory soliciting the needed money. The Nanyang Tobacco Company, for example, was assigned a loan of ¥500,000; the Sun Sun department store, ¥300,000; the Sincere and the Wing On department stores, ¥250,000 each; and the Commercial Press, ¥200,000. When businessmen refused to meet these and subsequent demands for loans and contributions, the revolutionary regime resorted to blackmail and kidnapping. The son of a wealthy indigo merchant was arrested as a counter-revolutionary; ¥500,000 was demanded for his release. The three-year-old son of the manager of the Sincere Company was kidnapped, and released only after a ¥500,000 contribution was delivered to the government. Such instances of extortion, often carried out under the pretext of anti-communism, created—as the American consul reported—"a veritable reign of terror among the money classes."[147]

The business community received some respite from the government's financial demands during the period of Chiang Kai-shek's retirement in late 1927. But the pressure for financial support resumed after Chiang returned to the government in January 1928. A tax of ¥30,000 was assessed each of Shanghai's eighty-three native banks, an amount so large that some of them were forced out of business. The China Merchants Steamship Navigation Company was bankrupted by government pressures. And the wave of kidnappings resumed. An American foreign service officer reported in February 1928 that "Chiang's subordinates in this area are once more resorting to the scheme of official blackmail and extortion similar to the system which prevailed during the summer of 1927."[148]

By June 1928, with the Northern Expedition nearly completed, the government was ready to make amends with the capitalists, and T. V. Soong admitted that "in time of war, we have perhaps been forced to resort to extraordinary means to raise funds."[149]

Government extortion from the financial and business classes never again reached the heights of gangsterism that had been attained during 1927 and 1928. The basic attitude of the regime toward these groups, however, did not change. As late as 1936, for example, the eminent economist H. D. Fong quoted a Japanese study, which held that the bureaucrats and militarists:

have gradually got the capital into their own hands, the commercial and industrial classes have been sucked dry, and an immense amount of harm has been done to the development of capitalism. (They) cannot bear the thought of any private ownership other than theirs. Whether it be the ownership of a large area of land, or the possession of mines supplying raw materials for industry, or the control of means of transport—they try to lay their hands on everything, from banking facilities to factories. All these lines are barred to those not connected with the militarists and bureaucrats—that is, to commercial and industrial men in general—and an immense amount of harm has been done to the development of capitalism as witnessed in other countries.

"The truth of these charges," Fong added, "cannot seriously be disputed."[150]

Although the Nanking regime viewed the business classes as a source of revenue, its relationship with the modern sector was, initially at least, highly ambiguous. Indeed, it took most of the decade for the regime to establish its ascendancy over these economic groups. This ambiguity was exemplified by the government's ties with the banks.

Throughout the decade, the regime had never contrived a means to meet its expenditures from such sources of revenue as taxation and state-operated enterprises. It was consequently forced to rely heavily on borrowing. During the period 1929–1937, an average of over one-fifth of the government's annual receipts were obtained through borrowing, either through the issue of government bonds or simply in the form of bank loans and overdrafts.

The relationship of the banking classes with the government was therefore close and proved to be extraordinarily lucrative for them. The government customarily sold bonds to the banks at less than face value—perhaps only 60–70 percent of face value—and at annual interest rates of 7–10 percent. The banks consequently realized large profits from loans to the government, the effective yield reaching 15–20 percent during the years 1927–1933. At times, the yield rose to 25 percent—as it did after the Manchurian Incident—although it fell to 12 percent by 1936.[151]

The practice of relying upon borrowed money was not sound fiscal policy. Of the government bonds issued at a face value of ¥1,465 million between 1927 and 1934, for example,

Table 10. Expenditure, Revenue and Deficit, 1929–1937
(in millions of yüan)

Year ending June 30	Expenditure (excluding balances at end of the period)	Revenue (non-borrowed, excluding balances at beginning of the period)	Deficit covered by borrowing	
			Amount	Percentage of expenditure
1929	434	334	100	23.0
1930	585	484	101	17.3
1931	775	558	217	28.0
1932	749	619	130	17.4
1933	699	614	86	12.3
1934	836	689	147	17.6
1935	941	745	196	20.8
1936	1,073	817	256	23.8
1937	1,167	870	297	25.4

Source: Arthur N. Young, "China's Fiscal Transformation, 1927–1937," *Strenuous Decade,* p. 102. See also Leonard G. Ting, "Chinese Modern Banks and the Finance of Government and Industry," *Nankai Social and Economic Quarterly* 8.3:592–594 (October 1935).

the government actually realized only ¥809 million.[152] In addition, an increasing percentage of the regime's annual expenditures—between 25 and 40 percent—was being committed to servicing this growing debt.[153]

The policy of borrowing had therefore become a Frankenstein's monster that threatened to kill its own creator. Nanking first attempted to control the costs of borrowing in 1932 by persuading bondholders to accept a reduction of interest payments to a uniform rate of 6 percent and, at the same time, lengthening the schedule of repayments. This measure saved the government about ¥100 million a year in servicing debts, and is the reason why the government borrowed relatively little during 1932 and 1933.[154]

To persuade the bondholders to accept this reorganization of the loans, the government had promised that it would contract no further domestic loans for four years. It was unable to fulfill this promise, and within the year it resumed a policy of borrowing to keep itself financially afloat.[155]

Nanking's two chief financial problems—that of dependence on private banking and that of reliance on borrowed money—were resolved by H. H. Kung. Kung replaced his brother-in-law, T. V. Soong, as finance minister in November 1933. And his first major move was to establish the government in control of the nation's banking community. During the depth of the depression in the spring of 1935, Kung asserted that, to aid the ailing industrial and banking firms, it would be necessary to expand the credit of a central banking group. To attain this end, he ordered the two principal private banks, the Bank of China and the Bank of Communications, to approximately double their credit capacity by accepting a new issue of government bonds as capital. Government capital in the Bank of China, for instance, was raised from ¥5 million to ¥20 million. By this crude expedient, Kung had in a single blow made the government the major shareholder in, and therefore the absolute controller of, those banks. Subsequently, this central banking group bought up a large quantity of the bank notes of the Chinese Industrial, the Ssu-ming, and the Chinese Commercial Banks, which it then suddenly presented to those banks for redemption. When the latter banks were unable to redeem the notes, they fell under the control of the government-related banking group.[156] Using similar devices, the government soon dominated the banking industry, controlling something approaching 70 percent of the nation's total banking resources.[157]

The political and economic significance of this governmental coup against the private banks has been aptly described by Y. C. Wang: "The shift of control from the hands of a small group of bankers to those of the government represented a basic change in the power structure of urban China. Managers of the large Chinese banks had been the only business group that had important political influence, and their eclipse therefore signified not only complete government domination over the Chinese financial world but also the end of the entrepreneurs as an independent pressure group."[158]

Kung had plotted this takeover of the banks in complete secrecy. Only he, Chiang Kai-shek, T. V. Soong, and a very few other government leaders knew of the scheme. Even Wang Ching-wei had not been privy to the secret. The banking community was, of course, outraged by the government's almost overt theft, but they were powerless. The final irony was that, after the takeover, the central banking group still did not grant additional credits to the business community as Kung had originally promised.[159]

Kung's next major move—designed to eliminate the necessity of borrowing—followed directly from the shift in November 1935 from a currency backed by silver to a managed currency. By the terms of the currency reform, the notes of the central banking group (the Central Bank of China, the Bank of China, the Bank of Communications, and later the Farmers Bank of China) were made the only legal currency of the country. No longer were provincial and private banks permitted to issue their own paper notes. Moreover, the government-controlled banks could now put out new issues of paper notes without the backing of silver.

This new currency system offered Kung an irresistible opportunity to put an end to governmental borrowing by simply printing more money. Legally the currency was henceforth to be backed 60 percent by gold, silver, or foreign exchange and 40 percent by paper securities. But the temptation to issue notes, particularly now in the absence of other legal tender in the country, was too great to be resisted. Rather than borrowing to maintain a balanced budget, the Finance Ministry had merely to demand new notes from the government-controlled banks on the security of new bond issues. As a result, the volume of bank notes rose; and Kung by 1937 had reduced governmental borrowing for general purposes to zero.[160]

H. H. Kung had thus largely solved, for the moment, the problem of government borrowing. At the same time, he had—albeit unintentionally—stimulated the inflationary trend that pulled the rural economy out of the depression. Moreover, the currency reform contributed to the political unification of the country, because businessmen in the still independent provinces of Kwangtung and Kwangsi favored Nanking's new notes over their own provincial money. Kung's fiscal policies must therefore be accounted an overwhelming success as of 1937.

The long-term success of the currency reform would depend, however, on Kung's ability to establish the stability of the new currency. And here the prognoses were less encouraging. Conceivably, with a continued favorable trade balance and with peace, Nanking could have brought its expenditures into line with its revenues. And perhaps the regime could have resisted the allurements of the printing press and thereby have restricted the money supply. It is significant, however, that the government's plans to establish a Central Reserve Bank, which was intended as the agency to control money and credit as means of stabilizing the currency, had been stillborn as a result of intra-bureaucratic squabbles.[161]

We can, of course, never know how successful Nanking's monetary policies might have been if there had been no war. But war did intervene, and the runaway inflation of the 1940s was directly related to the adoption of a managed currency. The currency reform of 1935 may therefore have been the single most fateful act of the Nationalist regime during its tenure in Nanking.

The Nationalists' insouciance in the face of the problems of economic development was manifested clearly in the regime's taxation policies, which were both regressive and inelastic. The fundamental defect, remedied only in 1941, was that the regime in 1928 had surrendered revenues from the land tax to the provincial government. This had been dictated by power realities at the time. By acquiescing in the persistence of this division of tax revenues, however, the government denied itself the right to tax the source of approximately 65 percent of the gross national product. In other words, if Nanking had reserved the land tax for itself, and had collected that tax efficiently, the fiscal problems of the 1930s could have been largely avoided.

Deprived of revenues from agriculture, Nanking depended for tax revenues almost entirely on the manufacturing and trade sectors. Consequently, the central government derived about 85 percent of its revenues from the sector of the econ-

Table 11.   Distribution of Revenues, 1929–1937 (in percent)

Year	Customs	Salt	Consolidated (consumer) and other taxes	Miscellaneous revenues
1929	53.5	9.0	11.0	26.5
1930	57.0	25.2	11.0	6.8
1931	56.1	26.9	12.2	4.8
1932	59.8	23.2	16.5	0.6
1933	53.1	25.8	15.9	5.2
1934	51.3	25.7	19.0	4.1
1935	47.3	22.4	17.3	12.9
1936	33.3	22.6	20.4	23.7
1937	43.4	22.7	22.2	11.7

Source: Young, *China's Nation-Building Effort,* p. 307.

omy that produced only 10 to 15 percent of the national income.[162] The capacity of trade and manufacturing to sustain the financial needs of the government and still make a profit was, of course, limited. Nevertheless, the government demand for revenues was relentless, with the result that the business community felt few incentives to expand.

"The primary purpose of the Chinese tariff," Cheng Yu-kwei has observed, "was the increasing of revenue collections, whereas protection of domestic industries was only its secondary aim."[163] Thus, the government tripled the tariff rates—but its thirst for money so overrode broader economic considerations, that it levied the duties impartially on exports and imports. Chinese business was consequently denied any especial advantage against foreign products, either at home or on the world market. Imported *raw* materials were also taxed at virtually the same rates as imported *finished* products. Raw cotton, needed by Chinese mills, for instance, had to pay almost the same duty as imported textiles. Chinese manufacturers vigorously protested Nanking's regressive tax policy, but to no effect.[164]

The burden of customs, salt, and consolidated taxes was whenever possible passed on to the consumer. As a result, taxes weighed inordinately upon the average consumer; and, relative to their ability to pay, resting lightly on the well-to-do.[165] A halting effort to remedy this fault in the system was made in late 1936 with the inauguration of an income tax. This had effect only on the salaries of government officials, and did not in fact remotely meet the problem of taxing the wealth of the country.[166] The regime displayed little initiative in seeking new sources of revenue. It listlessly went through the motions of accomplishing a cadastral survey. In practice, however, it simply maintained the pattern of taxation that had been bequeathed it by the Peking warlords. And, when financial needs increased, the regime simply tried to patch up the old system—as it did with the salt tax—or it raised the tax rates.[167]

The business community operated under the additional handicap that it could obtain investment capital from the banks only at such high rates that expansion was discouraged. Because the banks realized an annual return of at least 12–20 percent on loans to the government, a large part—70 percent—of all bank loans was channeled away from investments in commercial and industrial enterprises and into loans to the government. To obtain credit, private entrepreneurs were required to pay approximately 15–20 percent interest, a rate which, as Frank Tamagna observed, "most Chinese industries were unable to pay; as a result, industrial activity was turned into speculative ventures."[168]

The burdens imposed upon the private capitalists, and the obstacles to economic development created during the 1930s, resulted in large part from the peculiar military and political exigencies that confronted the government during the decade. But the regime's tendency to "milk" the resources of private entrepreneurs and indeed its impulse to dominate all enterprises that were successful or politically influential were not essentially different from earlier Chinese regimes, and its attitude therefore had deep historical roots.

The Nationalist government's tendency to dominate the economy at the expense of private capital had been fortified and to a degree legitimized, however, by the regime's ideology. Sun Yat-sen, for example, in the latter years of his life, had become a staunch proponent of state capitalism. "If we do not use state power to build up these enterprises," he asserted in his lectures on the Three People's Principles, "but leave them in the hands of private Chinese or of foreign businessmen, the result will be simply the expansion of private capital and the emergence of a great wealthy class with the consequent inequalities in society . . . The state should lead in business enterprises and set up all kinds of productive machinery which will be the property of the state."[169] The attraction of fascism and political authoritarianism during the 1930s, as well as the Chinese reaction to the apparent demise of laissez-faire during the world depression, also strengthened the Nationalists' resolve to institute a pervasive system of economic controls.

During the Nanking decade, therefore, there was a growing tendency for the government to participate in the economy and, in some kinds of productive enterprises, to replace private with state ownership. In 1932, for example, Nanking nationalized the important China Merchants Steam Navigation Company. Various governmental bureaus undertook to produce such diverse products as steel, machinery, electrical appliances, alcohol, wood oil, tungsten, and matches. A sizable chunk of the textile industry also fell under state control, either through direct investment or after mills went bankrupt and went into the receivership of the government-controlled banks.[170] The government's domination of the nation's banking was, of course, the chief expression of Nanking's growing "state capitalism." There was, therefore, a clear trend toward state domination of the modern sector of the economy. The extent of this domination on the eve of the war, however, ought not be exaggerated. For, although the government did effectively dominate the banking industry, it controlled only about 6 percent of the nation's modern manufacturing enterprises by 1936.[171] Thus, state control of industrial production, which became a prominent feature of Nationalist rule in the 1940s, had barely begun prior to the war with Japan. (The term "bureaucratic capitalism" has frequently been used to describe the Nationalist government's involvement in the economy. But there are so many problems of definition, and the whole treatment of bureaucratic capitalism has been so overlaid with political polemics, that I have thought it best here to avoid the epithet.)

What, in the final analysis, was the impact of the Nationalist government on the modern sector of the economy? In confronting this question, it should be frankly recognized that there existed so many imponderables that it may never be possible to answer this question definitively. We can only speculate, for instance, that Chinese industry might have developed markedly faster if it had not been burdened by ad hoc governmental levies, a regressive system of taxes, and exorbitant interest rates. And it is impossible to calculate the retardative effects of the depression, of the loss of the Manchurian markets, and of Japanese aggression.

What we do know, however, is that the growth of industrial production during the Nanking period was not markedly different from the average annual rate for the entire period from 1912 to 1936. And, indeed, even during the so-called depths of the warlord period, the rate of growth was commensurate with that under the Nationalists.[172]

Still, industrial production did increase, however modestly, during the Nanking decade, and this belies Douglas S. Paauw's contention that the Chinese economy "stagnated" under Nationalist rule.[173] The causes of the industrial growth during the decade are, however, still unclear. It may be speculated that the increases were attributable largely to foreign-owned factories in China. During the decade, foreigners provided approximately 63 percent of the total capitalization of China's factories; and Hou Chi-ming has stated that "foreign capital was largely responsible for the development of whatever economic modernization took place in China before 1937."[174] Moreover, the sharp acceleration of production after the depression of 1932–1935 was a consequence primarily of the generous harvests in 1936, which generated fresh demands from the farmers for industrial goods—and not of governmental policies.[175]

In view of these facts, all claims for the success of Nationalist "growth-inducing measures," as John Chang phrased it, must be viewed with the utmost suspicion. Indeed, it appears more probable that Nationalist policies, on balance, had a dampening effect on the productivity of Chinese-owned factories.

Class Basis of the Kuomintang

Was the Kuomintang an instrument of the landlord class and urban capitalist interests? Scholars with a penchant for class analysis, such as Ho Kan-chih and Barrington Moore, have contended that it was.[176] The research for this chapter suggests, however, that the generalization may be false.

When agents of the Kuomintang employed outright extortion and kidnapping against the commercial classes, when the policies of the regime patently worked to the disadvantage of the private entrepreneurs, when state-owned enterprises began competing with private capital, then it must be concluded that the urban economic interests were not controlling or significantly influencing the policies of the Nanking regime. Indeed, the strongest evidence that the Kuomintang was working in close collaboration with those interests has been the fact that the regime was heavily dependent on bank loans and that the banking interests profited immensely from this tie to the government. We have noted, however, that this financial liaison broke up in 1935. After H. H. Kung's banking coup, the leaders of the private banks felt that they had been robbed and cheated. But they were powerless. That they did not wield strong influence within the Kuomintang is obvious.

The quality of the relationship between the landlord class and the Kuomintang is less easy to discern. There is, without question, a plenitude of evidence that the regime did frequently act in the interests of rural gentry. Nanking scrupulously avoided policies of land redistribution; it did not enforce the provisions of the Land Law, which called for a reduction of rents; it even returned to the landlords those lands that had been confiscated by the communists. The regime also appeared to foster the control of the rural elite over the cooperatives. These attitudes and policies of the Kuomintang left the impression, recorded for example by the United States minister to China, that "the thesis then adopted by the Government appeared to be that the strength of the rural communities rested upon the old gentry, and that at all costs the power of the gentry should be restored."[177]

Undoubtedly the regime and the rural elite did share several interests in common. Both felt threatened by the mobilization of the masses; both feared a social and political upheaval in the villages; both feared communism. In these respects, the interests of the Kuomintang did conjoin with those of the landlords.

But their interests were not identical. For at least a century the local elites had been encroaching upward, assuming more of the tasks of local governance. The Nationalist regime, by contrast, was committed to a policy of extending its administrative, fiscal, and military controls downwards. After 1928, for example, each hsien was to be divided into from four to ten ch'ü each to be headed by an appointee of the provincial government.[178] Branch headquarters of the party were also penetrating to the local level. This progressive bureaucratization of control at the local level was not merely a formalization of the powers previously captured by the rural elites. Heads of ch'ü government in areas most thoroughly controlled by Nanking—that is, in the anti-communist, Bandit-Suppression Areas—for example, were made subject to the rule of avoidance. In other words, the rural elites were not permitted to preside over ch'ü government in their home provinces, where their personal power would be deeply entrenched and their interests might easily conflict with that of the governmental bureaucracy. Indicative of this growing bureaucratization and the decline of local-elite control in the Bandit-Suppression Areas was the change in these areas of the name of the offices in the ch'ü government from *kung-so* (a traditional term for local organizations controlled by the gentry and local elite) to *shu* (which was a standard appellation for a bureaucratic office).[179]

Financial control at the local level was the big bone of contention between the local elites and agents of the Nationalist regime. The local elites vigorously exercised their acquired right, for example, to levy surtaxes and t'an-k'uan in order to support security, construction, and other local programs. Seldom did they forward these revenues to the hsien authorities, and frequently they siphoned portions of these monies into their own pockets. As a consequence, the Nationalist authorities often viewed the rural elites as competitors rather than partners in local government[180]

Nationalist authorities were also concerned about the loss of revenues resulting from the wholesale evasion of taxes by the landlords. Kiangsu provincial authorities, for example, issued orders stating that such practices could not be tolerated, and landlords who persisted in defying these orders were smeared with the evil-sounding label, *t'u-hao lieh-shen*—"local bullies and evil gentry." So-called t'u-hao lieh-shen also diked flood plains near the rivers and then refused to pay taxes on the reclaimed lands. Disputes over the taxes on these polder fields, in some instances involving as much as 4,500 acres, sometimes led to armed confrontations between government agents and the local powers.[181] These confrontations with t'u-hao lieh-shen were, of course, only extreme manifestations of the disparities between government and landlord interests. As noted earlier, however, the unremitting search of the regime for tax revenue was creating economic distress for many landlords. The Fei clan, whose fortunes prospered until 1927 and then sharply declined, thus stands as a symbol of the tension existing in the relationship between the regime and the landlords as a class.

Control of police and military powers at the local level was another area of contention between the local elites and the regime. In the environment of social instability and banditry that pervaded the countryside since the early nineteenth century, local elites had formed numerous militia corps, ostensibly to maintain local defense. These militia enormously buttressed the power of the local elite—the best of whom merely profited from the irregular surtaxes that were levied to support the militia; the worst of whom used these petty armies to terrorize the region. These autonomous armed forces were an obstacle to Nationalist control at the local level, and throughout the decade governmental authorities worked to replace them with police, militia, and *pao-chia* units that were amenable to bureaucratic rather than gentry control. But even in Kiangsu, where Nationalist authority was most pervasive, the contest with the local elites was never fully decided.[182]

In a multiplicity of ways, therefore, the Nationalist regime was attempting to displace the local elite's control over the police, militia, taxation, and other matters of local government. "Nanking," Philip A. Kuhn has perceptively remarked, "was on a collision course with sub-county satraps who could neither insure local security nor transmit sufficient revenues upwards."[183]

To deny that the Nanking government was an instrument of landlord or urban-capitalist class interests is not to deny that the interests of the regime and those classes sometimes coincided. Each feared social revolution; each feared the communists. And, needless to say, the network of personal relationships did not stop at the edge of the bureaucracy, and landlords and capitalists were not blind to the officials' susceptibility to bribes. *Some* landlords and *some* capitalists were consequently able through the patronage of individual officials to win special favors. There frequently existed, therefore, a certain affinity between the Nationalist regime and the landlords and capitalists. At base, however, there was an inherent tension between them: the landlords and capitalists aspired to preserve the existing order; the regime, by contrast, was working to maximize its power and to construct a new political system. The long-term goals of the regime and of the landlord and capitalist classes were therefore fundamentally dissimilar.[184]

Chapter 6 **On the Eve of the War**

China in 1936 and 1937 was a markedly changed nation from what it had been a decade earlier. Despite widespread inefficiency and corruption, the country was being integrated politically and territorially to a degree not known since at least 1915. And in numerous ways, China was taking on the attributes of a modern nation. The law codes, for example, had been completely rewritten. The unequal treaties, in existence for nearly a century, had in most cases been abrogated. The educational system had grown impressively: according to official statistics, the number of students in primary schools had increased between 1931 and 1937 by 86 percent and by 94 percent in the universities.[1] And, for the first time in China's history, the currency of the nation was unified.

In a material way the changes—at least in the cities—were perhaps even more impressive. Modern-style office buildings had sprung up in many of the larger cities, and paved boulevards ran through what had been dense warrens of humanity. Electrical and water-supply systems had ramified through many major urban areas, and sanitation in some centers had noticeably improved. The growing presence of radios and rolled cigarettes, of movies and automobiles, of cabarets and

Western dress also testified to the impact of Western ways. As a team of American observers in 1935 reported, albeit with a bit too much enthusiasm: "In all fields, a vast change is coming over China: a modernization that, as compared with ten or even five years ago, marks many centuries."[2]

Many of the construction projects—such as the welter of statues, the arch bridges, and the ornate governmental structures—were questionable contributions to the program of national reconstruction. An American who was otherwise impressed by the "settling down" and "opening up" that he discerned, remarked for example that the "immense amount of money and labor spent on monuments, Spirit Valley Shrines, and national recreation parks in commemoration of events . . . makes one wonder how far the authorities have any real comprehension of the character or magnitude of the task that lies before them."[3] Yet, for many Chinese living in the cities, life had undoubtedly improved during the decade of Kuomintang rule. Western technology was increasing the amenities; the decline of prices meant a higher standard of living for persons on fixed salaries; and, for the politically non-involved, there was greater political stability than there had been in the preceding decade or was to be in the ensuing one. Not surprisingly, many Chinese today look back upon the Nanking period as a "golden decade." The really momentous change since the early 1930s, however, was a psychological one. Mid- and late-1936 marked the turning-point.

The New National Mood

The National Salvation Movement. One of the most burning political issues for China during the 1930s was how to respond to Japanese aggression. Following the Japanese attack on Manchuria in September 1931, an infuriated Chinese nation called for resistance to the invader, and the Nineteenth Route Army became national heroes after they defied the orders of Nanking by fighting the Japanese at Shanghai.

But Nanking had remained steadfast in the conviction that to become entangled in a war with Japan before the unification and reconstruction of the nation had been completed would be to invite certain disaster. "First unite within," Chiang Kai-shek had declared, "then resist the enemy without." The Nanking government therefore engaged in almost continual warfare during the 1930s, but its guns were pointed against the communists and "rebellious warlords" and seldom toward the Japanese.

By March 1933 Japan had forcibly occupied all four provinces in Manchuria. For a brief time in 1933, the Nationalist troops staged a heroic fight to prevent the spread of the Japanese south of the Great Wall. Resistance soon collapsed, however, and by May the Imperial Army was only thirteen miles from Peiping. Nanking at this point agreed to the humiliating terms of the Tangku Truce.[4] Thereafter, for three years, Nanking repeatedly granted concessions to the Japanese in an effort to buy time.

Whether or not this policy of appeasement was the wisest possible will perhaps always be debated. Many then as now were convinced that the swiftest way for the central government to unite the country would be to stand up to the Japanese and, if necessary, fight. What is not in question, however, is that Nanking's policy had the effect, in the short run at least, of broadening the already gaping chasm between the government and the public.

Despite the deep currents of anti-Japanese sentiment that coursed through China, public outrage against the Japanese after 1932 was muted. Nationalist repression scattered the leadership of anti-Japanese groups, radical students and professors were expelled or arrested, boycotts of Japanese goods were suppressed, and censors combed the press for every innuendo at which the hypersensitive Japanese might take offense. Hatred of the Japanese was ever close to the surface, but the years 1932 to 1935 formed an interlude during which domestic concerns overshadowed the Japanese problem.

The Japanese problem leaped abruptly to the forefront again in early 1935. For several months there had been auguries that a rapprochement between Nanking and Tokyo was in the making. China, for its part, offered to conclude a treaty of friendship with Japan on the condition that the principle of absolute equality between the two nations be respected. And, to the Japanese foreign ministry, this suggested that Nanking was prepared to exclude the Western powers from a role in China and to accept the economic, political, and military assistance and advice of the Japanese government. If the Japanese military had not suddenly intervened, the Sino-Japanese issue might have been resolved on these general terms.[5]

During 1935 the military in Japan were exerting increasing influence on the machinery of government. Above all, they felt that Japan must pursue a "positive" foreign policy and they consequently viewed with antipathy the Foreign Ministry's attempt to reach a settlement in China. Rather than bolster Chiang Kai-shek and the Nanking government, as the Foreign Ministry's policy would do, the army officers would weaken Chinese central authority wherever possible. Moreover, the Japanese Kwantung army had fully digested the gains of the Tangku Truce, and it was now restive and looking for new action.[6]

The Army therefore sabotaged the approaching rapprochement between Nanking and Tokyo by manufacturing a series of crises in north China, which culminated in June 1935 in the Ho–Umezu Agreement. In accordance with the terms of this agreement, all armies of the central government and all Kuomintang organizations were to be removed from Hopei. The agreement also called for the suppression of Blue Shirt activities in the province.[7]

Two weeks later, on June 27, a similar agreement between General Ch'in Te-ch'un and General Doihara Kenji resulted in the evacuation of much of Chahar by Nanking's military and party representatives. A further outgrowth of Japanese pressures was the promulgation by Nanking on June 10 of a "Goodwill Mandate," in which Nanking promised to punish all "discriminatory or provocative speeches or acts" against "friendly nations."[8]

These concessions merely tantalized the Japanese military, who were now acting with few restraints from the civilians in Tokyo. "The first step [of Japanese] national policy," declared the commander of the North China Garrison, General Tada Hayao, in September 1935, "is to make North China . . . a paradise for coexistence and mutual prosperity of the two nations." Other statements, emanating from Tokyo as well as the army in Tientsin, soon removed all doubt that the Japanese had determined to wrench from Nationalist authority the five provinces of Hopei, Shantung, Shansi, Chahar, and Suiyuan. There they would create an "autonomous" Chinese government in which Japanese political, financial, and economic control would be paramount.[9]

Chiang Kai-shek responded to these Japanese pressures by reaffirming his policy of appeasement. Addressing the Fifth Party Congress on November 12, 1935, Chiang declared, "We shall not lightly talk about sacrifice until we are driven to the last extremity which makes sacrifice inevitable."[10] Chiang, it is true, added a phrase asserting that there were limits to China's willingness to compromise. The emphasis, however, was still clearly on appeasement.

The students in north China had watched the erosion of Chinese authority with growing frustration and bewilderment. The Nanking government, it appeared, would acquiesce in Japanese domination of north China just as it had done in Manchuria. But political repression had taken a heavy toll, and the students had lost the organization and leadership that had characterized the student movement of 1931. During October and November 1935, however, new life was gradually breathed into the long-dormant student movement. By November 1, for example, several student groups in Peiping and Tientsin presented a petition to the central government requesting an end to political repression. They sought the freedoms of press, speech, and assembly and guarantees against unlawful arrest so that, they said, "we can fulfill our responsibilities" at a time of national danger.[11]

Not until General Ho Ying-ch'in came to Peiping on December 3, however, did the student movement again become a vital force. Ho Ying-ch'in had signed the humiliating agreement with Umezu just five months earlier, and the students now feared that he was in Peiping to surrender the five northern provinces to Japan. Furious with Nanking's pusillanimity, students of Peiping on December 9 demonstrated in the streets of the city, protesting the formation of so-called autonomous governments and demanding that civil war in the country be stopped so that the nation could unitedly fight against Japan. The police, commanded as a result of the Ho–Umezu Agreement by officers who were friendly to Japan, met the demonstrators with water hoses, pistol butts, and the blunt edges of their swords.[12]

The students were bested by the police that day, but on December 16 they organized a second demonstration, which, with almost 8,000 participants, was over twice as large as those at the height of the May Fourth Movement. And, by the end of the month, the student movement across the country had been jolted back to life. The events of this period were to go down in history as the December Ninth Movement.[13]

The banner of national salvation that the students had raised in December was soon taken up also by other segments of society. As early as December 27, 1935, a number of lawyers, journalists, and writers formed the Shanghai Cultural Workers National Salvation Association. Other groups dedicated to the cause of united national resistance to Japan—women, workers, professors, and merchants—soon formed their own national salvation associations. The movement remained relatively amorphous during the first half of 1936, but its members were intensely active. They evangelized the message of national salvation not only in the cities but even in the countryside where they lectured and staged propagandistic plays. Others worked to suppress Japanese smuggling, organized anti-Japanese boycotts, or, it was to be charged, carried on labor agitation in Japanese-owned factories.[14] Their publications also flourished; each issue of the *Ta-chung sheng-huo* (Mass life), for example, sold approximately 120,000 copies before it was banned, a circulation figure reached by no other Chinese periodical prior to that time.[15]

Nanking viewed this movement with embarrassment and suspicion. It was embarrassed, because the activities of the students violated the Goodwill Mandate. And it was suspicious, for there ran through the movement an anti-appeasement current so deep that it potentially at least posed a threat to the government. As even one of the right-wing, anti-communist student groups declared in February 1936, "We never support the present government blindly. We support the government that will resist the enemy. If the present government takes no steps to resist the enemy within the year, we also want to throw it out."[16]

Later in the spring, the movement became less overtly critical of the government—reflecting, perhaps, the Communist Party's decision at that time to strive for a united front with Chiang Kai-shek. Nevertheless, the national salvation movement was always to the "left" of the government. And its declaration in May 1936 that it would "use sanctions against any party or group" that weakened a united stand against Japan, demonstrated that its loyalty to Nanking remained tentative and conditional.[17]

Because of the national salvation movement's at least latent anti-government stance, the conjunction of three events in late May and early June 1936 might have, but significantly did not, put an end to Chiang Kai-shek's rule in Nanking. First, the national salvation movement was becoming organizationally cohesive. On May 29 a National Student Association, which was closely linked with the national salvation movement, was formed. Two days later, on May 31, sixty representatives from eighteen cities met in Shanghai and formed the All-China Federation of National Salvation Associations. Anti-Japanese sentiment was being woven into an organized political force.[18]

Second, events in north China were fanning national salvationist sentiment to new peaks of emotionalism. During the last two weeks of May, the Japanese suddenly began sending in shiploads of troops, tanks, and other equipment. The number of troop reinforcements was in dispute: the Japanese stated that only five thousand men had arrived; the word among the Chinese, however, was that fifty thousand had been unloaded. These reinforcements augured a new Japanese thrust in the north, and to many observers it appeared that a "second Mukden Incident" was in the making. In response to these developments, several thousand students in Tientsin demonstrated and declared a five-day strike. A bomb explosion on a railway bridge outside Tientsin heightened the tension in the city. Soon the demonstrations against the Japanese increase of troops spread to Peiping, then Shanghai, and even Canton, as both student and national salvationist groups added their weight to the protest.[19]

And, third, with the national salvation movement reaching an organizational and emotional peak, the two Southwest provinces, Kwangtung and Kwangsi, revolted.

Revolt of the Southwest. By the mid-1930s, Chiang Kai-shek's strategy of national unification was showing progress. Most of the great warlords, who had engaged in the civil wars of the period 1928–1931, were no longer prominent on the national scene. Feng Yü-hsiang, for example, resided in Nanking, effectively stripped of both political and military power. Yen Hsi-shan, who in any case was never as adventuresome in national politics as Feng, did retain power in Shansi, but he had been tamed and was now largely subservient to Nanking. Some provinces, such as Shantung, Szechuan, Yunnan, Honan, and Kweichow, still in 1935 retained greater or lesser degrees of independence of Nanking.

It was, however, Kwangtung and Kwangsi that were as a beam in Chiang Kai-shek's eye. These were the only provinces that in 1935 posed a potential challenge to the national preeminence of Nanking. In the province of Kwangtung, the Southwest authorities possessed a source of wealth which could rival that of the Yangtze basin. In the rulers of Kwangsi, Li Tsung-jen and Pai Ch'ung-hsi, they had military commanders of consummate ability whose hatred for Chiang

Kai-shek was legendary. And, in Hu Han-min, they had the one Kuomintang leader whose public stature still rivaled that of Chiang. As long as Kwangtung and Kwangsi remained independent of Nanking, Chiang Kai-shek's power was insecure.

The turning point in Nanking's relations with the Southwest was 1934. Until this time, Kwangtung and Kwangsi had fumed and scolded at Nanking, knowing that they were protected from Chiang Kai-shek's retribution by a protective buffer formed by a row of provinces that were themselves largely independent of the central government. With the suppression of the Fukien rebellion, however, armies loyal to Nanking hovered on the northern border of Kwangtung. Even more decisive had been the expulsion of the communists from Kiangsi in October of the same year. As the Nationalist troops pursued the retreating communist forces, Chiang was presented with a rich opportunity to extend his control to provinces that had hitherto remained beyond his grasp. The authorities in Kweichow, for example, granted the central government army access to the province to fight the communists. With his troops in the province, Chiang gained a purchase with which to exert pressure on the local administration. In this manner, the three provinces of Kweichow, Yunnan, and Szechuan quickly lost their freedom of maneuver, although they retained considerable administrative autonomy.[20]

As these southern provinces fell within Nanking's sphere of influence, the leaders of Kwangtung and Kwangsi perceived that Chiang Kai-shek was gaining a strategic advantage over them. They were furious, therefore, when units of the central government army remained encamped in Kweichow even after the communists had escaped farther to the west. In a telegram, they bitterly asked Chiang: "How is this exterminating communists?"[21] In addition to building up troop strength near the borders of Kwangtung and Kwangsi, Nanking was constructing a series of airfields in Hunan, and the Hankow–Canton railroad was being rushed to completion.[22]

Already Chiang's forces were within easy striking distance of the provincial capitals of Canton and Kweilin.

The cruelest blow came in the spring of 1935, when Kwei-chow, under pressure from Nanking, diverted the opium trade from Kwangsi. Until this time, opium from Szechuan and Yunnan had been shipped through Kwangsi, a trade that provided some ¥17 million in transit taxes each year.[23] This had been the largest single source of revenue for the Kwangsi authorities, whose own province was so impoverished that they were always on the brink of destitution.

The economic stability of both Southwest provinces was threatened also by a monetary crisis occasioned by Nanking's currency reform. After November 1935 the currencies issued by provincial banks were no longer regarded by the Nationalist government as legal tender and moreover were not exchangeable for foreign money. Although the Kwangtung and Kwangsi currencies continued to be legal in those provinces, the fact that they could not be exchanged for legal tender elsewhere resulted in a severe loss of fiscal confidence. The effects of the depreciated currency struck particularly hard in Kwangsi where, for example, the price of rice was at one time five times higher than normally.[24] Steadily, inexorably, Chiang's stranglehold on the Southwest was tightening.

As relations between Nanking and the Southwest worsened, attention focused on the frail figure of Hu Han-min. As long as Hu remained in the south, there was ever some question regarding the legitimacy of the Nanking government. Conversely, if Hu were to become reconciled with Nanking, Kwangtung and Kwangsi could easily be labeled rebels against the orthodox line of succession to Sun Yat-sen.

By late 1935 no one was certain whether Hu would remain in Hong Kong or return to Nanking. He had become almost completely alienated from Ch'en Chi-t'ang. Not only had General Ch'en stopped making even a show of respecting Hu's policy recommendations; he had also abruptly cut Hu's stipend in half. No longer could Hu afford the lavish establishment in Hong Kong, in which he reportedly employed some thirty servants, five secretaries, and two famed chefs. Thus, when Hu Han-min left in June 1935 for medical treatment in Europe, he was filled with pique and uncertain about his political future.[25] Chiang Kai-shek seized this occasion to invite Hu Han-min back to Nanking. In November 1935 Hu was named chairman of the Central Executive Committee—the highest post in the Kuomintang. (Chiang was named vice-chairman.) And, when Hu was returning from Europe in January 1936, one of Nanking's most prominent officials, Chü Cheng, rushed to Hong Kong to await Hu and to persuade him to move to Nanking.[26]

The Southwest authorities were deeply perturbed by these maneuvers. As Huang Hsü-ch'u, the leading civil authority in Kwangsi at that time, subsequently remarked, "If Hu went to Nanking, the Southwest's defensive screen would be lost and the ramparts would collapse." The Southwest therefore sent its own representative to Singapore to meet Hu before Chü Cheng could reach him. At the same time, both Ch'en Chi-t'ang and Li Tsung-jen showered Hu Han-min with assurances of their respect and goodwill.[27]

The Southwest won this duel for the affections of Hu Han-min. Presumably Hu's enmity for Chiang Kai-shek was even more deep-seated than his distaste for Ch'en Chi-t'ang. Yet Ch'en was sufficiently uncertain of Hu's loyalties that he prevailed on Hu to reside in Canton rather than in Hong Kong. And, once in Canton, Hu was kept a "virtual prisoner." The guards outside Hu's house, the American consul reported, were there "more to detain than to protect him."[28] For a time, at least, the Southwest had held the bulwarks against Chiang Kai-shek's centralizing tactics.

The catalyst in this turbid political mix was the sudden, unexpected death of Hu Han-min. On the evening of May 9, 1936, while playing chess at the home of his brother-in-law, Hu collapsed of a cerebral hemorrhage. Three days later, at the age of fifty-two, he died. Immediately following Hu's death, the Kwangtung authorities made public his last will and testament. Hu, it was officially reported, had been in a semi-coma since his stroke. Shortly before his death, however, his mind cleared, and he dictated a political testament that called for termination of dictatorial rule, resistance to Japan, and suppression of the communists.[29]

This document quickly became the subject of controversy, for it seemed to suit the political purposes of the Southwest authorities too neatly. It not only implied that Chiang Kai-shek was a rebel against the true doctrines of Sun Yat-sen, but, by urging resistance to Japan, it called for an end to the growing pressures on Kwangtung and Kwangsi. These political implications, together with the miraculously sudden lucidity of Hu's mind just before his death, caused many to believe that the will had been forged.[30]

As befitted a leader of the revolution and an intimate of Sun Yat-sen, Hu Han-min was honored by a lavish state funeral that lasted three days. Even Nanking proclaimed the nation in mourning for its erstwhile enemy, and it sent a high-level delegation consisting of Wang Ch'ung-hui, Sun Fo, and others to participate in the ceremonies.[31]

The significance of Hu's funeral lay not in the encomiums to the dead so much as in the negotiations affecting the future. For Nanking's delegation had closeted with the Southwest leaders and presented a demand that Kwangtung and Kwangsi now submit to the authority of the central government.[32]

For several months, the Southwest leaders had been discussing how they could resist Nanking's encroachments. Now Chiang Kai-shek had thrown down the gauntlet, and the Southwest leaders determined to meet the challenge in a desperate effort to preserve their regional power.[33] They moved precipitately. Their conversations with Wang Ch'ung-hui had taken place no earlier than May 25; and on June 1 mobilization orders were dispatched to the armies of both provinces.[34] There was therefore little time for scrupulous planning or preparations.

The extemporaneous character of the revolt is suggested by the fact that the leaders were not even certain what they should declare as a pretext for rebelling against central authority. Ch'en Chi-t'ang had at first proposed rebelling in the name of opposition to the "illegal constitution" that had been promulgated on May 5. The Kwangsi leaders laughed off this suggestion, however, recognizing that the draft constitution was anything but a visceral popular issue.[35] Finally they hit on the solution. As Huang Hsü-ch'u recalls: "But what purpose should we proclaim? To win the people's sympathy and still maintain righteousness, nothing surpassed 'resistance to Japan.' "[36] The Southwest would, in other words, join forces with the potentially powerful national salvation movement.

What was the ultimate goal of the Southwest leaders in rebelling? Even now, their motives are unclear, and it is possible that the Southwest had acted so hastily after receiving the demand to submit to Nanking's authority that they themselves were not clear regarding their goals. One interpretation, however, is that the Southwest hoped simply to embarrass Nanking; that by announcing their determination to fight Japan, Nanking would not dare attack a movement so apparently noble in its motives.[37]

Nanking was less certain that the Southwest's intentions were so relatively benign, and there is in fact evidence that the Southwest actually intended to overthrow the central government. According to one report, for example, Ch'en Chi-t'ang planned to organize a separate "anti-Japanese government"—a plan that was abandoned only after it became clear that regional militarists elsewhere in the country would not join the rebellion.[38] And the extremely agitated reaction to the rebellion of several of Kwangtung's own high-ranking members—the civilian elder-statesman Tsou Lu quickly left Canton, and several military officers were so outspokenly opposed that Ch'en Chi-t'ang placed them under surveillance[39]—at least suggests that the Southwest planned more than just a bluff to force Nanking to fight Japan.

(Li Tsung-jen—who should have been in a position to know —told a story about Ch'en Chi-t'ang that reinforces the impression that the Southwest authorities intended to overthrow the Nanking regime and illustrates how the warlords could be motivated by distinctly pre-modern calculations. According to Li, Ch'en had determined to revolt against Nanking after he had learned that the ancestors of Hung Hsiu-ch'üan, leader of the Taiping rebellion in the mid-nineteenth century, had been buried at their native place in Kwangtung at a point on top of "the mouth of a live dragon." Geomancers subsequently discerned, however, that the burial spot was a trifle too high. If the ancestors had been buried somewhat lower, they would have been located directly on the opening of the dragon's mouth—in which case Hung Hsiu-ch'üan, rather than dying in a defeated rebellion, would have been raised to the throne of a new dynasty. Hearing of this, Ch'en Chi-t'ang had bought the land from the Hung family and had reburied his mother's coffin at the precise opening of the dragon's mouth. This accomplished, Ch'en—who had hitherto always been excessively reluctant to become involved in politics outside his own province—had confidence that he could succeed in any undertaking, even in replacing Chiang Kai-shek as supreme leader of the nation.[40])

Whatever the intended strategy, the Southwest leaders had badly miscalculated. If they had aspired to topple the central government, they would, like the Fukien rebels, need the support of other potentially anti-Nanking militarists. In the event, however, none of them—from Ho Chien in the south to Sung Che-yüan in the north—gave even a hint of encouragement.

And if the Southwest leaders anticipated that the support of the Chinese masses would prevent Nanking from taking action against them, they were again proved wrong. Initially, it is true, there was some highly emotional popular support for the revolt. Students in Peiping staged a demonstration as evidence of its support, and publications of the national salvation movement declared that the incident was "a great victory for the anti-Japanese front."[41] Enthusiasm was dampened, however, when the public realized that the Southwest's anti-Japanese banner was merely a disguise for what was essentially just another factional power struggle. "Since the establishment of the Republic," observed the *Kuo-wen chou-pao,* "probably no civil war was greeted with more disgust and contempt than this one!"[42]

Most damaging to the credibility of the Southwest, perhaps, was the information—accurate in this instance—that Kwangsi had particularly close ties with the Japanese. Many of its military advisers were Japanese, and it had been buying airplanes, ammunition, machinery, and cement from Japan at bargain prices.[43] Li Tsung-jen and Pai Ch'ung-hsi doubtlessly deplored Japanese aggression as much as any other nationalistic Chinese; but in fortifying Kwangsi against their bête noire, Chiang Kai-shek, they had unquestionably compromised their anti-Japanese credentials.

The revolt of the Southwest lasted over three months, from June 1 to mid-September. Within days of the outbreak, however, it was apparent that the revolt would fail, and the only lingering question was how much the rebels could salvage from their forthcoming defeat.

Nanking was first apprised of trouble brewing in south China when on June 2 the leaders of Kwangtung and Kwangsi declared that China could no longer rely on the League of Nations to preserve her territorial sovereignty. Unless Nanking began a war of resistance, the telegram read, Peiping and Tientsin would be lost to Japan just as Manchuria had been three years previously. Two days later, still professing loyalty to the central government, the Southwest authorities demanded that the central government lead the nation's armies against Japan. At the same time, they changed the name of their armies to the Revolutionary Anti-Japanese National Salvation Army and began moving northward into Hunan province. By June 8 the vanguard of these forces had penetrated some sixty miles beyond the Kwangtung and Kwangsi borders.[44]

They were, however, to get no closer to the Japanese armies in north China. For, within days, at least ten government divisions blocked their passage. Some light skirmishes between the opposing armies broke out, but a civil war was avoided. Chiang Kai-shek had called their bluff, and the Southwest leaders—declaring that Nanking had unfortunately mistaken their motive, which was solely to fight the Japanese—on June 12 ordered their troops to stop the northward advance. The rebellion had stalled.[45]

For three weeks the troops of the Southwest and Nanking faced each other in southern Hunan, both sides anxious to avoid a trial of arms. The leaders of Kwangtung and Kwangsi knew that, without allies, their armies were no match for the central government forces. And Nanking feared that the renewal of civil war, especially if the fighting were protracted, might generate such strong political opposition that the regime could be overthrown.[46]

The first phase of the conflict, therefore, was resolved not on the battlefield but within the ranks of Ch'en Chi-t'ang's own troops. On July 4 forty pilots of the Cantonese air force suddenly flew to Hong Kong and thence defected to the central government with seven planes from Ch'en Chi-t'ang's air force. Four days later, General Yü Han-mou, retaining command of the Cantonese First Army, declared his loyalty to Nanking. Two Cantonese warships went over to the side of the central government on July 14. And on July 18 the entire remainder of Ch'en Chi-t'ang's air force—over 360 men with sixty-two airplanes—surrendered to the central government.[47]

Tai Li, incidentally, played a key role in at least the earliest of these defections. Slipping into Kwangtung disguised as a merchant, Tai contacted the air force officers, promising them ¥5 million and positions in the army of the central government if they would defect. H. H. Kung, then minister of finance, had initially balked at the exorbitant price that Tai had offered for these defections. As always, however, the rotund and complaisant "Daddy" Kung acquiesced. The flight of the first contingent of planes to Nanchang on July 4 was the result.[48]

By mid-July Ch'en Chi-t'ang's entire army was in virtual mutiny against him. His troops refused to fight their former comrades in the army of Yü Han-mou, which was now advancing on Canton. With the ground giving out from under him, Ch'en on July 18 boarded a British ship for Hong Kong, and the revolt of Kwangtung against the central government was over. (Ch'en had prepared well for this eventuality. On the ship with him were eighty large trunks that allegedly contained a sizable part of the province's silver reserves. And he had already stashed away in Hong Kong a fortune estimated at ￥30 million.[49] Warlordism, for some, was a highly profitable vocation.)

Kwangtung was now quickly incorporated into Nanking's scheme of administration. And on August 11 Chiang Kai-shek himself flew to Canton—his first visit there since the beginning of the Northern Expedition in 1926—to oversee pacification of the province and to direct the continuing operations against Kwangsi.

The central authorities' efforts to subjugate Kwangsi proceeded more slowly and with less success than they had in Kwangtung. The officers and men of the Kwangsi forces were closely tied by loyalty and respect to Li Tsung-jen and Pai Ch'ung-hsi, and no mass defections could be expected.[50] Chiang therefore endeavored to win over, not the underlings, but the Kwangsi leaders themselves by assuring them that they could retain the top military and civil posts in the Kwangsi administration if they would abandon their opposition to the central government. Following Ch'en Chi-t'ang's flight from Canton, Li Tsung-jen and Pai Ch'ung-hsi knew that Kwangsi could not hold off the central government forces. On July 24, therefore, they sent a telegram accepting the posts that had been offered them and requested Chiang to send an official to Nanking to administer the oaths of office on August 1.[51]

Peace might then have been restored to south China. But Chiang Kai-shek in late July felt himself in a much stronger position than two weeks earlier (before the collapse of Kwangtung) when he had first offered the appointments to Li and Pai. Rather than compromise with the Kwangsi leaders,

Chiang thought, he would eliminate Kwangsi regionalism once and for all. He therefore did not confirm Li and Pai's previous appointments and instead named them to nominally high posts which would, however, have transferred them from Kwangsi and stripped them of any real military power. The Kwangsi leaders rejected these new appointments, and civil war threatened the country once again.[52]

Li Tsung-jen and Pai Ch'ung-hsi did not have their hearts in this fight. They realized the military preponderance of the forces opposing them, but they were determined to retain if at all possible their power base in the province of Kwangsi. Their purpose in prolonging the struggle, therefore, was simply to improve their hands at the negotiation table. This relatively passive stance of the Kwangsi leaders was radically altered in mid-August, when veterans of the Nineteenth Route Army and the Fukien revolution arrived in the province to join the fight against Nanking. Li Chi-shen, Ts'ai T'ing-k'ai, Weng Chao-yüan, and Ou Shou-nien were among the most notable of these new arrivals. Ch'en Ming-shu and Eugene Ch'en were also reportedly hastening from abroad to participate in the reinvigorated rebellion.[53]

Ts'ai T'ing-k'ai quickly began organizing a new division of the Kwangsi army, composed in part of former Nineteenth Route Army soldiers who had rallied to the call of their former commander. At the same time, preparations were made for the formation of a "Chinese Republican People's Anti-Japanese National Salvation Military Government." Li Chi-shen, as in Fukien, was to be chairman of the new government, and Li Tsung-jen would hold the position of commander-in-chief of the army.[54]

It is unclear whether or not the military government was ever formally instituted. In any event, Li Tsung-jen and Pai Ch'ung-hsi were disinclined to carry on a bloody and bootless war against Chiang Kai-shek. They continued therefore to negotiate with Chiang's representatives, and by September 10 they had arranged the terms of a settlement. Kwangsi agreed to channel specified tax revenues to Nanking, but Nanking in return was to subsidize the Kwangsi army. Li Tsung-jen was confirmed in his command of the Kwangsi army, now using the title of pacification commissioner, and Huang Hsü-ch'u would retain control of the province's civil administration. Pai Ch'ung-hsi, however, would proceed to Nanking as a member of the standing committee of the military commission.[55]

On September 16 these three Kwangsi leaders took the oaths of their new offices. And, the same day, smarting from a sense of betrayal by Li and Pai, Ts'ai T'ing-k'ai and Li Chi-shen flew from Kwangsi to Hong Kong.[56] The revolt of the Southwest was over. Kwangsi retained much of its regional autonomy, but the rich and important province of Kwangtung was now securely under Nanking's control.

Chiang Kai-shek Becomes a National Leader. The Southwest rebellion caused a change in the national mood. With the collapse of the rebellion, it appeared that the nation had at last been unified. It was true that such provinces as Kwangsi, Shantung, Shansi, Szechuan, and Yunnan were still not fully responsive to the writ of the central government, yet neither were they sufficiently powerful to challenge the dominance of Nanking. Moreover, the suppression of the Southwest had been accomplished for the most part peacefully, which helped reassure the public—so weary of civil war—of the essential good faith of the Nanking leadership.

The element contributing most significantly to the new national mood was the fact that Chiang Kai-shek during the course of the rebellion had adopted an increasingly firm, if not exactly bellicose, stance toward Japan. The Southwest revolt, combined with the growing force of national salvationist sentiment, had forced Chiang on July 13 to proclaim that he would make no further concessions to the Japanese. China, he declared, was prepared to make the "ultimate sacrifice" of waging a war with Japan rather than tolerate further aggressions on her territorial integrity. As before, Chiang asserted that he still hoped to resolve the conflict peacefully; this time, however, he stressed the *limits* of appeasement rather than appeasement itself.[57]

This declaration was undoubtedly intended to defuse popular support for the rebelling Southwest, and many observers questioned the sincerity of his declaration.[58] It is now clear, however, that Chiang's attitude had in fact hardened toward Japan and that he was at last beginning to align himself with the anti-Japanese spirit of the nation.

Evidence of this is found in an extraordinary memorandum that he presented in secret to the Central Political Council on August 4, 1936. Here Chiang expressed a willingness to make far-reaching compromises in order to preserve peace with Japan. He was prepared to make "painful economic concessions" to Japan, and would even grant "special privileges" to Japan in Manchuria so long as Japan did not insist on legalizing the status of an "independent" Manchukuo. In a key article of the document, however, Chiang stipulated that if Japan anywhere encroached further upon Chinese territory, "armed resistance must be offered *without regard for the consequences.*"[59]

Chiang's new-found determination to block Japanese aggression was soon put to the test, for relations between the two countries were rapidly becoming inflamed. During August and September a series of murders of Japanese citizens in China infuriated the Japanese government, which complained that "anti-Japanese terrorism is becoming rampant throughout China."[60] First, mobs in Chengtu beat four Japanese, killing two of them. Then a druggist in Kwangtung, who had lived in China for twenty years and was married to a Chinese woman, was beaten to death by an angry anti-Japanese mob. In Shanghai, three sailors were shot down in the street and one of them died. Shortly afterwards, a consular policeman was found murdered in Hankow.[61]

Rather than retreat before this show of Chinese animosity, the Japanese seemingly went out of their way to aggravate Chinese sensitivities. In late October, for instance, the Imperial Army staged "autumn maneuvers" in north China. For ten days Japanese soldiers struck through Chinese territory, practicing street fighting in Peiping and Tientsin and rehearsing the takeover of centers of communication and transportation.[62] No nationalistic Chinese could mistake Japan's ultimate intentions.

Chinese patriotism was particularly aroused by the Japanese attempt in August to seize the province of Suiyüan. Under the slogan of "Mongolia for the Mongols," troops of Mongolians and Manchurians, armed and supported by the Japanese Kwantung Army, attempted to establish an "independent" state under the Mongolian Prince Teh (Te Wang). Chinese forces initially put up little resistance, but in November Nanking responded with unprecedented bellicosity. "The Japanese Kwantung Army," declared a government spokesman, "underestimates the determination of the Chinese people and their government. The time has ended when foreign nations could safely nibble away at Chinese territorial fringes. If the Kwantung Army think they can do this, they will come into contact with the forces of the Central Government, and, if they hope to localize the incident, they will be sadly mistaken. This would mean war."[63] True to these words, Chinese troops under the command of Fu Tso-i routed the invaders, and restored Suiyüan to Nanking's authority during November and December.

In the midst of these events, the Japanese ambassador Kawagoe Shigeru and the Chinese foreign minister Chang Ch'ün were locked in negotiations that lasted from September to December 1936. The Japanese military at this time held the upper hand in Tokyo, and Kawagoe therefore confronted Chang Ch'ün with what were perhaps Japan's maximal demands. These included recognition of the autonomy of an area in north China consisting of the five provinces of Hopei, Shansi, Shantung, Chahar, and Suiyüan; appointment by Nanking of Japanese advisers; and sharp reduction of tariffs on Japanese imports. Chang Ch'ün countered Kawagoe's demands with demands of his own. China, he asserted, would not negotiate unless Chinese sovereignty were fully respected and unless economic relations between the two countries were conducted on the principle of mutual benefit.[64]

Not since 1932 had relations with Japan been as strained as they became during these last three months of 1936. It appeared to some that war was imminent. Yet Nanking did not bend. Suiyüan remained in Nationalist hands, and the negotiations with Kawagoe broke off in early December with no compromises having been extracted.

The combination of these several political events—the firm resistance to Japanese pressure and the enhanced unity of the country after the defeat of the revolt of the Southwest, together with the improving economic conditions in the country —had an extraordinary psychological impact on the Chinese people. "At the moment," Nathaniel Peffer reported in October 1936, "Chinese are inclined to a mood of confidence and impassioned patriotism." And the *Ta-kung pao* editorialized in December, "In the period of the last few months, the people's confidence seems as though it was revived from the dead."[65]

Even the intellectuals' opposition to the regime was being tempered. "Where they were red or pink previously," the *China Weekly Review* observed in November, "they are only ruddy now." It is true that many intellectuals and a great many of the youth never became wholly reconciled to the Kuomintang. Yet they, like other Chinese, were being swayed by nationalistic passions, and they now seemed more prone to overlook the persistence of governmental maladministration and police repression than they had been in earlier years.[66]

The chief political beneficiary of this new national mood was Chiang Kai-shek. For years Chinese had misdoubted the man, thinking that his expressed determination to unify the nation before he would fight Japan was only a cowardly excuse to suppress domestic rivals. Now, however, with the warlords subdued and the communists seemingly defeated, Chiang was acting true to his words. Suddenly the public viewed the Generalissimo as a resolute and farseeing leader, one who had braved derision and criticism because he had perceived that it would be calamitous to fight Japan when Chinese were still fighting among themselves.

Indeed, a personality cult was growing around him. His fiftieth birthday on October 29, 1936, for example, was made the occasion for extravagant acclaim. For the greater part of a year preparations had been made for this signal event. An enormous campaign, "probably the most extensive ever staged in the land,"[67] was launched to raise money to buy airplanes as the nation's gift to its leader. At first, most contributions were mandatory—officials, for example, had a specified portion of their salaries deducted—and the campaign reeked of the coercive money-raising schemes that were familiar to all Chinese. By October, however, the popular attitude toward Chiang had so changed that there was apparent in the celebrations a spark of spontaneous enthusiasm.[68]

It is always difficult in such matters to sort out the genuinely popular elements from those that are officially inspired. The following quotation is, however, an interesting and not too extraordinary example of the acclaim being accorded Chiang Kai-shek in late 1936. It was entitled, "The Chinese Have Found Their Leader":

For a quarter of a century, we, like Diogenes, have been carrying a lantern in broad daylight to search everywhere for our Leader . . . We have been a herd of sheep without a shepherd, left to perish from the stormy weather and devoured by the marauding tigers. "Come out, our Leader! Come out, our Leader!" But this cry, though echoed and re-echoed throughout the whole country, brought no response and no Leader to us . . .

But in the background and amidst the pitch darkness, we saw a bright figure steadily arising to dwarf all the other ugly figures surrounding him. [A reference to the Kuomintang?] We rubbed our eyes and made certain if our vision was true.

After a long waiting and desperate search, we, to our great joy, have at long last found our Leader. The small bright figure which we saw a few days ago has now grown to a real giant, and the erstwhile star has transformed itself into a radiant sun. Basking under its sunshine, we have regained our customary composure and peacefulness, we have recovered our lost confidence and hope, we have had no more fear of the storm and tigers, and we have united in our strength as well as our purpose.[69]

Such fulsome praise must be discounted by half. Nevertheless, the point is that Chiang Kai-shek was being viewed by a large part of the Chinese population as a true and inexpendable national leader even before the Sian Incident.

That the Sian Incident occurred, however, points out the truth that support for Chiang was not universal. There had remained an ambiguity in his hardening attitude toward Japan, for he remained convinced that the communists were a greater evil than the Japanese. Some observers therefore were suspicious of Chiang even in late 1936, thinking that—despite Nanking's new stance toward the Japanese—he was still committed to the patently bankrupt policy of forcing national unity before resisting foreign aggression.[70]

And Chiang Kai-shek had, in fact, never wavered in his determination to complete the extermination of the Red Army. As a consequence, even during the Japanese-inspired offensive against Suiyüan, he had pressed ahead with his preparations for a "final" push against the communists. He had committed none of the central-government armies to the fighting; instead he moved three of his crack divisions under the command of Hu Tsung-nan into Kansu for an offensive against the Soviet area. The airplanes that had been presented to the nation on his birthday were flown, not to the anti-Japanese front in Suiyüan but to the anti-communist headquarters at Sian. And in late November, when nationalistic passions were at a feverish pitch, his police agents in Shanghai arrested seven leaders of the National Salvation Association—who subsequently became known as the Seven Gentlemen (*ch'i chün-tzu*)—presumably for their outspoken advocacy of a united anti-Japanese front between the communists and the Kuomintang.

Few were more perturbed or more directly affected by Chiang Kai-shek's anti-communist obsession than the soldiers of the Northwest Bandit-Suppression Forces under the command of Chang Hsüeh-liang. Routed from Manchuria after 1931, these troops were now stationed in Shensi and Kansu, their ostensible objective being to eradicate the last vestiges of communism in China. But these natives of Manchuria had little zeal for their task. Under the agitation of militant young officers, the soldiers felt their real enemy was the Japanese who had occupied their home provinces. And they had learned that the communists were not only fearsome opponents but were true patriots. Chang Hsüeh-liang shared these sentiments of his men, and by autumn 1936 the Bandit-Suppression Forces had virtually joined hands with the communists in a spirit of common enmity to the Japanese. The city of Sian thereafter became the focal point of the anti-Japanese movement. A branch of the National Salvation Association was formed there in October. And mass meetings, sometimes with as many as 12,000 demonstrators marching in the streets, proclaimed slogans calling for resistance to Japan and for an end to civil war.

These events infuriated Chiang Kai-shek. He was convinced that he could eliminate the communist nemesis with one last assault. He therefore rejected Chang Hsüeh-liang's entreaties to cooperate with the communists in fighting the Japanese in Suiyüan. Instead, he flew to Sian in late October, and personally ordered Chang Hsüeh-liang to launch an attack against the communists. A month passed, and the offensive did not materialize. Thus, on December 4 he again flew to Sian, determined to force the recalcitrant Manchurians into battle. After a week of fruitless exhortations and harangues, Chiang stripped Chang Hsüeh-liang of his command, replaced him with the loyal Chiang Ting-wen and ordered that the anti-communist offensive begin on December 12.

This sudden turn of events forced the hand of the Manchurians. In a series of events that are too well known to be detailed here, the militants under Chang Hsüeh-liang staged a coup, taking Chiang Kai-shek prisoner in the pre-dawn hours of December 12. Their goal was to force Chiang to halt the civil war, remove restrictions on "patriotic" political activities, and convene a national conference to determine future policy toward Japan. For two weeks, although in danger of his life, Chiang apparently refused to agree to these demands. Only after the communists interceded was Chiang released. On December 25, limping from a painful back injury incurred when he had tried to escape the mutineers, Chiang flew back to Nanking.

A fascinating and perhaps the most significant aspect of the Sian Incident was the Chinese public's response. When news of Chiang's kidnapping on December 12 had been announced, a pall of gloom had fallen over most of the nation. Children, it was reported, could not sleep; soldiers wept; and illiterates badgered those who read the newspapers in order to learn the most recent dispatches from Sian. And, when Chiang was released, a flood of relief and joy spread over the country. Happy demonstrators paraded through the streets, and the air reverberated with the sound of firecrackers.[71]

As evidenced by this public display, Chang Hsüeh-liang and the radical Manchurian officers had misjudged Chiang Kai-shek's new stature as a national leader. Most thinking citizens probably sympathized with the thrust of Chang Hsüeh-liang's demands, which was that China should fight the Japanese rather than other Chinese. Yet they had also acquired trust in Chiang Kai-shek, believing that he was irreplaceable in this period of national crisis.

The Sian Incident produced no clear denouement in national policy or in Kuomintang–communist relations. On the one hand, it appeared as if Nanking's hatred of the communists remained as firm as before the incident. Preparations for the trial of the "Seven Gentlemen" continued; the blockade of the soviet areas was resumed; and the rebellious Manchurian troops in Shensi–Kansu were replaced by forces known to be loyal to Chiang Kai-shek.

At the same time, however, Chiang could not totally disregard national sentiment, and he moved gradually toward rapprochement with the forces of Mao Tse-tung. Actual fighting with the communists did not recur; the name "Bandit-Suppression Forces" was quietly dropped from the title of the army in the northwest; the allegedly pro-Japanese Chang Ch'un was replaced as foreign minister; and the communists were invited to send representatives to the National People's Congress that was scheduled for November 1937.

When the fighting at the Marco Polo Bridge erupted on July 7, 1937, the united front between Yenan and Nanking had still not been consummated. But the foundation for cooperation had been laid. China was readying for war. Never had Chiang Kai-shek's popularity been greater.

A Balance-Sheet of the Decade

Much that has been written in the early chapters of this study has pointed to negative aspects of Kuomintang rule. Yet, when the first rifle shot sounded at the Marco Polo Bridge, twelve miles west of Peiping, on the night of July 7, 1937, China was unquestionably more unified and better armed than at any time during the preceding decade. What conclusions may then be drawn regarding the achievements of the Nationalists?

Despite the paucity of scholarly studies of the Nanking period, there does exist one clearly distinguishable school of interpretation. This interpretation has been strikingly summarized by Paul K. T. Sih. "Policy," Sih contends, "was sound; leadership was intelligent. Had it not been for the outbreak of the Resistance War against the Japanese invasion in July 1937, China would have been able to attain the status of a new, modern society, whereby the Principles of the Three Peoples would have been fully realized."[72] My own interpretation differs sharply from that of Sih. Yet it must be admitted that, on the surface at least, there were indications that the political system being created by the Nationalists might have proved viable if the war with Japan had not intervened.

In assessing Nationalist achievements, we must be cautious not to demand the impossible. It would be fatuous, for example, to expect that any government, however vigorous and enlightened, could have created—even if there had not been the obstacles of civil war, foreign aggression, and economic depression—a "modern" state and a "developed" economy during a ten-year span of time. Modernization is still poorly understood by the social scientists, but all agree that it is a slow process. Everett E. Hagen, for example, an economist seeking the sources of modernization in socio-psychological conditions, perceives the process as requiring several, perhaps four or five, generations.[73] Many scholars have challenged his analysis in its various details, but the fact that a scholar of Hagen's insight sees the modernization process as such a protracted one should deter us from measuring the accomplishments of the Nationalists against standards of development that are wholly unrealistic.

Moreover, we in the United States may be cautioned against harsh judgments of the Nationalist regime by our own government's inability to implement the programs of road beautification, ghetto renewal, or environmental improvement. And the United States is immeasurably more wealthy, technologically advanced, and free of strife than was Nationalist China.

Conversely, it would be a mistake to attribute all the positive developments during the decade to the Nationalists. China, prior to the Kuomintang's succession to power, had already been swept into the vortex of world change. The Nationalist regime claimed credit for attaining tariff autonomy and for the end of the unequal treaties. Yet these achievements were already a foregone conclusion when Chang Tso-lin reigned in Peking. Similarly, modern education, social change, industrialization, modern banking, improved sanitation, and electrical systems had all to a greater or lesser extent been implanted and were developing during the 1920s. We would totally distort our perspective on the Nationalists' highway construction program, for example, if we forgot that the nation's roads had extended from less than two thousand to almost thirty thousand kilometers in just the six years prior to Nationalist rule—that is, during the period that is regarded as the depth of warlordism. And, perhaps most significant, the nation was possessed of an educated elite that had been broadly exposed to both Western knowledge and values. Change, therefore, had developed a momentum of its own before the Kuomintang came to power.

It is from these perspectives that we should view what was probably Nanking's chief contribution to China's development: it had made considerable progress in riveting together the framework of a Chinese state. As compared with March 1929, for example, when it controlled only 8 percent of the nation's area and 20 percent of the population, the Nationalist government on the eve of the war with Japan could credibly claim to govern 25 percent of the area and 66 percent of the population of China.[74] True, such statistics disguise the fact that the loyalties of many officials and army commanders in the areas "controlled" by Nanking were exceedingly tenuous. And historians will perhaps always wonder if even this measure of unity had not been purchased at an excessive price. No doubt the tendency toward regionalism could not have been arrested without considerable reliance upon force. But might not the regime's expenditures of life, money, and property have been markedly reduced if it had relied more on the means of political, economic, and social reconstruction, and less on the military?

Despite such nagging questions, it remains true that the Nationalist authorities had made progress toward creating one of the primary conditions for a viable political system: political control over a unified territory. And viewed superficially, it appears as though they had forged an environment within which the forces of social and economic change could develop. It is therefore possible, as Paul Sih and others have contended, that the Nationalists were on the threshold of creating a rich and strong nation when the Japanese invasion began. But: *caveat lector!*

The following tale has a moral. In 1935 Tso Shun-sheng, a long-time member of the China Youth Party and critic of the Kuomintang, went to Nanking to take up a teaching position in the Central Political Institute. Tso, who had not been in the capital for several years, remarked to Ting Wei-fen, a leading member of the Institute, that he was very favorably impressed by the changes and improvements that had been effected in the capital city by the Nationalist government. Ting replied: "All this is only on the surface. You don't know the inside situation yet."[75]

What was the "inside situation"? One of the most critical problems in creating a modern political system is to accommodate into politics the numerous and diverse social groups that become politically alert and active during the modernization process. During the transition from a traditional agrarian society, increasing numbers of people move to the cities, literacy and education become widespread, and the masses at all levels of society are touched by the galvanizing effects of nationalism. As a result of these and other forces, the masses tend to acquire a political consciousness, and to demand a role in the political process.

When social mobilization of this kind occurs, the ruling power must adopt one of two strategies. It may, in the first instance, choose to demobilize these new forces. This is usually accomplished with political repression or socioeconomic reforms, either of which methods has the effect of defusing the political potential of the masses. Or second, it may choose to develop institutions that incorporate the new social forces into the political process so that they acquire a sense of community with the government and with the rest of society. One or the other of these strategies must be *effectively* employed. Otherwise, the governing regime loses its legitimacy, and the politically mobilized forces in society build up a sense of frustration and alienation. Political differences then easily erupt into naked conflict.[76]

The Nationalist authorities, after being confronted with the realities of social mobilization in 1926–27, rejected the latter alternative; they chose not to expand political participation. They sought rather to demobilize the newly activated segments of society. In the cities, intellectuals, students, and professional and industrial workers who agitated for a political role were denied any institutionalized means by which to vent their discontents or to develop a sense of identity with the state. These measures worked effectively upon the industrial workers, and the labor movement was as a result eviscerated as an independent political force. Among the other segments of urban society, however, demobilization was never accomplished completely, and significant elements in the urban population were converted into active enemies of the regime.[77]

In the countryside, the regime similarly attempted to perpetuate a politically inert peasantry. The mass organizations that had been spawned during the Northern Expedition were either proscribed or rendered politically impotent. And, despite an avowed commitment to local self-rule and representative constitutional government, the regime either perpetuated the feudalistic domination of local landlords or inserted its own bureaucratic control over the stirring masses. The Nationalist regime's determination to forestall political and social revolution in the villages might have been of marginal significance if it had even slightly alleviated the discontentments of the farmers. If, for instance, the regime had prevented the local authorities from arbitrarily exacting t'an-k'uan, or if it had protected the rural population from the numerous and unpredictable forms of confiscation and conscription, then it might have defused the sources of discord, banditry, and rebellion in the villages. But the regime did not accomplish even these elementary reforms. Unrest among the farmers continued therefore to percolate.

In traditional society, the failure to alleviate the distress of the peasantry was usually only of local consequence. By the end of the 1930s, however, it had become likely that the endemic discontentments of the farmers would eventually lead to wide-scale revolt. The reasons that rural discontent had now acquired a more menacing potential are, first, that the ineluctable forces of modernization—manifested, for example, in increased trade, new opportunities for employment, and rapid means of communication—caused the farmers to sense alternatives to their current existence. And second, a political movement—the communists—now existed that had learned to translate peasant dissatisfaction into political power. New factors, in other words, had been introduced into the political equation. At the same time, the Nationalist regime's demonstrated and continuing administrative ineffectiveness, its emphasis upon urban at the expense of rural matters, and its apparent determination to perpetuate the existing socioeconomic order in the villages, did not portend meaningful improvements in the lives of the masses. Thus, in 1937, the countryside remained as a veritable powder keg.[78]

Nor had the Nationalists succeeded in mending the frayed social fabric of the nation. True, the leadership had been acutely conscious of the need to create an integrated cultural and ethical community. The Blue Shirts, for instance, had emphasized that a "new national culture" must underlie all other attempts at national reconstruction. And Chiang Kai-shek regarded the New Life Movement as his principal tool in forging a new nation. But these efforts to achieve cultural integration bore little fruit. To the extent that the New Life Movement did have results, they were limited to the cities and to the military services. Even there it did not acquire a momentum of its own, because few officials regarded the movement with any seriousness. Indeed, even in the highest reaches of government, the prohibitions of the movement were blithely disregarded.[79]

In recording the Nationalists' failure to implant a new and unified system of values throughout the nation, I do not mean to suggest that the task was an easy one. Yet it does seem that the Nationalist strategy of doing so was poorly conceived and wretchedly implemented. For the official slogans enjoining unity, sacrifice, and obedience were too obviously self-serving. And the majority of the officials who mouthed those slogans were too transparently hypocritical.[80] If, by contrast, the regime had not tried to attain the goal of spiritual unity by means of moralistic sloganizing and political repression but had with true dedication undertaken to improve the economic and political condition of the nation, then a sense of moral community might indeed have been engendered in the wake of these reforms.

The sense of national commitment that in some measure did come into being after late 1936, when Chiang Kai-shek began to take a hard line against Japanese pressures, illustrates how ready the Chinese people were to respond to a dedicated and high-minded leadership. That popular response had, however, resulted from popular self-delusion, for the members of the Nationalist regime had not suddenly undergone a spiritual transformation. And, when it became manifest during the early years of the war against Japan that the Nationalists were still concerned above all to perpetuate themselves in power, the unity and commitment of the Chinese people was again shattered.

Finally, the persistence of "yamenization" in the governmental administration raises doubts regarding the Nationalist attempt to create a viable political system and regarding the future stability of the regime. Efforts had been made to remedy this malady of yamenization. The Central Political Institute, a school designed to train future officials, produced 6,000 graduates between 1932 and 1936. A Commission on Administrative Efficiency was created in 1934; a system of supervisory specialists (*hsing-cheng tu-ch'a chuan-yüan*) was imposed over the hsien governments;[81] and after Chiang Kai-shek took over the post of premier in 1935, increasing numbers of non-Kuomintang personnel (for example, Wong Wen-hao, Wu Ting-ch'ang, and Chang Kia-ngau) were being recruited for administrative positions in the central government. There was some evidence that these and other measures were bringing some order and efficiency to the administration. The financial administration in both Kiangsu and Chekiang were reportedly improved by early 1936 as a result of new appointments in the provincial departments of finance. And several political writers commented that the government was no longer as "chaotic, incompetent, and divided" as it had been in earlier years.[82]

Leonard Hsü, who was senior counsellor in the Ministry of Industries, offered an assessment of the rural reconstruction program in September 1936 that was perhaps applicable to most areas of administration at the end of the decade. Hsü insisted that "in the last few months" there had been signs that the quality of administration had been improving. He admitted, nevertheless, "There are plenty of plans, but they are mostly on paper; largely because, in the planning, the practical factors of personnel, finance and skill-available have been neglected."[83] And the Control Yüan's declaration in late 1937 that the elimination of corruption was one of the most urgent tasks of government during the war with Japan testifies to the persistence of that problem throughout the Nanking period.[84] Even Arthur Young, who has never been in the forefront of the regime's detractors, acknowledges that "accomplishments [in improving the civil service system] were mostly on paper by 1937."[85]

It is probable that the quality of Nationalist administration had improved to a modest degree in some sections of the bureaucracy and in some areas of the country. Yamenization, nevertheless, remained a problem of the utmost gravity. Just how serious a problem was suggested by Chiang Kai-shek in September 1936: "If we do not weed the present body of corruption, bribery, perfunctoriness, and ignorance, and establish in its stead a clean and efficient administration, the day will soon come when the revolution will be started against us as we did against the Manchus."[86]

The problem one encounters in assessing the Nationalist record of creating a viable political system during the Nanking period is that there were on the eve of the war both positive and negative forces at work. Were the improvements discernible in 1936 and 1937 sufficiently deep-rooted that they could in the long-run overcome the forces of ineffective administration, corruption, and factionalism? There can be no certain answer to this question, and we should frankly admit that any conclusions drawn about the Nationalist regime during the Nanking decade will be at least partially subjective.

Certainly, the overthrow of the regime was not inevitable. The fact that it survived the depression of 1932–1935 shows how an inefficient, corrupt, and unpopular regime could muddle through. Yet the failure (or the unwillingness) of the Nationalists to broaden political participation, to pacify the peasantry by means of socioeconomic reforms, to foster a pervading sense of moral community, and to create a responsible and effective administration did at least portend continuing political instability.

We cannot conclude a discussion of the strengths and weaknesses of the Nanking regime without attempting to make a judgment of Chiang Kai-shek. The degree to which an individual political leader influences the course of history remains debatable; there can be no dispute, however, that Chiang Kai-shek was a preponderating force within the Nationalist regime. As an American foreign service officer accurately observed in 1934, "The shadow of Chiang Kai-shek extends over this whole scene. Sitting at Peiping, I would have been unwilling to believe that he dominated the Government set-up here to the extent that is now so apparent. Where his interest touches, there you will find a certain governmental activity; elsewhere, if not paralysis, at least a policy of drift."[87]

Chiang was, indeed, one of the regime's principal sources of strength. Even at the end of the Nanking decade, the Chinese people sensed little loyalty for, nor did they tend to identify with, the party or the government. But Chiang personally had won the trust and respect of much of the nation.[88] The precise reasons for this personal popularity are unclear. He was not a charismatic figure, and he was anything but a demagogue. In addressing a public gathering, he was aloof, stiff, superior. His speeches were instructional sermons, often laced with moralistic recriminations against his listeners; they ignited few emotional flames. Even in private he remained cool and distant. He was, it has been remarked, "as talkative as Calvin Coolidge."[89] During meetings he seldom joined in the discussions. He listened attentively while the others expressed opinions. Then, the discussion over, he would peremptorily and without inviting comment announce his decision.[90] People did not love Chiang Kai-shek, but they were impressed by him.

During the early years of the decade it was widely believed that Chiang hungered for power for the sake of power alone. The *Ta-kung pao* in 1930 described him as an "uneducated, incompetent" leader, whose actions had plunged the nation into civil war and caused the people untold miseries.[91] By the end of the decade, however, he was widely regarded as the one Kuomintang figure who transcended the petty factional jealousies within the party, and who alone could hold together the divisive regime during a war with Japan.

Chiang Kai-shek's strengths were monumental; neither were his weaknesses small. Intolerant of differing opinions, he surrounded himself with subordinates, too many of whom were minions. When piqued, he had a fierce and awful temper, and subordinates who brought unpleasant facts to his ear were often subjected to verbal flayings that they never forgot. Few men of ability or conviction could withstand this kind of treatment, with the consequence that the most powerful man in the government was frequently isolated from the best informed opinions and from the realities of the national situation.[92]

Chiang has frequently won praise for his singleness of purpose, but this quality was balanced by the narrowness of his methods. He believed that the fundamental solution to China's problems lay in remolding the values and attitudes of the people. But his understanding of human motivation and mass psychology was incredibly shallow. He believed that moral preachments would suffice to change social behavior.[93] He was convinced that immorality was the cause of economic poverty rather than vice versa.[94] Thus he sermonized and he harangued. But he neglected the social and economic sources of the nation's problems.

And, when moral preachments failed, he instinctively turned to the use of force. H. H. Kung recalls, "I frequently said to the Generalissimo, 'Don't rely too much on military

power!' ''[95] Chiang even admitted he had erred in thinking
that force could overcome all obstacles.[96] Despite this intro-
spective insight, coercion remained a major instrument of his
policies. One wonders how many civil wars, how many assassinations, how many bloodied heads China might have been
spared if Chiang had better understood the motivations of
more ordinary men.

To a degree, also, Chiang Kai-shek must be held accountable for the administrative shortcomings of his government.
For Chiang did not understand institutions. He did not know
how to delegate responsibility. He ignored channels of authority; he might, depending on his mood and interests, intervene
in any governmental matter, large or small. He treated the
national treasury as a personal bank account. ''The real
authority of the government went wherever the Generalissimo
went,'' Franklin Ho recalls. ''In terms of authority he was the
head of everything.''[97] As a consequence, institutions withered; organizational and individual initiative died.

Personalistic government can, of course, be efficient, and the
Nanking regime sometimes moved with astonishing speed
when touched by the hand of Chiang Kai-shek. Arthur Young,
then adviser to the Ministry of Finance, recounted the occasion when the government adopted the gold standard for the
customs tariff. This was an extremely consequential move, for
it involved the establishment of a new unit of monetary exchange. Nevertheless, after receiving the approval of the
Central Political Council, which was chaired by Chiang, the
matter was ''brought up, enacted and dispatched within forty-
eight hours''—apparently without reference to any other governmental bodies that might have claimed a legitimate interest in the decision. This demonstrated, Young claimed, that
the ''Chinese government is not as cumbersome as it appears.''[98]

The shortcomings of one-man rule often do not appear in
the short-run. One-man rule, however, is potentially the most
unstable of all governments. Strong, enduring governance
requires complex institutions. The question of succession to

leadership, for example, is fundamental and inevitable in all political systems; and where institutions are weak, the question may have no ready answer. The consternation and infighting that took place during the Sian Incident amply revealed that such stability as China did enjoy by 1936 was inseparable from the person of Chiang Kai-shek.

Regimes that have developed highly articulated and complex organizations are also more likely, over the long-run, to respond creatively to new challenges than are regimes dominated by non-institutionalized procedures. Individuals have specific strengths and abilities, and as they mature, they become "set in their ways." Regimes dominated by individuals are accordingly little more flexible than the man at the top. Organizations, to the contrary, tend as they mature to become more complex and—providing that they have developed in a non-static environment—are consequently more able to cope with a variety of changing tasks.[99]

Even during the relatively short tenure of the Nationalist government in Nanking, this lack of flexibility had already appeared as a liability. Chiang had displayed a certain genius during the initial years of the regime. He balanced clique against faction; he knew when to cajole and when to use force. These were the means that he had used in rising to power, and they were the means that he employed in ruling the nation. But, as two writers unkindly (but perhaps not too wrongly) phrased it, he was "an economic ignoramus."[100] He also felt constrained by political organizations; he lacked a comprehension of state planning; he was unable to unify and discipline his own followers; and perhaps most consequential, he did not understand politics involving the masses.

Chiang Kai-shek was undoubtedly a remarkable man. That he even survived the challenges and intrigues of the Nanking period was testimony to the strength of his character and abilities; that he emerged from those trials with his powers enhanced was a mark of his extraordinary talents. His talents, however, were best suited to the old China. In the game of warlord politics, he was a master. But China was in the process of change, and the rules of the game of politics were changing accordingly. Chiang displayed little talent for the new game. Thus Chiang, who was primarily responsible for the Nationalist government's continued existence, also contributed to the essential instability that characterized the regime throughout the Nanking decade.

Chapter 7 Social Traits and Political Behavior in Kuomintang China

The theme of revolutionary failure has infused each of the preceding chapters. In our search for the causes of this failure, we have discerned that the Nationalist movement even before 1927 had never been molded into a cohesive or disciplined political movement. This historic fact would, in any case, have created major problems for the party after its ascendancy to national power in 1927. The problems were worsened, however, by two further developments. First, the multifarious character of the Nationalist movement became even greater when the so-called northern mandarins and various warlords leaped onto the Kuomintang bandwagon at the moment of revolutionary success. And second, the Kuomintang's purge of the communists and the radical left meant that the movement deprived itself of both the personnel and ideas that might have enabled it to cope, in a fundamental way, with the political and economic disintegration afflicting the political system.

Yet the symptoms of the revolutionary failure—ineffectual administration, corruption, factionalism, and political repression—were not unique to the Nationalist movement. During at least the latter half of the Ch'ing dynasty, for example, officials had flagrantly enriched themselves from the public purse, had employed incompetent relatives, and had concentrated their energies on maintaining clique ties rather than on administering state affairs in the public interest. And under the warlord regimes of the early Republican period, too, these characteristics of governmental conduct persisted. At Peking, both bureaucrats and members of parliament were largely indifferent to the public welfare and concentrated instead on garnering the political and financial perquisites of office.[1] It is patent therefore that the sources of those symptoms, and the fundamental causes of the Nationalist failure to fashion a viable political system, must lie elsewhere than in the Kuomintang itself.

In the following pages, I shall attempt to show that those causes lay in the weakness of China's political institutions and in the persistence of China's traditional political culture.

Weak Political Institutions

During the traditional period, when the dynasties were at their height, the bureaucratic administration was normally held accountable for its performance by the emperors. Political institutions were strong, for there existed, as Joseph Levenson discerned, a dynamic tension between the emperorship and the bureaucracy.[2] The emperor and the bureaucracy were not, then, one. And the emperors endeavored to maintain the distinction by cultivating non-bureaucratic political forces —such as the aristocracy, eunuchs, and Manchus—to counterbalance and control the bureaucracy. It was only when the tension between the emperorship and the bureaucracy became slack, when the emperors' base of power exterior to the administration weakened (or when the emperor became associated with dominant groups within the administration), that the bureaucrats were no longer constrained to perform effectively. When this occurred, the dynasties entered the phase of decline, characterized by ineffectual administration, gross corruption, and uncontained factionalism.

Neither the revolution of 1911 nor of 1927 succeeded in

recreating political institutions sufficiently strong that they could impose accountability upon the members of the government. Chiang Kai-shek seemingly strived to do so. His periodic crackdowns on corruption, punctuated by the executioner's gunshot, were evidence of his desire to impose discipline upon the bureaucracy. And the organizing of the Blue Shirts was his attempt to create a counterbalancing force against the civil administration. But Chiang, like an emperor during the waning phase of a dynasty, was so dependent on his officials that he was unable to control them sufficiently to restore vitality to the government.

Governmental accountability need not, of course, be imposed only from above. Liberal democracy in the West, for example, is predicated on the belief that the force of public opinion, transformed into political power by means of representative parliaments, organized interest groups, and a powerful free press, will suffice to control and give direction to the executive and administrative branches of government. And the administration in such one-party regimes as Soviet Russia may be made accountable by the party operating outside the bureaucracy.

In Nanking China, neither the public nor the Kuomintang imposed effective constraints on the Nationalist administrators. The Kuomintang after 1927 never acquired the vitality nor the autonomy necessary to discipline the bureaucracy. Although "radicals" in the Kuomintang had attempted to subordinate the governmental administration to party control, they were quickly disarmed. As early as 1928 the Central Executive Committee rejected proposals that the party exercise direct control over the bureaucracy. According to Patrick Cavendish, this decision was attributable to Chiang Kai-shek, who "emphasized above all the need to protect the administration from party interference . . . The party's rule below the Centre was henceforth to be restricted to 'propaganda' in the widest sense of the term."[3] The Kuomintang was as a consequence rendered powerless to supervise the government, and indeed the party by the end of the decade had almost ceased to be a political force—only 10 percent of the two million members continuing to be active in the party.[4] "According to my observation," Arthur Young has remarked about the Nanking period, "the Kuomintang Party as such was far less important than the government as a factor in national affairs in those years, and was tending to decrease in importance and become almost nominal."[5]

Nor was the Nationalist bureaucracy accountable to organs of popular will. Never during the Nanking period was life breathed into the National Assembly or hsien assemblies. The labor unions and mass organizations had either been eliminated or made over into docile tools of the regime. Even the dominant economic strata in the country, the landlords and the urban capitalists, did not (as was suggested in Chapter 5) effectively influence the policies of the Nanking government.

The Nationalist regime tended therefore to be neither responsible nor responsive to political groups or institutions outside the government. It became, in effect, its own constituency, ruling in the interests of its own members. As a consequence, the activities of the governmental administration, which ostensibly served the needs of the larger society, were in fact directed to maximizing the power, prestige, and wealth of the bureaucrats themselves.

This is not to contend that the Nanking government operated in a vacuum, isolated from the multifarious forces of the broader society. For, in order to preserve its political power, the government did sometimes respond to influences from without. The student and national salvation movements, for example, grew into a force that prompted the regime to abandon its policy of appeasing Japan. And, in the villages, the most powerful landlords blunted the edge of the regime's drive for tax revenue by such schemes as removing their lands from the tax registers. Yet neither the landlords, nor the urban capitalists, nor the students were able to generate sufficient organizational strength that they could ensure continued accountability by the government in either policy formation or administrative practice.

Politically Relevant Social Traits

The weakness of her political institutions was a necessary but not sufficient condition for the ineffectual administration, corruption, and factionalism in the governments of modern China. Being largely unconstrained by extra-governmental forces, the bureaucrats might have displayed any number of patterns of behavior. Not all Chinese bureaucrats, for example, ignored the public welfare or enriched themselves through corruption. But that ineffectual administration, corruption, factionalism, and political repression did tend to characterize modern Chinese government generally, and the Nationalist government in particular, suggests that there were forces impelling the officials into those modes of political behavior.

The analysis in the following pages is premised on the assumption that the political behavior of Chinese bureaucrats working within weak political institutions was determined in large degree by the social traits that they acquired before they became members of the bureaucracy. In this section, therefore, I shall discuss several dominant characteristics of Chinese social behavior. Then, in the following sections, I shall attempt to show how these behavioral tendencies were manifested in the conduct of Nationalist officialdom.

Before proceeding to this discussion, however, it is necessary to add a few cautionary notes. First, the study of Chinese political culture is still at an exceedingly primitive level. As a consequence, the attempt here to generalize about modal patterns of Chinese behavior probably does not reflect what may be broad divergencies between the behavioral traits of different strata within Chinese society. It may be, for example, that there are significant differences between the personality types of different regions of China. Or perhaps the social and behavioral traits I shall discuss are class-specific, typical only of, say, China's middle and upper classes.

Second, the traits are presented only as abstractions. There were, of course, wide individual variations from these modal behavioral traits. It would be a mistake, therefore, to attribute to any specified Chinese individual the traits that are here attributed to a group.

And, finally, the traits are presumably not qualitatively different from those in other societies. In every society, for example, there are authority and dependency relationships. The Chinese in this regard were not alone. I contend no more than that each society or culture is characterized by certain general behavioral traits and that there are shadings of difference between the modal behavioral patterns of different societies. There may be universalities in human behavior, but a Spaniard is not a Russian is not an Indian is not a Chinese. Cultural differences, even if subtle, are real.

Having stressed the tentative nature of all the following generalizations about Chinese social traits, let us venture into the study of Chinese political culture.

China was a status-oriented society in which social relationships tended to be structured vertically; all social relationships, that is, tended to be between individuals who acted as either a superior or a subordinate in the relationship. This superior-subordinate pattern—or, as I prefer to call it, the "authority-dependency pattern"—is a key to all the ensuing analysis. In this society, the individual acquired a sense of personal identity not so much from a sense of his personal worth or individual attainments as from a realization of his relative position, or status, in a vertically tiered society.

The prototypical Chinese authority figure was the father. A Chinese father would probably be warm, informal, and sometimes playful with a son during the child's early years. Later, however, the father assumed the attributes of a disciplinarian: frequently stern, remote, and demanding the strictest obedience to his wishes. The father would often punish the son not only with harshness but sometimes even with cruelty. Morton Fried recalled of his investigations in central China that "Although [he] never witnessed any physical punishment of a child under three or four years old, worse than a mild shaking, he saw many older children, particularly male, being beaten, sometimes with a stick. With increased discipline, the father and son move apart, often never to meet again on any ground of true warmth.''[6] And Richard Solomon notes that ''Chinese parents felt they could only control their children by developing in them a sense of anxiety ('fear') about contravening parental instructions. The response of unconditional obedience was a goal to be strived for.''[7] A father typically loved his son, of course, but he expressed this love not in the form of overt affection, but in caring for the material needs of the child and in the stern insistence that he prepare himself diligently for the tasks of adulthood.[8]

Perhaps the most intriguing of all Chinese authority figures was the mother-in-law, who frequently adopted toward her new daughter-in-law a harsh, unfeeling, and even tyrannical attitude. Marion J. Levy, Jr., has observed how the mother-in-law became the central figure in the life of a new bride. A marriage, he said, was actually consummated twice: once on the night of the wedding with her husband, and again the next morning when she rose early to prepare breakfast for and comb the hair of her husband's mother.[9] And C. K. Yang has spoken of the ''raw subjugation'' of the young girl to her mother-in-law during the early years of her marriage.[10] Not infrequently mothers-in-law treated their sons' wives with such cruelty that the girls felt that their only escape was by suicide. And it is probable that the highest rate of suicide in China prior to the communist period was among that age group of women who would have recently married.[11]

The tyrannical behavior of so many mothers-in-law—there were, of course, atypical mothers-in-law who treated their sons' wives with affection and warmth—is at first sight puzzling, for it would seem that women who had experienced the agony of daughter-in-law-hood would have resolved to treat their own daughters-in-law in a more kindly manner. Such an expectation is erroneous, because it fails to take into consideration either the accepted behavior of Chinese authority figures or the psychological forces that the pattern of social relationships engendered. A Chinese woman was permitted to savor few of the satisfactions of the status-oriented society.

Throughout their lives, women were subordinated to the authority of others. As a consequence, Francis Hsü states, such a woman "merely waits for her chance to 'take it out on' her daughter or daughter-in-law."[12]

Other authority figures tended to adopt similar behavioral traits: the teacher toward the student, employer toward employee, landlord toward tenant. In all these relationships, although not necessarily in the same degree as that of a father toward his son, the superior in the relationship tended to be remote, strict, arbitrary, and unchallengeable.

What made one person an authority figure and another a dependency figure? To generalize, the chief determinants of status were sex, age, wealth, and proximity to power.[13] Within the family, sex and age tended to be the factors that were decisive in determining authority status. Thus brothers dominated sisters, and elder brothers dominated younger brothers.[14] In non-kin relationships, wealth and proximity to power were relatively decisive. These factors were variables, however, and a different mix of these variables could resolve relationships in different ways. For example, the wife of a wealthy landlord would be received obsequiously by a male of lesser economic standing, but that same lady might be highly respectful toward an aged but impoverished member of the village. Whatever the mix of these variables, the resulting relationship was almost always vertical rather than horizontal.

The vertical structure characterized even the relationship between persons that would in most respects be regarded as peers. There were, of course, some relations between friends that were based entirely upon mutual affection and that bore no distinction between superior and subordinate.[15] Yet true friendship, based upon mutual affection and that bore no trace of status differentiation or of exploitation, was a rarity in the life of an individual. "Chinese society has been based on the . . . assumption," Wolfram Eberhard has observed, that "no two persons are ever equal; always one is higher than the other."[16] And Richard Solomon has remarked that "there are few real 'peer' relations in traditional Chinese society.''[17]

My own experience has confirmed these observations. Recently, for example, I asked an associate researcher at the Academia Sinica about his relationship with other associate researchers with whom (so far as I could discern) he enjoyed a friendly relationship that bore no mark of status differentiation. This was not true, he told me. There was, he said, always an implicit awareness among these nominal equals of their respective relationships to the head of the institute. And the relative proximity to the head of the institute affected the quality of their relationships to each other, a scholar closer to the head of the institute assuming the role of authority figure over those who were more remote.

The subordinates in these vertically structured relationships tended to assume an attitude of dependence on the authority figure. The preeminent Chinese characteristic, Francis Hsü has suggested, is not self-reliance, but reliance upon others.[18] Chinese learned that the individual could not cope with the world alone. They therefore did not generally strive for personal autonomy but learned rather that security and contentment could only be attained by reliance upon others. This was true of both authority and dependency figures. For, while dependents looked to authority figures for assistance and protection, authority figures expected that their dependents would act loyally, obey unquestioningly, and render support should the need arise. Thus the relationship was reciprocal if not egalitarian, and the system was characterized not just by dependency, but *mutual* dependency.

The sense that the individual possessed few resources and abilities to deal with the world alone was implanted at an early age. During infancy, the child was carried about by the mother or an older child until he was able to walk; the adventurous mishaps that might have resulted from crawling around on all fours were discouraged by the child's authority figures. Later, the child was seldom encouraged to think that he could solve problems through his own initiative. Within the family, the child learned that security was realized only by the strictest obedience to authority: experimentation on one's own was discouraged, and the child was taught to learn through imitation of one's elders. In school, rote memorization was the universal pedagogical technique. And the child was admonished that, when he had a run-in with another child, he should streak for home rather than slug it out on his own. They were taught not to fight, Margery Wolf has observed, "even if it is to defend himself or his property."[19] Indeed, the child was not encouraged to venture far beyond the family compound, where he might investigate, learn for himself—get into trouble, perhaps—and generally to develop his initiative and sense of independence.

This socialization process that accustomed the child to the status-oriented society left a deep mark upon the personality and behavioral patterns of the adult. Mature Chinese tended, for example, to be excessively submissive in their relations with authority figures. There was, as Solomon phrased it, an "indirection in dealing with superiors, great reluctance to criticize, and an over-willingness to please those in power."[20] And Francis Hsü, writing of the overt behavior of Chinese, concluded that "the first outstanding quality is an explicitly submissive attitude toward authority."[21] Authority figures neither expected their subordinates to be capable of independence and creativity, nor did they reward it. And dependency figures were therefore reluctant to exercise their own initiative, sensing security in passivity and obedience.

The behavior of a Chinese in his role as an authority figure was utterly different from his conduct when filling the role of a dependent. Now he was proud, dominating, overbearing, inconsiderate. Describing the conduct of supervisors in a factory in Szechuan, Shih Kuo-heng wrote that "whenever they pass by [they] have a habit of shouting at workers to 'hurry up,' without even looking at the work at all. These same supervisors when they give orders are blustering and rude as if ordering slaves. Other officers, even assistant engineers, often go beyond the call of duty to give superfluous directions, seemingly merely to show that they have the power to give orders.'"[22] Such conduct typified the attitude of superiors toward subordinates at all levels of the social hierarchy. As Solomon concluded, "To assert authority was to affirm one's right to be the superior figure in the relationship . . . For a superior *not* to be assertive in the use of authority would be to create 'confusion.' "[23] In this status-oriented society, the failure to assert dominance and precedence could easily be mistaken for weakness or the lack of status.

Persons reared in such a status-oriented society sensed little difficulty in adjusting from the role of a dependency figure in one set of social relationships to that of an authority figure in another set. Children were constrained to act as dependency figures towards their parents, but at the same time they learned from their parents how they should act when they themselves assumed the role of an authority figure. Thus an elder brother would play out the role of an authority figure in his relations with his younger brothers and sisters. "It is not unusual," Morton Fried observed during his field studies, "to see an older brother of twelve or fourteen strike a brother who is two or three years his junior. Only cases of flagrant persecution will arouse parental interference."[24] In similar fashion, the father—so awesome at home—would become a humble dependency figure vis-à-vis his superiors when he was at work. And the stern all-knowing village schoolmaster scraped and bowed before the provincial director of education.

Role-playing is common and accepted behavior in all societies. In a status-oriented society like China's, however, where a person's sensed identity was almost wholly determined by relative status, the differentiation of roles was essential to maintenance of the social structure. Dependency figures might resent the treatment they received at the hands of their superior, but the structure was durable, because every dependency figure welcomed the satisfactions accompanying authority status when they themselves acted as authority figures.[25]

Yet another behavioral trait resulting from the authority-dependency pattern was the tendency for each individual to wrap himself in a network of personal relationships. Because the individual had never been encouraged to be self-reliant, he acquired the feeling that security and contentment could be derived only with the help of others. One of Solomon's interviewees, for example, explained that the most important thing obtained from friends was "their sympathy and support. A person cannot take care of things all by himself. If he has friends who come and help him, encourage him and support him, then things can be dealt with effectively."[26] Thus, wherever he went, in all areas of activity, the individual purposively, if not consciously, built up the personal relationships that might someday be useful.

The vital force in these relationships was *jen-ch'ing,* or "human feelings." No value in Chinese morality was more stressed than to *chiang jen-ch'ing,* or "have concern for human feelings." To "have concern for human feelings" meant not simply to express warm sentiments toward another person, but to act as a person who understood the way of being a truly human being in relationship to another human being. Throughout his life, a Chinese would endeavor to establish *jen-ch'ing* relations with persons of consequence in his life; doing so, he created that network of relationships upon which he could confidently rely for aid and security.

The means by which Chinese implanted *jen-ch'ing* becomes clearer in the light of Yang Lien-sheng's perceptive observation: "When a Chinese acts, he normally anticipates a response or return. Favors done for others are often considered what may be termed 'social investments,' for which handsome returns are expected."[27]

The element of good fellowship did, of course, infuse the kind of personal relationships discussed here. Yet when a Chinese extended a dinner invitation, gave a New Year's gift, or helped someone or someone's son obtain a job, a "social investment" had been made. And, should the recipient of such favors later refuse—if asked—to repay that investment, he would open himself to one of the harshest accusations in the

Chinese language: *t'a pu-chiang jen-ch'ing*—"He has no concern for human feelings!"

The final behavioral trait that we need to discuss here was the relative lack of commitment to abstract principles. "Resolute committal to a cause," Francis Hsü has written, "is missing from the Chinese social conscience." They are opportunistic, he adds, "because, being so irretrievably tied to their primary relations, they are prone to think of right or wrong, truth or untruth, justice or injustice, in relative terms. *The only absolutes are those which revolve about concrete duties toward specific individuals.*"[28]

This is not to argue that Chinese did not concern themselves with such matters as social improvement or justice for all men. Indeed, Chinese valued universalistic principles, and they honored men who acted upon those principles. Yet, when they organized in support of a cause, they tended to structure themselves on the basis of personal ties to a much greater extent than on the basis of a common ideological commitment.[29] As a consequence, most Chinese in their conduct found themselves inextricably enmeshed in a web of personal relationships. Lacking self-reliance, conscious of their inclusion in and responsibility to larger social groups, and painfully sensitive to the demands and pressures of *jen-ch'ing,* they would—*should there be a conflict*—sacrifice abstract principle to personal relationship.

The following sections will be devoted to a discussion of the various ways in which members of the Kuomintang frequently let particularistic values obstruct their commitment to abstract principles. Yet it cannot be stressed too strongly that this behavioral trait was not limited to members of the Kuomintang but was pervasive throughout Chinese society. H. D. Fong has provided apt illustration of this fact from his 1932 study of the cotton industry:

The whole system of management among Chinese owned mills is usually polluted by ignorance, factionalism, and squeeze . . . The whole plant, worth millions of dollars, may be entrusted to a manager who knows nothing about spinning. The latter, usually the trusted appointee of the most influential stockholder, has frequently neither a grasp of the technical complexity of spinning and weaving, nor a knowledge of cost accounting, financing and marketing. Instead he delegates his duties to the subordinates, and relies upon the good turn of luck for the mill's profits. In such a mill, the head of the spinning or weaving department, oftentimes a close friend or relative of the manager or the stockholder, considers his job as the source of squeeze, but delegates in turn his duties to one of the foremen, who, although skilled in mechanics, lacks scientific training.[30]

Chinese, when they became officials in the Nanking regime, acted in much the same way. But then they imperiled not just the livelihood of a few stockholders but of the nation.

Ineffectual Administration

Government office represented, for most ambitious Chinese, the acme of accomplishment. Just as during the Ch'ing dynasty when youth had studied the Confucian classics with the intent not of becoming philosophers but of passing the civil service examinations, so students in the Republican period aspired above all else to become officials.[31]

An official in China was more than just a bureaucrat. That he should view himself as a civil *servant* was inconceivable. An official, so close to the ultimate source of power in Chinese society, was the Chinese authority figure *par excellence*. In becoming an official, therefore, a Chinese acted as he had learned authority figures properly act: domineering, arbitrary, and often inconsiderate. "Arrogance," C. K. Yang has written, "was built into the status system of the traditional social structure; it was an institutionalized prerogative of the high-status group of scholar-officials, a part of their personality pattern in normal social life. They were hardly likely to drop their domineering traits when they entered the bureaucracy where the added power and prestige would only enhance such traits."[32]

These behavioral traits directly affected the quality of an official's administrative work. In this status-oriented society, it was essential that an official not confuse the differences of status by engaging in activities that were appropriate to persons of lesser status. Therefore, just as Chinese factory managers avoided involvement with the technological complexities of production or cost accounting, the official would not deign to study first-hand the peasants' problems, nor to learn the details of water conservancy, nor to supervise the maintenance of tax records. And the official of the National Economic Council, who "refused to get himself wet" while inspecting dikes, was merely acting in a manner appropriate to his status.[33] Officials were, therefore, often woefully ignorant of the problems under their jurisdiction. And this was true at all levels of administration. "One can only be surprised," remarked Franklin Ho, who joined the government in 1936, "to know just how unaware people at the top were of what was going on, how little they knew of the actual conditions in the country."[34]

Despite their ignorance, it was appropriate to the authority status of the officials to write memoranda, draw up regulations, draft plans, and issue orders. One devastating indictment of governmental administration at the local level charged that section chiefs issued orders without investigating actual conditions in the villages and that supervising officials disregarded the practicality of these documents' contents, paying attention only to the literary style.[35] And the head of a ministry in Nanking complained that "heaps of well-phrased and well-printed reports are piled up every place. But when one reads the contents, one is wholly disheartened!"[36]

In this world of status and documents, officials tended to lose sight of the goal of administrative output. "Administration degenerates," C. M. Chang wrote in 1936, "into mere correspondence. The result is that politics too often end where it should begin, with the assertion of intentions. A clever magistrate is one who engages a good secretary who has at his command an excellent literary style which, like charity, covers a multitude of sins . . . An old hand at the game knows that since the orders are so numerous, no one is expected to take them seriously."[37] Hsu Dau-lin recalls that "Party resolutions were treated in the same way that government officials treated government documents: everything was done on paper only, and as soon as it was on paper it was forgotten."[38]

Unaccountable to forces outside the government, the officials tended to be concerned less with administrative goals than with bureaucratic means. "The Kuomintang," wrote Searle Bates in 1932, "seems to use most of its income and energy in making its own wheels go around, with little benefit in public service."[39] And Melville Kennedy, in a detailed study of the Training and Organization Bureaus of the Kuomintang between 1927 and 1931, found that the efforts of the party bureaucrats "appeared to focus mainly on the structure and regulations of the Party instead of on the Party as the national unifier and the agent for economic and social betterment." There was, Kennedy concluded, "a characteristic preoccupation of the Party with its own operations and functional requirements to the virtually complete exclusion . . . of the purpose of national political unification."[40]

Contributing to the absence of administrative effectiveness was the tendency of officials to avoid taking independent initiative that might seem to challenge the superior. "The prerequisite for a successful magistrate," C. M. Chang asserted, "is the possession of an ability to ingratiate himself with his superiors by his attentions and a show of deference. Only in very exceptional cases does he find himself promoted merely on the basis of his being a good advisor."[41] Frequently, therefore, a lower-level official possessed the technological know-how or was sufficiently familiar with actual conditions in the villages that he knew the directives of his superior were impractical or wrong-headed. Yet, as a dependent in the official hierarchy, it would be inappropriate for him to bring this to the attention of his superior. Just as a son would not "talk back" to his father, a subordinate official avoided giving the impression that he was challenging the authority status of his superior by demonstrating greater insight or knowledge. It was better to let the project end in disaster than to correct his boss. Passivity, Hsu Dau-lin recalls, was not severely reprimanded, for the superior's most acute fear was not of negligence but of insubordination.[42] Sidney Gamble also noted that most district magistrates "showed but little initiative . . . Their general motto seemed to be 'maintain order, produce the usual revenue, make changes only on orders from above!' "[43]

The contention here is not that the Nationalists' bureaucracy completely and utterly neglected the goals of administrative output. This was manifestly not true. Yet administrative output patently received secondary priority in the bureaucrats' order of concerns.

Corruption

Where the system of supervision is lax and when legal retribution is uncertain, there will probably be some form of corruption. Corruption, therefore, was not unique to the Nationalist regime—as recent enquiries into the New York City police force have made painfully evident. In Nationalist China, however, the institutional constraints against corruption were much weaker than in New York. And there was, moreover, a centuries-long tradition of governmental corruption so that social attitudes were often exceedingly indulgent. Thus there were few impediments to official malfeasance. Not surprisingly, therefore, the typical Nationalist bureaucrat sought to *sheng-kuan fa-ts'ai*—to acquire wealth through corruption. As a newspaper editorialist observed, "In Chinese politics, the basic principle is that the government is established for the rulers, not for the people. The officials' goal is to collect taxes and to attain wealth. For example, in maintaining local order, their goal is not to strive for the people's livelihood, but to protect sources of revenue . . . Government is a kind of economic function."[44]

To fathom the motivation of a corrupt official, it must be recalled that a Chinese who became an official was attaining indisputable authority status. He was acquiring not responsibilities but prerogatives. Like a father or a mother-in-law, the official felt that he was now due the deference, the benefits, and the amenities appropriate to his status.

This view was expressed with remarkable candor shortly after the Nationalist government was established in Nanking. Members of the State Council had proposed a salary increase for themselves. Feng Yü-hsiang opposed the raise, saying that people were now threatened with famine, and that the members of the council should provide relief to the drought-stricken areas before they raised their own salaries. But Tai Chi-t'ao replied: "Some people say that we should live a life of extreme simplicity and frugality. But we have followed Sun Yat-sen, and the revolution has passed through many adversities. Now the revolution has succeeded, and it is only right that we enjoy things a little."[45]

In all probability, however, the hedonistic desire to "enjoy things a little" was not the only or even the primary reason why an official indulged in corrupt practices. For in Chinese society, where status was all-important, wealth was a primary attribute of status. Without a fine home, without servants, without the financial ability to pick up the bill at the end of an expensive banquet, an official would feel—and his associates would also conclude—that he did not measure up to his position. "The important thing for the Chinese great man," Francis Hsü has written, "is to maintain his distinction from his fellow men. This is done by ceremonial pomp, cloistered residences, and a battery of guards, who are not protectors but symbols of rank. In fact, the wider his distance from the people, the higher is the hero's prestige."[46] Officials, in greater or lesser degree, sought the things that would mark themselves off from the common people and from bureaucrats of lesser rank. Those marks of status could easily require more money than they could afford from strictly legitimate sources. In addition, the material goods of the West had become important distinguishing marks of the superior man—and these cost even more than the traditional badges of status.[47] This explains, in part at least, why official corruption may have become more rampant under the Kuomintang than in earlier periods.

An official, moreover, could not be content if his high status was merely temporary. Not only for himself but for his family, he would have to ensure the perpetuation of high status after leaving office. And this could best be done by accumulating wealth. This responsibility to his primary group, even more than to himself, made corruption virtually a moral imperative.[48]

Another reason impelling an official to become corrupt was the financial cost of maintaining his network of *jen-ch'ing*. Entertainment of his colleagues and superiors in the bureaucracy, essential for the maintenance of good personal relations, might make such heavy demands on an official's purse that he would have to dip into public monies. His superiors might also expect, if not demand, sizable gifts or other forms of remuneration for their continued patronage. Should an official not comprehend these niceties for maintaining a network of personal relations, he would probably be quickly replaced by someone with a better understanding of bureaucratic practice. "It is," a contemporary noted, "both difficult and foolish to be honest in the officialdom at this time."[49]

The strongest external pressures impelling the official to indulge in corrupt practices came, however, from his family. According to Wang Cheng, even Western-educated members of the Kuomintang who had acquired universalistic standards of conduct, "soon discovered that they could not in any significant measure escape the tenacious hold of the family over them. The moment they secured some small power in or through the Kuomintang (for example, a position within the party structure or a governmental post), their relatives, the majority of their friends, and even their professional associates assumed that this power would be put in part at least to the furtherance of family ends. To fail to do so was, in almost everyone's eyes, a failure of character or at the very least of good sense."[50]

The kind of pressures that family relationships could exert

upon an official was poignantly illustrated by Franklin Ho's uncle. This uncle had helped finance Ho's graduate study in the United States. And, after Ho accepted a government position in 1936, he showed up at Ho's office asking that Ho help him attain the life-long ambition of becoming a hsien magistrate. Ho knew that his uncle was not remotely qualified for such a position; yet he was deeply indebted to the uncle for his past financial support.[51]

How would an official resolve this dilemma between demands of public responsibility and familial loyalties and obligations? If Ho refused the uncle's request, the uncle and most of the family would believe that Ho had become uppitty during his study abroad, that he no longer "had concern for human feelings." Moreover, Ho might in the future require the help or support of his family—but this help might be denied him if he now refused his uncle's request.

In this particular case, Ho turned down the uncle's request. "We struggled over [the request] in Nanking," Ho recalled, "and finally he left, extremely angry. Oh, he was mad."[52] Franklin Ho had braved this wrath. More often, however, the demands of kinship and friendship superseded the principle of bureaucratic impersonality. It became a common occurrence that a newly appointed head of a ministry would fire all the old employees, and would replace them with his own people. With personal rather than objective criteria determining the selection of personnel, many of Nanking's bureaucrats were but poorly qualified; moreover, the practice resulted in a grossly inflated and unwieldy bureaucracy.[53] "Where . . . two relatives could do the job as well as one," Wang Cheng noted, "two jobs were created."[54]

One wonders how a hsien magistrate felt when he saw peasants under his jurisdiction living in destitution while he was squeezing as much as ¥100,000 a year from local tax revenue. We can only speculate. It is probable, however, that the magistrate would sense little empathy for the peasants, because they lay outside his web of personal relationships.

Another interpretation is suggested by T. W. Adorno in his

work, *The Authoritarian Personality*. Persons reared in an authoritarian and status-oriented environment, Adorno observed, tend to display "a desperate clinging to what appears to be strong," and a "contempt for the allegedly inferior and weak."[55] Although Adorno's study has been briskly criticized by recent scholarship for a variety of reasons, this quotation displays an insight that has much relevance to the Chinese situation. For the corrupt magistrate, who was excessively conscious of status relationships, would view the common farmers as inferior beings. The farmers did indeed suffer, but—so the magistrate might reason—they were accustomed to such suffering. The magistrate himself, on the other hand, occupying authority status, had a right to income that would enable him to live as a scholar and official ought.

These remarks regarding the psychology of the corrupt official are, of course, conjectural, and much research remains to be done in this field of political sociology. That our remarks may have some basis in the realities of Chinese psychology was, however, suggested by Liu Chien-ch'ün: "The greatest short-coming of the Chinese is that they are unwilling to put themselves in the place of others [that is, to empathize with others]. In thinking of others, they always rationalize their own actions and blame others for everything."[56]

Factionalism

One must, in seeking an explanation of the continual factionalism that splintered the Kuomintang, purge the idea that factional struggles were caused primarily by conflicts over principle or policy. We ought, of course, not deny that Chinese were sometimes passionately and selflessly committed to a "cause." This may, for example, have been true of some factional leaders like Hu Han-min, the Ch'en brothers, or the Thirteen Princes of the Blue Shirts. But the common run of factional members (like most people in most societies) were more concerned with maintaining a home and family and with getting on in the world than with creating a more equitable society.

In addition, when Chinese organized in support of a cause, they displayed a strong tendency to structure the group or faction on the basis of personal ties. The whole pattern of authority-dependency relationships, mutual dependency, and *jen-ch'ing* was thereby established. It was therefore incumbent upon the factional followers to support the factional leader in his cause (and, as was frequently the case, even when the leader switched causes). And, at the same time, the factional leader was expected to provide for his followers.

There was not necessarily a conflict between the personal and impersonal goals of the faction members. But in Chinese society, where the *sheng-kuan fa-ts'ai* mentality was deeply entrenched, the personal goals of the members usually—and especially after the faction had worked its way into power—began to overshadow their commitment to the impersonal goals. Chiang Kai-shek and his coterie provide, perhaps, the preeminent example of this strain between group principles and personal aggrandizement. Chiang himself seems to have been little concerned with personal enrichment and was probably firmly committed to broad national goals. Yet he also condoned flagrant corruption and notorious inefficiency on the part of his officials and military commanders as long as they remained loyal to him.

In large degree, therefore, factions tended to be groups tied together by a network of personal relationships, whose chief purpose had become the enhancement of the power, prestige, and wealth of the faction members. As a newspaper editorialist phrased it: ''Within the party, there is only the formation of alliances, the jealous enmities, the charges and countercharges among the large factions and small cliques. Persons with inflated ambitions to be leaders become sycophants toward those above them who are important persons in the major factions; whereas, toward those below them, they simply seek some backing among those who will cast ballots in electing them [to higher office]. The important persons [in the party] also use this kind [of sycophant] as a tool for their own advancement. Everyone, big and little, does nothing but act for his personal advancement, and certainly does not engage in any practical work among the oppressed lower-level masses."[57]

Americans, even though they are familiar with the meaninglessness of much of their own major parties' campaign oratory, find it difficult to grasp that Chinese factional struggles were not usually the result of deep differences of political views. Yet participants in the events of the decade give convincing testimony that differences over ideology or policy had little if anything to do with the formation of factions:

1. Hsu Dau-lin: "The C.C. and the Whampoa cliques, which both controlled numerous followers in the party at the top as well as at the bottom, were engaged in a relentless race to expand their influence into local governments, government banks, and public enterprises . . . But even they were primarily interested in seizing positions and influence in government and business; *party ideology and political programs were not topics of their quarrel.*"[58]

2. Franklin Ho, who was himself a member of Tao She, which was organized in 1936, wrote: "The Tao She was organized to make its bid for power. It had no program, no platform. Like the Whampoa and C.C. cliques, *it was purely and simply a clique bidding for power within the Party.*"[59]

3. And Liu Chien-ch'ün asserted that *"Any [factional] struggle is not a struggle resulting from differences of policy, but is a struggle for the rice bowl.*"[60]

By the mid-1930s many Chinese intellectuals, who had witnessed repeated revolutions and civil wars, began to sense how meaningless ideology was to the politicians. They therefore refused to support anti-Kuomintang groups—however much they disliked the Kuomintang—because they realized that another revolution would merely harm the people without bringing improvements. The *Ta-kung pao* wrote: "Chinese civil wars are quite different from those in the West. For, although Chinese civil wars are called revolutionary, and they advocate specific political goals, they are actually private power struggles . . . Since 1911 . . . all wars have proclaimed a political goal, but in fact they were personal conflicts."[61] And the *I-shih pao,* a highly respected liberal paper published in Tientsin, declared: "Revolutions in China have been intended merely to get rid of rivals and as a means to obtain political power, because there has been hardly any conflict of principle or ideology. Revolution is wasteful, because it merely switches around the politicians and their posts without drastically bringing new political ideology or political accomplishments."[62]

Although ideology held little meaning for most of China's political actors, they by no means ignored it. For example, hundreds and perhaps thousands of articles and books were written about interpretations of Sun Yat-sen's doctrine. But these ideological polemics and doctrinal explications were little more than froth covering the struggle for office and political power. And Wang Ching-wei, when out-of-power from 1928 to 1932, spearheaded his attack on Chiang Kai-shek with the demands for a multi-party system and the elimination of corruption. After becoming premier in 1932, however, Wang whistled a different tune. He asserted then that the legalization of non-Kuomintang parties at that stage of the revolution would be to ignore the tragic historical lessons since the revolution of 1912 and would plunge China back into a period of warlordism. Meanwhile, Wang's faction settled into government posts, and the name of his reorganization clique became—in at least some circles—almost a byword for corruption and nepotism. Witnessing the transformation wrought on Wang's faction after it attained power, one editorial writer commented that this "truly causes us to feel that political principles are valueless."[63]

Political Repression

One of the important aspects of Chinese social relationships was that conflicts between individuals were seldom resolved through reasoned, face-to-face debate and compromise. Instead, social harmony was to be preserved by silent submission to the decision of an authority figure. Fathers, for example, desired and to a large degree expected absolute obedience from their sons. Failure to receive such unqualified and unquestioning obedience would often cause the father to become infuriated, and to thrash or in some other way inflict harsh punishment on the recalcitrant youth. If a boy as he became older refused to submit to his father, it often led to a breaking-off of the relationship: they would cease to talk to each other; or, in extreme cases, the son would leave home.[64]

In other social relationships, too, the authority of the superior had to be preserved from all taint of criticism or challenge. In school, for example, a young pupil quickly learned that the teacher must be treated as though he knew all the answers; the teacher's facts or interpretations were not open to question. And what would happen in a job if the subordinate criticized the superior to his face? "The boss might misunderstand," a Chinese typically replied: "*he might think the subordinate was opposing him,* or not obeying his orders. He might get angry and then conflict would develop; and possibly the outcome would be bad for the subordinate."[65] At the base of authority figures' responses to criticism was their belief or fear that criticism represented a challenge to or rebellion against their authority status. Because of the primary importance of status to an individual's sense of self-identity, he would react to challenge with all the forces at his command.

An important aspect of Chinese responses to conflict situations is that there was little expectation that these conflicts could be "talked out" or that differences could be resolved through calm and rational debate. Emotions ran close to the surface in China, and conflicts often produced noisy and even dramatic scenes. Quarrels between neighbors would become a spectacle for the entire street to enjoy; marital disagreements might end with the husband striking the wife, or with the wife, cleaver in hand, chasing the husband from the house. The growing child was offered many such examples teaching him that social conflicts must be wholly avoided by submitting passively to authority, or they would erupt in fearful confrontations. Seldom was a Chinese offered a model that would teach him that differences of opinion could be resolved through calm and rational debate.

In the political sphere, there was also but slight expectation that opposition could be resolved through discussion and compromise. When someone expressed criticism of a governmental policy, therefore, the governmental leadership would not perceive that criticism could spring from a legitimate difference of opinion but rather would view it as a rejection of the political authority of the government.

The question of political dominance, in short, suffused all disputes over policy and ideology and partially explains why ideology assumed importance in the Chinese political world. As an editorialist for the *Ta-kung pao* remarked, officials "believe that the secret on how to swim in the bureaucratic sea is to avoid distinguishing between right or wrong or adhering to fixed principles . . . [But] they regard dissenting opinions as opposition and debate as a quarrel."[66]

And Wu Ching-ch'ao, a noted sociologist at Tsinghua University, observed, "Chinese do not maintain an attitude of [objective] discussion . . . In a discussion in China, if someone advocates an idea, it seems as though he falls in love with it and would live with it forever. This kind of person is pleased with people who support his view, and he calls them friend or comrade. But towards those who criticize his view he becomes angry and they . . . become his enemies . . . He not only says such persons lack learning, he says that they lack moral character."[67]

The fact that ideological disagreement was viewed as a symbol of political dissidence helps explain why the Kuomintang leadership was obsessed with the goal of "unity of thought." In a typical statement, Chiang Kai-shek declared, "Unity of thought is more important than anything. If we want the nation to be strong and to be independent and free, then the first task is to plan for the unity of the Chinese people's thought, and to firmly establish Sun Yat-sen's Three People's Principles as the nation's only thought so that they will not again desire a second system of thought to create disorder in China.''⁶⁸

In the eyes of the Kuomintang, advocates of a doctrine other than the official orthodoxy did so because they had *ssu-i* —selfish ambitions. Persons who differed from or criticized the regime were therefore not merely misguided; they were immoral. Such persons, declared Chiang in a vein characteristic of Chinese political discourse, were ''perverse'' and ''opportunistic,'' they did not possess ''innate goodness'' (*liang-chih*), and were simply ''struggling for power.''⁶⁹ It was appropriate therefore—just as a father punished a disobedient son—for the Kuomintang to take firm repressive measures against its critics and opponents. Political objectivity was never a virtue under the Kuomintang. The concept of ''leaning to one side'' was not invented by Mao Tse-tung.

In this chapter, it has been suggested that the failure of the Nationalist regime to create a stable and effective system of rule was fundamentally, albeit not solely, attributable to two factors. First, its political institutions were weak, in the sense that there existed no effective means to supervise, control, and discipline—to impose direction and accountability upon—the personnel within those institutions. This had the effect, as it would have had in any cultural setting, of leaving the members of the government essentially free to rule in the interests not primarily of society but of themselves.

And second, some of the dominant traits of Chinese social behavior proved to be particularly inimical to the development of effective governmental administration. It is true that the purges deprived the Nanking regime of many of its most progressive members; and the infusion of ''northern mandarins'' caused a sudden coagulation in the Kuomintang bloodstream of many of the traditional bureaucratic practices. It would surely be a mistake, nevertheless, to search for the sources of Nationalist weaknesses only within the Kuomintang itself, for both the Ch'ing and warlord governments were characterized by essentially the same administrative pathology. Thus the Nationalists' failure to create an effective and stable system of rule resulted not from, say, some unique ideological or moral fallibilities but was the fruit rather of long historical and cultural development.

There is a tragic irony in the fact that the political culture, which proved so disastrous for the Kuomintang, had served the Chinese well during the traditional period. Dominant traits—such as the authority-dependency pattern of social relationships, the individual's inordinate submissiveness toward authority, the stress on personal relationships, the relative lack of commitment to abstract principles—had contributed to the unparalleled stability of a great culture. And it must be presumed that these traits had become dominant and had endured so lastingly, because the people themselves found them to be generally satisfactory. (I, for one, believe that these traits contributed in at least as great measure to the contentment of the Chinese people as have the more universalistic, egalitarian, and individualistic values to the people of the United States.) Yet these same traits acted like a millstone around the neck of Chinese society during the transition to what-we-call modernity.

The nub of the problem was that China's political culture was well suited to a relatively slowly changing agrarian society but was less well suited to the needs of modernization. In the Ming and Ch'ing dynasties, for example, the role of government was largely limited to preserving peace and maintaining the sources of revenue. The functions of government were therefore essentially negative, and such traits as the willingness to subordinate principles to personal relationships contributed to the admirable stability of the time. During the Nanking period, by contrast, economic and social changes were demanding that government assume a more dynamic role in society. Now it was essential that the government effectively lead in developing the infrastructure—corporate laws, systems of communication, standardization of weights and measures, and so on—upon which a modern economy builds. Now it was essential that the government devise ways of dealing with the newly mobilized social and economic groups. These tasks required a positive, active, and innovative system of government—required administrative behavior that conflicted with the values and practices of the Chinese traditional political culture. But personality, social behavior, and social structures are highly resistant to change. Governments come and go, but these building blocks of culture remain. They are not, to be sure, eternal verities. Yet they change only by gradual erosion and accretion.

This persistence of the political culture has been as pregnant with consequences for the Chinese Communist Party as it was for the Kuomintang. We have already noted that the Kuomintang purges of the late 1920s had a filtering effect. Those who remained in the Kuomintang were preponderantly the careerists, those for whom *sheng-kuan fa-ts'ai* held a strong attraction. The Kuomintang, in other words, was left with members most of whom displayed the modal characteristics that were described in this chapter.

Conversely, the communists, those who had been filtered out of the Kuomintang by the purge, probably did not in strong degree possess the modal traits of Chinese social behavior. If they had been primarily concerned with attaining official status and the perquisites of office, they surely would not have been attracted by perils of the revolutionary endeavor in Kiangsi. They tended therefore to be persons more imbued with idealism and social purpose than those who remained within the ranks of the Kuomintang. This, at least, is the impression that was conveyed by the Edgar Snows, Evans Carlsons, and Harrison Formans—by the vast majority of Westerners who gained access to the Soviet areas during the 1930s and the 1940s.[70]

After the communists' victory, the dominant social traits of the traditional political culture began to emerge within the ranks of the Communist Party. For, when the Communist Party became the ruling power of the nation, it and not the

Kuomintang was the source of careerist and material gratification. No doubt the communists were more successful than the Kuomintang in creating strong political institutions before they gained national power—the communists' relatively long administrative experience in Yenan was thus an advantage that had been denied the Kuomintang. And after 1949, the Communist Party strived valiantly to maintain quality control of its new members. For a time during the 1950s it looked as though they had succeeded in screening out the carriers of the old political culture. But the task was gargantuan. The Communist Party grew from a membership of 1.2 million in 1945, to 5.8 million by the end of 1950, to 17 million by 1961.[71] Manifestly, it was neither practicable nor possible to admit into the party only persons possessing the values and behavioral traits of the veterans of the Long March. As a consequence, the leadership of the party increasingly during the early 1960s voiced complaints against official corruption, bureaucratization, and the growing gulf between the cadre and masses. "Some cadres," it was said, "are too concerned with rank and position"; and there were official admissions that "arrogant careerists and degenerate elements" were active in the party.[72] By 1966 Doak Barnett concluded that the party leadership's struggle against bureaucratism "appears to have been a losing battle."[73]

The Cultural Revolution appears to have been Mao Tsetung's supreme effort to prevent the traditional political culture from suffocating the revolution that he had nursed to maturity. He had observed the experience of Chiang Kai-shek, and he was determined that his revolution not fall victim to the traditional cultural influences as had the Kuomintang.

Mao, however, has recognized that the political culture is tenacious. "Reactionary thought . . . inherited from the past," he has warned, "still exists in the minds of a considerable number of people, and cannot be transformed quickly. Its transformation needs time, a long period of time." In fact, he cautioned that the evil traits of the old society will continue even after "one, two, three, or four great cultural revolu-tions."[74] Mao, obviously, has perceived that traditional val-ues and attitudes must be thoroughly transformed; a modern Chinese state cannot coexist with the old political culture. Realization of this truth had been denied Chiang Kai-shek.

Notes, Bibliography,
Glossary, and Index

Abbreviations Used in the Notes

CWR   *China Weekly Review*
KMTS   "Chung-kuo kuo-min-tang shih tzu-liao hui-pien," ts'e 9
KWCP   *Kuo-wen chou-pao*
Nankai *Nankai Social and Economic Quarterly*
NCH   *North China Herald*
SHHW   *She-hui hsin-wen*
STKL   *Shih-tai kung-lun*
TFTC   *Tung-fang tsa-chih*
TKP   *Ta-kung pao*
TLPL   *Tu-li p'ing-lun*

Many of the Chinese periodicals referred to in the notes were not paginated sequentially throughout the journal. As a consequence, different articles or sections of a journal frequently began with page one.

While in Taiwan undertaking research for this study, I interviewed a number of persons who had participated in the events of the Nanking period. Soon after starting these interviews, I discovered that my informants were reluctant to be candid in their revelations of past events unless they were assured of anonymity. I was sympathetic to their concerns. I have therefore not revealed the identity of my informants who are still living, but have simply indicated "interview" in the notes when information was obtained through personal conversation.

Notes

Foreword

1. Philip A. Kuhn, " 'Local Self-Government' under the Republic: Problems of Control, Autonomy, and Mobilization" (Paper prepared for the Research Conference on Local Control and Protest during Ch'ing Period, East–West Center, University of Hawaii, 1971), p. 41, to be published in *Conflict and Control: Social Process in Late Imperial China,* ed. Frederic Wakeman, Jr., with Carolyn Grant (Berkeley, University of California Press, in press).

2. Ernest P. Young, "The Hung-hsien Emperor as a Conservative Modernizer" (Paper prepared for the Research Conference on Intellectuals and the Problems of Conservatism in Republican China, Dedham, Mass., 1972), p. 12.

3. Talcott Parsons, "Some Reflections on the Place of Force in Social Process," in *Internal War,* ed. Harry Eckstein (New York, Free Press of Glencoe, 1964), p. 34.

4. Lin Yü-sheng, "Radical Iconoclasm in the May Fourth Period and the Future of Chinese Liberalism," in *Reflections on the May Fourth Movement: A Symposium,* ed. Benjamin I. Schwartz (Cambridge, Mass., East Asian Research Center, Harvard University, 1972), p. 27.

5. Ernest P. Young, p. 6.

6. C. K. Yang, *A Chinese Village in Early Communist Transition* (Cambridge, Mass., Massachusetts Institute of Technology Press, 1959), p. 114.

1. "The Revolution Has Failed"

1. *China Year Book, 1928,* pp. 1373, 1374.

2. Franklin L. Ho, "The Reminiscences of Ho Lien (Franklin L. Ho)" as told to Crystal Lorch, unpub. ms., postscript dated July 1966 (Special Collections Library, Butler Library, Columbia University), p. 438.

3. Quoted in [Yang Kung-]ta, "Fa-hsi-ssu-t'i chih mi" (The fascist riddle), *Shih-tai kung-lun* 16:11 (July 15, 1932).

4. League of Nations Archives, Report of Ludwig Rajchman, Feb. 5, 1930, p. 7.

5. Gauss to Johnson, Sept. 16, 1934, State Dept. 893.00/12842, p. 1.

6. Interview; Chou Fo-hai, "Chin-hou te ko-ming" (The revolution from now on), *Hsin-sheng-ming* 1.1:11–12 (January 1928); *Ch'en-pao* (Morning post), Jan. 11, 1928, in Hatano Ken'ichi, comp., *Gendai Shina no kiroku* (Peking, 1924–1932), January 1928, pp. 110–111. This last item is based on a reporter's interview with Ho Ying-ch'in.

7. James Robert Shirley, "Political Conflict in the Kuomintang: The Career of Wang Ching-wei to 1932" (Ph.D. diss., University of California, 1962), p. 3; Huang Shao-hung, *Wu-shih hui-i* (Hangchow, 1945), p. 183.

8. C. Martin Wilbur, "Military Separatism and the Process of Reunification under the Nationalist Regime, 1922–1937," *China in Crisis*, ed. Ping-ti Ho and Tang Tsou (Chicago, University of Chicago Press, 1968), I, 224–225n; Melville Talbot Kennedy, Jr., "The Kuomintang and Chinese Unification, 1928–1931" (Ph.D. diss., Harvard University, 1958), pp. 136–137.

9. *Ch'en-pao*, Jan. 11, 1928, in Hatano, *Kiroku*, January 1928, pp. 110–111.

10. Sa Meng-wu, "I-tang chih-kuo" (Using the party to rule the nation), *Hsin-sheng-ming* 1.4:8 (April 1, 1928). On lax Kuomintang recruiting policy, see also: Patrick Cavendish, "The Rise of the Chinese Nationalist Party and the Foundation of the Nanking Regime: 1924–1929" (Ph.D. diss., Cambridge University, 1968), p. 213; Ts'un-tung, "Tang te min-chu-hua yü ch'ün-chung-hua" (The democratization and mass-ization of the party), *Ko-ming p'ing-lun* 12:15 (1928).

11. Ho Ying-ch'in, "Chin-hou chih Chung-kuo kuo-min-tang" (The Chinese Kuomintang from now on), *Chung-yang pan-yüeh-k'an* 2:100–102 (October 1927); *Ch'en-pao*, Jan. 11, 1928 in Hatano, *Kiroku*, January, 1928, pp. 110–111.

12. "Hui-fu ko-ming ching-shen ho chi-lü" (Restore revolutionary spirit and discipline), *Chiang tsung-t'ung yen-lun hui-pien* (Taipei, 1956), IX, 53 and 55. See also Chou Fo-hai, "Chin-hou te ko-ming," *Hsin-sheng-ming* 1.1:2 (January 1928).

13. Ch'en Kung-po, *So-wei san-tz'u tai-piao ta-hui chia-chih te ku-liang*, 2nd ed. (Shanghai, 1929), p. 14; Jürgen Domes, *Vertagte Revolution: Die Politik der Kuomintang in China, 1923–1937* (Berlin, 1969), p. 748.

14. *NCH*, Apr. 14, 1928, p. 48. See also *NCH*, Apr. 14, 1928, p. 52; and *NCH*, July 28, 1928, p. 138.

15. Dau-lin Hsu, "Chinese Local Administration under the National Government: Democracy and Self-government" (unpub. ms.), chap, 2, p. 46; *TKP*, Nov. 5, 1934, editorial, p. 2.

16. *NCH*, May 2, 1929, p. 342.

17. Liu Chien-ch'ün, *Fu-hsing Chung-kuo ko-ming chih lu* (n.p., 1934), p. 113.

18. Wang Cheng, "The Kuomintang: A Sociological Study of Demoralization" (Ph.D. diss., Stanford University, 1953), p. 147.

19. Fu Yüan, "Wo-men te i-chiu-erh-pa nien" (Our 1928), *Kung-hsien* 1.4:4 (Jan. 5, 1928); [Ma] Chi-lien, "Kuo-nan fang-hsing wei-ai" (The national emergency has just started and no prospect of surcease), *KWCP* 9.25: articles p. 4 (June 27, 1932).

20. *NCH*, Nov. 10, 1928, p. 212; Ho Kan-chih, *Chung-kuo hsien-tai ko-ming shih* (Peking, 1957), I, 118–119; "I-pao i-pao chih pu-k'o (The impermissibility of transforming violence with violence), *TKP* editorial, reprinted in *KWCP* 7.33: editorials p. 1 (Aug. 25, 1930).

21. Ho Ying-ch'in, "Chin-hou chih Chung-kuo kuo-min-tang," p. 102. See also Huang Shao-hung, pp. 183–184; Patrick Cavendish, "The 'New China' of the Kuomintang," in Jack Gray, ed., *Modern China's Search for a Political Form* (London, 1969), p. 141.

22. Shen Ch'ing-chen, "Chung-kuo ko-ming te shih-pai yü ch'i ch'u-lu" (The defeat of the Chinese revolution and its way-out), *Shih-tai kung-lun* 2.45:11 (Feb. 2, 1934).

23. Hu Shih, "Hsin-wen-hua yün-tung yü kuo-min-tang" (The new culture movement and the Kuomintang), in *Jen-ch'üan lun-chi* (Shanghai, 1931), p. 135. See also *Ch'en-pao*, Jan. 10, 1929, in Hatano, *Kiroku*, January 1929, p. 103.

24. For a specific example of this effect, see pp. 52–53.

25. See, e.g., *Ch'en-pao*, Feb. 11, 1928, in Hatano, *Kiroku*, February 1928, pp. 151–154.

26. *NCH*, Jan. 28, 1930, p. 132; ibid., Feb. 11, 1930, p. 205.

27. Wang Cheng, pp. 143–146.

28. *TKP* editorial, Nov. 5, 1934, pp. 2–3.

29. Li Lu-chou, *Kuo-min cheng-fu te cheng-chi* (Shanghai, 1934), p. 182. See also Hung-mao Tien, *Government and Politics in Kuomintang China, 1927–1937* (Stanford, 1972), pp. 22–24; *I-shih pao* editorial, reprinted in *KWCP* 9.23: editorials pp. 8–9 (June 13, 1932).

30. Mei Ssu-p'ing, "Wu-ch'üan hsien-fa te ching-shen chi yün-yung te fang-fa" (The spirit of the five-power constitution and the method of implementing it), *Hsin-sheng-ming* 1.3:4 (March 1, 1928); Yang Yu-chiung, "I-tang chih-kuo chih li-lun te chi-ch'u" (The theoretical basis of party-rule), *Chung-yang pan-yüeh-k'an* 22:95 (1928).

31. Hung-mao Tien, *Government and Politics,* p. 21.

32. Li Lu-chou, p. 79. Because so few persons attained office through the examinations, the economic feasibility of the examination system was highly dubious. It was estimated that the Examination Yüan spent ¥20,000 for each man selected for office (ibid.). This is a good example of the bureaucracy that exists for the benefit of the bureaucrats themselves.

33. Huang Shao-hung, p. 233. See also Hu Shih, "Kung-k'ai chien-chü i" (On open recommendations), *TKP*, March 4, 1934, reprinted in *KWCP* 11.10: articles p. 1 (March 12, 1934).

34. "Hsiu-ming nei-cheng yü cheng-ch'ih li-chih" (Reform internal ad-

ministration and rectify rule by officials), *Chiang tsung-t'ung ssu-hsiang yen-lun chi* XI, 130.

35. "Chiao-fei yao shih-kan" (To exterminate the communists, we must work effectively), *Chiang tsung-t'ung ssu-hsiang yen-lun chi* XI, 137.

36. Dau-lin Hsu, chap. II, p. 49.

37. "Fa-k'an tz'u" (Inaugural statement), *Wen-hua chien-she* 1.1:3 (Oct. 10, 1934).

38. Gideon Chen, *Chinese Government Economic Planning and Reconstruction since 1927* (China Institute of Pacific Relations, 1933), p. 24 and passim. Ting Wen-chiang remarked that "the more reconstruction organizations established, the fewer are the results." "Chung-kuo cheng-chih te ch'u-lu" (The way out for Chinese government), *TLPL* 11:6 (July 31, 1932). On the relationship between the central and provincial administrations, see Hung-mao Tien, *Government and Politics,* pp. 89–95.

39. Gideon Chen, p. 9.

40. Ibid., pp. 25–26.

41. "Hsin-sheng-huo yün-tung san-chou-nien chi-nien kao ch'üan-kuo t'ung-pao shu" (A report to the nation on the third anniversary of the New Life Movement), *Chiang tsung-t'ung ssu-hsiang yen-lun chi,* XXV, 56.

42. Lin Yutang, *My Country and My People* (New York, 1935), p. 182.

43. J. S. Nye, "Corruption and Political Development: A Cost-Benefit Analysis," *American Political Science Review* 61.2:417–427 (June 1967).

44. Gunnar Myrdal, *Asian Drama: An Inquiry into the Poverty of Nations* (New York, 1968), pp. 951–952.

45. Ho Ying-ch'in, "Chin-hou chih Chung-kuo kuo-min-tang," p. 102.

46. *NCH,* Nov. 17, 1928, p. 249; *TKP* editorial, reprinted in *KWCP* 10.44: editorials p. 4 (Nov. 6, 1933); *TKP* editorial, reprinted in *KWCP* 7.7: editorials pp. 5–6 (Feb. 24, 1930); Hsiung Shih-li "Wu-ch'ih wu-chiao" (No food, no education), *TLPL* 95:14 (April 8, 1934); Franklin L. Ho, "Reminiscences" p. 291; Kennedy, p. 67; [Ma] Chi-lien, "Kuo-nan fang-hsing wei-ai," p. 6; *Shun-t'ien shih-pao* (Shun-t'ien times) editorial, reprinted in Hatano, *Kiroku,* September 1928, p. 255.

47. *STKL* editorial, reprinted in *KWCP* 9.22: editorials p. 6 (June 6, 1932); Chün-heng, "Cheng-chih ling-hsui te ssu-hsin" (The selfishness of the political leaders), *TLPL* 61:10 (July 30, 1933).

48. H. D. Fong, *Industrial Capital in China* (Tientsin, 1936), p. 47. See also *TKP,* Dec. 15, 1934, editorial p. 2.

49. Franklin L. Ho, "Reminiscences," p. 291.

50. Interview. It is of some interest that persons who he said were not corrupt were Hu Han-min, Wang Ching-wei, and the brothers Ch'en Kuo-fu and Ch'en Li-fu. Li Lu-chou, p. 75, also remarked that there were a few incorrupt officials in the regime, but these did not customarily hold important positions.

51. *TKP* editorial, reprinted in *KWCP* 7.48: editorials pp. 1–2 (Dec. 8, 1930); [Ma] Chi-lien, "Hsien-cheng neng chiu Chung-kuo?" (Can constitutional government save China?), *KWCP* 9.18: articles p. 6 (May 9, 1932). Ch'en Chih-mai, by contrast, stated that corruption, albeit still rampant,

was not as bad as under the warlords. "Lun cheng-chih t'an-wu" (On governmental corruption), *TLPL* 184:4 (Jan. 5, 1936).

52. See, e.g., *Shih-shih hsin-pao* ("The China Times") editorial, reprinted in *KWCP* 9.28: editorials p. 1 (July 18, 1932).

53. Quoted in Ting Wen-chiang, "So-wei 'chiao-fei' wen-t'i" (The so-called bandit-extermination problem), *TLPL* 6:3 (June 26, 1932).

54. *Shih-shih hsin-pao*, Oct. 21, 1930, sect. 2, p. 1.

55. "Chiao-fei yao shih-kan," *Chiang tsung-t'ung ssu-hsiang yen-lun chi*, XI, 137.

56. Chiang Chung-cheng, "Ti-erh-ch'i ko-ming chih k'ai-shih," *Ch'ien-t'u* 2.2:1 (Feb. 1, 1934).

57. I have seen references to new laws that were promulgated in each year between 1930 and 1937. See, e.g., *Ch'en-pao* editorial, reprinted in *KWCP* 13.12: editorials p. 6 (March 30, 1936).

58. Huang Shao-hung, pp. 298–299.

59. Wu Chih-kan, "Nankin seifu Ō-Bei ha no taigai tainai seisaku to saikin no Nei-Etsu kanken" (The foreign and domestic policies of the Nanking government's European-American clique and recent relationships between Nanking and Canton), *Shanhai* 958:3 (June 1936).

60. C. M. Chang, "Impeachments of the Control Yuan," *Chinese Social and Political Science Review* 19.3 and 4: 524–534 (January 1936).

61. Li Lu-chou, p. 88. These figures may be only approximate, for the scholarly quality of this source is dubious. Li Lu-chou's figures regarding impeachments do, however, correspond closely with a reliable work that has, incidentally, been banned in Taiwan. See Fu Chi-hsüeh, et al., *Chung-hua min-kuo chien-ch'a-yüan chih yen-chiu* (Taipei, 1967), pp. 217–218, 220–226. The general validity of the information detailed here is attested also by C. M. Chang, "Impeachments," pp. 534–538; T'ang Chi-ho, "Wu-nien-lai te chien-ch'a-yüan" (The Control Yüan during the past five years), *TFTC* 34.1:151–153 (Jan. 1, 1937); and Wang Lü-keng, "Chung-kuo chih chien-ch'a chih-tu" (China's supervisory system), *TFTC* 32.17:173–176 (Sept. 1, 1936).

62. Wang Hsin-ming, "Ch'iang-hua tang-chih yü chi-hsü hsün-cheng" (Strengthen party-rule and continue political tutelage), *Wen-hua chien-she* 2.2:21 (Nov. 10, 1935).

63. Fu Ch'i-hsüeh, chart 31, pp. 220–226.

64. "Nan-ching cheng-cheng chih nei-mu" (The inside story of Nanking's political struggles), an article dated July 5 [1934] from unspecified newspaper, in Yokota Minoru Newspaper Collection (Tōyō Bunko); "Chien-yüan cheng-yüan k'ang-cheng chü-lüeh" (The struggle between the Control Yüan and the Executive Yüan intensifies), *Chiang-nan cheng-pao* (Kiangnan truth), Oct. 7, 1934, in Yokota Collection. This case deserves further study, for it provides ready access to the struggles that existed behind the scenes in Nanking. See, e.g., issues of *STKL* in 1934. Also, see C. M. Chang, "Impeachments," pp. 359–365.

65. Report of Capt. J. M. McHugh on reconnaissance of Kiangsi and Hunan in December 1934, State Dept, 893.00/12948, p. 14; Peck to State, State Dept., 893.00/12617. p. 3.

66. *NCH,* May 20, 1930, p. 297.

67. *Ching-pao* (Capital post), Feb. 26, 1929, in Hatano, *Kiroku,* February 1929, p. 293.

68. *NCH,* May 20, 1930, p. 297.

69. Liu Chen-tung, "Chung-kuo ch'u-lu wen-t'i" (The question of China's way-out), *KWCP* 10.24:2 (June 19, 1933).

70. Tsiang T'ing-fu "Kuo-min-tang yü kuo-min-tang-yüan" (The Kuomin-tang and Kuomintang members), *TLPL* 176:14 (Nov. 10, 1935).

71. *TKP* editorial, reprinted in "Min-pien shih-chi" (Preliminary record of the Fukien rebellion), *KWCP* 10.47: articles p. 10 (Nov. 27, 1933); and *TKP* editorial, reprinted in *KWCP* 10.47: editorials p. 1 (Nov. 27, 1933). During these years, such sentiments were not a rarity.

72. Tsi-an Hsia, *The Gate of Darkness: Studies on the Leftist Literary Movement in China* (Seattle, 1968), pp. 164–165; *China Forum* 2.1:12 (Feb. 11, 1933); *CWR* 63.3:94 (Dec. 17, 1932); Harriet Cornelia Mills, "Lu Hsün: 1927–1936, The Years on the Left" (Ph.D. diss., Columbia University, 1963), pp. 291–292.

73. *China Critic* 6.6:165–166 (Feb. 9, 1933); *China Forum* 2.1:9–10 (Feb. 11, 1933). For other reports of prison conditions, see *China Forum* 2.2:15–16 (March 1, 1933) and 2.3:13–14 (March 27, 1933); and Mills, pp. 301–311.

74. *China Forum* 2.2:14 (March 1, 1933), and 2.3:13 (March 27, 1933); Jerome B. Grieder, *Hu Shih and the Chinese Renaissance* (Cambridge, Mass. 1970), pp. 272–279.

75. For emotion-filled accounts of this episode, see *China Forum* 2.7:1–7 (June 19, 1933), and 2.8:1 (July 14, 1933).

76. *CWR* 65.4:146 (June 24, 1933); Mills, p. 297.

77. *CWR* 65.4:146–147 (June 24, 1933).

78. Mills, p. 299.

79. "Lan-i-she to chiao-yü ch'üan" (The Blue Shirts usurp the power of education), an article dated June 17, [1934?] from unspecified newspaper, in Yokota Collection. A partial listing of episodes of suppression of students is in Lo I and Huang Chi-ch'ing, et al., *Chung-kuo fa-hsi-ssu t'e-wu chen-hsiang,* p. 16. A brief but good picture of the "white terror" in educational circles is in John Israel, *Student Nationalism in China, 1927–1937* (Stanford, 1966), pp. 98–100.

80. *TKP* editorial, Dec. 9, 1934, pp. 2–3.

81. Chang Ch'i-yün, *Tang-shih kai-yao* (Taipei, 1953), II, 580.

82. Ssu-ma Hsien-tao, *Pei-fa hou chih ko-p'ai ssu-ch'ao* (Peiping, 1930), pp. 152–157.

83. *NCH,* Aug. 6, 1927, p. 221.

84. Lin Yutang, *A History of the Press and Public Opinion in China* (Chicago, 1936), p. 126.

85. Chang Ching-lu, *Chung-kuo hsien-tai ch'u-pan shih-liao* (Peking, 1954–1959), II, 510–517. Numerous supplementary regulations to the Press Law were promulgated throughout the 1930s. See Lee-Hsia Hsu Ting, "Government Control of the Press in Modern China, 1900–1949: A Study of Its

Theories, Operations and Effects" (Ph.D. diss., University of Chicago, 1969), pp. 34–38; and *Chinese Year Book, 1936–1937,* pp. 524–534.

86. Chang Ching-lu, II, 190–205, and III, 144–164; Lin Yutang, *History of the Press,* p. 173.

87. Chang Ching-lu, II, 205–254.

88. Lee-Hsia Hsu Ting, p. 189. Ting derived this figure from the eight lists in the Chang Ching-lu volumes which, she observes, sometimes overlap but which also do not exhaust the number of banned works.

89. *KWCP* 8.31: editorials p. 5 (Aug. 10, 1931); *KWCP* 12.5: editorials p. 4 (Jan. 28, 1935); *KWCP* 7.10: editorials p. 6 (Mar. 17, 1930); *KWCP* 12.5: editorials p. 4 (Jan. 28, 1935).

90. *NCH,* Oct. 13, 1934, p. 173; Lin Yutang, *History of the Press,* pp. 170–171.

91. H. J. Timperley, "Makers of Public Opinion about the Far East," *Pacific Affairs* 9:225 (June 1936). Other examples in Lin Yutang, *History of the Press,* p. 177; Lee-Hsia Hsu Ting, pp. 187, 194.

92. See, e.g., *NCH,* Dec. 31, 1929, p. 536.

93. *China Year Book, 1934,* p. 663.

94. The fullest and best discussion of this incident is in Lee-Hsia Hsu Ting, pp. 218–223. See also Lin Yutang, *History of the Press,* pp. 171–172; Li P'u-k'ou, recorded by Ch'in Ling-yün' " "Ts'ung so-wei 'ch'i-chün-tzu' t'an tao 'chiu-kuo-hui' " (The so-called seven gentlemen and the National Salvation Association), *Ch'un-ch'iu* 144:6 (July 1, 1963).

95. Timperley, p. 224. Edgar Snow also commented on this aspect of censorship in "The Ways of the Chinese Censor," *Current History* 42.4:381–386 (July 1935).

96. Cheng-chih, "Chung-kuo wei-shem-ma mei-yu yü-lun?" (Why doesn't China have a public opinion?), *KWCP* 11.2: articles pp. 2–4 (Jan. 1, 1934); *TKP* editorial, reprinted in *KWCP* 11.50: editorials p. 1 (Dec. 17, 1934).

97. Huang Shao-hung, p. 238; Edgar Snow, "Ways of the Chinese Censor," p. 381; Vernon Nash and Rudolf Löwenthal, "Responsible Factors in Chinese Journalism," *Chinese Social and Political Science Review* 20.3:420–426 (October 1936); Lin Yutang, *History of the Press,* p. 174.

98. Nash and Löwenthal, p. 424; Lee-Hsia Hsu Ting, p. 181; Lin Yutang, *History of the Press,* pp. 163–164.

99. Lin Yutang, *History of the Press,* pp. 177–178; Lee-Hsia Hsu Ting, p. 243; *TKP* editorial, reprinted in *KWCP* 11.50: editorials p. 1–2 (Dec. 17, 1934).

100. *Howard L. Boorman,* ed., *Biographical Dictionary of Republican China* (New York, 1967–1971), III, 320.

101. "Hsiu-k'an te hua" (Words upon ceasing publication), *STKL* 155/156:79 (March 22, 1935).

102. Quoted in *NCH,* Dec. 4, 1935, p. 389.

2. Fascism in the Kuomintang

1. On the emperors' use of these diverse groups to control the civil bureaucrats, see Joseph R. Levenson, *Confucian China and Its Modern Fate,* Vol.

II, *The Problem of Monarchical Decay* (Berkeley, University of California Press, 1964), pp. 35–50.

2. This essay, the Chinese title of which is "Kung-hsien i-tien cheng-li pen-tang te i-chien," may be found in Liu Chien-ch'ün, *Fu-hsing Chung-kuo ko-ming chih lu*, pp. 95–181. The following discussion of Liu Chien-ch'ün's ideas is drawn entirely from that essay.

3. "Tang-nei t'uan-chieh shih wo-men wei-i te ch'u-lu" (Our only solution is for the party to unite), *Chiang Tsung-t'ung ssu-hsiang yen-lun chi* XI, 44.

4. "Chiang Chieh-shih tz'u kuo-fu chu-hsi" (Chiang Kai-shek resigns chairmanship of the national government), *KWCP* 8.50: articles pp. 1, 4–5 (Dec. 21, 1931). Chiang did not, however, resign from the Central Executive Committee of the Kuomintang.

5. "Ranisha no gainen to sono tokumu kōsaku ni tsuite" (The concept of the Blue Shirts and their special service operations; prepared by the General Headquarters of the Expeditionary Army in China, 1940), n. p.

6. "Ranisha no soshiki to hanmen kōnichi katsudō no jitsurei" (The organization of the Blue Shirts and examples of anti-Manchukuo, anti-Japanese activities), in *Ranisha ni kansuru shiryō* (Materials on the Blue Shirts), p. 11; and [Iwai Eiichi], *Ranisha ni kansuru chōsa* (An investigation of the Blue Shirts; issued by the Research Division of the Foreign Ministry), p. 6.

7. The sources provide slightly different versions of the events leading to the formation of the organization. Compare "Ranisha no gainen"; Ch'en Shao-hsiao, *Hei-wang-lu* (Hong Kong, 1966), p. 9; Kan Kuo-hsün, "Chui-ssu Liu Chien-ch'ün, ping shih lan-i-she," *Chuan-chi wen-hsueh* 21.3:19.

8. Morohashi Tetsuji, *Dai Kan-Wa jiten* (Chinese-Japanese dictionary; Tokyo, 1955–1966), II, 1574. Chü-wai-jen, "Chi tang-nien ch'uan-shuo-chung te 'shih-san t'ai-pao'," pt. 7, p. 10.

9. The nine names that appear most frequently as Thirteen Princes were: Ho Chung-han, K'ang Tse, Teng Wen-i, P'an Yu-ch'iang, Tai Li, Liu Chien-ch'ün, Cheng Chieh-min, Hsiao Tsan-yü, and Kuei Yung-ch'ing. Others who have been mentioned by various authors as being Thirteen Princes are: Feng T'i, Chou Fu, Tseng K'uo-ch'ing, T'eng Chieh, Liang Kan-ch'iao, Ko Wu-ch'i, Tu Hsin-ju, Chiang Hsiao-hsien, and Hu Tsung-nan. Compare: "Ranisha no gainen"; Ch'en Shao-hsiao, p. 14; and Chü-wai-jen, pt. 1, p. 5.

10. F. F. Liu, *A Military History of Modern China* (Princeton, 1956), pp. 53–59; interview.

11. Tien-wei Wu, "Chiang Kai-shek's March Twentieth Coup d'Etat of 1926," *Journal of Asian Studies* 27.3:586–587 (May 1968); Boorman, II, 64–65; C. Martin Wilbur and Julie Lien-ying How, eds., *Documents on Communism, Nationalism, and Soviet Advisers in China, 1918–1927* (New York, 1956), pp. 200, 260, 263; and interview. Ch'en Shao-hsiao, pp. 31–32, states that the initial organization formed by the left-leaning cadets was called the Huo-hsing-she. I have seen no corroboration elsewhere.

On the Sunists' reliance on the writings of Tai Chi-t'ao, see Iwai, p. 16. An exposition of Tai's writings is in Herman William Mast, III, "An Intellectual Biography of Tai Chi-t'ao, 1890–1927" (Ph.D. diss., University of Illinois, 1970), pp. 285–299. See also Boorman, III, 202.

12. Franklin Ho, "Reminiscences," p. 305.

13. Ch'en Kung-po, *So-wei san-tz'u tai-piao ta-hui,* pp. 35–36.

14. A secret publication of the Blue Shirts allegedly reported that approximately one-half of the Whampoa graduates remained loyal to Chiang Kai-shek in 1935. (See "Ranisha no soshiki," pp. 21–22.) According to this report, Whampoa men were divided into the following camps by percent:

Chiang Kai-shek	35	Reorganizationist clique (Wang	
Various generals responsive to		Ching-wei)	3
Chiang Kai-shek's authority	15	Third Party	2
Communist Party	10	Manchuria-Mongolia	1
Kwangtung-Kwangsi	10	Unclear	20
Northwest (Yen Hsi-shan,			
et al.)	4		

15. T'ung Jun-chih, "Chung-kuo min-tsu te chih-li" (The intelligence of the Chinese race), *TFTC* 26.3:67–76 (Feb. 10, 1929).

16. Jerry Bernard Seps, "German Military Advisers and Chiang Kai-shek, 1927–1938" (Ph.D. diss., University of California, Berkeley, 1972), pp. 35, 82, 160, and passim; Karl Mehner, "Die Rolle deutscher Militärberater als Interessenvertreter des deutschen Imperialismus und Militarismus in China (1928–1936)" (Inaugural dissertation, Karl-Marx-Universität, Leipzig, 1961), pp. 69–71, 99–100, 118–121, and passim. See also F. F. Liu, p. 75; Ch'en Shao-hsiao, p. 26; *Chung-kuo chin-tai cheng-chih chien-shih* (Chung-nan, republished 1950), p. 99.

17. Ch'en Po-ta, *Jen-min kung-ti Chiang Chieh-shih* (Peking, 4th ed., 1954), p. 72.

18. Seps, p. 281.

19. "Ranisha no soshiki," pp. 3, 5.

20. "Kuo-min-tang yü fa-hsi-ssu-t'i yün-tung" (The Kuomintang and fascism), *SHHW* 4:274 (Aug. 24, 1933).

I am of the considered opinion that *She-hui hsin-wen* was a Blue Shirt publication. The reader should be warned, however, that the question of the political alignment of this periodical may be in doubt. Boorman, I, 436, states that it was a publication of the CC clique. The Boorman volumes cannot, however, be accepted as definitive. The *China Forum* (2.12:4 [Oct. 22, 1933]), on the contrary, referred to *She-hui hsin-wen* as "Chiang Kai-shek's local Blue Jacket sheetlet." *China Forum,* however, was probably not clear regarding the distinction between the Blue Shirts and the CC clique. (See, e.g., 2.2.:4–5 [March 1, 1933]). The most conclusive evidence to hand is: that Chiang Chien-jen, a known Blue Shirt, has been identified by a knowledgeable informant as editor of the journal; and that writers in the *Ch'ing-nien chün-jen* (an anti-Chiang organ published in Kwangtung) stated that *She-hui hsin-wen* was a Chinese fascist organ (1.13:2 [Sept. 30, 1933])—and by "Chinese fascist" they meant the Blue Shirts (see, e.g., 1.7:5 [June 30, 1933] and 2.16:19 [Aug. 31, 1934]). This conclusion is supported by the fact that the editorial policy of the *She-hui hsin-wen* corresponds almost exactly with the writings in *Ch'ien-t'u* (a single exception is noted below, pp. 51–52, which was unquestionably a Blue Shirt publication. On the relationship of *Ch'ien-t'u* with the Blue Shirts, see Ch'en Shao-hsiao, p. 44.

21. Interview.

22. Iwai, p. 187.

23. "Kuo-min-tang yü fa-hsi-ssu-t'i yün-tung," *SHHW* 4:274.

24. Ch'en Ch'iu-yün, "Fa-hsi-ssu-t'i yü Chung-kuo" (Fascism and China), *Ch'ien-t'u* 2.2:1 (Feb. 1, 1934). *Ch'ien-t'u* was indisputably a Blue Shirt publication.

25. "Chin-jih chiao-shih ying-yu te jen-shih yü tse-jen" (The awareness and responsibilities that today's teachers ought to have), speech delivered by Ho Chung-han, recorded by Chang Ming, *Ch'ien-t'u* 1.8:1 (Aug. 1, 1933). On Ho Chung-han, see Boorman, II, 64–67.

26. Editorial, *SHHW* 3:147 (April 30, 1933).

27. Ch'en Ch'iu-yün, "Fa-hsi-ssu-t'i chu-i yü Chung-ko," p. 3.

28. Iwai, p. 188.

29. Liu Chien-ch'ün, *Yin-ho i-wang* (Memories at Yin-ho; Taipei, 1966), p. 235. See also Liu's analogy between marriage and unquestioning commitment to the leader. Ibid.

30. "Ranisha no soshiki," p. 5.

31. "Kuo-min-tang yü fa-hsi-ssu-t'i yün-tung," p. 275.

32. Liu Chien-ch'ün, *Fu-hsing Chung-kuo ko-ming chih-lu,* pp. 34–35.

33. Ch'en Ch'iu-yün, "Fa-hsi-ssu-t'i chu-i yü Chung-kuo," p. 3.

34. "Wu-ch'üan ta-hui hsüan-ch'uan ta-kang" (Propaganda program of the 5th party congress), Oct. 21, 1934, in Yokota Collection.

35. Editorial, *SHHW* 3:226 (May 15, 1933). Emphasis added.

36. Iwai, pp. 38–39.

37. *NCH,* Oct. 17, 1934, p. 113; *China Year Book, 1935,* p. 96.

38. Chang Yün-fu, "Wen-hua t'ung-chih te i-i chi fang-fa" (The meaning and method of cultural control), *Ch'ien-t'u* 2.8:7 (Aug. 1, 1934).

39. Ju Ch'un-p'u, "Wen-hua t'ung-chih te ken-pen i-i yü min-tsu ch'ien-t'u" (The basic meaning of cultural control and the future of the nation), *Ch'ien-t'u* 2.8:4 (Aug. 1, 1934).

40. Chang Yün-fu, p. 2.

41. Editorial, *SHHW* 3:306 (May 30, 1933); editorial, *SHHW* 3:354 (June 9, 1933); Chang Yün-fu, p. 4; Liu Ping-li, "Nung-ts'un fu-hsing te i-i" (The meaning of rural regeneration), *Ch'ien-t'u* 1.9:3 (Sept. 1, 1933).

42. Editorial, *SHHW* 3:354 (June 9, 1933).

43. Li Ping-jo, "Chung-kuo li-shih-shang te wen-hua t'ung-chih" (Cultural control in Chinese history), *Ch'ien-t'u* 2.8:3–8 (Aug. 1, 1934); and Chang Yün-fu, pp. 3–4.

44. "Ranisha no soshiki," p. 5.

45. Yü Wen-wei, "Chung-hua min-tsu hsien-tsai hsü-yao ho-chung chiao-yü" (What kind of education does the Chinese nation now need), *Ch'ien-t'u* 1.7:4 (July 1, 1933).

46. Lü K'o-jen, "She-hui-min-chu-chu-i shih-fou k'o-i chiu Chung-kuo?" (Can social-democracy save China?), *SHHW* 3:435 (June 24, 1933).

47. Editorial, *SHHW* 3:354 (June 9, 1933).

48. "Ranisha no soshiki," p. 25.

49. Iwai, p. 188.

50. Editorial, *SHHW* 5:9 (Oct. 6, 1933).

51. Ju Ch'un-p'u, "Wen-hua t'ung-chih te ken-pen i-i yü min-tsu ch'ien-t'u," pp. 8, 11.

52. Editorial, *SHHW* 4:339 (Sept. 6, 1933); editorial, *SHHW* 3:306–307 (May 30, 1933); Chang Yün-fu, p. 11.

53. "Chin-jih chiao-shih ying-yu te jen-shih yü tse-jen," p. 1.

54. Ibid., pp. 1–3; Ch'iu Ch'un, "Chiao-yü yü Chung-hua min-tsu-hsing chih kai-tsao" (Education and the rebuilding of China's national character), *Ch'ien-t'u* 1.7:1–12 (July 1, 1933); Yü Wen-wei, pp. 1–6.

55. Yü Wen-wei, p. 3. Emphasis added.

56. Ch'iu Ch'un, pp. 8–10; and I Ching, "Min-tsu chiao-yü te yao-i" (The essential meaning of national education), *Ch'ien-t'u* 1.7:3–4 (July 1, 1933).

57. Lin Shih-ts'un, "Kuo-chia tsung-tung-yüan (General mobilization of the nation), *Ch'ien-t'u* 2.2:4 (Feb. 1, 1934); Ch'iu Ch'un, p. 10.

58. Yü Wen-wei, pp. 3–6; Ch'iu Ch'un, p. 10.

59. Yü Wen-wei, pp. 3–6; Ch'iu Ch'un, pp. 11–12; and I Jen, "Chung-kuo ko-ming chin-chan-chung chih chiao-yü wen-t'i" (The educational question in the development of the Chinese revolution), *Ch'ien-t'u* 2.1:3–7 (Jan. 1, 1934).

60. Ch'iu Ch'un, p. 11.

61. Yü Wen-wei, pp. 2–6.

62. Iwai, p. 190.

63. Iwai, pp. 215–217.

64. Iwai, p. 190.

65. "So-wei chi-k'ou shou-t'ien (The so-called per-capita land distribution), *SHHW* 6:269 (Feb. 27, 1934); and *SHHW* 6:301 (March 6, 1934); editorial, *SHHW* 11:328 (June 21, 1935); Ying-lung, "Nung-ts'un chien-she wen-t'i-chung te chi-chien shih" (Several matters related to the question of rural reconstruction), *SHHW* 11:350 (June 21, 1935).

66. Liu Ping-li, p. 3; and Pai-yü, "Fei-ch'ang-t'ai te Chung-kuo nung-ts'un shuai-lo yü fu-hsing te hsien-chüeh wen-t'i" (The abnormal decline of Chinese agriculture and the primary questions for restoration), *Ch'ien-t'u* 1.9:9 (Sept. 1, 1933).

67. Hsü T'ai-k'ung, "Wu-shih-nien p'ing-chün ti-ch'üan lun" (Land equalization in fifty years), *Ch'ien-t'u* 2.4:8 (April 1, 1934).

68. Ibid., p. 5.

69. Ibid., p. 6; see also Pai-yü, p. 11. Since the existing land taxes in provinces controlled by Nanking already amounted to anywhere from 2.93 to 6.62 percent of the land value, the Blue Shirt formula would not appear to have been an effective means of forcing landlords to sell their lands. The existing land law stipulated that the land tax should not exceed 1 percent of the land value. See *Chinese Year Book, 1935–36*, p. 845.

70. Liu Ping-li, p. 4; Sun Po-chien, "Chung-kuo nung-ts'un-chung te po-hsiao kuan-hsi yü nung-ts'un ching-chi te chiang-lai" (The exploitative re-

lationships in China's villages and the future of the rural economy), *Ch'ien-t'u* 1.9:11 (Sept. 1, 1933).

71. "Ranisha no soshiki," pp. 19, 23. See also "Ranisha ni tsuite" (On the Blue Shirts).

72. See, e.g., Kao Ch'ing-chai, "Chung-kuo ko-ming yü wo-men te lu-hsien" (The Chinese revolution and our line), *Ch'ien-t'u* 2.1:5 (Jan. 1, 1934); editorial, *SHHW* 3:98–99 (April 21, 1933); editorial, *SHHW* 3:163 (May 3, 1933).

73. Ch'en Ch'iu-yün, "San-min-chu-i yü fa-hsi-ssu-t'i" (The three people's principles and fascism), *Ch'ien-t'u* 2.4:6 (April 1, 1934); "Fa-hsi-ssu-t'i yü Chung-kuo ko-ming" (Fascism and the Chinese revolution), *SHHW* 4:413 (Sept. 18, 1933). For similar comments on the compatibility of fascism and the Three People's Principles, see: Kao Ch'ing-chai, "Chung-kuo ko-ming yü wo-men te lu-hsien," p. 5; "Kuo-min-tang yü fa-hsi-ssu-t'i yün-tung" (The Kuomintang and the fascist movement), *SHHW* 4:258 (Aug. 21, 1933); editorial, *SHHW* 4:403 (Sept. 18, 1933).

74. Interview.

75. Interview with Liu.

76. Iwai, p. 131.

77. "Ranisha no gainen."

78. Iwai, pp. 60–61; interview; Chü-wai-jen, pt. 2, p. 4. "Ranisha no soshiki," p. 22, states that five guarantors were needed, but this statement is not corroborated elsewhere.

79. Chü-wai-jen, pt. 2, p. 5; Ch'en Shao-hsiao, p. 9.

80. Interview.

81. Interview; Ch'en Shao-hsiao, p. 40.

82. Interview.

83. Iwai, p. 49. The size of this body may have varied considerably during the lifetime of the Blue Shirts. Ch'en Shao-hsiao, p. 9, states that there were nine full members and three reserve members; "Ranisha no gainen" records fifteen members.

84. Iwai, pp. 49–50. "Ranisha no gainen" states that a representative conference of the Blue Shirts recommended a list of thirty to Chiang, from which he picked fifteen to serve on the committee.

85. Iwai, p. 50. Ch'en Shao-hsiao, p. 10, states that the standing committee consisted initially of only three members.

86. The men who served as executive secretary were: T'eng Chieh (March 1932–January 1933), Ho Chung-han (January 1933–August 1934), Feng T'i (August 1934–October 1935), Liu Chien-ch'ün (October 1935–September 1937), and K'ang Tse (September 1937–April 1938). See Ch'en Shao-hsiao, p. 14.

87. There is no unanimity in the sources regarding the precise titles of these administrative sections. Compare: Iwai, p. 50; Ch'en Shao-hsiao, p. 10; "Ranisha no gainen."

88. Iwai, pp. 112–130. All membership figures in this section were presumably for 1935.

89. Iwai, pp. 50, 244; Chü-wai-jen, pt. 2, p. 5.

90. Iwai, pp. 76–78.
91. Chü-wai-jen, pt. 1, p. 5; Iwai, p. 47; "Ranisha no gainen."
92. Iwai, pp. 47–48.
93. Iwai, pp. 116–117.
94. Kan Kuo-hsün, p. 19. Kan maintains that the Fu-hsing-she was not brought into existence until July 1934. This is an important observation. I have, however, seen no corroborating evidence in other sources.
95. Iwai, pp. 9–10.
96. Interview.
97. The author calling himself "Outsider" states as fact that the original name was the Blue Shirt Society (lan-i-she); this was subsequently changed to Li-hsing-she, although, he remarks, few persons knew of this change; and not long afterwards the name was changed to Fu-hsing-she. See Chü-wai-jen, pt. 1, p. 5. The account in Ch'en Shao-hsiao, p. 8, states flatly that the name Chung-hua fu-hsing-she (Chinese revival society) was adopted after rejecting the alternatives of Li-hsing-she and Chiu-wang-she (Salvation society). Kan Kuo-hsün, p. 19, by contrast, maintains that the name Fu-hsing-she did not exist until July 1934.
98. Interview with Liu.
99. Iwai, pp. 74–75; "Ranisha no soshiki," p. 26.
100. Interview.
101. "Ranisha no soshiki," p. 23; Iwai, p. 70.
102. Interview.
103. Interview.
104. Interview.
105. "Ranisha no soshiki," pp. 23–24.
106. Interviews; Iwai, p. 75.
107. "Ranisha no soshiki," p. 26.
108. Ibid., pp. 24–25.
109. Iwai, pp. 150–155; Ch'en Shao-hsiao, pp. 40–41, 69–70; *Chinese Year Book, 1936–37*, p. 528; Boorman, II, 65. The Boorman volumes rarely mention the Blue Shirts, not even in the entries on Ho Chung-han and Tai Li. The sole reference to the Blue Shirts that I have thus far discovered states that Chou Fo-hai was associated with the movement (I, 407). This, to the best of my knowledge, is erroneous.
110. Iwai, pp. 157–158. See also Ch'en Shao-hsiao, p. 41; and Kan Kuo-hsün, pp. 19–20.
111. "Chiang Kai-shek Developing a Fascism à la Chine," *CWR* 68.10:387 (May 5, 1934); *China Year Book, 1934,* p. 300.
112. Interview.
113. Iwai, pp. 156–159; Ch'en Shao-hsiao, p. 41; Israel, p. 99.
114. "Chiang Kai-shek Developing a Fascism à la Chine," p. 387; James C. Thomson, Jr., *While China Faced West: American Reformers in Nationalist China, 1928–1937* (Cambridge, 1969), p. 168; Israel, pp. 99–100.
115. Ch'en Shao-hsiao, p. 54.
116. Samuel C. Chu, "The New Life Movement, 1934–1937," *Researches in the Social Sciences on China,* ed. John D. Lane (New York, 1957), pp. 3–4.

117. Iwai, p. 166.

118. Ou-yang Tsung, *Chung-kuo nei-mu* (Shanghai, 1941), p. 17; Chü-wai-jen, pt. 2, p. 4. George E. Taylor remarked that both the New Life Movement and the National Economic Reconstruction Movement "had their origins in military circles . . . A strong authoritarian conception of the State lies behind both movements." "The Reconstruction Movement in China," *Problems of the Pacific, 1936,* ed. W. L. Holland and Kate L. Mitchell (Chicago, n.d.), p. 404.

119. Iwai, pp. 22–27.

120. Samuel C. Chu, p. 5. These ninety-five rules are listed in *Hsin-sheng-huo yün-tung hsü-chih* (Nanking, 1935), pp. 216–220.

121. "Hsin-sheng-huo yün-tung chih yao-i" (The essential meaning of the New Life Movement), *Chiang tsung-t'ung ssu-hsiang yen-lun chi* XII, 109–110.

122. Ibid., p. 110.

123. Iwai, pp. 37–38.

124. "Hsin-sheng-huo yün-tung chih yao-i," p. 111.

125. Iwai, pp. 36–39.

126. Interview.

127. Kan Kuo-hsün, pp. 19–20.

128. Thomson, p. 177.

129. Thomson, p. 183.

130. Samuel C. Chu, p. 8.

131. "Chiang Kai-shek Developing a Fascism à la Chine," p. 387.

132. *NCH,* Aug. 15, 1934, p. 238.

133. *NCH,* May 30, 1934, p. 304; "Hsin chiao-t'ung hsi yü lan-i-she chih an-chung tou-fa" (The undercover combat between the new communications clique and the Blue Shirts), dated April 4, [1934], in Yokota Collection.

134. See, e.g., Ch'en Li-fu, "Hsin-sheng-huo yün-tung fa-wei" (The budding of the New Life Movement), *TFTC* 32.1: (*tung*)25–29 (Jan. 1, 1935). See also Thomson, p. 157.

135. Johnson to State, May 21, 1937, State Dept. 893.00/14127, encl. 2, pp. 12–13. See also Thomson, p. 180.

136. Iwai, pp. 47, 167–168.

137. Chiang Chung-cheng, "Ti-erh-ch'i ko-ming chih k'ai-shih," *Ch'ien-t'u* 2.2:1. The following discussion of the Pieh-tung-tui is largely based on: Chü-wai-jen, pt. 1, p. 5, and pt. 2, pp. 5, 21; Shih Pu-chih, "Ching-kang-shan te feng-huo" (The beacon fire of Ching-kang mountain), pt. 9, *Ch'un-ch'iu* 158: 24–25 (Feb. 1, 1964); Ch'en Shao-hsiao, pp. 47–54; and *NCH,* Oct. 31, 1934, p. 196.

138. Ch'en Shao-hsiao, pp. 47–48. The Pieh-tung-tui was officially established on Oct. 3, 1933. See Ch'en Shao-hsiao, pp. 48, 51–52, 58; Iwai, p. 247; Shih Pu-chih, p. 24.

139. The lesser figure is in Iwai, p. 148; 20,000 is the estimate of Shih Pu-chih, p. 25. According to Iwai, a Large Corps was divided into four Medium Corps (*chung-tui*), each of which were divided into four Branch Corps (*chih-*

tui). A Branch Corps was in turn divided into four Small Corps (*hsiao-tui*), which comprised sixteen men each.

140. Ch'en Shao-hsiao, pp. 48–49; Iwai, p. 148.

141. Ch'en Shao-hsiao, pp. 49–50; Shih Pu-chih, p. 24.

142. *NCH*, Oct. 31, 1934, p. 196.

143. *NCH*, Nov. 7, 1934, p. 235.

144. Ibid.

145. Shih Pu-chih, p. 24.

146. *NCH*, Nov. 7, 1934, p. 235.

147. Shih Pu-chih, p. 24.

148. *NCH*, Nov. 7, 1934, p. 235.

149. Thomson, p. 115; Tsiang T'ing-fu, "Tui kung-ch'an-tang pi-hsü te cheng-chih ts'e-lüeh" (Necessary political measures regarding the communist party), *TLPL* 11:7 (July 31, 1932).

150. *NCH*, Oct. 31, 1934, p. 170.

151. Ku-wu, "Ti-yü-li te lao-sao-hua" (Grumblings from hell), *TLPL* 113:13 (Aug. 12, 1934).

152. *NCH*, Oct. 31, 1934, p. 170.

153. Ch'en Shao-hsiao, pp. 51–54; Iwai, pp. 131, 146, 149.

154. Initially another Blue Shirt leader, Teng Wen-i, headed a separate special service unit in Chiang's Nanchang headquarters. But in 1934 Tai also assumed direction of that unit. The brief remarks here on Tai's career are based upon *Tai Yü-nung hsien-sheng nien-p'u* ([Taipei], 1966), passim; supplemented by Chü-wai-jen, pt. 10, p. 19; Ch'en Kung-shu, "Chiang-fei t'e-wu nei-mu i-pan" (An aspect of the inner history of bandit Chiang's special services), in Lo I and Huang Chi-ch'ing, *Chung-kuo fa-hsi-ssu t'e-wu chen-hsiang* (n.p., 1949), pp. 83–91; and Iwai, p. 251.

Tai Li's biography is in Boorman, III, 205–207. Like many entries in the Boorman volumes, the one on Tai must be used with care. For example, Tai was born in 1897, not 1895 as the Boorman entry states; and Tai was a member of Whampoa's sixth, not fourth, class.

155. See, e.g., "CC tokumu kōsaku no enkaku" (1940); "Hsin-kuo-min-tang tsu an-sha chi-kuan" (The New Kuomintang organizes an assassination organization), *SHHW* 3:165 (May 3, 1933).

156. Tai Li, *Cheng-chih Cheng-t'an* (n.p., 1938). A similar and equally fascinating work that was presumably also used by the Blue Shirts was Wang P'ei-huai, *Ko-ming te pao-chien* (n.p., 1936).

157. Tai Li, pp. 2–3.

158. Tai Li, pp. 61–62. The version here is an abbreviated paraphrase of the original.

159. Tai Li, chaps. 4 and 5.

160. Tai Li, p. 127.

161. *Tai Yü-nung hsien-sheng nien-p'u*, p. 25. Ch'en Shao-hsiao, pp. 105–106.

162. "Ranisha no gainen."

163. Ch'en Shao-hsiao, pp. 71–76. For a description of the shooting, see "Shanghai Shocked by Murder of Noted Chinese Scholar, Yang Chuan," *CWR* 65.4:146–147 (June 24, 1933).

164. *Shen-pao,* Nov. 14, 1934, p. 3; *Shen-pao,* Nov. 17, 1934, p. 3; Ch'en Shao-hsiao, pp. 77–85; "Shih-an yü lan-she 'wen-hua t'ung-chih'" (The Shih case and the blue society's cultural control), from *Chung-hsing jih-pao,* Nov. 18, 1934, in Yokota Collection; Chü-wai-jen, pt. 24, p. 4; and "Ranisha no soshiki," pp. 42–43.

165. *CWR* 66.7:282 (Oct. 14, 1933).

166. See, e.g., Hu Han-min, "Lun so-wei fa-hsi-ssu-t'i" (On so-called fascism), *San-min-chu-i yüeh-k'an* 1.5:18–22 (May 15, 1933); Hu Han-min, "Tsai min-chu te k'ou-hao-hsia chi-ho-ch'i-lai" (Join together under the slogan of democracy), *San-min-chu-i yüeh-k'an,* 5.1:34–36 (Jan. 15, 1935).

167. *NCH,* Oct. 18, 1933, p. 92.

168. Name and date of newspaper unclear, in KMTS; *Jen-min jih-pao,* Nov. 22, 1933, p. 2.

169. Interview.

170. Doki Naohiko, "Shina seikyoku no kiki" (The crisis of the Chinese political situation), *Tōa* 6.5:45 (1933).

171. "Ranisha no kaiso shugi no tenkō nara ni saikin no dōkō," p. 4, in *Ranisha ni kansuru shiryō.*

Ch'en Shao-hsiao, pp. 8–10, suggests that the anti-Japanese aspects of the Blue Shirt "Program" had been proposed by Chiang Kai-shek in 1932 merely as window-dressing, without any intention at least immediately of carrying out a program of resistance to Japan. It is incontestable, however, that at least after 1934 the Blue Shirts were a major concern of the Japanese in north China and Manchuria. This was evidenced not only by the secret intelligence reports of the Japanese regarding specific Blue Shirt activities, but also in the arrests of Blue Shirts by Japanese (*NCH,* Nov. 13, 1935, p. 262) and the provision in the Ho-Umezu agreement of June 1935 calling for suppression of the Blue Shirts which were "inimical to Sino-Japanese relations." T. A. Bisson, *Japan in China* (New York, 1938), p. 55.

172. Iwai, p. 234; "Ranisha no kaiso shugi no tenkō," pp. 15–21; "Ranisha no soshiki," pp. 33–43; and "Ranisha ni tsuite," pp. 11–12.

173. Iwai, p. 229.

174. James Bertram, *First Act in China: The Story of the Sian Mutiny* (New York, The Viking Press, 1938), p. 142.

175. "Communist Declaration of Unity" issued by the Chinese Soviet Government and the Central Committee of the Chinese Communist Party, quoted in Lawrence K. Rosinger, *China's Wartime Politics, 1937–1944* (Princeton, Princeton University Press, 1944), p. 67. This reference, and that in note 174 above, were brought to my attention by W. F. Elkins, "'Fascism' in China: The Blue Shirts Society 1932–1937," *Science and Society* 33.4:432 (Winter 1969).

176. Chü-wai-jen, pt. 2, p. 5. On dissolution of the Blue Shirts, see also Ch'en Shao-hsiao, pp. 58–68.

177. Lyman P. Van Slyke, *Enemies and Friends: The United Front in Chinese Communist History* (Stanford, 1967), pp. 84–85.

178. Ch'en Shao-hsiao, p. 67.

179. Ch'ien Tuan-sheng, *Government and Politics,* pp. 126–128, 130.

180. S. J. Woolf, "Did a Fascist Economic System Exist?", in *The Nature of Fascism,* ed. S. J. Woolf (New York, 1969), p. 119.

181. N. Kogan, "Fascism as a Political Ssystem," in *The Nature of Fascism,* p. 16.

182. A. James Gregor, *The Ideology of Fascism: The Rationale of Totalitarianism* (New York, The Free Press, 1969), p. 12. The failure of scholarship thus far to discern the generic characteristics of fascism has been trenchantly expressed also by Henry Ashby Turner, Jr., "Fascism and Modernization," *World Politics* 24.4:547–564 (July 1972).

183. George L. Mosse, "Fascism and the Intellectuals," in *The Nature of Fascism,* p. 208.

184. This discussion is drawn largely from *The Nature of Fascism,* and particularly the contribution by N. Kogan, pp. 11–18. Objections to a definition of fascism based upon ideological traits are raised in "Discussion— Fascism and Polity," in *The Nature of Fascism,* pp. 51–61, a discussion which simply emphasizes the difficulty, if not impossibility, of establishing a definitive definition of fascism.

185. N. Kogan, p. 17, states: "Racism was not an essential characteristic of fascism." On racism in Italian fascism, see the sophisticated analysis of Gregor, pp. 241–282.

186. J. Solé-Tura, "The Political 'Instrumentality' of Fascism," in *The Nature of Fascism,* p. 44.

187. That principles had been sacrificed to political power by the Blue Shirts is evidenced in quotations below, p. 305.

188. "CC dan ni kansuru chōsa," pp. 101–102; "Ranisha no gainen"; Ch'en Shao-hsiao, pp. 44, 46.

189. Interview with Liu.

3. The Fukien Rebellion

1. Dau-lin Hsu, chap. 1, notes p. 1.

2. Edgar Snow, *Red Star over China* (New York, 1938), p. 166.

3. Materials on the history of the Nineteenth Route Army are in Ch'iu Kuo-chen, *Shih-chiu lu-chün hsing-wang shih* (Hong Kong, 1969). Ch'iu, although a former member of the Nineteenth Route Army, is frequently critical of the top command. See also Teng Ch'ang, "Shih-chiu lu-chün chien-shih" (A short history of the Nineteenth Route Army), *SHHW* 9:216–221 (Nov. 21, 1934); Hatano Ken'ichi, *Gendai Shina no seiji to jimbutsu* (Tokyo, 1937), pp. 81–86.

4. Other officers associated with Ch'en's command during the 1920s and who later participated in the rebellion were Mao Wei-shou, Ou Shou-nien, and Huang Ch'i-hsiang. See Hatano, *Seiji to jimbutsu,* p. 82.

5. Sakurai Kōzō, "Shina no shakai minshutō to torikeha" (China's social-democratic party and liquidationist clique), *Tōa* 6.7:59 (July 1, 1933).

6. Hsi-yün, "Ts'ung AB t'uan shuo tao she-min-tang" (The A.B. Corps and the social democratic party), *SHHW* 5:310 (Nov. 30, 1933). Ch'en was at this time in possession of considerable amounts of money—he may indeed have been one of the richest men in China. (Teng Ch'ang, p. 219). The source

of his money is uncertain. An unfriendly source states that he obtained part of it from corruption when he was head of the government in Kwangtung; he also allegedly engaged in such illegal operations as the opium trade. It is doubtful that much credence can be put in these specific accusations. The fact of his considerable wealth is, however, attested by the fact that his investments in the Kuo-hua Bank in Shanghai made him the principal stockholder. (Teng Ch'ang, p. 219; editorial, *SHHW* 5:338–339 (Dec. 6, 1933); Hatano, *Seiji to jimbutsu,* p. 90.

7. *"Tu-shu tsa-chih* fa-k'an te i-ko kao-pao" (A notice upon the inaugural publication of *Tu-shu tsa-chih*), *Tu-shu tsa-chih* 1.1:5 ([April, 1931]).

8. The A.B. Corps had been born of the anti-communist sentiment that spread within the Kuomintang following the death of Sun Yat-sen in March 1925. A group of young Kuomintang members, many of whom had recently returned from studying in Europe and the United States (like Tuan Hsi-p'eng and Ch'eng T'ien-fang) formed the Youth Work Corps (Ch'ing-nien kung-tso t'uan). This group increasingly received aid and encouragement from the leadership of the Kuomintang as Chiang Kai-shek's enmity for the communists grew. For a brief time, the name of the group was changed to the Extirpate Communism Corps (Ch'an-kung t'uan). And during 1926 the name A.B. Corps was adopted.

In late 1926, after the revolutionary armies of the Northern Expedition reached the Yangtze Valley, the Organization Department of the Kuomintang sent Tuan Hsi-p'eng to Kiangsi. There, he was to reorganize the entire party structure in order to remove communist influences. Kiangsi thereafter became the center of A.B. Corps activities.

Chiang Kai-shek's headquarters were transferred to Nanchang, Kiangsi, in early 1927. And the acting head of Chiang's Organization Department, Ch'en Kuo-fu, found the organization of the A.B. Corps ideally suited to his own anti-communist activities. It is ironic therefore that Ch'en Kuo-fu and other future members of the CC clique participated actively, if only for a brief time, in the A.B. Corps, and rendered it financial support.

The ideology of the A.B. Corps during the early period of its existence was an ill-defined admixture. The doctrines of Sun Yat-sen were joined with the extreme nationalism of the China Youth Party, which stressed that communism was unsuited to China because China had no capitalists. There was also a dash of left-wing radicalism, suggested by their slogans, "distribution to alleviate impoverishment" and "overthrow local rascals and oppressive gentry."

Ch'en Kuo-fu's association with the A.B. Corps was short-lived. By June 1927 this "right-wing" of the Corps had withdrawn and had formed the CC clique, which now began a separate existence. The remaining "left-wing" thereafter constituted the A.B. Corps. Under the leadership of Wang Li-hsi, the Corps became a highly cohesive organization, reputedly even more tightly disciplined than the Communist Party. Its activities expanded to every hsien in Kiangsi, and reached even into Anhwei and Nanking. After the communists dominated large parts of Kiangsi, the Corps maintained its secret organization there, and fought vigorously for control of the province.

Sources: Hsiao-ts'en, "AB t'uan tsai Chiang-hsi" (The A.B. Corps in Kiangsi), *SHHW* 3:116–118, 133–135 (April 24 and 27, 1933) ; Wang Chien-min, *Chung-kuo kung-ch'an-tang shih-kao* (Taipei, 1965), II, 528, 538–539; Sakurai Kōzō, pp. 58–59; *CC dan ni kansuru chōsa* (Special Investigative Section at Shanghai of the Japanese Embassy in China, 1939), pp. 7–8, 23; Ronald S. Suleski, "The Fu-t'ien Incident, December 1930," *Early Communist China: Two Studies* (Ann Arbor, 1969), pp. 2–4 and passim.

9. Hsi-yün, p. 310.

10. Hu vigorously denied that he was a member of the A.B. Corps, asserting that he was a "free person" (*tzu-yu jen*), independent of political affiliations. (*SHHW* 1:322 [Nov. 15, 1932]). Mei Kung-pin was also associated with the editing of these two journals. (Hatano, *Seiji to jimbutsu,* p. 91). Both journals were soon shut down by Shanghai's ardent censors.

11. In March 1932, several of the Trotskyites, including P'eng Shu-chih, Li Chi, Liu Jen-ching, and Yen Ling-feng joined the staff of the Shen-chou kuo-kuang-she. (Hatano, *Seiji to jimbutsu,* p. 90; Sakurai Kōzō, pp. 60–61). The participation of the Trotskyites was denied in "Pien-che te hua" (Words of the editor), *Tu-shu tsa-chih* 2.5:1–2 [1932]). Since 1929 a small number of Chinese had organized in support of Trotskyite views—a movement that received its greatest impetus after Ch'en Tu-hsiu was expelled from the Communist Party. The Trotskyites led a tragic existence. They were opposed by the Communist Party—which denigrated them as "Liquidationists" (*ch'ü-hsiao p'ai*) ; they were harried by the Kuomintang police; and were fragmented within by incessant factional squabbles. This group—even at its height numbering no more than 400 members—received a mortal blow during 1932, when both Ch'en Tu-hsiu and P'eng Shu-chih were arrested.

12. Sakurai Kōzō, pp. 59–60; Hatano, *Seiji to jimbutsu,* p. 90; *Hsien-tai shih-liao,* ed. Hai-t'ien Publishing Co. (2nd ed., 1933), I, 280; Teng Ch'ang, p. 220.

13. This is the interpretation of Teng Ch'ang, p. 220. See also Hsi-yün, p. 311.

14. Ch'iu Kuo-chen, p. 123.

15. A study of the incident does exist, but it does not come to grips with the internal relations of the Nanking leadership at the time. See Paul O. Elmquist. "The Sino-Japanese Undeclared War of 1932 at Shanghai," *Papers on China* 5:39–74 (1951). The Tōyō Bunko has a rich store of works on this incident.

16. *CWR* 60.1:43 (March 5, 1932).

17. Ch'ien-chün-hsiao-tsu, "Ts'ai T'ing-k'ai te 'wei-pa' " (Ts'ai T'ing-k'ai's tail), *SHHW* 5:276 (Nov. 24, 1933) ; Teng Ch'ang, p. 220.

18. Ibid. The open letter is reproduced in Ch'iu Kuo-chen, pp. 62–63.

19. H. L. Stimson memorandum of conversation with Sir John Hope Simpson, head of the National Flood Relief Commission, State Dept. 893.48/585 (July 8, 1932).

20. *NCH,* Aug. 3, 1932, p. 176.

21. Editorial, *SHHW* 5:19 (Oct. 6, 1933) ; Liu Chien-ch'ün, p. 237.

22. Lei Hsiao-ts'en, *San-shih nien tung-luan Chung-kuo* (Hong Kong, 1955), p. 213.

23. I-jan, "Chi Teng Yen-ta yü so-wei ti-san-tang" (Recollections of Teng Yen-ta and the so-called third party), *Ch'un-ch'iu* 283:10 (April 16, 1969); Hsiao Wen-che, *Hsien-tai Chung-kuo cheng-tang yü cheng-chih* (Nanking, 1946), pp. 48–50; Boorman, III, 263; Wang P'ei-huai, p. 226.

24. *Hsien-tai shih-liao*, I, 264–266; Boorman, III, 263.

25. Ni Kuo-ch'ang, "Ti-san-tang te ts'ung-ch'ien" (The third party's past), *SHHW* 2:167 (Feb. 7, 1933); "T'an P'ing-shan ch'ien-lai Shang-hai" (T'an P'ing-shan sneaks into Shanghai), *SHHW* 2:338 (March 12, 1933); *Hsien-tai shih-liao*, I, 264–265; Boorman, III, 219–220.

26. Ni Kuo-ch'ang, pp. 166–167. This source states that Teng actually transformed the Third Party into a Social Democratic Party. If this is true, the organizational consequences are not clear.

27. *Hsien-tai shih-liao*, I, 265; Ni Kuo-ch'ang, p. 167. The name of the party was also changed to Chinese Kuomintang Provisional Action Committee (Chung-kuo kuo-min-tang lin-shih hsing-tung wei-yüan-hui). The term Kuomintang was incorporated in the new name, because the party continued to profess that the doctrines of Sun Yat-sen, when combined with Marxism, represented the highest principles of the Chinese revolution. See *Chung-kuo hsin-min-chu yün-tung-chung te tang-p'ai* (Shanghai and Hong Kong, 1946), p. 42; Hsiao Wen-che, p. 48. This latter source (pp. 50–55) reprints the program of the Third Party, which was adopted by a party congress on Sept. 1, 1930. This official document was actually a summary of an essay by Teng Yen-ta, entitled "Our Political Advocacy." See *Teng Yen-ta hsien-sheng i-cho* (Hong Kong, 1949).

28. *Chung-kuo hsin-min-chu yün-tung chung te tang-p'ai*, p. 42; Ni Kuo-ch'ang, p. 147; Hatano, *Seiji to jimbutsu*, p. 77.

29. *Hsien-tai shih-liao*, I, 265.

30. Boorman, III, 264 dates Teng's execution on Nov. 29. Kao Yin-tsu, by contrast, puts the execution on Dec. 16. See Kao Yin-tsu, *Chung-hua min-kuo ta-shih chi* (Taipei, 1957), p. 362. This latter date is corroborated by Chin Tien-jung, "Hsi-nan lao-chiang Liu Yün-huan chuan-chi" (Biography of the southwest's old general Liu Yün-huan), *Ch'un-ch'iu* 170:7 (Aug. 1, 1964).

31. Ou-yang Tsung, et al., *Chung-kuo nei-mu* (Shanghai, 1941), p. 29; Chang Chih-i, *K'ang-chan chung te cheng-tang ho p'ai-pieh* (Chungking, 1939), p. 54; Chin Tien-jung, p. 7.

32. *Hsien-tai shih-liao*, I, 266.

33. Ni Kuo-ch'ang, pp. 182–183; *Hsien-tai shih-liao*, I, 183 and 266; "Fukken shinseifu no juritsu o chūshin ni zenshi mata fuku dai dōyō no chinchō" (The establishment of a new government in Fukien as an emphatic sign of renewed turmoil in all of China), *Shina jihō* 20.1:35 (Jan. 1, 1934).

34. "Ti-san-tang tsai Min pan hsün-k'o-pan" (The third party in Fukien runs a training class), *SHHW* 2:418 (March 27, 1933); "Ti-san-tang te chung-hsin i Min" (The bulk of the Third party moves to Fukien), *SHHW* 3:4–5 (April 3, 1933).

35. Tseng Ou-kuang, "Cheng-ch'üan jao-jang chung te Min-sheng fei-huo" (Fukien banditry in the political turmoil), *SHHW* 1:243 (Nov. 3, 1932).

36. *NCH*, Aug. 3, 1932, p. 170.

37. George Babcock Cressey, *China's Geographic Foundations: A Survey of the Land and Its People* (New York, 1934), pp. 334–347.

38. Wei-tsung, "Shih-chiu lu-chün yü Fu-chien cheng-ch'üan" (The Nineteenth Route Army and political power in Fukien), *SHHW* 1:26–28 (Oct. 7, 1932); Tseng Ou-kuang, "Cheng-ch'üan jao-jang chung te Min-sheng fei-huo," *SHHW* 1:242–244 (Nov. 3, 1932); Victor C. Falkenheim, "Provincial Administration in Fukien, 1949–1966" (Ph.D. diss., Columbia University, 1973), chap. 3.

39. Tseng Ou-kuang, p. 242; *NCH*, Sept. 14, 1932, p. 409; *NCH*, Dec. 7, 1932, p. 370; *NCH*, Nov. 2, 1932, p. 169; Huang Hsü-ch'u, "Kuang-hsi yü chung-yang nien-yü-nien-lai pei-huan li-ho i-shu," pt. 20, *Ch'un-ch'iu* 123:15 (Aug. 16, 1962).

40. *NCH*, Jan. 4, 1933, p. 11; Ch'iu Kuo-chen, p. 110.

41. Fu Po-ts'ui, "Nung-min yü t'u-ti wen-t'i" (The farmers and the land question [A speech to the farmers' first representative conference, July 6, 1933]), *Lung-yen yüeh-k'an* (Lung-yen monthly) 1:19–20 (Sept. 9, 1933); "Min-luan ch'ien-hou chih ko-fan-tung-p'ai chien-chi" (Collected clippings on counter-revolutionary cliques before and after the Fukien disturbance; unpub. collection), sec. 3–4; K'un-lin, "Ti-san tang chih tsai Fu-chien" (The third party in Fukien), *SHHW* 3:52–54 (April 12, 1933); Kuang-chiu, "Min-hsi she-hui-chu-i shih-yen-ch'ü" (The socialist experimental area in western Fukien), *SHHW* 2:215–216 (Feb. 16, 1933).

42. Huang Ch'iang, "Tsai Min-pien chung te Ch'en Ming-shu yü wo" (Ch'en Ming-shu and I in the Fukien Rebellion), *Ch'un-ch'iu* 131:2 (Dec. 16, 1962); Ku-shu-chih, "Ch'en Chiang Ts'ai yü ti-san-tang-jen te chieh-ho Min-pien yu pao-fa tao wa-chieh," pt. 1, *Ch'un-ch'iu* 96:3 (July 1, 1961). See also Ts'ai T'ing-k'ai, *Ts'ai T'ing-k'ai tzu-chuan* (Hong Kong, 1946), I. 374.

43. "Ti-san-tang te chung-hsin i Min," *SHHW* 3:4–5; Ku-shu-chih, pt. 1, p. 3.

44. "Min-hsi shan-hou wei-yüan-hui shih-cheng ta-kang" (The administrative program of the Western Fukien Reconstruction Council), *Lung-yen yüeh-k'an* 1:31–33 (Sept. 1, 1933). All the other articles and documentary materials in this volume of *Lung-yen yüeh-k'an* are also pertinent here. See also Wu Tan-yün, "Min-hsi shan-hou wei-yüan-hui tsui-chin shih-cheng kai-k'uang chi ch'i t'u-ti wen-t'i" (The Western Fukien Reconstruction Council's most recent administrative situation and its land question), *TFTC* 30.24:64–68 (Dec. 16, 1933).

45. [P'an] Han-nien, "Shih-chiu lu-chün-fa te 'sheng-ch'an ta-chung cheng-ch'üan' yü t'u-ti cheng-kang" (The political sovereignty of the producing masses and land program of the Nineteenth Route Army lords), *Tou-cheng* 28:6–12 (Sept. 30, 1933); "Lun Chung-hua su-wei-ai chung-yang cheng-fu so-kung-pu te tui shih-chiu lu-chün te hsieh-ting" (On the agreement with the Nineteenth Route Army promulgated by the Chinese Soviet Central Government), *Tou-cheng* 48:12 (Feb. 23, 1934).

46. *NCH,* Nov. 15, 1933, p. 249; Pai Ming-hsin, "Lung-yen ts'an-kuan-t'uan jih-chi" (Diary of the Lung-yen observer corps), *Hsia-ta chou-k'an* ("The University of Amoy Weekly") 13.9:7–17 (Nov. 25, 1933).

47. *NCH,* Jan. 31, 1934, p. 166. The disciplined conduct of the Nineteenth Route Army was frequently contrasted with the pillaging and coarse conduct of soldiers of the central government army when Foochow fell. See, e.g., Nelson Trusler Johnson to Wang Ching-wei, March 3, 1934, *Foreign Relations of the United States, 1934,* III, 468–469; State Dept. 893.00 P. R. Foochow/73, Feb. 5, 1934, pp. 22.

48. Report by Huang Ch'iang, June 12, 1933, entitled "Chang-Lung lu-cheng chi Lung-yen k'uang-ch'ang shih-ch'a chi" (Notes on an inspection of the Chang-Lung road administration and the Lung-yen mines), printed in *T'ing-chin tsa-chih* 2:13 (July 15, 1933); "Lung-yen fen-ch'u erh-shih-erh nien hsia-pan nien shih-cheng chi-hua" (The Lung-yen branch office's administrative plan for the second half of 1933), *Lung-yen yüeh-k'an* 1:21 (Sept. 1, 1933).

49. "Min-hsi chün-cheng t'e-hsün" (The special lesson of the Western Fukien military government), *SHHW* 4:168 (Aug. 3, 1933). An American State Department official reported that the merchants were taxed "to the breaking point." See State Dept. 893.00 P.R. Foochow/72, Jan. 5, 1934, p. 22.

50. "Min-pien yü Min-sheng jen-min" (The Fukien rebellion and the people of Fukien), *SHHW* 6:413 (March 27, 1934). A similar folk song is reproduced in "Min-luan ch'ien-hou chih ko fan-tung-p'ai chien-chi," sec. 4.

51. Ch'iu Kuo-chen, p. 86; Lei Hsiao-ts'en, pp. 224–225.

52. Tseng Ou-kuang, p. 244; "Ch'en Ming-shu chih hsing-ts'ung" (Ch'en Ming-shu's trail), *SHHW* 1:220 (Oct. 31, 1932); "Ch'en Chen-ju hsien-sheng tsai Fu-chou ko-chieh huan-ying ta-hui yen-chiang-tz'u" (Ch'en Ming-shu's speech to the all-circles welcoming assembly at Foochow), *T'ing-chin tsa-chih* 2:11 (July 15, 1933).

53. "Ch'en Ming-shu jih-ch'ang kung-k'o" (Ch'en Ming-shu's daily lessons), *SHHW* 5:5 (Oct. 3, 1933); Ch'ü-yüan, "Hsi-nan te ming-cheng an-tou" (The overt and covert struggles in the southwest), *SHHW* 3:232 (May 15, 1933).

54. "Ch'en Chen-ju . . . yen-chiang-tz'u," p. 11. This welcoming assembly was also reported in Yang-wu, "Ch'en Ming-shu ju-Min-hou chih Min-chü" (The situation in Fukien after Ch'en Ming-shu entered Fukien), *SHHW* 3:409–410 (June 18, 1933).

55. Ts'ai T'ing-k'ai, *Tzu-chuan,* pp. 378–389; "Fukken shinseifu no juritsu o chūshin ni zenshi mata fuku daidōyō no chinchō," pp. 26–27. Fukien reportedly received ¥600,000 from Nanking and ¥300,000 from Kwangtung each month. See "Min-pien shih-chi," *KWCP* 10.47:1.

56. Ts'ai T'ing-k'ai, *Tzu-chuan,* p. 378; "Min-pien shih-chi," p. 1.

57. Ibid., p. 2; "Fukken dokuritsu mondai" (The question of Fukien independence), *Tōa* 7.1:139–140 (Jan. 1, 1934).

58. *Shih-shih hsin-pao,* Nov. 16, 1933, p. 1; ibid., Nov. 18, 1933, p. 1; ibid., Nov. 25, 1933, p. 1; Juan Fang-hua, *Chung-kuo ch'ih-huo ssu-shih nien* (Taipei, 1967), p. 277; "Fukken hitorida mondai," p. 139.

59. *Nan-hua jih-pao* (South China daily), Nov. 23, 1933, in KMTS.

60. *Hsiang-kang chung-hsing pao* (The Hong Kong restoration post), Nov. 21, 1933, in KMTS; "Min-pien shih-chi," p. 2.

61. Ch'iu Kuo-chen, p. 124. See also "Min-pien shih-chi," p. 2.

62. "Fukken dokuritsu mondai," p. 140; [No title or date], in KMTS. In taking these actions, the office of the pacification commissioner stated: "The Nanking Government has stopped the provision of military supplies to the Nineteenth Route Army. In order to maintain the lives of several ten-thousand people, it is necessary to take over temporarily the Customs organization, using this authority in order to fulfill military needs." I-sheng, "Min-yu hui-hsiang lu" (Reminiscences of a trip to Fukien), serialized in *Kung-shang jih-pao* (Industry and commerce daily), pt. 9, in KMTS.

63. *Fan-Chiang yün-tung shih* (n.p., 1934), p. 670.

64. The most detailed description of the meeting is in *Kung-shang jih-pao*, Nov. 23, 1933, in KMTS. See also "Min-pien shih-chi," p. 2; Hsiao-chao, "Ts'an-cha Fu-chou jen-min tai-piao ta-hui chi" (Notes on attending the Foochow people's representative conference), *TLPL* 84:5–9 (Jan. 7, 1934); "Fukken hitorida mondai," pp. 140–141.

65. State Dept. 893.00 P.R. Foochow/71, pp. 10–11; Burke to Johnson, Nov. 24, 1933, State Dept. 893.00/12599, p. 8.

66. *Jen-min jih-pao*, Nov. 22, 1933, sec. 1, p. 2. See also "Min-pien shih-chi," p. 2.

67. *Kung-shang jih-pao*, Nov. 23, 1933, in KMTS; Gauss to State, Dec. 5, 1933, State Dept. 893.00/12610, p. 9; "Min-pien hsü-chi" (Notes continued on the Fukien rebellion), *KWCP* 10.48: articles p. 2 (Dec. 4, 1933); Ch'iu Kuo-chen, p. 137.

68. The council was composed of most of the leading figures in the revolutionary movement. Most lists of the membership include: Li Chi-shen, Ch'en Ming-shu, Chiang Kuang-nai, Ts'ai T'ing-k'ai, Feng Yü-hsiang (who, when he failed to come to Foochow, was replaced by Yü Hsin-ch'ing), Hsü Ch'ien, Fang Chen-wu, Eugene Ch'en, Tai Chi, Li Chang-ta, and Ho Kung-kan. See Ch'iu Kuo-chen, p. 135; *Fan-Chiang yün-tung shih*, p. 663; "Min-pien hsü-chi," p. 2. Significantly, the revolutionaries' newspaper listed Huang Ch'i-hsiang as a member. *Jen-min jih-pao*, Nov. 22, 1933, sec. 1, p. 2.

69. *Chūka minkoku Fukken shō dokuritsu no shinsō* (n.p., 1934); Lei Hsiao-ts'en, p. 216.

70. Alexander Ivanovich Cherepanov, *Notes of a Military Advisor in China*, tr. Alexandra O. Smith (Taipei, 1970), p. 25.

71. Lei Hsiao-ts'en, p. 214; P'ing-neng, "Min-pien tsu-chih kai-k'uang shih-lu" (The true record of the situation at the organization of the Fukien rebellion), *SHHW* 6:202 (Feb. 12, 1934).

72. "Cheng-fu ch'eng-li hsüan-yen" (Declaration announcing establishment of the government), *Jen-min jih-pao*, Nov. 22, 1933, sec. 1, p. 2.

73. "Tui-wai hsüan-yen" (Declaration to the foreign powers), *Jen-min jih-pao*, Nov. 23, 1933, sec. 1, p. 2.

74. "Tui-wai hsüan-yen"; "Jen-min cheng-kang" (People's political program), reprinted in "Min-pien hsü-chi," p. 2.

75. Ibid.; Ch'iu Kuo-chen, pp. 133–134.

76. P'ing-neng, pp. 200–203; Hatano, *Seiji to jimbutsu*, p. 80; Wei-chung, "Min ti-ssu-tang te ho-ts'ung-lien-heng" (Conflicts within Fukien's Fourth party), *SHHW* 5:296 (Nov. 27, 1933).

77. Hatano, *Seiji to jimbutsu*, pp. 74, 80–81; Wei-chung, pp. 296–297; Ch'iu Kuo-chen, p. 136.

78. Wei-chung, pp. 296–297.

79. Ch'iu Kuo-chen, p. 136.

80. Ibid.; *Jen-min jih-pao*, Nov. 22, 1933, p. 11; *KWCP* 10.50: events p. 3 (Dec. 18, 1933); State Dept. 893.00 P.R. Foochow/72, Jan. 5, 1934, p. 10.

81. Hu Ch'iu-yüan, *Tsai T'ang San-ts'ang yü Fu Shih-te chih chien* (Taipei, 1962), p. 17.

82. Ku-shu-chih, pt. 3, pp. 7–8; interview.

83. Interview. Hatano, *Seiji to jimbutsu*, pp. 71–75, also indicates the general character of the conflict among the revolutionaries.

84. "Ti-san-tang shang liu cheng-p'ai" (The Third party still retains an orthodox clique), *SHHW* 5:309 (Nov. 30, 1933).

85. Ku-shu-chih, pt. 3, p. 8. See also Hu Ch'iu-yüan, *Tsai T'ang San-ts'ang*, pp. 17–18.

86. "Fukken dokuritsu mondai," pp. 142–145; *Chūka minkoku Fukkenshō dokuritsu no shinsō; Fan-Chiang yün-tung shih*, p. 663.

87. "Sheng-ch'an-tang shang-wei cheng-shih ch'eng-li" (The producers' party still has not been formally established), *SHHW* 5:471 (Dec. 30, 1933); *Kung-shang jih-pao*, Dec. 4, 1933, in KMTS. Sources on the formation of the Sheng-ch'an-tang: Ku-shu-chih, pt. 3, p. 7; Hu Ch'iu-yüan, *Tsai T'ang San-ts'ang*, p. 17; and interview.

88. Lei Hsiao-ts'en, pp. 214, 215, 217; Hu Ch'iu-yüan, *Tsai T'ang San-ts'ang*, p. 17; "Fukken shinseifu," p. 28; *Nan-hua jih-pao*, date unclear, in KMTS.

89. Lei Hsiao-ts'en, p. 221. Lei does not explicitly name Soong Ch'ing-ling, but the implication is clear.

90. Interview; Hatano, *Seiji to jimbutsu*, p. 75.

91. A good discussion of the political system in Kwangtung was prepared by Joseph W. Ballantine in a State Dept. report, "Political system of Kwangtung Province," Sept. 21, 1932, 893.00/12182.

92. "Hu Han-min ch'u-kuo chi" (Notes on Hu Han-min's departure from the country), June 19, 1935, in Yokota Collection; Kao Hsin-min, "Hu Han-min yü hsin kuo-min-tang" (Hu Han-min and the New Kuomintang), *SHHW* 1:2 (Oct. 4, 1932).

93. During these preparations for rebellion, the Southwest had sent a representative to Fukien asking the Nineteenth Route Army to participate. Ts'ai T'ing-k'ai had been skeptical that the New Kuomintang would act in good faith, but Chiang Kuang-nai had gone to Canton to discuss plans with the Southwest leaders. Ts'ai T'ing-k'ai, *Tzu-chuan*, pp. 378–379; "Min-pien shih-chi," p. 1.

On the New Kuomintang, see; Kao Hsin-min, "Hu Han-min yü hsin kuo-min-tang," pp. 2–4; Hatano, *Seiji to jimbutsu*, pp. 66–67.

94. The fifteen articles of the agreement are quoted in Huang Hsü-ch'u,

"Yüeh-Kuei-Min san-sheng lien-meng nei-mu yü ching-kuo" (The inside story and development of the alliance between Kwangtung, Kwangsi, and Fukien), *Ch'un-ch'iu* 256:26 (March 1, 1968). See also Huang Hsü-ch'u, "Kuang-hsi yü chung-yang nien-yü-nien-lai pei-huan li-ho i-shu," pt. 20, *Ch'un-ch'iu* 123:15 (Aug. 16, 1962). The author of these articles was chairman of Kwangsi province, the province's third-ranking authority, and was also a signatory to the agreement. His numerous contributions to *Ch'un-chiu* constitute a valuable and relatively reliable source on events in Southwest China.

95. Huang Hsü-ch'u, "Yüeh-Kuei-Min," p. 26.

96. Ch'i-yü, "Yüan-lao shih-li liang-p'ai chüeh-lieh chih hsü-mu" (Prologue to a split between the yüan-lao and military cliques), *SHHW* 4:10 (July 3, 1933).

97. Huang Hsü-ch'u, "Kuang-hsi yü chung-yang," pt. 20, pp. 15–16.

98. See below, pp. 120–123.

99. The telegrams are quoted in *Fan-Chiang yün-tung shih,* pp. 671–672. Regarding emissaries, see: "Min-pien hsü-chi," p. 5.

100. British Foreign Office, Further Correspondence respecting China, F 204/3/10, enclosure, Phillips to Sir M. Lampson, Dec. 2, 1933; Huang Hsü-ch'u, "Pa Kuei i-wang lu" (Reminiscences of Pa-Kwei), pt. 25, *Ch'un-ch'iu* 192:16 (July 1, 1965); Kao-shan I-hao, "San-chi ch'eng-hsiung hua nan-t'ien (A tale of three heroes of south China named Chi), pt. 7, *Ch'un-ch'iu* 214:22 (June 1, 1966).

101. Huang Hsü-ch'u, "Kuang-hsi yü chung-yang," pt. 20, p. 16; Huang Hsü-ch'u, "Pa Kuei," p. 16.

102. Huang Hsü-ch'u, "Kuang-hsi yü chung-yang," pt. 21, p. 4.

103. Kao-shan I-hao, p. 22.

104. Huang Hsü-ch'u, "Kuang-hsi yü chung-yang," pt. 21, p. 5.

105. *Kung-shang jih-pao,* Nov. 23, 1933, in KMTS; "Min-pien hsü-chi," p. 5; Hsüan-ts'un, p. 8; Huang Hsü-ch'u, "Kuang-hsi yü chung-yang," pt. 20, p. 16.

106. *Kung-shang jih-pao,* Nov. 23, 1933, in KMTS; Ballantine to Legation, State Dept. 893.00/12635; Gauss to State, Dec. 5, 1933, State Dept. 893.00/12610, p. 6.

107. *Nan-hua jih-pao,* Nov. 27, 1933, in KMTS; *Jen-min jih-pao,* Nov. 24, 1933, sec. 1, p. 3; "Min-ni ch'ien-tu pu-i" (For the Fukien rebels to shift their capital will not be easy), *SHHW* 6:42 (Jan. 12, 1934); "Yueh-Min tai-piao ts'o-shang shih-chü chin-hsing" (The progress of discussions on the current situation between Kwangtung and Fukien representatives), in KMTS.

108. *KWCP* 10.49: events p. 3 (Dec. 11, 1933). The central government had initially invited two eminent Kuomintang members, Ts'ai Yüan-p'ei and Tai Chi-t'ao, to join the delegation. These men enjoyed a broader reputation than did Chang Chi. But both declined the honor. In fact, it was reported that Tai "vigorously declined" the offer. I have discovered no explanation for this intriguing by-play. *Chung-hsing jih-pao,* Nov. 26, 1933, and *Kung-shang jih-pao,* Nov. 28, 1933, both in KMTS.

109. *Chung-hsing jih-pao,* Dec. 12, 1933, in KMTS. See also *KWCP* 11.1: events pp. 1–2 (Jan. 1, 1934).

110. On December 28 Hu specifically proposed such an alliance, but the thought was implicit in all his writings during the Fukien rebellion. Hsüan-ts'un, "Ch'üan Min hui-t'ou shuo Kang Hu" (Encouragements to Fukien to change policies; Speaking of Hu Han-min), *SHHW* 6:8 (Jan. 3, 1934); "Ch'üan Ch'en Li teng ch'e-ti ho-tso" (Encouraging Chen Ming-shu, Li Chi-shen, et al., to cooperate closely), in KMTS; Huang Hsü-ch'u, "Pa Kuei," p. 16. Huang Hsü-ch'u, "Kuang-hsi yü chung-yang," pt. 20, p. 16.

111. Feng Yü-hsiang, *Wo so-jen-shih te Chiang Chieh-shih* (Hong Kong, 1949), p. 39; *Kung-shang jih-pao*, Nov. 26, 1933, in KMTS; *Shen-pao*, Nov. 26, 1933, p. 2. Chiang Kai-shek pressed Feng to manifest his support by visiting Nanking, but Feng adamantly refused.

112. "Hokushi seikyoku no dōkō o kanru" (A look at trends in the north China political situation), *Shina jihō* 20.2:35–36 (Feb. 1, 1934).

113. Ibid., pp. 36, 39.

114. Peck to State, Dec. 8, 1933, State Dept. 893.00/12617, p. 2; "Hokushi seikyoku," p. 39.

115. Yi-yun Shen Huang, "My Husband and I: Personal Reminiscences of an Eminent Chinese Woman," condensed, ed., and tr. T. K. Tong (unpub. ms. in Special Collections Library, Butler Library, Columbia University, preface dated 1960), pp. 428–430; *Shen-pao*, Nov. 23, 1933, p. 7.

116. Yi-yun Shen Huang, pp. 429–430; Hsu Dau-lin, "Comments," *China in Crisis*, I, 275–276.

117. All newspapers and many periodicals in early 1934 carried reports on Sun Tien-ying's revolt. See, e.g., "Sun Tien-ying p'an-pien chih yen-chung-hsing" (The seriousness of Sun Tien-ying's uprising), *SHHW* 6:86 (Jan. 21, 1934).

118. Hu Ch'iu-yüan, *Fei-pang chi-t'uan kung-jan shan-tung cheng-chih ch'ing-suan wen-t'i* (Taipei, 1963), p. 39.

119. Ts'ai T'ing-k'ai, "Ts'ung k'u-men chung fen-tou i ch'iu-sheng" (From out of despair struggle to seek life), *T'ing-chin tsa-chih* 3:1–2 (Sept. 20, 1933); and [P'an] Han-nien, "Shih-chiu lu-chün-fa te 'sheng-ch'an ta-chung cheng-ch'üan' yü t'u-ti cheng-kang," *Tou-cheng* 26:6–12, NCH, Oct. 4, 1933, p. 7; ibid., Jan. 3, 1934, p. 31; Ts'ai T'ing-k'ai, *Tzu-chuan*, pp. 378–379.

120. Tso-liang Hsiao, *Power Relations within the Chinese Communist Movement, 1930–1934* (Seattle, 1961–1967), II, 684; Hatano Ken'ichi, *Chūgoku kyōsantō shi, 1933* (Tokyo, 1934), pp. 262–263; Kung Ch'u, *Wo yü hung-chün* (Hong Kong, 1954), p. 363.

121. Huang Ch'iang, "Tsai Min-pien-chung te Ch'en Ming-shu yü wo" (Ch'en Ming-shu and I in the Fukien rebellion), *Ch'un-ch'iu* 131:3 (Dec. 16, 1962).

122. Kung Ch'u, p. 363, quotes part of the letter. Hu Ch'iu-yüan states that Chu Wen-shan was the person responsible for establishing initial contact between the two parties. *Tsai T'ang San-ts'ang*, p. 17.

123. Kung Ch'u, p. 364; Lei Hsiao-ts'en, p. 214; Hsiao Tso-liang, I, 248–249, 255. Hatano, *Chūgoku kyōsantō shi, 1933*, pp. 260–263, is doubtless inaccurate in any details (See Hu Ch'iu-yüan, *Fei-pang chi-t'uan*, pp. 38–45). According to some sources, the agreement could not be implemented until the

Chinese Soviet had obtained the approval of the Comintern. See Lei Hsiao-ts'en, p. 215; name and date of newspaper not specified, in KMTS; "Fukken jimmin seifu no kaishō" (Dissolution of the Fukien people's government), *Shina jihō* 20.2:17 (Feb. 1, 1934).

The text of the agreement is in Hsiao Tso-liang, II, 676; and Wang Chien-min, II, 601. The version of the agreement in Hsiao is slightly but not significantly more complete than that in Wang.

124. This supplementary agreement has never been published, but it was mentioned in Article One of the preliminary agreement. Hatano, *Chūgoku kyōsantō shi*, p. 262, states that Ts'ai T'ing-k'ai met in early December with Chu Teh, P'eng Te-huai, and Lin Piao, at which time they agreed upon the areas to be controlled by the Red Army. See also Ku-shu-chih, pt. 3. p. 6.

125. William F. Dorrill, "The Fukien Rebellion and the CCP: A Case of Maoist Revision," *China Quarterly* 37:36 (January–March 1969); Wang Chien-min, II, 602.

126. Lun Chung-hua su-wei-ai chung-yang cheng-fu so-kung-pao te tui shih-chiu lu-chün te hsieh-ting" (The agreement with the 19th Route Army promulgated by the Chinese Soviet Central Government), *Tou-cheng* 48:12 (Feb. 23, 1934).

127. Ch'en Yün, "Fu-chien tsu-chih 'jen-min ko-ming cheng-fu' yü ch'ih-se kung-hui tsai Fu-chien te jen-wu" (The organization of a 'peoples revolutionary government' in Fukien and the responsibilities of the red unions in Fukien), *Su-ch'ü kung-jen* 5:1–5 (Dec. 25, 1933).

128. Hu Ch'iu-yüan, *Fei-pang chi-t'uan*, p. 39; *Chung-hsing jih-pao*, Dec. 11, 1933, in KMTS.

129. "Lun Chung-hua su-wei-ai," p. 12. A general amnesty for all prisoners except murderers, robbers, and so on, was issued on December 1. See State Dept 893.00 P.R. Foochow/72, Jan. 5, 1934, p. 7.

130. "Lun Chung-hua su-wei-ai," p. 12; Ch'iu Kuo-chen, p. 143.

131. "Chung-kuo kung-ch'an-tang chung-yang wei-yüan-hui wei Fu-chien shih-pien ti-erh-tz'u hsüan-yen" (Second declaration of the CCP Central Committee regarding the Fukien rebellion), *Tou-cheng* 45:1 (Feb. 2, 1934).

132. Ch'en Yün, p. 2; "Chung-kuo kung-ch'an-tang chung-yang wei-yüan-hui wei Fu-chien shih-pien kao ch'üan-kuo min-chung" (Statement of the CCP Central Committee to the masses of the nation regarding the Fukien rebellion), *Tou-cheng* 38:2 (Dec. 12, 1933).

133. Tso-liang Hsiao, II, 684. A similar appeal to Fukien was made in a second telegram dispatched as late as Jan. 13, 1934—although this second telegram did not clearly promise that the communists would offer military cooperation. See ibid.

134. "Chung-kuo kung-ch'an-tang . . . kao ch'uan kuo min-chung," p. 3.

135. "Chung-kuo kung-ch'an-tang ti-erh-tz'u hsüan-yen," p. 1; "Lun Chung-hua su-wei-ai," pp. 12–13.

136. Tso-liang Hsiao, II, 687. Emphasis added.

137. William Dorrill has examined the circumstances surrounding the communists' reevaluation of their policy during the rebellion. My examination of the evidence supports his admittedly tentative conclusion that Mao and a

majority of the Kiangsi leadership had not advocated closer unity with Fukien. During the rebellion, advocacy of an alliance with Fukien was labeled a "right-opportunist error." It is significant that writings by the Communist Party (presumably controlled by the Po Ku faction) at that time devoted little effort or space to rebutting this rightest deviation. Judging from the space allotted in these writings, a far more serious and threatening deviation came from the "left revolutionaries," who were opposed to any alliance with any non-communist forces. See "Lun Chung-hua su-wei-ai," p. 9; Ch'en Yün, p. 2. It seems certain, therefore, that Mao's support for the Fukien revolutionaries appeared only long after the People's Revolutionary Government had been defeated.

138. Kung Ch'u, p. 367.

139. *Fan-Chiang yün-tung shih*, p. 670; Juan Fang-hua, *Chung-kuo ch'ih-huo ssu-shih-nien* (Taipei, 1967), I, 278.

140. *Shih-shih hsin-pao*, Nov. 19, 1933, p. 1; ibid., Dec. 2, 1933. These reports may have been accurate, for the same charge was made almost a year earlier. See "Fu-chien Ch'en Kuo-hui chih hsien-chuang" (The current situation of Fukien's Ch'en Kuo-hui), *SHHW* 1:445 (Dec. 3, 1932).

141. *Chung-hsing jih-pao*, Dec. 9, 1933, in KMTS; "Min-ni tsai Hu ts'ai-pan chün-hsü (Fukien rebels buy up military supplies in Shanghai), *SHHW* 5:438 (Dec. 24, 1933).

142. Lei Hsiao-ts'en, p. 222.

143. Interview.

144. Lei Hsiao-ts'en, pp. 222–223.

145. *Chung-hsing jih-pao*, Nov. 22, 1933, in KMTS.

146. The communists did criticize Fukien for not having taken more positive measures against both Japan and Chiang Kai-shek. But this did not imply that Fukien was any more in collusion with Japan than with Chiang. See Sheng-lun, "Fu-chou yü Jui-chin" (Foochow and Jui-chin), *KWCP* 12.9: articles, pp. 7, 9 (March 11, 1935).

147. Ch'iu Kuo-chen, pp. 157–160; Ku-shu-chih, pt. 4, p. 7; Hu Ch'iu-yüan, *Fei-pang chi-t'uan*, pp. 82–83.

148. The wealthy classes, however, had panicked. The closure of the banks, followed by rumors that everything would be communized, caused many of the rich to pack their movable possessions and flee the province. Lei Hsiao-ts'en, pp. 216–217; *Kung-shang jih-pao*, Nov. 27, 1933, in KMTS.

This drain on the wealth of the province was of sharp concern to the Fukien authorities, and they immediately moved to stop the flow. As early as November 22 they restricted travelers' luggage to one or two pieces for each person. Two days later, persons leaving the province were required to obtain traveling permits, and each branch of the Public Security Office could issue but ten a day. *Jen-min jih-pao*, Nov. 23, 1933, sec. 2, p. 1. The authorities also forestalled a run on the banks after they reopened, restricting withdrawals to 10 percent of an individual's total deposit. *Kung-shang jih-pao*, Nov. 27, 1933, in KMTS. The authorities at the same time attempted to allay public disquiet. Non-agricultural private property, they promised, would not be expropriated, and private commercial and industrial enterprises would be protected and encouraged. Ibid., *KWCP* 10.49: events p. 2 (Dec. 11, 1933).

149. The full text of this declaration is in "Min-min-fu ti-erh-tz'u hsüan-yen ch'üan-wen" (Full text of the Fukien People's Government's second declaration), name of paper unclear, Dec. 24, 1933, in KMTS. First mention of the federal principle appeared in a document, "Stages of Constructing a National Producers' Government, reported from Amoy on Dec. 13. See *KWCP* 10.50: events p. 3 (Dec. 18, 1933).

150. Ku-shu-chih, pt. 3, p. 6; Huang Hsü-ch'u, "Kuang-hsi yü chung-yang," pt. 20, p. 16; Ts'ai T'ing-k'ai, *Tzu-chuan*, p. 383; *NCH*, Feb. 7, 1934, p. 205.

151. Huang Chen-hsia, "Ts'ung chün-shih-shang kuan-ch'a Min-pien" (Looking at the Fukien rebellion from the vantage of military science), *Shen-pao yüeh-k'an* 3.2:32 (Feb. 15, 1934); Lei Hsiao-ts'en, pp. 220–221.

152. See above, p. 117; also *NCH*, Jan. 10, 1934, p. 38.

153. Lei Hsiao-ts'en, p. 221.

154. Huang Chen-hsia, p. 31.

155. Ts'ai T'ing-k'ai, *Tzu-chuan*, p. 383.

156. Huang Chen-hsia, pp. 31–32; Lei Hsiao-ts'en, p. 214. Estimates of the actual numerical strengths of the two armies vary widely. Huang Chen-hsia, p. 33, puts the size of Fukien forces at 65,000 men and Nanking forces at 150,000. A Japanese estimate gives Nanking 84,000 and Fukien 75,000 (*Chūka minkoku Fukkenshō dokuritsu no shinsō*). Wang Chien-min, II, 606, puts Fukien's strength at something over 40,000 men, which accords with most other estimates.

157. Wang Chien-min, II, 607; *KWCP* 10.49: events p. 1 (Dec. 11, 1933); *Kung-shang jih-pao*, Dec. 2, 1933, in KMTS.

158. Wang Chien-min, II, 606; Lei Hsiao-ts'en, p. 221, *K'an-ting Min-p'an chi-lüeh* (n.p., n.d.), pp. 1–15; Franklin to State, State Dept. 893.00/12654, p. 1; State Dept. 893.00 P.R. Foochow/72, Jan. 5, 1934, p. 17.

159. "Min t'uan-t'i fen-fen hu-yü chih-chih cha-Min" (Kukien group appeals to halt the bombing of Fukien), name and date of newspaper unclear; a diary of the three-day bombing of Foochow, *Kung-shang jih-pao*, Dec. 29, 1933; both in KMTS.

160. *Kung-shang jih-pao*, Jan. 18, 1934; and *Chung-hsing jih-pao*, Feb. 1, 1934; both in KMTS.

161. *NCH*, Jan. 31, 1934, p. 166; State Dept. 893.00 P. R. Foochow/73, Feb. 5, 1934, pp. 8–21. The fence-sitting posture of the navy throughout the rebellion is discussed in State Dept. 893.00 P.R. Foochow/72, Jan. 5, 1934, pp. 11–13.

162. Ku-shu-chih, pt. 4, p. 7; Nan-pin, "Min-pien ching-kuo" (Development of the Fukien rebellion), *TFTC* 31.4:67–68 (Feb. 16, 1934); *Kung-shang jih-pao*, Jan. 20 (?), 1934, in KMTS.

163. *China Year Book, 1934*, p. 378; *NCH*, Jan. 24, 1934, p. 118.

164. *Kung-shang jih-pao*, Dec. 4, 1933; and ibid., Jan. 19, 1934; both in KMTS.

165. Ts'ai T'ing-k'ai, *Tzu-chuan*, p. 380; Interview; Huang Hsü-ch'u, "Kuang-hsi yü chung-yang," pt. 20, p. 16. Other sources remarking on the poor morale of the army are: Huang Ch'iang, "Tsai Min-pien-chung te Ch'en

Ming-shu yü wo" (Ch'en Ming-shu and I in the Fukien rebellion), *Ch'un-ch'iu* 131:3 (Dec. 16, 1962); Huang Chen-hsia, pp. 31–32; *Kung-shang jih-pao,* Jan. 19, 1934, in KMTS.

166. Ts'ai T'ing-k'ai, *Tzu-chuan,* p. 383.

167. Ch'iu Kuo-chen, p. 137; Ku-shu-chih, pt. 1, p. 3; State Dept. 893.00 P. R. Foochow/72, Jan. 5, 1934, p. 8.

168. Ku-shu-chih, pt. 4, p. 7; Lei Hsiao-ts'en, p. 223. See also *Kung-shang jih-pao,* Jan. 18(?), 1934, in KMTS.

169. Ku-shu-chih, pt. 4, p. 7; Ch'iu Kuo-chen, pp. 137–138; Lei Hsiao-ts'en, p. 223; and interview.

170. Ku-shu-chih, pt. 3, p. 8; *NCH,* Feb. 13, 1934, p. 238; Ts'ai T'ing-k'ai, *Tzu-chuan,* p. 383; and interview.

171. Ku-shu-chih, pt. 5, p. 11. Hu Ch'iu-yüan states that Hsü's execution was at least partially due to other, but unspecified, reasons than his participation in the rebellion. *Fei-pang chi-t'uan,* p. 71. Photographs of the execution are in *TFTC* 31.8 (April 16, 1934).

172. Hu Chow-yuan [Hu Ch'iu-yüan], "The Nineteenth Route Army," *Amerasia,* May 1937, pp. 130–131; *NCH,* Jan. 2, 1935, p. 33; *KWCP* 11.7: events p. 2 (Feb. 5, 1934).

173. *NCH,* Feb. 7, 1934, p. 205; "Min-pien-hou chu-ni chih hsing-ts'ung" (The activities of the various rebels after the Fukien rebellion), *SHHW* 4:99 (Jan. 1, 1935); Ts'ai T'ing-k'ai, *Hai-wai yin-hsiang chi* (Record of impressions abroad) (Hong Kong, 1935); "Ts'ai T'ing-k'ai shih pu-yüan ts'an-chia" (Ts'ai T'ing-k'ai does not wish to participate), name of newspaper unspecified, June 11, 1936, in Yokota Collection.

174. "Min-pien-hou chu-ni," pp. 98–99; "Ch'en Chen-ju yü Hsü Ch'ien ho mou" (Ch'en Ming-shu and Hsü Ch'ien plot together), *SHHW* 6:357 (March 8, 1934).

175. *NCH,* Jan. 24, 1934, p. 117.

176. Gauss to State, Dec. 5, 1933, State Dept. 893.00/12610, p. 2.

178. "Min-pien shih-chi," p. 12; *NCH,* Jan. 3, 1934, p. 1.

179. See, e.g., Hu Shih, "Fu-chien te ta-pien-chü" (General situation of the rebellion in Fukien), *TLPL* 79: 2–4 (Dec. 3, 1933); editorial, *Shen-pao,* Nov. 23, 1933, p. 5.

180. This effect of the Japanese threat was frequently remarked during the period. Nelson Johnson, the U.S. ambassador, suggested in 1936 that one of the "chief factors" that had prevented civil war in the preceding six years was "the desire to avoid giving the Japanese military an overt excuse for aggression. Johnson to Secretary of State, July 13, 1936, State Dept. 893.00/ 13610, p. 11. See also Wang Yün-sheng "Che liang-nien" (These two years), *KWCP* 10.37: articles p. 6 (Sept. 18, 1933); Tsiang T'ing-fu "Chiu-i-pa—liang-nien i-hou" (Sept. 18—two years later), *TLPL* 68:3 (Sept. 17, 1933).

4. Democracy and Dictatorship

1. Domes, pp. 311–320; Ch'ien Tuan-sheng, *The Government and Politics of China* (Cambridge, Mass., 1961), pp. 133–139.

2. Yang Yu-chiung, "Pen-tang cheng-chih chien-she chih li-lun te kuan-ch'a" (A view of the theory of our party's political reconstruction), *Chung-yang pan-yüeh-k'an* 2.1:35 (Oct. 1, 1928).

3. Ch'ien Tuan-sheng, *Government and Politics,* pp. 296–297.

4. Wu Ching-ch'ao, "Chung-kuo te cheng-chih wen-t'i" (The question of China's political system), *TKP,* Dec. 30, 1934, pp. 2–3; Liang Shu-ming, "Chung-kuo tz'u-k'o shang pu tao yu hsien-fa ch'eng-kung te shih-hou" (China at this moment has still not reached the time when a constitution can succeed), *TKP,* April 22, 1934, sec. 1, p. 2; and Hsü Ch'ih-p'ing, "Hsien-cheng k'o-i k'ai-shih le ma?" (Can constitutional government be instituted?), *TLPL* 176:9–11 (Nov. 10, 1935).

5. Tsiang T'ing-fu, "Lun chuan-chih ping ta Hu Shih-chih hsien-sheng" (On despotism and also a reply to Hu Shih), *TLPL* 83:4 (Dec. 31, 1933). See also Tsiang, "Ko-ming yü chuan-chih" (Revolution and despotism), *TLPL* 80:2–5 (Dec. 10, 1933).

6. Hu Shih, "Chien-kuo yü chuan-chih" (Nation-building and despotism), *TLPL* 81:2–5 (Dec. 17, 1933).

7. Tsiang T'ing-fu, "Nan-ching te chi-hui" (Nanking's opportunity), *TLPL* 31:1 (Dec. 18, 1932).

8. Chang Hung, "Chuan-chih wen-t'i p'ing-i" (An unbiased discussion of the question of despotism) *TLPL* 104:10 (June 10, 1934).

9. Ch'ien Tuan-sheng, "Min-chu cheng-chih hu? Chi-ch'üan kuo-chia hu?" (Democratic government? Or a totalitarian state?). *TFTC* 31.1:23 (Jan. 1, 1934).

10. Examples of these arguments are: Ch'eng Jui-lin "Chung-kuo kuo k'o shih-hsing hsien-cheng hu" (Can China indeed institute constitutional government?), *Wen-hua chien-she* 2.2:16 (Nov. 10, 1935); Chu Wei-ju, "Te-mo-k'o-la-hsi te ch'ien-t'u" (The future of democracy), *STKL* 111:9–13 (May 11, 1934).

11. Ch'ien Tuan-sheng, "Te-mo-k'o-la-hsi wei-chi chi chiang-lai" (The peril and future of democracy), *Kuo-li Wu-han ta-hsüeh she-hui k'o-hsüeh chi-k'an* ("Quarterly Journal of Social Science") 1.1:50 (March 1930).

12. Ch'ien Tuan-sheng, "Min-chu cheng-chih hu? Chi-ch'üan kuo-chia hu?," p. 17.

13. Ibid., pp. 22, 23.

14. Ibid., p. 24.

15. Ting Wen-chiang remarked that everyone, of both leftist and rightist political views, was attracted by the model of a controlled economy. "Shih-hsing t'ung-chih ching-chi te t'iao-chien" (The conditions for the implementation of a controlled economy), *TLPL* 108:18 (July 8, 1934). See also Ch'eng T'ien-fang, "Min-chu yü tu-ts'ai" (Democracy and dictatorship), *STKL* 150:13 (Feb. 8, 1935); Ch'ien-chi, "T'ung-chih ching-chi wen-t'i" (The question of a controlled economy), *KWCP* 10.39: articles pp. 1–4 (Oct. 2, 1933).

16. Chang Chin-chien, "Tu-ts'ai chu-i lun" (On dictatorship), *Wen-hua chien-she* 1.2:28 and 31 (Nov. 10, 1934).

17. Ibid., pp. 29–30.

18. Ch'en Chih-mai, "Tsai lun cheng-chih te she-chi" (Again on the planning of a political system), *TLPL* 205:4 (June 14, 1936).

19. I have discussed the difference between these traditions, with specific reference to Mao Tse-tung, in "Mao, Marx, and the Future Society," *Problems of Communism,* May–June 1969, pp. 21–26. See also Wolfram Eberhard, *Moral and Social Values of the Chinese: Collected Essays* (Taipei, 1971), pp. 8–13.

20. Ch'ien Tuan-sheng, "Min-chu cheng-chih hu? Chi-ch'üan kuo-chia hu?" p. 23.

21. Ch'en Chih-mai, "Min-chih chu-i te yen-pien" (The evolution of democracy), *TFTC* 33.17:43 (Sept. 1, 1936).

22. Chou Fo-hai, "Min-ch'üan chu-i te ken-chü ho t'e-chih," (The basis and special characteristics of the doctrine of popular sovereignty), *Hsin-sheng-ming* 1.2:11 (Feb. 1, 1928).

23. Sa Meng-wu, "I-tang chih-kuo" (Party rule), *Hsin-sheng-ming* 1.4:5 (April 1, 1928).

24. Wu Ching-hsiung and Huang Kung-chüeh, *Chung-kuo chih-hsien shih* (Shanghai, 1937), p. 735.

25. Wu Ching-hsiung, "Chung-hua min-kuo hsien-fa ts'ao-an te t'e-se" (The special character of the constitutional draft), *TFTC* 33.13:10 (July 1, 1936).

26. Chang Fo-ch'üan, "Lun kuo-min cheng-chih fu-tan" (On the burden of national government), *KWCP* 10.33: articles p. 5 (Aug. 21, 1933).

27. Chin Tseng-ku, "Shih-nien-lai chih Chung-kuo ssu-hsiang-chieh" (China's intellegentsia during the past ten years), *Yü-chou hsün-k'an* 1.2:11 (Dec. 25, 1934).

28. See, e.g., Mei Ssu-p'ing, "Wu-ch'üan hsien-fa te ching-shen chi ch'i yün-yung te fang-fa" (The spirit of the five-power constitution and the method of its implementation), *Hsin-sheng-ming* 1.1:4–5 (Jan. 1, 1928); Yang Yu-chiung, "Pen-tang cheng-chih chien-she chih li-lun te kuan-ch'a," *Chung-yang pan-yüeh-k'an* 2.1:37 (Oct. 1, 1928).

29. Wu Ching-ch'ao, "Chung-kuo te cheng-chih wen-t'i," p. 2. Others, however, saw this support for democracy eroding. See, e.g., [Chang] Fo-ch'üan, "Hsün-cheng yü chuan-cheng" (Political tutelage and absolutism), *KWCP* 11.36: articles p. 4 (Sept. 10, 1934).

30. P'eng Hsüeh-p'ei, "I-chiu-san-i nien Chung-kuo cheng-chih" (Chinese politics in 1931), *Tu-shu tsa-chih* 2.1:6 (n.d.). P'eng, incidentally, joined the Nationalist government shortly after writing this article.

31. Chang Fo-ch'üan, "Hsün-cheng yü chuan-cheng," *KWCP* 11.36:4.

32. J. L. Talmon, *The Origins of Totalitarian Democracy* (New York, Frederick A. Praeger, 1960), p. 1.

33. *I-shih pao* editorial, reprinted in *KWCP* 10.23: editorials p. 7 (June 12, 1933).

34. Hu Tao-wei, "Chung-kuo te ch'i-lu" (China's fork in the road), *KWCP* 12.6: articles p. 4 (Feb. 18, 1935).

35. Ming-hsia, "Wo tui min-chih te i-chien" (My view of democracy), *Yü-chou hsün-k'an* 2.8:1–4 (July 25, 1935).

36. Hu Shih, "Tsai lun chien-kuo yü chuan-chih" (Again on nation-building and despotism), *TLPL* 82:5 (Dec. 24, 1933).

37. Ibid., p. 4.

38. Ibid., p. 5.

39. Ibid., pp. 4–5.

40. Hu Shih, "I-nien-lai kuan-yü min-chih yü tu-ts'ai te t'ao-lun" (The discussion on democracy and dictatorship during the past year), *TFTC* 32.1:16 (Jan. 1, 1935); Hu Shih, "Tsai t'an-t'an hsien-cheng" (Again discussing constitutional government), *TLPL* 236:5–7 (May 30, 1937).

41. Hu Shih, "China's Chances of Survival," *People's Tribune* 16.5:378–379 (March 1, 1937).

42. Chang Hsi-jo, "Min-chu cheng-chih tang-chen shih yu-ch'ih te cheng-chih ma?" (Is democracy really a childish political system?), *TLPL* 239:3–6 (June 20, 1937). Much the same criticism of Hu Shih's view was made by Chün-heng, "Hsien-cheng te t'iao-chien" (The conditions of constitutional government), *TLPL* 238:2–4 (June 13, 1937).

43. Hao Chang, *Liang Ch'i-ch'ao and Intellectual Transition in China, 1890–1907* (Cambridge, Mass., Harvard University Press, 1971), pp. 189–206; Benjamin Schwartz, *In Search of Wealth and Power: Yen Fu and the West* (Cambridge, Mass., The Belknap Press of Harvard University Press, 1964), pp. 240–242, and passim.

44. *Hsien-tai shih-liao,* I, 278; see, e.g., Jen Chung-min, "Kuo-min fu-hua chi ch'i kai-ko" (The decay of the people and their renovation), *Chung-yang pan-yüeh-k'an* 1.17:33 (Feb. 15, 1928); Yung-ni, "Ts'ung fan-hsing chung ch'iu ch'u-lu" (Seek a way out through introspection), *TLPL* 54:2–6 (June 11, 1933); editorial, *SHHW* 6:290–291 (March 6, 1934).

45. Hu Shih, "Ch'üan-kuo chen-ching i-hou" (After the nation is shaken up), *TLPL* 41:6 (March 12, 1933).

46. Shen T'ung, "Min-tsu te yu-sheng" (Races' survival of the fittest), *TLPL* 84:9–11 (Jan. 7, 1934).

47. T'ung Jun-chih, "Chung-kuo min-tsu te chih-li" (The intelligence of the Chinese race), *TFTC* 26.3:67–76 (Feb. 10, 1929).

48. Fritz Stern, *The Politics of Cultural Despair: A Study in the Rise of the Germanic Ideology* (Berkeley, University of California Press, 1961), see esp. the introduction and pp. 267–294.

49. [Ma] Chi-lien, "Chiu-fen chung-chung chih tang-kuo" (The embattled party-state), *KWCP* 9.4: articles p. 1 (Jan. 18, 1932).

50. *I-shih-pao* editorial, reprinted in *KWCP* 10.23: editorials p. 8 (June 12, 1933).

51. See, e.g., ibid.; *TKP* editorial, reprinted in *KWCP* 10.23: editorials pp. 3–4 (June 12, 1933); *TKP* editorials, reprinted in *KWCP* 10.22:5–6 (June 5, 1933).

52. Ting Wen-chiang, "Chung-kuo cheng-chih te ch'u-lu" (The way out for Chinese government), *TLPL* 11:4 (July 31, 1932).

53. "Nan-ching kuo-min-tang ti-ssu-tz'u ch'üan-kuo tai-piao ta-hui" (The Nanking Kuomintang's 4th party congress), *KWCP* 8.47: articles p. 5 (Nov. 30, 1931).

54. *KWCP* 8.49: events p. 14 (Dec. 14, 1931). A complete list of the delegates, as of January 1932, is in *Ch'en-pao,* Jan. 22, 1932, in Hatano, *Kiroku,* January 1932, pp. 287–289.

55. *TKP,* April 4, 1932, in Hatano, *Kiroku,* April 1932, pp. 53–55; *NCH,* April 4, 1932, p. 10. These demands were expressed in a telegram to Wang Ching-wei on March 27, 1932.

56. *KWCP* 9.11: events p. 7 (March 21, 1932) lists 114 new delegates. The total number of delegates was over 400. *Ch'en-pao,* April 16, 1932, in Hatano, *Kiroku,* April 1932, p. 225.

57. *KWCP* 9.14: events p. 6 (April 11, 1932); *NCH,* April 5, 1932, p. 10.

58. *CWR* 60.7:215 (April 16, 1932).

59. *KWCP* 9.14: events p. 6 (April 11, 1932); *NCH,* April 5, 1932, p. 10; *NCH,* April 12, 1932, p. 50.

60. *TKP* editorial, reprinted in *KWCP* 9.15:7 (April 18, 1932). The largest number of delegates to attend a session was 159. *KWCP* 9.15: events p. 1 (April 18, 1932).

61. *Ch'en-pao,* April 16, 1932, in Hatano, *Kiroku,* April 1932, pp. 224–227, gives an animated description of the proceedings. See also *Hsien-tai shih-lao,* I, 113–117.

62. *KWCP* 9.15: events p. 5 (April 18, 1932).

63. *KWCP* 9.17: events p. 9 (May 2, 1932).

64. [Ma] Chi-lien, "Hsien-cheng neng chiu Chung-kuo?" (Can constitutional government save China?), *KWCP* 9.18:2 (May 9, 1932). Wang made this statement on April 25, 1932.

65. Ibid.; *KWCP* 9.17: events p. 2 (May 2, 1932). On Sun Yat-sen's prescriptive model for political tutelage, and on the vicissitudes of local self-government during the Nanking period, see Ch'ien Tuan-sheng, *Government and Politics,* pp. 296–297; and Hung-mao Tien, *Government and Politics,* pp. 93–94.

66. Wang Chü-yüan, "San-chung-ch'üan-hui ch'ien chih ko-fang-mien" (Circumstances prior to the 3rd plenum), *SHHW* 1:509 (Dec. 15, 1933); Ballantine to State, Dec. 28, 1932, State Dept. 893.00/12283, pp. 5–7.

67. Domes, p. 491, note 52.

68. *NCH,* Sept. 14, 1929, p. 397.

69. The text is in *KWCP* 9.17: events p. 9 (May 2, 1932). Sun was particularly anxious to enlist the support of the Kwangtung leaders, Ch'en Chi-t'ang and Hu Han-min, who since Chiang Kai-shek returned to government in January 1932 had reverted to their customary truculence toward Nanking. See *KWCP* 9.19: events pp. 7–8 (May 16, 1932).

70. The central government was at a nadir in the latter half of 1932, and Sun Fo's political stock rose accordingly. The government was disorganized and demoralized after it fled to Lo-yang at the time of the Shanghai fighting; popular disgust with the regime was also greater than at any time previously. Moreover, Wang Ching-wei had resigned as premier in August 1932, ostensibly in protest against Chang Hsüeh-liang's failure to resist the Japanese in Manchuria. With Wang absent, Chiang Kai-shek was even more vulnerable to the charge of dictatorship. Presumably Chiang hoped to allay these various

discontents by enlisting Sun Fo into the government and by tolerating Sun's demands for a constitution.

71. Wu Ching-hsiung and Huang Kung-chüeh, pp. 86–87. The document had been signed in advance by twenty-six other members of the Central Executive Committee.

72. Wu Ching-hsiung and Huang Kung-chüeh, pp. 725–726.

73. Chang Chih-pen, as related to Ch'en Hsiu-feng, *Chung-kuo li-hsien ku-shih* (Taipei, 1966), pp. 50–51.

74. The original version of Sun's resolution is in Wu Ching-hsiung and Huang Kung-chüeh, pp. 717–722. English summaries of this and the final, revised version are in *China Year Book, 1933*, pp. 252–253, 255–256.

75. *KWCP* 10.1: chronology p. 1 (Jan. 1, 1933).

76. *KWCP* 10.4: events p. 4 (Jan. 23, 1933).

77. See Sun Yat-sen, *Fundamentals of National Reconstruction* (Taipei, 1953), pp. 9–16.

78. Ibid., pp. 27–30.

79. The text of this and other major drafts prepared between 1933 and 1936 are reproduced in Wu Ching-hsiung and Huang Kung-chüeh, appendices, pp. 793–1002.

80. See articles 32, 38, 71, and 76 of the draft constitution, ibid., pp. 894–902.

81. Ibid., p. 890.

82. Ibid., pp. 891–893.

83. Chang Chih-pen, *Chung-kuo li-hsien ku-shih*, p. 78; Chang Chih-pen, "Hsien-fa ts'ao-an wei-yüan-hui chih shih-ming chi ts'ao-an-chung ying-hsing yen-chiu chih wen-t'i" (The mandate of the constitutional drafting committee, and questions in the draft that should be studied), *TFTC* 30.7: 11–19 (April 1, 1933).

84. Wu Ching-hsiung and Huang Kung-chüeh, pp. 564–565, 772.

85. Ibid., pp. 781–782.

86. Ibid., p. 783.

87. Ibid., pp. 489–490. For biographical background on Wang, see Boorman, III, 376–378.

88. Wu Ching-hsiung and Huang Kung-chüeh, pp. 765–766.

89. For an apt example of this ambiguity, see Sun Yat-sen, *Fundamentals of National Reconstruction* (Taipei, China Cultural Service, 1953), pp. 15–16.

90. Ch'ien Tuan-sheng, *Government and Politics* p. 301.

91. *KWCP* 11.9: summary comments, p. 2 (March 5, 1934); Wang Han-chang, "Shen-men shih-chü-chung te tsung-li-chih wen-t'i" (Deep concern regarding the question of the tsung-li system in the current situation), *STKL* 107:5 (April 13, 1934); *China Year Book, 1935*, p. 96.

92. "Chiang Chieh-shih chih hsin-sheng-huo yün-tung" (Chiang Kai-shek's New Life Movement), name and date of newspaper not indicated, Yokota Collection.

93. Wang Han-chang, p. 7.

94. Chiang made this statement on March 1, 1934. *KWCP* 11.9: events p. 1 (March 5, 1934); *China Year Book, 1935*, p. 96.

95. *KWCP* 11.33: events p. 2 (Aug. 20, 1934).

96. Hsiao Ch'ing, "Fan-tui Nan-ching chao-k'ai ti-wu-tz'u ch'üan-kuo tai-piao ta-hui" (Oppose Nanking's convening of the 5th party congress), *Ch'ing-nien chün-jen* 2.16:9 (Aug. 31, 1934); editorial, *San-min-chu-i yüeh-k'an* 4.4:16 (Oct. 15, 1934).

97. Hu Han-min et al., telegram to Central Executive Committee, Sept. 8, 1934, *San-min-chu-i yüeh-k'an* 4.4:1–2 (Oct. 15, 1934).

98. "Chiang Chieh-shih chung-ta k'ung-pu" (The great fear of Chiang Kai-shek), name of newspaper not indicated, Aug. 17, 1934; "Lan-i-she chüeh-t'ui Chiang Chieh-shih chiu-jen kuo-min-tang tsung-li" (The Blue Shirts determinedly push Chiang Kai-shek to assume the post of tsung-li), name of newspaper not indicated, Aug. 19, 1934; "Fan-Chiang ko-p'ai chi-chi yün-jang" (All anti-Chiang factions actively brew a plot), *Chiang-nan cheng-pao*, Oct. 7, 1934; and "Fan-Chiang ko-p'ai ch'eng-chi t'u-jan fa-ch'i" (All anti-Chiang factions grasp the occasion to suddenly rise up), name and date of newspaper not indicated; all in Yokota Collection.

99. "Fan-Chiang ko-p'ai chi-chi yün-jang" in Yokota Collection.

100. Ibid.; "Ou-Mei p'ai chi Hu kuei-hua" (The European-American clique gathers in Shanghai to prepare plans), name of newspaper not indicated, Sept. 25, 1934, in Yokota Collection.

101. *China Year Book, 1935,* p. 99.

102. *NCH,* Oct. 17, 1934, p. 113.

103. Chiang's pretext for this action was that many of the nation's top military commanders urged postponement, because a congress would interfere with the military campaign against the communists, that was, they said, on the verge of final and complete success. This concerted expression of concern was obviously not spontaneous, and Kwangtung authorities suggested that Chiang had told his commanders to send him these telegrams so that he would have a face-saving gesture for further postponing the congress. Postponement was illegal, for a party congress could only legally be postponed once, and this was the second time the 5th congress had been cancelled. See *TKP*, Oct. 26, 1934, p. 3; editorial, *San-min-chu-i yüeh-k'an* 4.5:1–2 (Nov. 15, 1934); *China Year Book, 1935,* pp. 100–102.

104. Wu Ching-hsiung and Huang Kung-chüeh, pp. 577–578, 783.

105. The original text is in ibid., pp. 978–1002; a translation is in *China Year Book, 1936,* pp. 150–155.

106. Ch'ien Tuan-sheng, *Government and Politics,* p. 122.

107. [Ma] Chi-lien, "Hsien-cheng neng chiu Chung-kuo ma?" (Can constitutional government save China?), *KWCP* 9.18: articles pp. 1–2 (May 9, 1932).

108. "Min-pien hsü-chi," p. 7; *TKP* editorial, reprinted in *KWCP* 11.1: editorials pp. 2–3 (Jan. 1, 1934).

109. *I-shih-pao* editorial, reprinted in *KWCP* 10.23: editorials p. 7 (June 12, 1933).

110. Peck to State, Dec. 8, 1933, State Dept. 893.00/12617, p. 2.

111. Wang Han-chang, "Shen-men shih-chü-chung te tsung-li chih-tu wen-t'i," *STKL* 107:7.

5. Nanking and the Economy

1. Ta-chung Liu and Kung-chia Yeh, *The Economy of the Chinese Mainland: National Income and Economic Development, 1933–1959* (Princeton, 1965), p. 66; Albert Feuerwerker, *The Chinese Economy, 1912–1949* (Ann Arbor, 1968), p. 8 and passim.

2. Increases of cultivable land and population:

Year	Land area (in millions of *shih-mou*)	Year	Population (in millions)
1685	740 (±100)	1650	100–150
1766	950 (±100)	1750	200–250
1873	1,210 (± 50)	1850	410 (±25)
1893	1,240 (± 50)	1873	350 (±25)
1913	1,360 (± 50)	1893	385 (±25)
1933	1,470 (± 50)	1913	430 (±25)
		1933	500 (±25)

Figures from Dwight H. Perkins, *Agricultural Development in China, 1368–1968* (Chicago, 1969), pp. 216, 240.

3. Liu and Yeh, pp. 34–37.

4. See note 2. Ramon Myers points out that average farm size decreased by 32 percent in the more densely populated areas of China between 1870 and 1930; 36 percent in north China during the same period; and 6 percent in the rice region of south China between 1910 and 1930. See Myers, "Land Distribution in Revolutionary China: 1890–1937," *The Chung Chi Journal* 8.2:62–63 (May 1969).

5. Perkins, pp. 186–189 and passim; Myers, *Chinese Peasant Economy*, pp. 207–210, 212–213.

6. John Lossing Buck, *Land Utilization in China* (New York, 1964), pp. 458–461.

7. A dissenting voice from this generalization is that of Myers, "Land Distribution," pp. 64–65, who sees no "distress signs" in rural China during normal times, and estimates that, in five provinces studied, "per capita grain equivalents [consumed] were 60 percent above the required minimum."

8. Buck, p. 387.

9. R. H. Tawney, *Land and Labour in China* (New York, 1932), p. 72.

10. Compare Yang Sueh-chang, "China's Depression and Subsequent Recovery, 1931–36: An Inquiry into the Applicability of the Modern Income Determination Theory" (Ph.D. diss., Harvard University, 1950), p. 162; Liu Ta-chung, *China's National Income, 1931–36: An Exploratory Study* (Washington, D.C., 1946), p. 22; Buck, pp. 312–321, 344.

11. Foreign investments more than doubled between 1928 and 1930 (from ¥100 million to ¥202 million annually), and remittances from overseas Chinese increased from ¥215.6 million to ¥316.3 million. See Yang Sueh-Chang, p. 118.

12. Yang Sueh-Chang, pp. 182–183, 194; Cheng Sen-yü, "Chung-kuo mien-fang chih-yeh te wei-chi" (The crisis in China's cotton spinning industry), *TFTC* 33.20 :64–65 (Oct. 16, 1936).

13. Exports from China Proper to the four northeastern provinces were valued at ¥100 million in 1931. In 1935, the amount had declined to ¥35 million. See *Chinese Year Book, 1937,* pp. 618–619, and esp. table 3, p. 620.

14. A considerable literature is developing on the silver question and Sino-American relations. See: Dorothy Borg, *The United States and the Far Eastern Crisis of 1933–1938* (Cambridge, Mass., 1964), pp. 121–137; Cheryl Payer, "Western Economic Assistance to Nationalist China, 1927–1937" (Diss. in progress, Harvard University), chap. 2; Michael B. Russell, "American Silver Policy and China, 1933–1936" (Ph.D. diss., University of Illinois, 1972); Arthur N. Young, *China's Nation-Building Effort, 1927–1937* (Stanford: 1971), pp. 223–229.

15. Yang Sueh-Chang, p. 205.

16. H. D. Fong, "Toward Economic Control in China," *Nankai* 9.2 :354–357 (July 1936). For data on silver exports and estimates on amounts of smuggled silver, see Yu-Kwei Cheng, *Foreign Trade and Industrial Development of China: An Historical and Integrated Analysis through 1948* (Washington, D.C., 1956), pp. 262–263.

17. Mo-yen, "Shang-hai chin-jung k'ung-huang te hui-ku yü ch'ien-chan" (Glances backward and forward regarding the Shanghai financial panic), *TFTC* 33.22 :33–43 (Nov. 16, 1936); *Wage Rates in Shanghai,* by Bureau of Social Affairs, The City of Greater Shanghai (Shanghai, 1935), p. 53.

18. Ibid., p. 62.

19. See below, pp. 227–228.

20. W. Y. Lin, *The New Monetary System of China: A Personal Interpretation* (Chicago, 1936), p. 54.

21. Johnson to State, Sept. 19, 1931, State Dept. 893.00 P.R./48, p. 24; *China Year Book, 1932,* pp. 385–387; Yang Sueh-Chang, p. 151; H. D. Fong, "Toward Economic Control," p. 304.

22. Yang Sueh-Chang, pp. 149, 156–157.

23. See, e.g., Ou Pao-san, "Min-kuo erh-shih-erh-nien te Chung-kuo nung-yeh ching-chi" (China's agricultural economy in 1933), *TFTC* 31.11 :7–16 (June 1, 1934).

24. Chang P'ei-kang, "Min-kuo erh-shih-san-nien te Chung-kuo nung-yeh ching-chi" (The Chinese argicultural economy in 1934), *TFTC* 32.13 :135 (July 1, 1935); Kao T'ing-tzu, *Chung-kuo ching-chi chien-she* (Shanghai, 1937), p. 115–116; Chang P'ei-kang, "Chin-nien-lai te tsai-huang" (Calamities in recent years), *TLPL* 150.12–13 (May 12, 1935); Chang P'ei-kang, "Min-kuo erh-shih-ssu-nien te Chung-kuo nung-yeh ching-chi" (China's agricultural economy in 1935), *TFTC* 33.8 :23–26 (April 16, 1936).

25. Chang P'ei-kang, "Min-kuo erh-shih-san-nien te Chung-kuo nung-yeh ching-chi," p. 134.

26. Computed from table 7 in Liu Ta-chung, *China's National Income,* pp. 20–21. See also Yen Chung-p'ing et al, *Chung-kuo chin-tai ching-chi shih t'ung-chi tzu-liao hsüan-chi* (Peking, 1955), p. 360.

27. Liu Ta-chung, *China's National Income,* pp. 10, 35–40. The actual decline of agriculture's contribution to the national product was less drastic when measured in 1931 prices, declining from a high of ¥26.64 billion in 1932 to a low of ¥23.34 billion in 1934—a decline of only 12 percent. But we are here concerned primarily with the fiscal effects of the depression, for which the figures in current prices are a better indicator.

28. The actual statistical figure was 4.8 percent. See Wu Chih-hsin, "Chung-kuo nung-min li-ts'un wen-t'i" (The problem of Chinese farmers leaving the villages), *TFTC* 34.15:19 (Aug. 1, 1937). Many similar studies, but less extensive in scale, were made during this same period, most of which concluded that emigration was larger than 4.8 percent.

29. Chang Yu-i, ed., *Chung-kuo chin-tai nung-yeh shih tzu-liao,* III (Peking, 1957), 882.

30. Ai-lien, "Ju-tz'u Kuei-chou" (This is Kweichow), pt. 2, *TLPL* 118:13, 16 (Sept. 16, 1934).

31. Nien-fei, "Chü-pien chung te ku-hsiang—Wu-chin nung-ts'un" (My old home town in a time of rapid change—the village of Wu-chin), *TFTC* 33.6:117–118 (March 16, 1936).

32. Hsiu-chen, "Ku-hsiang chih chin-hsi" (My old home town, past and present), *TLPL* 122:8–11 (Oct. 14, 1934). For other evidence of decreased land values, see *Problems of the Pacific, 1933: Economic Conflict and Control,* ed. Bruno Lasker and W. L. Holland (Chicago, 1934), p. 298.

33. Hsü Hsieh-hsiang, "Ju-tz'u t'ien-t'ang" (Thus is heaven), *TLPL* 124:8–11 (Oct. 28, 1934). See also Chang Yu-i, p. 602.

34. Muramatsu Yuji, "A Documentary Study of Chinese Landlordism in the Late Ch'ing and the Early Republican Kiangnan," *Bulletin of the School of Oriental and African Studies* 29:3:574–575 (1966).

35. Wu Shih-ch'ang, "Keng-che k'en yu ch'i t'ien ma?" (Is the tiller willing to possess his land?), *TLPL* 175:7 (Nov. 3, 1935).

36. Wang Tz'u-fan, "Nung-ts'un ti-chu yü shih-p'in-min" (A village landlord and the urban poor), *TLPL* 106:5–8 (June 24, 1934).

37. See, e.g., Wu Ching-ch'ao, "Lun ti-chu te tan-fu" (On the burdens of landlords), *TLPL* 175:8–10 (Nov. 3, 1935).

38. Chang Yu-i, pp. 728–730. For suggestive evidence that large land concentrations tended to decrease in the period 1928–1933, see Yen Chung-p'ing, pp. 283, 286 (tables 20 and 23).

39. Ramon H. Myers, *The Chinese Peasant Economy: Agricultural Development in Hopei and Shantung, 1890–1949* (Cambridge, Mass., 1970), pp. 207–210 and passim.

40. The wealthy and the extraordinarily poor in this village paid even smaller parts of their income to the government. See Amano Motonosuke, *Shina nōgyō keizai ron,* II (Tokyo, 1942), 199–201. Note that the land taxes in this village were unusually light.

41. Myers, *Chinese Peasant Economy,* p. 64. On the land tax in the Ch'ing period, see Yeh-chien Wang, "The Fiscal Importance of the Land Tax during the Ch'ing Period," *Journal of Asian Studies* 30.4:829–842 (Aug. 1971).

42. Amano, II, 15. In 1935, for example, the land tax provided 77.5 percent of the hsien revenue in Kiangsu, and 70.4 percent in Anhwei. In Chekiang, by contrast, only 27 percent of hsien revenue was from the land taxes. See also Fang Hsien-t'ing, p. 960.

43. Buck, p. 312.

44. Buck, p. 324.

45. This discussion of the tax system in Chekiang is based on Franklin L. Ho, "Land Tax in Chekiang," *Monthly Bulletin on Economic China* 7.1:1–14 (Jan. 1934). For corroboration regarding increase of surtaxes, see *Chechiang hsin-chih*, comp. Chiang Ch'ing-yün (Hangchow, 1936), II, 22b.

46. Franklin L. Ho, "Land Tax in Chekiang," pp. 3–4. C. M. Chang reported seventy-three surcharges in Chekiang—but 147 kinds of surtaxes in Kiangsu. See C. M. Chang, "A New Government for Rural China: The Political Aspect of Rural Reconstruction," *Nankai* 9.2:274 (July 1936). See also chart in Chang Yu-i, p. 16. Provinces under Nanking's control tended to have a greater number of surcharges than other provinces.

47. Computed from data in Sun Tso-ch'i, *Chung-kuo t'ien-fu wen-t'i* (Shanghai, 1935), pp. 171–173.

48. Franklin L. Ho, "Land Tax in Chekiang," p. 3.

49. League of Nations, Council Committees on Technical Cooperation between the League of Nations and China, *Report of the Technical Agent on His Mission in China from the Date of His Appointment until April 1st, 1934* (Geneva, 1934), p. 20. Franklin Ho also found that three hsien paid only ¥0.21–0.30 in combined main tax and surtaxes; ten paid ¥0.31–0.40; and eleven paid more than ¥1.00 per mou. "Land Tax in Chekiang," p. 4.

50. Chin Feng, "Tu Chiang-su Che-chiang nung-ts'un tiao-ch'a" (Having read the investigations of villages in Kiangsu and Chekiang), *KWCP* 12.14: articles p. 2 (April 15, 1935). Sun Tso-ch'i, pp. 171–173, gives a breakdown of the main tax and total surtaxes for each hsien in Kiangsu.

51. Franklin L. Ho, "Land Tax in Chekiang," p. 3.

52. Myers, *Chinese Peasant Economy*, p. 268.

53. Buck, p. 324.

54. Computed from data in Fang Hsien-t'ing, pp. 952–954.

55. H. D. Fong, "Toward Economic Control in China," *Nankai* 9.2:359 (July, 1936); Wu Ching-ch'ao, "Ti-fang chien-she te i-hsien shu-kuang" (A ray of hope in local reconstruction), *TLPL* 201:43–44 (May 17, 1936). See also *Problems of the Pacific, 1936*, p. 161.

56. Y. C. Wang, *Chinese Intellectuals and the West, 1872–1949* (Chapel Hill, 1966), p. 458.

57. This discussion of t'an-k'uan is based on Amano, II, 39–47; and Cheng Shu-t'ang, "Jih-ch'ü yen-chung te nung-ts'un t'an-k'uan wen-t'i" (The increasingly serious problem of village t'an-k'uan), *TFTC* 32.24:49–58 (Dec. 16, 1936).

58. Myers, *Chinese Peasant Economy*, p. 64.

59. Wan Kuo-ting, "Chung-kuo t'ien-fu wu-k'an chi ch'i kai-ko ch'ien-t'u" (A bird's-eye view of China's land taxes and their future reform), *Ti-cheng yüeh-k'an* 4.2/3:145–147 (March 1936).

60. See, e.g., Sun Tso-ch'i, pp. 359–367; *Ti-cheng yüeh-k'an* 4.2/3 (March 1936), which is a special issue devoted to various aspects of the land tax; Myers, *Chinese Peasant Economy,* p. 272; Hung-mao Tien, *Government and Politics,* pp. 163–166.

61. Franklin L. Ho, "Land Tax in Chekiang," p. 11.

62. Sidney D. Gamble, *Ting Hsien: A North China Rural Community* (Stanford, 1968), p. 167.

63. Franklin L. Ho, "Land Tax in Chekiang," pp. 8–11. There is a considerable literature in Chinese on the means of tax evasion. See, e.g., Sun Tso-ch'i, pp. 357–370.

64. Fang Hsien-t'ing, pp. 346–347.

65. Letter from Buck to Arthur Young, Jan. 28, 1959, cited in Arthur N. Young, *China's Wartime Inflation, 1937–1945* (Cambridge, Mass., Harvard University Press, 1965), p. 22.

66. Fang Hsien-t'ing, p. 1115.

67. Meng Wei-hsien, "Tung-t'ing-hu pin chih nung-min sheng-huo" (Living conditions of farmers in the area bordering Tung-ting lake), *TFTC* 33.8:115 (April 16, 1936); Sun Tso-ch'i, pp. 186–188; Kuan Yü-jun, "Nung-ts'un ching-chi i-hsi-t'an" (An evening's chat on the village economy), *TLPL* 132:12 (Dec. 23, 1934). The author of this last article points out that, despite the relatively low taxes, the farmer was in straitened circumstances.

68. Franklin L. Ho, "Rural Reconstruction in China," *Nankai* 9.2:523–524 (July 1936).

69. Myers, *Chinese Peasant Economy,* p. 269.

70. Ho Lien and Li Jui, *Ts'ai-cheng hsüeh* (Shanghai, 1935), pp. 257–262, 267–273; *China Year Book, 1931–32,* p. 488.

71. Gamble, pp. 178, 184; C. M. Chang, "Tax Farming in North China: A Case Study of the System of Auctioned Revenue Collection made in Ching-hai Hsien, Hopei Province," *Nankai* 8.4:824–852 (January 1936).

72. Chi-chen, "Ku-hsiang chih chin-hsi" (My old home town: past and present), *TLPL* 122:11 (Oct. 14, 1934).

73. Y. C. Wang, *Chinese Intellectuals,* pp. 429–433; *China Year Book, 1934* pp. 539–540; *China Year Book, 1935,* pp. 488–489, 533–534. Also relevant here is S. A. M. Adshead, *The Modernization of the Chinese Salt Administration, 1900–1920* (Cambridge, Mass., Harvard University Press, 1970), passim.

74. Y. C. Wang, *Chinese Intellectuals,* p. 459. The increase in the cost of salt is shown in the following table of index numbers (from Chang P'ei-kang, "Wo-kuo nung-min sheng-huo ch'eng-tu te ti-lo" [The decline in the Chinese farmers' standard of living], *TFTC* 34.1:124 [Jan. 1, 1937]):

Year	Peiping	Shanghai
1931	100.0	100.0
1932	96.2	84.0
1933	101.1	95.5
1934	109.7	126.2

75. *China Year Book, 1934,* p. 539.

76. The figures are only approximate. The price of salt in Ting hsien was ¥12.50 per picul. Gamble, p. 113, estimates that the average person consumed six catty annually. Fang Hsien-t'ing, p. 931, however, estimated that Chinese ate twelve catty a year. The table in Amano II, 199–200, suggests that salt consumption varied greatly among the various income-level groups.

The figures on household income are derived from Charles R. Roll, Jr., "Rural Inequality in China, 1934" (draft chapter for Ph.D. diss., Harvard University, written in 1972).

77. Hsü Hsieh-hsiang, "Ju-tz'u t'ien-t'ang," pp. 10–11; Li Ching-han, "Shen-ju min-chien te i-hsieh ching-yen yü kan-hsiang" (Several experiences and impressions derived from going among the people), *TLPL* 179: 10–11 (Dec. 1, 1935); Ch'en T'i-ssu, "Hsiang chü jih-chi" (A diary of living in a village), *TFTC* 32.18:100–101 (Sept. 16, 1935).

78. Li Ching-han, pp. 10–11. On "earth salt," see also *Chinese Year Book, 1937,* p. 421.

79. Quoted in Hung-mao Tien, *Government and Politics,* p. 168. See also Arthur N. Young, who wrote of the Nanking period, "Whenever revenue needs increased, the first thought was to raise rates or add a surtax that was supposedly temporary but in practice was not easily ended. Thus various tariff rates were raised and general surtaxes added, bringing about rates that often reduced revenue and caused smuggling that was hard to control." (Young, *China's Nation-Building Effort,* p. 144.)

80. Myers clearly indicates in his study that governmental functions at the local level increased and that this led to increased taxes. (*Chinese Peasant Economy,* pp. 63–65, 87, 120–121.) Note, however, that in a concluding chapter he develops an estimate showing that the village tax burden did not significantly change from 1930 to 1937 (pp. 265–268). He candidly admits that the tax burden may have been greater than he assumed. But his conclusion is inexplicable, because it flies in the face of his own evidence.

81. In his conclusion, Ramon Myers wrote: "Local government spent too much for expanding the police force and not enough for building roads and fostering local industry . . . In attempting to do so much, the bureaucracy became enlarged, inefficient, and extravagant in its use of public monies." Myers also quotes, apparently with approval, a Chinese scholar who wrote that most of the "extra tax revenue" was being spent simply for "maintaining the existence of the local bureaucratic organizations." (Myers, *Chinese Peasant Economy,* p. 271. See also ibid., p. 87.)

82. Chia Wen-chin, "Sui-Hsüan chih shih-hsien chi ch'i shou-fu" (The loss of Sui-ting and Hsüan-han hsien and their recovery), *TLPL* 89:17 (Feb. 25, 1934). According to another account, a local resident in Kiangsi pointed to the farmers toiling in a field, and remarked, "For this kind of people, communism is really a bright hope." This same native said that the communist army in Kiangsi gained in strength because the communist-suppression forces sold their weapons to the communists. Mao Tzu-shui, "Nan-hsing tsa-chi" (Random notes on a trip in the south), *TLPL* 18:18 (Sept. 18, 1932).

83. Ku-wu, "Ti-yü-li te lao-sao-hua," p. 13.

84. Ch'en Chen-han, "Cheng-fu yin-hang hsüeh-shu chi-kuan yü fu-hsing nung-ts'un" (Government banks, academic institutions, and revival of the villages), *KWCP* 10.46: articles p. 4 (Nov. 20, 1933). See also *TKP* editorial, reprinted in *KWCP* 10.15: editorials pp. 3–4 (April 17, 1933).

85. Yeh-ko, "Min-nan te nung-ts'un tsa-hsieh" (Random writings on villages in southern Fukien), *TFTC* 33.8:108–109 (April 16, 1936).

86. *NCH*, April 15, 1930, p. 89.

87. *China Year Book, 1936*, p. 32; Domes, pp. 605, 607. The bulk of railway construction was accomplished late in the decade. Only 2,404 kilometers were built from 1928 to May 1936, but 4,188 kilometers were constructed in the two-and-a-half years from May 1936 to December 1938.

88. Hsiung Shih-li, "Wu-ch'ih wu-chiao" (Without food, without education), *TLPL* 95:13 (April 8, 1934). On Hsiung Shih-li, see Boorman, II, 116–117.

The crowning blow to many farmers came after they had constructed the roads over their lands, for they sometimes had to continue paying taxes on the land commandeered for the roads. Franklin L. Ho, "Rural Economic Reconstruction," pp. 533–534.

89. Samuel C. H. Tang, "The Need of Co-ordination in China's Transport," *Monthly Bulletin on Economic China* 7.10:411 (October 1934). Ch'ao-shu, "Hsien hsing-cheng kai-chin" (Advances in hsien administration), *TLPL* 219:7 (Sept. 20, 1936).

90. "T'ui-chin cheng-chih chu-chung nung-ts'un chien-she" (Promote political and rural reconstruction), *Chiang tsung-t'ung ssu-hsiang yen-lun chi* XIII, 94; *CWR* 77.6:206 (July 11, 1936).

91. League of Nations, *Report of the Technical Agent*, Annexes, p. 76, quoted in Samuel C. H. Tang, p. 411.

92. Franklin L. Ho, "Reminiscences," p. 121.

93. *Problems of the Pacific, 1936*, ed. W. L. Holland and Kate L. Mitchell (Chicago, n.d.), p. 153; Kao T'ing-tzu, p. 130.

94. Quoted in George E. Taylor, "The Reconstruction Movement in China," *Problems of the Pacific, 1936*, p. 396.

95. For a succinct historical account of the cooperative movement in China, see *Chinese Year Book, 1936–37*, pp. 1272–1276. On statistical growth of the movement, see Frank M. Tamagna, *Banking and Finance in China* (New York, 1942), p. 189; *Chinese Year Book, 1937*, pp. 808–809, 811; Franklin L. Ho, "The Agricultural Economy of China: Comments," *The Strenuous Decade: China's Nation-Building Efforts, 1927–1937*, ed. Paul K. T. Sih (New York, 1970), p. 198.

96. Approximately three-fourths of the cooperatives performed credit functions. Of all cooperatives, 59 percent were exclusively credit societies, while the rest were involved also in producer and consumer cooperative functions. Tamagna, p. 189; *Chinese Year Book, 1936–37*, p. 1280; Chen Han-seng, "Cooperatives as a Panacea for China's Ills," *Far Eastern Survey* 6.7:75 (March 31, 1937).

97. The precise extent of farmer indebtedness is uncertain. John Lossing Buck's study, p. 464, based on a survey of 143 hsien, concluded that 39 per-

cent of the families were in debt. A government study, however, completed about the same time as Buck's in late 1933, reported that 56 percent in 850 hsien owed money. See Li Ching-han, "Chung-kuo nung-ts'un chin-jung yü nung-ts'un ho-tso wen-t'i" (China's rural finances and the problem of rural cooperation), *TFTC* 33.7:15–16 (April 1, 1936). These figures are cited also in Tamagna, p. 203.

98. "Cooperation among Farmers: Mr C. F. Strickland's Report to Universities China Committee—Communism Definitely Rejected," *NCH,* May 4, 1936, p. 396.

99. Buck, p. 463; Tamagna, p. 205; Li Ching-han, "Chung-kuo nung-ts'un chin-jung," p. 16. Li Ching-han also recorded that 64.7 percent of all loans were for a period of six to twelve months, and 12.6 percent were for less than six months. Few loans were therefore used for long-term capital investments.

League of Nations, *Report of the Technical Agent,* p. 21, noted that the average interest rate was 35 percent and often exceeded 100 percent.

100. Li Ching-han, "Chung-kuo nung-ts'un chin-jung," p. 16, based on a broad survey of rural financial conditions, provides the following percentage breakdown of sources of credit in 1933:

Rich farmers	45.0
Merchants	17.3
Landlords	9.0
Pawnshops and native shops	8.9
Cooperatives	1.3
Miscellaneous	1.1
	82.6

Tamagna, p. 203, states that, during the period 1933–1935, cooperatives provided 1 percent of the total credit. Yen Chung-p'ing, p. 345, indicates that 2.6 percent of the loans were granted by cooperatives in 1934.

101. Credit-granting cooperatives obtained the bulk of their capital from banks that charged 8–14 percent in interest annually. See Tamagna, pp. 189, 195; *Problems of the Pacific, 1936,* pp. 158–159.

102. *Problems of the Pacific, 1936,* p. 159; Chen Han-seng, "Cooperatives as a Panacea," p. 75; Tamagna, p. 194.

103. Chen Han-seng, "Cooperatives as a Panacea," p. 75; Tamagna, p. 194; *Agrarian China: Selected Source Materials from Chinese Authors* (Chicago, 1938), p. 208. Fei Hsiao-t'ung noted that, in a village in Kiangsu, many borrowers did indeed default. The resulting losses contributed to the failure of the cooperative in that village. See Fei Hsiao-t'ung, *Peasant Life in China: A Field Study of Country Life in the Yangtze Valley* (New York, E. P. Dutton and Company, 1939), p. 281.

104. *Agrarian China,* p. 216.

105. *Problems of the Pacific, 1936,* p. 390. Other examples are in *Agrarian China,* p. 213, and Franklin L. Ho, "Agricultural Economy," p. 198.

106. W. D. H. Campbell, "Some Practical Proposals for Chinese Co-

operatives," *Nankai* 10.1:82 (April 1937). Campbell was associated with the National Economic Council.

107. *Agrarian China*, pp. 215–216.

108. *Chinese Year Book, 1936–37*, pp. 1290–1291; *Chinese Year Book, 1937*, p. 818.

109. Buck, p. 194; Feuerwerker, *Chinese Economy*, p. 35; Yen Chung-p'ing, p. 262.

110. *Problems of the Pacific, 1936*, pp. 157–158; George E. Taylor, p. 391; T. H. Shen, *Agricultural Resources of China* (Ithaca, Cornell University Press, 1951), p. 100.

111. Tsiang T'ing-fu, "Tui kung-ch'an-tang," p. 7.

112. League of Nations, *Report of the Technical Agent*, p. 18.

113. Ibid., pp. 28–29.

114. *Problems of the Pacific, 1936*, p. 391.

115. The effects of the green revolution in West Pakistan have been summarized as follows: "The benefits of the Green Revolution, just like the benefit from industrialization, has gone to a comparatively narrow segment of society, to the bigger landowners, money lenders, and urban investors . . . The masses of smaller farmers have not benefited. Indeed they may well be worse off . . . Social and political tension [has been] increased by the wide disparity between what the masses have got and what the better-off classes have got from development." Sir Arthur Gaitskell, "Foreword," in Leslie Nulty, *The Green Revolution in West Pakistan: Implications of Technological Change* (New York, Praeger Publishers, 1972), p. vii. Francine R. Frankel arrived at essentially similar conclusions in *India's Green Revolution: Economic Gains and Political Costs* (Princeton, Princeton University Press, 1971).

116. Franklin L. Ho, "Rural Economic Reconstruction," p. 484, 502–503; *China Year Book, 1934*, p. 771; *China Year Book, 1935*, p. 60; T. H. Shen, "First Attempts to Transform Chinese Agriculture, 1927–1937," *Strenuous Decade*, p. 206.

117. Payer, untitled chapter on League of Nations activity in China. As a result of the fighting with Japan, the work of the council did not begin formally until Nov. 1933.

For monographic studies on the National Economic Council, see: Tao Siu, *L'Oeuvre du Conseil National Economique Chinois* (Nancy, 1936); and Norbert Meienberger, *Entwicklungshilfe unter dem Völkerbund: Ein Beitrag zur Geschichte der internationalen Zusammenarbeit in der Zwischenkriegszeit unter besonderer Berücksichtigung der technischen Hilfe an China* (Winterthur, Switzerland, 1965).

118. League of Nations, *Report of the Technical Agent*, pp. 11–12.

119. Rajchman, letter to Dragoni, Aug. 4, 1934, League of Nations archives, R.5687. It appears that there had from the beginning been a fundamental misunderstanding of the role of the council. Chiang Kai-shek in 1931 had clearly stated that the council was to be an "advisory board." (*Report of the Technical Agent*, p. 11.) But Ludwig Rajchman, in defining the powers of

the council in 1934, made no allusion to mere advisory functions (ibid., pp. 14–15).

120. *Chinese Year Book, 1937,* p. 252; Franklin L. Ho, "First Attempts to Transform Chinese Agriculture, 1927–1937: Comments," *Strenuous Decade,* pp. 234–235.

121. Ibid., p. 236; *Chinese Year Book, 1937,* pp. 250–251. Six thousand square miles, or an area measuring about 80 miles by 80 miles, did not represent a significant portion of China's total farm area.

122. Payer, citing League of Nations Archives, R.5673.

123. Payer, citing League of Nations Archives, 5711.

124. See, e.g., T. H. Shen, "First Attempts," pp. 214–232.

125. Franklin L. Ho, "First Attempts . . . Comments," p. 235, notes that some of the universities and the missionaries engaged in extension work, but that these efforts were "small in scope and symbolic in results."

126. Young, *China's Nation-Building Effort,* p. 75; Dau-lin Hsu, chap. 1, p. 19.

127. Dau-lin Hsu, chap. 1, pp. 1–4.

128. Dau-lin Hsu, chap. 1, p. 22.

129. Kao T'ing-tzu, *Chung-kuo ching-chi chien-she* (Shanghai, 1937), p. 122–123.

130. Huang Shao-hung, pp. 232–239.

131. Young, *China's Nation-Building Effort,* p. 252, and appendices 12 and 13.

132. *Chinese Year Book, 1937,* pp. 778–779.

133. Young, *China's Nation-Building Effort,* p. 250.

134. Ibid., pp. 152, 237.

135. *Problems of the Pacific, 1936,* p. 166. It should be noted that the informant providing this information did feel that the farmers had received considerable indirect benefits from the government. Dison Hsueh-Feng Poe, in an essay strongly favorable to Kuomintang efforts during the Nanking period, also stated: "In all fairness it must be admitted that . . . there was comparatively little accomplishment in the attempts of improving popular economic life, and that nevertheless arduous efforts so far as possible were made and some foundation was laid." Poe, "Political Reconstruction, 1927–1937," *Strenuous Decade,* p. 72.

136. Myers, *Chinese Peasant Economy,* p. 271.

137. Hu Shih, "Ts'ung nung-ts'un chiu-chi t'an tao wu-wei te cheng-chih" (Rural relief: a discussion of *wu-wei* government), *TLPL* 49:2–6 (May 7, 1933).

138. Paul M. A. Linebarger, *The China of Chiang Kai-shek: A Political Study* (Boston, 1941), p. 106. Although Linebarger's study was published in 1941, its section on the agrarian situation was based in large part on materials of the pre-war years.

139. Yuan-li Wu, "Industrial Development and Economic Policy," *Strenuous Decade,* pp. 242–243.

140. Chang Kia-ngau, "Toward Modernization of China's Currency and Banking, 1927–1937," *Strenuous Decade,* pp. 150–160.

141. Feuerwerker, *Chinese Economy,* p. 17.

142. John K. Chang, "Industrial Development of China, 1912–1949," *Journal of Economic History* 27.1:75 (March, 1967) ; Yuan-li Wu, pp. 239–240.

143. Liu Ta-chung, *China's National Income,* p. 12.

144. John K. Chang, p. 81.

145. Harold R. Isaacs, *The Tragedy of the Chinese Revolution,* 2nd rev. ed. (Stanford, 1961), pp. 111–151.

146. Parks M. Coble, "The Shanghai Commercial, Financial, and Industrial Elite and the Kuomintang, 1927–1929" (seminar paper, University of Illinois, 1971), p. 11.

147. Coble, p. 16.

148. Coble, pp. 24–25.

149. Coble, p. 27.

150. H. D. Fong, "Industrial Capital in China," *Nankai* 9.1:73 (April 1936).

151. Ibid., pp. 590–591; Young, "China's Fiscal Transformation," p. 108. According to Leonard G. Ting, the yield on loans had been estimated as high as 30–40 percent. See Leonard G. Ting, "Chinese Modern Banks and the Finance of Government and Industry," *Nankai* 8.3 :595.

152. Leonard G. Ting, p. 591.

153. Young, "China's Fiscal Transformation," p. 118; Y. C. Wang, *Chinese Intellectuals,* p. 456.

154. Young, "China's Fiscal Transformation," pp. 109–110.

155. Y. C. Wang, *Chinese Intellectuals,* p. 453.

156. Hsieh Chü-tseng, "I-chiu-san-wu-nien Shang-hai pai-yin feng-ch'ao kai-shu" (A survey of the silver unrest in Shanghai, 1935), *Li-shih yen-chiu* (Historical researches), 1965, no. 2, pp. 95–96.

157. Chang Kia-ngau, pp. 155–156. A certain amount of guess-work is involved in determining the size of the government's participation in the banking industry. I arrived at the approximate figure of 70 percent on the basis of the fact that the four principal government-related banks in 1936 held 59 percent of the aggregate assets of Chinese banks; and that the government also held direct or indirect control of a sizable group of other modern banks, savings institutions, and trusts. See Tamagna, pp. 185–187; and Ch'en Po-ta, *Chung-kuo ssu-ta-chia-tsu* (Hong Kong, 1947), pp. 22–23.

158. Y. C. Wang, *Chinese Intellectuals,* p. 449.

159. Ibid., p. 450; Chang Kia-ngau, p. 156.

160. Young, "China's Fiscal Transformation," p. 108. The government did in 1937 borrow for specific projects, such as the financial rehabilitation of Szechuan and Kwangtung.

161. Chang Kia-ngau, pp. 164–165.

162. Douglas S. Paauw, "The Kuomintang and Economic Stagnation, 1928–37," *Journal of Asian Studies* 16.2 :217 (February 1957). See also Y. C. Wang, *Chinese Intellectuals,* p. 462.

163. Yu-Kwei Cheng, p. 61. See also Young, *China's Nation-Building Effort,* p. 307.

164. Young, "China's Fiscal Transformation," pp. 116–117; Y. C. Wang, *Chinese Intellectuals,* pp. 460–462; Y. C. Wang, "Free Enterprise in China: The Case of a Cigarette Concern, 1905–1953," *Pacific Historical Review* 29:404, 411–412 (November 1960).

165. Myers, *Chinese Peasant Economy,* pp. 121–122; Young, "China's Fiscal Transformation," p. 117.

166. Ibid.; Ta-chung Liu, "China's Fiscal Transformation, 1927–1937: Comment," *Strenuous Decade,* p. 126.

167. Douglas S. Paauw, "The Kuomintang and Economic Stagnation," p. 217; Young, "China's Fiscal Transformation," p. 117.

168. Tamagna, p. 212; Y. C. Wang, *Chinese Intellectuals,* p. 489.

169. Quoted in Young, *China's Nation-Building Effort,* p. 294.

170. Ibid., p. 295; Yuan-li Wu, "Industrial Development and Economic Policy," *Strenuous Decade,* pp. 245–246; Ch'en Po-ta, *Chung-kuo ssu-ta-chia-tsu,* pp. 80–81; Y. C. Wang, *Chinese Intellectuals,* p. 49.

171. K'ang Chung-p'ing, "Lun kuan-liao tzu-pen chu-i" (On bureaucratic capitalism), *Ch'ün-chung,* II.39:14 (October 7, 1948).

172. Hou Chi-ming wrote: "Contrary to common belief, the modern sector of the economy grew continuously, not sporadically. All the indicators (except railroads) . . . [show] a constant rate of growth in the long run. This was achieved despite drastic changes on the political scene: the Manchu government (up to 1911), the Peking government (1912–1926), and the National government (1927–1937)." See Chi-ming Hou, *Foreign Investment and Economic Development in China, 1840–1937* (Cambridge, Mass., Harvard University Press, 1965), pp. 125–127.

John Chang cites an average annual growth rate of 9.3 percent for the period 1931–1936, and states that this represented a "surge" of industrial expansion that he attributes substantially to Nanking's policies. In fact, however, this figure reflects a 14.2 percent rate of growth in Manchuria. The actual rate of growth of 6.5 percent in China proper for those six years hardly justifies being characterized as a "surge." See John Chang, p. 68 and passim; Yuan-li Wu, "Industrial Development and Economic Policy," *Strenuous Decade,* pp. 239 and 326 note 6.

173. Douglas S. Paauw, "The Kuomintang and Economic Stagnation, 1928–1937," *Journal of Asian Studies,* XVI, 2:213–220 (February 1957).

174. Chi-ming Hou, p. 130. In fairness to Hou, it should be added that he does not believe that, in the long run, foreign enterprises grew at a faster rate than did Chinese enterprises. His argument in support of this latter contention is, however, weakly supported by evidence; he himself presents the argument only as a set of "tentative hypotheses." See Chi-ming Hou, pp. 138–150.

175. Yang Sueh-Chang, pp. 230–241.

176. Ho Kan-chih, pp. 119–123; Barrington Moore, Jr., *Social Origins of Dictatorship and Democracy: Land and Peasant in the Making of the Modern World* (Boston, Beacon Press, 1966), pp. 187–201.

177. Thomson, p. 31.

178. Ch'ien Tuan-sheng, *Min-kuo cheng-chih shih* (Shanghai, 1946), II, 665–669.

179. Kuhn, pp. 48–49, 62.

180. Kuhn, pp. 61–62.

181. *Chiang-su sheng cheng-fu kung-pao* (Kiangsu provincial government gazette) 32:13–14 (May 7, 1928) and 36:18–22 (June 4, 1928).

182. Kuhn, p. 61. The pao-chia was a system of local control using the methods of collective responsibility and organization of defense forces. See Hung-mao Tien, *Government and Politics,* pp. 101, 111–112.

183. Kuhn, p. 64.

184. Apt illustration of this tension between landlords and the regime has been offered by Doak Barnett. Describing the rural situation in Szechuan in 1948, Barnett observed that the impulse for change and reform came solely from a few idealistic governmental administrators. The changes they sought were resisted, however, by landlords in the hsien council. A member of the hsien government remarked to Barnett: "The Council members . . . are all men of wealth, education, and leisure. They are conservative and aren't interested in changing the *status quo*. The *status quo* is not bad at all from their own personal point of view, which is the only point of view most of them have." A. Doak Barnett, *China on the Eve of Communist Takeover* (New York, Frederick A. Praeger, 1963), p. 154.

6. On the Eve of the War

1. Domes, p. 590. It should be noted that education remained a privilege reserved for the elite: in 1937, 21.7 million students were enrolled in the primary schools, and only 48,516 students in the universities.

2. Quoted in Tamagna, p. 54.

3. "Notes on China," received informally from Francis Pickens Miller, 1934, State Dept. 893.00/12656B, p. 5.

4. According to the terms of this agreement, a demilitarized zone was to be created in an area between the Great Wall and a variable line running slightly north of Peiping and Tientsin. The "demilitarization" of the area was utterly spurious: Chinese and Japanese armies would indeed be evacuated, but Japanese troops were still permitted in specified cities of the area under the provisions of the 1901 Boxer Protocol. Moreover, peace and order were to be maintained in the demilitarized zone by a police force friendly to Japan. The text of the truce is in Bisson, pp. 44–45.

5. James B. Crowley, *Japan's Quest for Autonomy* (Princeton, 1966), pp. 211–212 and passim; Domes, pp. 628–633.

6. Crowley, pp. 212–217; Bisson, p. 54.

7. Domes, pp. 633–634; Bisson, pp. 55–57.

8. Bisson, pp. 57–67.

9. Bisson, pp. 71–77; Crowley, pp. 217–230.

10. *CWR* 77.7:231 (July 18, 1936).

11. Bisson, p. 113; Israel, pp. 114–115.

12. Bisson, pp. 113–116; Israel, pp. 119–123. A fascinating statement of the events and ideology of the student movement, from the students' eye-level is

"The Student Movement: Transmitting a Copy of the Report of the Peiping Student Union," State Dept. 893.00/13546, May 19, 1936, pp. 1–49.

13. Israel, pp. 110–156; Bisson, pp. 110–124; Nym Wales, *Notes on the Chinese Student Movement, 1935–1936* (mimeographed, 1959), pp. 26–34, 41–52, and passim.

14. Takayanagi Torao, *Kōnichi jimmin sensen undō no tembō* (Shanghai, 1936), pp. 128–187 and passim. On the student aspect of the movement, see Israel, pp. 159–162.

15. Boorman, III, 320; Mu Hsin, *Tsou T'ao-fen* (Hong Kong, 1959), p. 154, cites a circulation of 200,000.

16. Israel, p. 141.

17. Bisson, pp. 136–137. The question of communist involvement inevitably arises in a discussion of the national salvation movement. That there was communist influence is certain. The shift of the movement to advocacy of a united front between the communists and Nanking occurred contemporaneously with the communists' own change of policy on this question—an improbable coincidence. And Mu Hsin, pp. 185–186, states that communists had begun to infiltrate the publishing organization of Tsou T'ao-fen, one of the movement's leaders, from about March 1936. I think, however, that John Israel, p. 155, was correct in observing that "The question of direct CCP control is less important than the fact that large numbers of student leaders almost automatically followed the party line because it appeared to be the only road to national salvation." See also Lyman P. Van Slyke, *Enemies and Friends: The United Front in Chinese Communist History* (Stanford, 1967), p. 70.

18. Israel, p. 158; Takayanagi Torao, pp. 121–123.

19. *KWCP* 13.22: events pp. 1–3 (June 8, 1936), Bisson, pp. 137–138.

20. Robert A. Kapp, "Provincial Independence vs. National Rule: A Case Study of Szechwan in the 1920s and 1930s," *Journal of Asian Studies* 30.3:542–547 (May 1971).

21. Huang Hsü-ch'u, "Kuang-hsi yü chung-yang," pt, 22, p. 15.

22. Atcheson to State, June 21, 1935, State Dept. 793.94/7096; Johnson to Secretary of State, June 18, 1936, State Dept. 893.00/13610, p. 4.

23. Peck to State, July 7, 1936, State Dept. 893.00/13674, p. 3.

24. Ibid., pp. 3–4; Spiker to Johnson, July 6, 1936, State Dept. 893.00/13648, pp. 27–28.

25. "Hu Han-min ch'u-kuo chi" (Notes on Hu Han-min's departure from the country), June 19, 1935, Yokota Collection.

26. Huang Hsü-ch'u, "Kuang-hsi yü chung-yang," pt. 24, p. 16.

27. Ibid.; Huang Hsü-ch'u, "Pa-Kuei," pt. 25, pp. 17–18.

28. State Dept. 893.00 P.R./110, p. 10.

29. State Dept. 893.00 P.R./116, June 19, 1936, pp. 17–18. The will is translated in *NCH*, May 27, 1936, p. 364.

30. Chu-ch'eng, "Che-i-nien" (This year), *KWCP* 14.1: articles p. 3 (Jan. 1, 1937); Spiker to Johnson, June 3, 1936, State Dept. 893.00/13582, p. 8.

31. *NCH*, May 27, 1936, p. 364.

32. Chü-wai-jen, pt. 21, p. 11; Huang Hsü-ch'u, "Kuang-hsi yü chung-yang," pt. 24, p. 17. An interesting sidelight to these negotiations was Chiang Kai-shek's flat denial that such negotiations had occurred. "It is contrary to the Chinese practice," Chiang declared, "to talk about Party and political affairs while they are on such a solemn mission. Only those who do not understand the nature of the Chinese people would spread such rumours" (Johnson to Secretary of State, June 18, 1936, State Dept. 893.00/13610, p. 7 note). Manifestly, duplicity by government leaders was not invented by the Pentagon.

33. The sources disagree regarding which of the Southwest leaders took the lead at this time. Most contemporary reports state that Pai Ch'ung-hsi assumed the initiative, virtually running amuck, it was alleged, in his fury at Nanking. (See, e.g., Spiker to Johnson, July 6, 1936, State Dept. 893.00/13648, pp. 3–6.) I am inclined to accept the accounts of the Kwangsi leaders, which state that Ch'en Chi-t'ang was the prime mover of the rebellion. Ch'en had always exercised extreme caution in his governance of Kwangtung, but it seems probable that, with his back against the wall, he threw off all his customary restraint. According to this interpretation, the Kwangsi leaders realized their disadvantages vis-à-vis Nanking, but knew that the future of Kwangsi was irrevocably linked with that of Kwangtung. See "The Reminiscences of General Li Tsung-jen," with the assistance of Dr. T. K. Tong, 2nd English version, 1964 (unpub. ms. in Special Collections Library, Butler Library, Columbia University), chap. 31, pp. 10–12; Huang Hsü-ch'u, "Pa-Kuei," pt. 25, p. 18; and Huang Hsü-ch'u, "Kuang-hsi yü chung-yang," pt. 24, p. 17. See also Yung-sou, "Chiang Li ti-i-tz'u li-ho nei-mu" (The inside story of the first break-up and reconciliation between Chiang and Li), *Ch'un-ch'iu* 62:3 (Feb. 1, 1960); Gauss to Johnson, June 11, 1936, State Dept. 893.00/13613, pp. 2–3.

34. Johnson to Secretary of State, June 18, 1936, State Dept. 893.00/13610, p. 10.

35. Huang Hsü-ch'u, "Pa-Kuei," pt. 25, p. 18.

36. Huang Hsü-ch'u, "Kuang-hsi yü chung-yang," pt. 24, p. 17.

37. Suggested by Gauss to Johnson, June 11, 1936, State Dept. 893.00/13613, p. 3.

38. Huang Hsü-ch'u, "Kuang-hsi yü chung-yang," pt. 24, p. 17.

39. Spiker to Johnson, July 6, 1936, State Dept. 893.00/13648, p. 5; Johnson to Secretary of State, June 18, 1936, State Dept. 893.00/13610, p. 9.

40. Li Tsung-jen added that the Kwangsi group had joined Ch'en Chi-t'ang only with reluctance. Kwangsi feared being isolated from Kwangtung and thought that, by joining the revolt, they could restrain Ch'en. Li Tsung-jen, "The Reminiscences of Li Tsung-jen," with the assistance of T. K. Tong, 1964, 2nd English version (unpub. ms. in Special Collections Library, Butler Library, Columbia University), chap. 31, pp. 10–11.

41. *CWR* 77.4:150–152 (June 27, 1936); *Chung-kuo tsai t'ung-i chung*, ed. Liu Ch'ün (n.p., 1937), pp. 43–54 and passim.

42. "Yüeh-Kuei wen-t'i chih chan-k'ai" (The unfolding of the Kwangtung-Kwangsi question), *KWCP* 13.24: articles p. 1 (June 22, 1936).

43. *KWCP* 13.23: events p. 5 (June 15, 1936); Spiker to Johnson, June 3, 1936, State Dept. 893.00/13582, p. 12.

44. The two telegrams are reproduced in *KWCP* 13.23: events p. 2 (June 15, 1936). See also State Dept. 893.00 P.R./118, p. 14.

45. *TKP*, June 13, 1936, sheet 1, p. 3; *TKP*, June 19, 1936, sheet 1, p. 3; Huang Hsü-ch'u, "Kuang-hsi yü chung-yang," pt. 24, p. 17; Peck to State, July 7, 1936, State Dept. 893.00/13674, p. 8. Domes, p. 528, states that the Southwest authorities in a circular telegram on June 12 called on the nation to revolt against the Nanking government. I have been unable to corroborate this statement. It is, moreover, inconsistent with other telegrams being dispatched by the Southwest authorities at almost the same time.

46. Peck to State, July 7, 1936, State Dept, 893.00/13674, p. 11.

47. State Dept. 893.00 P.R./119, pp. 10–11; Huang Hsü-ch'u, "Kuang-hsi yü chung-yang," pt. 24, pp. 17–18; Huang Hsü-ch'u, "Pa-Kuei," pt. 25, p. 18; State Dept. 893.00 P.R./119, pp. 10–11; *TKP*, June 5, 1936, sheet 1, p. 3; *TKP*, June 19, 1936, sheet 1, p. 3.

48. Chü-wai-jen, pt. 21, pp. 11–12. See also Ch'en Shao-hsiao, p. 91.

49. *CWR* 77.13:461 (Aug. 29, 1936); Hoover to State, Aug. 7, 1936, State Dept. 893.00/13689, p. 1.

50. Four Kwangsi planes did defect on August 14 by flying to Kwangtung. The pilots of these planes were, however, Cantonese. *KWCP* 13.33: events p. 2 (Aug. 24, 1936); Cheng Tzu-hsiang, "Wo tang-nien shuai-ling Kuang-hsi k'ung-chün ch'i-i tsu-ch'eng Chiang Li Pai ch'i-chan-yen-ho te ching-kuo" (My experiences when I led the Kwangsi air force to defect thereby forcing Chiang, Li, and Pai to negotiate a peace settlement), *Ch'un-ch'iu* 72:2–5, 25 (July 1, 1960); *CWR* 77.13:456 (Aug. 29, 1936).

51. Li Tsung-jen and Pai Ch'ung-hsi on July 13 were offered the posts of commissioner and assistant commissioner of pacification, and Huang Hsü-ch'u was offered the provincial chairmanship. Huang Hsü-ch'u, "Kuang-hsi yü chung-yang," pt. 24, p. 18.

52. Ibid. *TKP* provides a good account of the day-by-day negotiations and disputes during this period and throughout the rebellion.

53. *KWCP* 13.34: events pp. 1–2 (Aug. 31, 1936); Spiker to Johnson, July 6, 1936, State Dept. 893.00/13648, pp. 29–33.

54. *Shina tōmen no jūyō mondai,* prepared by Tōyō Kyōkai chōsato (Tokyo, 1936), p. 14.

55. For terms of the peace settlement, see Domes, pp. 531–532.

56. *TKP*, Sept. 16, 1936, sec. 1, p. 3; *TKP*, Sept. 17, 1936, sec. 1, p. 3.

57. "Yü-wu chih hsien-tu" (The limits of resisting humiliations), *Chiang tsung-t'ung ssu-hsiang yen-lun chi* XIII, 382.

58. *Chung-kuo tsai t'ung-i chung,* pp. 72–75.

59. Domes, p. 644. Emphasis added.

60. *CWR* 78.4:117 (Sept. 26, 1936).

61. These and other anti-Japanese incidents are described in detail in Chou K'ai-ch'ing, *K'ang-chan i-ch'ien chih Chung-Jih kuan-hsi* (Taipei, 1962), pp. 211–248.

62. Ibid., pp. 133–134; *CWR* 78.9:305–306 (Oct. 31, 1936).

63. F. F. Liu, p. 114. See also Chou K'ai-ch'ing, pp. 134–142; Domes, pp. 645–646.

64. The Chang-Kawagoe negotiations are discussed in detail in Chou K'ai-ch'ing, pp. 67–105. See also Domes, pp. 642–644.

65. *New York Times,* Oct. 4, 1936, p. 25; *TKP,* Dec. 13, 1936, sec. 1, p. 2. See also Chu Ch'eng, "Che i-nien" (This year), *KWCP* 14.1: articles pp. 1–5 (Jan. 1, 1937); *KWCP* 13.48: editorials p. 1 (Dec. 7, 1936).

66. *CWR* 78.10:330 (Nov. 7, 1936). On student attitudes, see Chu-ch'eng, pp. 4–5; and *New York Times,* Oct. 4, 1936, pt. 7, p. 25.

67. *CWR* 76.7:218 (April 18, 1936).

68. *TKP,* Dec. 13, 1936, sec. 1, p. 2 (editorial).

69. *CWR* 78.13:452 (Nov. 28, 1936). The author of this piece, T. S. Young had previously criticized the regime freely and caustically. He may therefore not have been a government propagandist but simply a private citizen with an unfortunate penchant for purple prose. For other evidence of genuine enthusiasm for Chiang's leadership at this time, see *NCH,* Nov. 4, 1936, pp. 173, 177, 184; and *TKP,* Dec. 13, 1936, sec. 1, p. 2.

70. The following discussion of events relating to the Sian Incident is based largely on Bisson, pp. 154–191; Van Slyke, pp. 71–91; and James M. Bertram, *First Act in China* (New York, The Viking Press, 1938).

71. Chu-ch'eng, p. 4; *TKP,* Dec. 27, 1936, sec. 1, p. 2 (editorial).

72. *Strenuous Decade,* p. xx. Others who more or less adhere to this interpretation are F. F. Liu (see e.g., p. 102), and Jürgen Domes (see, e.g., pp. 682, 701–702). See also the assessment which on balance is favorable to the Kuomintang, in Arthur N. Young, *China's Nation-Building Effort,* pp. 422–430.

73. Everett E. Hagen, *On the Theory of Social Change: How Economic Growth Begins* (Homewood, Ill., The Dorsey Press Inc., 1962), pp. 210, 218.

74. Domes, table 22, facing p. 680.

75. Tso Shun-sheng, "The Reminiscences of Tso Shun-sheng (1893–)," as told to Julie Lien-ying How, (unpub. ms. in Special Collections Library, Butler Library, Columbia University, 1965), p. 116.

76. Samuel P. Huntington, *Political Order in Changing Societies* (New Haven, 1968), pp. 1–92 and passim.

77. John Israel's study of the student movement, already cited, provides a fine case study of the Nationalist regime's efforts to suppress elements of the population that were becoming politically active. On Nationalist handling of the labor movement, see Walter E. Gourlay, " 'Yellow' Unionism in Shanghai: A Study in Kuomintang Technique in Labor Control, 1927–1937," *Papers on China* 7:103–135 (1953); Joseph Fewsmith, "Authoritarian Rule in Kuomintang China: The Nanking Decade, 1927–1937" (Master's thesis, University of Chicago, 1973), pp. 95–127.

78. For an insightful discussion of the peasants' condition, and how they responded to impoverishment and oppressive government, see Lucien Bianco, "Les Paysans et la Révolution: Chine, 1919–1949," *Politique Étrangère,* 2:117–141 (1968). The political effects of a failure to ameliorate peasant dissatisfaction have also been indicated by Samuel P. Huntington: "If the

countryside supports the political system and the government, the system itself is secure against revolution and the government has some hope of making itself secure against rebellion. If the countryside is in rebellion, both system and government are in danger of overthrow." See Huntington, p. 292.

79. Tso Shun-sheng recalled that, even in the offices of the Officers' Moral Endeavor Corps, Yang Yung-t'ai had told him to pay no attention to the prohibition on smoking ("The Reminiscences of Tso Shun-sheng," p. 124). And it has long been rumored that Madame Chiang Kai-shek continued to smoke even at the height of the New Life Movement. More significant, the officials failed to promote the New Life Movement unless exposed to the prodding eye of Chiang Kai-shek. See Ma Chi-lien, "Kuan-yü tu-ts'ai" (Regarding dictatorship) *KWCP* 12.5: articles p. 2 (Jan. 28, 1935).

80. For caustic appraisals of officials promoting the New Life Movement, see Fu Meng-ch'eng, "Cheng-fu yü t'i-ch'ang tao-te" (Government and the promotion of morality), *TKP,* Nov. 25, 1934, editorial pp. 2–3; "Hsin-sheng-huo yün-tung chou-nien kan-yen" (Thoughts on the anniversary of the New Life Movement), editorial from *TKP, KWCP* 12.7: editorials pp. 3–4 (Feb. 25, 1935).

81. Hung-mao Tien, *Government and Politics,* pp. 24–26, 107–108; Chou Hsien-min, "Chin-nien kai-ko ti-fang cheng-chih chih te-shih" (Achievements and failures in the reform of local administration in recent years), *KWCP* 13.2: articles p. 17 (Jan. 6, 1936).

82. Hu Hsien-su, "Nan-yu tsa-kan" (Random impressions on a trip to the south), *KWCP* 13.7: articles p. 9 (Feb. 24, 1936); *TKP* editorial, reprinted in *KWCP* 13.49: editorials p. 4 (Dec. 24, 1936); Chu-ch'eng, p. 1.

83. Leonard S. Hsü, "Rural Reconstruction in China," *Pacific Affairs* 10.3:263 (September 1937). Punctuation modified.

84. Fu Ch'i-hsüeh, p. 163.

85. Young, "China's Fiscal Transformation," p. 120.

86. *NCH,* Sept. 16, 1936, p. 482.

87. Gauss to Johnson, Sept. 16, 1934, State Dept. 893.00/12842, p. 1; see also Ch'ien Tuan-sheng, *Government and Politics,* p. 149.

88. Franklin L. Ho, "Reminiscences," p. 439.

89. Thomson, p. 181.

90. Franklin L. Ho, "Reminiscences," p. 130.

91. *TKP* editorial, reprinted in *KWCP* 7.25: editorials p. 2 (June 30, 1930).

92. See, e.g., Tso Shun-sheng, p. 274; K'ung Hsiang-hsi, "The Reminiscences of K'ung Hsiang-hsi (September 11, 1800–)," as told to Julie Lien-ying How (unpub. ms. in Special Collections Library, Butler Library, Columbia University, 1961), p. 71; Shih-hsin, "Shih-ts'ung sheng-huo chi-wang pu-i" (Addenda to Reminiscences on the life of a bodyguard), *Ch'un-ch'iu* 133:7 (Jan. 16, 1963).

93. On one occasion, for example, he saw a ten-year-old boy smoking on the street. He went to the child's parents and admonished them for failing to discipline the child. After this, Chiang claimed, small children seldom smoked in that village. This incident proved to Chiang that "the transformation of

customs and the reconstruction of society is certainly not a difficult task."
Chiang tsung-t'ung ssu-hsiang yen-lun chi XII, 108.

94. See, e.g., Chiang Kai-shek, "The Cause and Cure of Rural Decadence," in Wang Ching-wei and Chiang Kai-shek, *China's Leaders and Their Policies* (Shanghai, China United Press, 1935), pp. 31–32.

95. K'ung Hsiang-hsi, p. 72.

96. "Hsin-sheng-huo yün-tung chih yao-i," *Chiang tsung-t'ung ssu-hsiang yen-lun chi* XII, 111.

97. Franklin L. Ho, "Reminiscences," p. 160.

98. Conversation between Minister Johnson and Arthur N. Young, May 15, 1930, State Dept. 893.01/395, p. 2.

99. Huntington, pp. 13–20.

100. H. R. Ekins and Theon Wright, *China Fights for Her Life* (New York, Whittlesey House, 1938), p. 27. Much the same view was expressed, if less cuttingly, by *I-shih pao* editorial, reprinted in KWCP 9.23: editorials p. 8 (June 13, 1932).

7. Social Traits and Political Behavior in Kuomintang China

1. Andrew James Nathan, "Factionalism in Early Republican China: The Politics of the Peking Government, 1918–1920" (Ph.D. diss., Harvard University, 1970), pp. 99–102.

2. Levenson, II, 25–116.

3. Cavendish, "The 'New China' of the Kuomintang," p. 161.

4. The source of these figures was a statement by Ch'en Li-fu in 1938. See "Influential Elements in the Kuomintang (and National Government)" dated Jan. 24, 1943, in *The Amerasia Papers: A Clue to the Catastrophe of China* (Washington, D.C., Government Printing Office, 1970), I, 236.

5. Young, *China's Nation-Building Effort*, p. 424.

6. Morton H. Fried, *Fabric of Chinese Society: A Study of the Social Life of a Chinese County Seat* (New York, 1953), p. 47.

7. Richard H. Solomon, "Mao's Effort to Reintegrate the Chinese Polity: Problems of Authority and Conflict in Chinese Social Process," *Chinese Communist Politics in Action*, ed. A. Doak Barnett (Seattle, 1969), pp. 284–285.

8. Marion J. Levy, Jr., *The Family Revolution in Modern China* (New York, 1968), pp. 166–175; Margery Wolf, "Child Training and the Chinese Family," *Family and Kinship in Chinese Society*, ed. Maurice Freedman (Stanford, 1970), pp. 40–41; Richard H. Solomon, *Mao's Revolution and the Chinese Political Culture* (Berkeley, 1971), pp. 39–81.

9. Levy, p. 105 and passim.

10. C. K. Yang, *The Chinese Family in the Communist Revolution* (Cambridge, Mass., 1959), p. 107; also ibid., pp. 22–29, 106.

11. Levy, p. 117; C. K. Yang, pp. 107–110.

12. Francis L. K. Hsü, *Under the Ancestors' Shadow: Chinese Culture and Personality* (New York, 1948), p. 265.

13. Compare Francis L. K. Hsü, *Under the Ancestors' Shadow*, pp. 267–271.

14. Margery Wolf, p. 53, has shown that the relationships between brothers

are complex, for initially the elder must yield to the younger. Later, however, the older brother assumes the power to dominate the relationship.

15. Fried, p. 226.

16. Wolfram Eberhard, *Moral and Social Values of the Chinese: Collected Essays* (Taipei, 1971), p. 6.

17. Solomon, "Mao's Effort," p. 297. This view is corroborated by Robert Henry Silin, "Management in Large-Scale Taiwanese Industrial Enterprises" (Ph.D. diss., Harvard University, 1970), p. 42.

18. Francis L. K. Hsü, *Americans and Chinese: Two Ways of Life* (New York, 1953), pp. 99–103, 279, and passim. Richard Solomon's research, cited elsewhere in this chapter, has also been based on the conclusion that the "dependency orientation toward authority" is one of the fundamental facts of social behavior. My study accepts this conclusion, but it also lays greater relative emphasis upon the authority figure and the Chinese tendency to aspire to authority status than does Solomon.

19. Wolf, pp. 54–55. See also Hsü, *Americans and Chinese,* pp. 79–80.

20. Solomon, *Mao's Revolution,* p. 112.

21. Hsü, *Under the Ancestor's Shadow,* p. 260.

22. Shih Kuo-heng, *China Enters the Machine Àge: A Study of Labor in Chinese War Industry* (Cambridge, Mass., 1944), pp. 118–119.

. 23. Solomon, "The Chinese Revolution," p. 166.

24. Fried, p. 61. See also Solomon, *Mao's Revolution,* p. 112: "An elder brother is a Son with his father, but a Father with his younger brother."

25. Hsü, *Under the Ancestors' Shadow,* p. 265.

26. Solomon, "Mao's Effort," p. 299.

27. Lien-sheng Yang, "The Concept of *Pao* as a Basis for Social Relations in China," *Chinese Thought and Institutions,* ed. John K. Fairbank (Chicago, 1957), p. 291.

28. Hsü, *Americans and Chinese,* pp. 357, 379. Emphasis added.

29. Nathan, chap. 2, esp. pp. 73–74, is highly suggestive on this point.

30. H. D. Fong, *Cotton Industry and Trade in China* (Tientsin, 1932), I, 319.

31. *TKP* editorial, reprinted in *KWCP* 11.37: editorials p. 1 (Sept. 17, 1934).

32. C. K. Yang, "Some Characteristics of Chinese Bureaucratic Behavior," *Confucianism in Action,* ed. David S. Nivison and Arthur F. Wright (Stanford, 1959), p. 149.

33. Payer (in chapter on League of Nations activities in China).

34. Franklin L. Ho, "Reminiscences," p. 144.

35. Yü Hsüeh-lun, "Chung-kuo sheng-cheng yü hsien-cheng chih mao-tun chi ch'i chiu-ch'i (The contradictions in provincial and hsien administrations and their solution), *KWCP* 10.34: articles p. 3 (Aug. 28, 1933).

36. Shen Yen, "Chin-jih li-chih pai-huai yüan-yin chi cheng-tun fang-fa" (The reasons for the current ruination of rule by low-level officials, and methods of reform), *KWCP* 10.15: articles p. 6 (April 17, 1933).

37. C. M. Chang, "A New Government for Rural China: The Political Aspect of Rural Reconstruction," *Nankai* 9.2:272 (July 1936).

38. Dau-lin Hsu, chap. 1, p. 32.

39. M. Searle Bates, "Toward an Understanding of Chinese Politics," *Pacific Affairs* 5.3:223 (March 1932).

40. Kennedy, p. 4 of summary.

41. C. M. Chang, p. 266.

42. Dau-lin Hsu, chap. 2, p. 45.

43. Gamble, p. 9. See also Hung-mao Tien, p. 212.

44. *Ching-pao* (Capital press), June 23–25, 1930, in Hatano, *Kiroku,* June 1930, p. 307. Emphasis added.

45. Feng Yü-hsiang, pp. 11–12.

46. Hsü, *Americans and Chinese,* p. 152.

47. Shen Yen, p. 4.

48. Hagen, p. 82.

49. *CWR* 78.3:90 (Sept. 19, 1936). Wang Cheng, p. 38, has emphasized the degree to which power and policy were determined within the Kuomintang by informal relations—what he called the "covert power structure"—rather than within the formal structures of government. He knew this was true, to some extent, in Western democracies. But "what seems . . . to have been the distinguishing characteristics of the Kuomintang were (a) the extent to which the covert system of controls submerged and nullified the formal structure, and (b) the fact that *the covert system existed and operated almost exclusively on the basis of interpersonal relations*" (emphasis added).

50. Wang Cheng, pp. 143–144.

51. Franklin L. Ho, "Reminiscences," pp. 136–137.

52. Ibid., p. 137. On the tensions that existed between principles of bureaucratic impersonality and societal pressures, see C. K. Yang, "Some Characteristics," pp. 156–159.

53. Huang Shao-hung, p. 233; Hu Shih, "Kung-k'ai chien-chü i" (On public recommendations), *KWCP* 11.10: articles p. 1 (March 12, 1934); *TKP,* Nov. 5, 1934, p. 2 (editorial).

54. Wang Cheng, p. 145.

55. T. W. Adorno et al, *The Authoritarian Personality* (New York, Harper and Row, 1950), pp. 367, 971.

56. Liu Chien-ch'ün, *Fu-hsing Chung-kuo ko-ming chih lu,* p. 115. See also Fan Jen, "Chung-kuo-jen te t'ung-ch'ing-hsin" (Compassion of the Chinese), *TFTC* 39.8:13–16 (June 30, 1943).

57. *Hsin-ch'en-pao* (New morning press), Jan. 10, 1929, in Hatano, *Kiroku,* January 1929, p. 102.

58. Dau-lin Hsu, chap. 1, p. 31.

59. Franklin L. Ho, "Reminiscences," p. 314.

60. Liu Chien-ch'ün, *Fu-hsing Chung-kuo ko-ming chih lu,* p. 39.

61. *TKP* editorial, reprinted in *KWCP* 9.35: editorials, p. 1 (Sept. 5, 1932).

62. *I-shih pao* editorial, reprinted in *KWCP* 10.46: editorials p. 6 (Nov. 20, 1933).

63. [Ma] Chi-lien, "Hsien-cheng neng chiu Chung-kuo ma?" *KWCP* 9.18: articles p. 3 (May 9, 1932).

64. Solomon, *Mao's Revolution,* pp. 116–121.

65. Solomon, "Mao's Effort," p. 289.

66. *TKP* editorial, reprinted in *KWCP* 8.9: editorials p. 7 (March 9, 1931).

67. Wu Ching-ch'ao, "Yü-lun tsai Chung-kuo ho-i pu fa-ta" (Why isn't public opinion well developed in China?), *TLPL* 87:3–4 (Jan. 28, 1934).

68. "Chung-kuo chien-she chih t'u-ching" (The path of China's reconstruction), *Chiang tsung-t'ung yen-lun hui-pien,* IX, 94.

69. "Tzu-shu yen-chiu ko-ming che-hsüeh ching-kuo te chieh-tuan" (Stages traversed in studying revolutionary philosophy), *Chiang tsung-t'ung yen-lun hui-pien,* X, 50.

70. Kenneth E. Shewmaker, *Americans and Chinese Communists, 1927–1945: A Persuading Encounter* (Ithaca, 1971), esp. pp. 20–179.

71. Peter S. H. Tang and Joan M. Maloney, *Communist China: The Domestic Scene, 1949–1967* (South Orange, N.J., Seton Hall University Press, 1967), pp. 144–145.

72. *The Politics of the Chinese Red Army: A Translation of the Bulletin of Activities of the People's Liberation Army,* ed. J. Chester Cheng (Stanford, The Hoover Institution, 1966), p. 553; "Quarterly Chronicle and Documentation," *China Quarterly* 20.171 (October–December 1964).

73. A. Doak Barnett, *Cadres, Bureaucracy, and Political Power in Communist China* (New York, Columbia University Press, 1967), p. 38.

74. Jerome Ch'en, ed., *Mao Papers: Anthology and Bibliography* (London, Oxford University Press, 1970), pp. 139, 144–145. For other evidence indicating the Maoist realization that the persistence of the old political culture was having invidious effects on the revolutionary forces, and the consequences of this realization in the cultural revolution, see Solomon, *Mao's Revolution,* pp. 406–431 and passim.

Bibliography

Agrarian China: Selected Source Materials from Chinese Authors. Comp. and tr. by the Research Staff of the Secretariat, Institute of Pacific Relations. Chicago, University of Chicago Press, 1938.

Amano Motonosuke 天野元之助. *Shina nōgyō keizai ron* 支那農業經濟論 (The Chinese farm economy). 2 vols. Tokyo, 1940–1942.

Bisson, T. A. *Japan in China.* New York, The Macmillan Co., 1938.

Boorman, Howard L., ed. *Biographical Dictionary of Republican China.* 4 vols. New York, Columbia University Press, 1967–1971.

Borg, Dorothy. *The United States and the Far Eastern Crisis of 1933–1938.* Cambridge, Mass., Harvard University Press, 1964.

Buck, John Lossing. *Land Utilization in China,* 2nd printing. New York, Paragon Book Reprint Corp., 1964.

Cavendish, Patrick. "The Rise of the Chinese Nationalist Party and the Foundation of the Nanking Regime: 1924–1929." Ph.D. diss., Cambridge University, 1968.

—— "The 'New China' of the Kuomintang," *Modern China's Search for a Political Form.* Ed. Jack Gray. London, Oxford University Press, 1969.

CC dan ni kansuru chōsa C. C. 團に關する調査 (An investigation of the CC clique). Prepared by the Special Investigative Section at Shanghai of the Japanese ministry in China. 1939.

   A 112-page study of the CC clique, dealing primarily with the period down to 1936.

"CC tokumu kōsaku no enkaku" CC 特務工作ノ沿革 (The development of the CC clique's special service work). Marked "Top secret." 1940.

   A Japanese government report.

Chang, C. M. "A New Government for Rural China: The Political Aspect of Rural Reconstruction," *Nankai Social and Economic Quarterly* 9.2: 239–295 (July 1936).

Chang Ch'i-yün 張其昀. *Tang-shih kai-yao* 黨史概要 (Survey of party history). 5 vols. Taipei, 1953.

Chang Chih-i 張執一. *K'ang-chan chung te cheng-tang ho p'ai-pieh* 抗戰中的政黨和派別 (Political parties and factions in the war of resistance). Chungking, 1939.

Chang Chih-pen 張知本, as related to Ch'en Hsiu-feng 陳秀鳳. *Chung-kuo li-hsien ku-shih* 中國立憲故事 (The story of the preparation of a constitution in China). Taipei, 1966.
　　　Cursory in coverage, but adds detail to the study by Wu Ching-hsiung and Huang Kung-chüeh.

Chang Ching-lu 張靜廬. ed. *Chung-kuo hsien-tai ch'u-pan shih-liao* 中國現代出版史料 (Historical materials on publishing in contemporary China). 4 vols. Peking, 1954–1959.

Chang, John K. "Industrial Development of China, 1912–1949," *Journal of Economic History* 27.1: 56–81 (March 1967).

Chang Yu-i 章有義. *Chung-kuo chin-tai nung-yeh shih tzu-liao* 中國近代農業史資料 (Historical materials on modern Chinese agriculture). Vol. III, 1927–1937. Peking, 1957.

Che-chiang hsin-chih 浙江新志 (New Chekiang provincial gazetteer). Comp. Chiang Ch'ing-yün 姜卿雲. Hangchow, 1936.

Chen, Gideon. "Chinese Government Economic Planning and Reconstruction since 1927." Preliminary paper prepared for the Fifth Biennial Conference of the Institute of Pacific Relations, to be held at Banff, Canada, Aug. 28, 1933. China Institute of Pacific Relations, 1933.

Ch'en Kung-po 陳公博. *So-wei san-tz'u tai-pai ta-hui chia-chih te ku-liang* 所謂三次代表大會價值的估量 (An assessment of the value of the so called third party congress). 2nd ed. Shanghai, 1930.

Ch'en Po-ta 陳伯達. *Chung-kuo ssu-ta-chia-tsu* 中國四大家族 (China's four great families). Hong Kong, 1947.

———— *Jen-min kung-ti Chiang Chieh-shih* 人民公敵蔣介石 (People's enemy: Chiang Kai-shek). Peking, 1st ed., 1948; 4th ed., 1954.

Ch'en Shao-hsiao 陳少校 (pseud. of Ch'en Fan 陳凡). *Hei-wang-lu* 黑綱錄 (Record of the black net). Hong Kong, 1966.

Cheng Yu-kwei. *Foreign Trade and Industrial Development of China: An Historical and Integrated Analysis through 1948*. Washington, D. C., The University Press of Washington, D. C., 1956.

Cherepanov, Alexander Ivanovich. *Notes of a Military Advisor in China*. A draft translation by Alexandra O. Smith. Ed. Harry H. Collier and Thomas M. Williamsen. Taipei, (U. S. Army) Office of Military History, 1970.

Chiang Kai-shek 蔣介石. *Chiang tsung-t'ung yen-lun hui-pien* 蔣總統言論彙編 (The collected speeches of President Chiang). Taipei, 1956.

———— *Chiang tsung-t'ung ssu-hsiang yen-lun chi* 蔣總統思想言論集 (The collected thoughts and speeches of President Chiang). Taipei, 1966.

Ch'ien-t'u 前途 (Future). Hankow and Shanghai, 1933–1937.
　　　A Blue Shirt publication; edited by Liu Ping-li.

Ch'ien Tuan-sheng 錢端升. *Min-kuo cheng-chih shih* 民國政制史 (History of the political system under the Republic). Shanghai, 1946.

———— *The Government and Politics of China.* Cambridge, Mass., Harvard University Press, 1961.

China Forum. Shanghai, 1933–1934.

China Weekly Review. Shanghai, 1927–1938.

China Year Book. Tientsin, Shanghai, 1928–1936.

Chinese Social and Political Science Review. Peiping, 1927–1938.

Chinese Year Book. Shanghai, 1936–37, 1937.

Ch'ing-nien chün-jen 青年軍人 (Young soldier). Canton, 1933–1935.

> An apparently official publication of the Kwangtung regime, it was strongly opposed to Nanking.

Ch'iu Kuo-chen 丘國珍. *Shih-chiu lu-chün hsing-wang shih* 十九路軍興亡史 (A history of the rise and fall of the Nineteenth Route Army). Hong Kong, 1969.

Chou K'ai-ch'ing 周開慶. *K'ang-chan i-ch'ien chih Chung-Jih kuan-hsi* 抗戰以前之中日關係 (Sino-Japanese relations prior to the war of resistance). Taipei, reprinted 1962.

Chu, Samuel C. "The New Life Movement, 1933–1937," *Researches in the Social Sciences on China,* ed. John E. Lane. New York, Columbia University, East Asian Institute Studies no. 3, 1957.

Chūka minkoku Fukkenshō dokuritsu no shinsō 中華民國福建省獨立之眞相 (True situation in the independent Chinese province of Fukien). N.p., 1934.

> Consists of only two large sheets but comprises a detailed map showing the location of military forces in Fukien in the first week of January 1934; also provides an organizational chart of the rebel government and list of leading officials.

Chūgoku kankei Nihonbun zasshi ronsetsu kiji mokuroku 中國關係日本文雜誌論說記事目錄 (Tables of contents of Japanese journals related to China). 2 vols. Tokyo, Tōyō Bunko, 1964–65.

Ch'un-ch'iu 春秋 ("The Observation Post"). Hong Kong, 1957–1971.

> Contains numerous articles and personal memoirs relating to modern Chinese history. These articles are of very mixed quality, but the journal is an important research source.

Chung-kuo chin-tai cheng-chih chien-shih 中國近代政治簡史 (A survey history of modern Chinese politics). Ed. Chün-ta tsung-hsiao cheng-chih-pu 軍大總校政治部. Chung-nan, republished 1950.

Chung-kuo hsin-min-chu yün-tung chung te tang-p'ai 中國新民主運動中的黨派 (Parties and cliques within China's new democracy movement). Shanghai and Hong Kong, 1946.

"Chung-kuo kuo-min-tang shih tzu-liao hui-pien" 中國國民黨史資料彙編 (Collected materials on Chinese Kuomintang history). Unpub. collection, Hoover Institute, 9 ts'e.

> A collection of documents and newspaper clippings on selected episodes of Kuomintang history, 1923–1934.

Chung-kuo tsai t'ung-i chung 中國在統一中 (China in unity). Ed. Liu Ch'ün 劉群. N.p., 1937.

A collection of articles representing the views of the national salvation movement at the time of the December Ninth student unrest and during the ensuing months of 1936.

Chung-yang pan-yüeh-k'an 中央半月刊 (The central bi-weekly). Nanking, 1927–1928.

Stated purpose of this journal was to clarify Kuomintang doctrine and eliminate factionalism. Strongly opposed to the Reorganization clique; contains articles by Chiang Kai-shek, Hu Han-min, and Sun Fo.

Chü-wai-jen 局外人. "Chi tang-nien ch'uan-shuo-chung te 'shih-san t'ai-pao' " 記當年傳說中的 '十三太保' (Reminiscences of the legendary thirteen princes), pts. 1–24, *Ch'un ch'iu*, vols. 95–118 (June 16, 1961–June 1, 1962).

Ch'üan-kuo t'u-ti tiao-ch'a pao-kao kang-yao 全國土地調查報告綱要 (Summary of the national land investigation report). Comp. T'u-ti wei-yüan-hui. N.p., 1937.

An extensive official survey, begun in late 1935, of land conditions throughout the nation.

Coble, Parks M. "The Shanghai Commercial, Financial, and Industrial Elite and the Kuomintang, 1927–1929." Seminar paper, University of Illinois, 1971.

Crowley, James B. *Japan's Quest for Autonomy: National Security and Foreign Policy, 1930–1938*. Princeton, Princeton University Press, 1966.

Domes, Jürgen. *Vertagte Revolution: Die Politik der Kuomintang in China, 1923–1937*. Berlin, Walter de Gruyter and Co., 1969.

Elmquist, Paul O. "The Sino-Japanese Undeclared War of 1932 at Shanghai," *Papers on China* 5: 39–74 (1951). Cambridge, Mass., East Asian Research Center, Harvard University.

Fan-Chiang yün-tung shih 反蔣運動史 (History of the Anti-Chiang movement). Ed. Chung-kuo ch'ing-nien chün-jen she 中國青年軍人社. [Canton], 1934.

Fang Hsien-t'ing 方顯廷, ed. *Chung-kuo ching-chi yen-chiu* 中國經濟研究 (Researches on the Chinese economy). Changsha, 1938.

A collection of articles on the economy by many of China's leading students of the economy. A source of prime importance for the period of the 1930s.

Far Eastern Survey. New York, American Institute of Pacific Relations, 1932–1937.

Feng Yü-hsiang 馮玉祥. *Wo so jen-shih te Chiang Chieh-shih* 我所認識的蔣介石 (The Chiang Kai-shek that I know). Hong Kong, 1949.

Feuerwerker, Albert. "Industrial Enterprise in Twentieth-Century China: The Chee Hsin Co.," *Approaches to Modern Chinese History*, ed. Albert Feuerwerker, et al. Berkeley, University of California Press, 1967.

——— *The Chinese Economy, 1912–1949*. Ann Arbor, Center for Chinese Studies, University of Michigan, 1968.

Fong, H. D. (Fang Hsien-t'ing). *Cotton Industry and Trade in China*. Tientsin, Nankai Institute of Economics, Nankai University, 1932.

———— "Industrial Capital in China," *Nankai Social and Economic Quarterly* 9.1: 27–94 (April 1936).

———— "Toward Economic Control in China." *Nankai Social and Economic Quarterly* 9.2: 296–397 (July 1936).

Fu Ch'i-hsüeh 傳啓學, et al. *Chung-hua min-kuo chien-ch'a-yüan chih yen-chiu* 中華民國監察院之研究 (Researches on the Control Yuan in the Chinese Republic). Taipei, 1967.

    This work was published with support from the Harvard-Yenching Institute; subsequently it was banned in Taiwan.

Gamble, Sidney D. *Ting Hsien: A North China Rural Community.* Stanford, Stanford University Press, 1968.

Grieder, Jerome B. *Hu Shih and the Chinese Renaissance: Liberalism in the Chinese Revolution, 1917–1937.* Cambridge, Mass., Harvard University Press, 1970.

Hatano Ken'ichi 波多野乾一. *Gendai Shina no kiroku* 現代支那之記錄 (Records of contemporary China). 23 reels. Peking, 1924–1932.

———— *Chūgoku kyōsantō shi, 1933* 中國共產黨史 (History of the Chinese Communist Party, 1933). Tokyo, 1934.

———— *Gendai Shina no seiji to jimbutsu* 現代支那の政治と人物 (The politics and personalities of contemporary China). Tokyo, 1937.

    This is the most detailed study of the domestic politics of the 1930s. It is, unfortunately, fraught with inaccuracies.

Ho, Franklin L. (Ho Lien). "Land Tax in Chekiang," *Monthly Bulletin on Economic China* 7.1: 1–14 (January 1934).

———— "Rural Economic Reconstruction in China," *Nankai Social and Economic Quarterly* 9.2: 496–535 (July 1936).

———— "The Reminiscences of Ho Lien (Franklin L. Ho)" as told to Crystal Lorch, postscript dated July 1966. Unpub. ms. in Special Collections Library, Butler Library, Columbia University.

Ho Kan-chih 何幹之. *Chung-kuo hsien-tai ko-ming shih* 中國現代革命史 (History of the modern Chinese revolution). Peking, 1957.

Ho Lien 何廉 and Li Jui 李銳. *Ts'ai-cheng hsüeh* 財政學 (The study of financial administration). Shanghai, 1935.

Hsia, Tsi-an. *The Gate of Darkness: Studies on the Leftist Literary Movement in China.* Seattle, University of Washington Press, 1968.

Hsiao, Tso-liang, *Power Relations within the Chinese Communist Movement, 1930–1934.* 2 vols. Seattle, University of Washington, 1961.

Hsiao Wen-che 蕭文哲. *Hsien-tai Chung-kuo cheng-tang yü cheng-chih* 現代中國政黨與政治 (The parties and politics of contemporary China). Nanking, 1946.

Hsieh Chü-tseng 謝菊曾. "I-chiu-san-wu-nien Shang-hai pai-yin feng-ch'ao kai-shu 一九三五年上海白銀風潮概述 (A survey of the silver unrest in Shanghai, 1935), *Li-shih yen-chiu* 歷史研究 (Historical researches), 1965, no. 2, pp. 79–96.

Hsien-tai shih-liao 現代史料 (Contemporary historical materials). Ed. Hai-t'ien Publishing Co. 2nd ed. [Shanghai], 1933.

Hsin-sheng-huo yün-tung hsü-chih 新生活運動須知 (Essential information about the New Life Movement). Comp. Hsin-sheng-huo ts'ung-shu she. Nanking, 1935.

Hsin-sheng-ming 新生命 (New Life). Shanghai, 1928–1930.

> Edited by Chou Fu-hai with financial backing from Chiang Kai-shek, it was devoted to discussions of Kuomintang doctrines and to introducing Western writings on sociology and economics. Initially enjoyed a broad circulation.

Hsin-yüeh 新月 (Crescent moon). Shanghai, 1928–1930.

Hsu, Dau-lin. "Chinese Local Administration under the National Government: Democracy and Self-Government versus Traditional Centralism." Unpub. ms.

Hsü, Francis L. K. *Under the Ancestors' Shadow: Chinese Culture and Personality*. New York, Columbia University Press, 1948.

—— *Americans and Chinese: Two Ways of Life*. New York, Henry Schuman, 1953.

Hu Ch'iu-yüan 胡秋原. *Tsai T'ang San-ts'ang yü Fu-shih-te chih chien* 在唐三藏與浮士德之間 (Between Hsüan-tsang and Faust). Taipei, 1962.

—— *Fei-pang chi-t'uan kung-jan shan-tung cheng-chih ch'ing-suan wen-t'i* 誹謗集團公然煽動政治清算問題 (The bloc of slanderers publicly incite a political purge). Taipei, 1963.

Huang Hsü-ch'u 黃旭初. "Kuang-hsi yü chung-yang nien-yü-nien-lai p'ei-huan li-ho i-shu" 廣西與中央廿餘年來悲歡離合憶述 (Reminiscences of the vicissitudes of relations between Kwangsi and the central government during the past twenty-odd years), pts. 20–24, *Ch'un-ch'iu*, vols. 123–127 (Aug. 16–Oct. 16, 1962).

—— "Pa-Kuei i-wang lu" 八桂憶往錄 (Pa-Kuei memoirs), pt. 25, *Ch'un-ch'iu* 192: 15–18 (Aug. 1, 1965).

Huang Shao-hung 黃紹竑. *Wu-shih hui-i* 五十回憶 (Recollections at the age of fifty). 2 vols. Hangchow, 1945.

> Useful, albeit somewhat sketchy, reminiscences by a former high official in both the Kwangsi and Nanking regimes.

Huang, Yi-yun Shen. "My Husband and I: Personal Reminiscences of an Eminent Chinese Woman," condensed, ed., and tr. by T. K. Tong. Unpub. ms. in Special Collections Library, Butler Library, Columbia University, preface dated 1960.

Huntington, Samuel P. *Political Order in Changing Societies*. New Haven, Yale University Press, 1968.

Isaacs, Harold R. *The Tragedy of the Chinese Revolution*. 2nd rev. ed. Stanford, Stanford University Press, 1961.

Israel, John. *Student Nationalism in China*. Stanford, Hoover Institution, Stanford University Press, 1966.

[Iwai Eiichi 岩井英一]. *Ranisha ni kansuru chōsa* 藍衣社ニ關スル調査 (An investigation of the Blue Shirts). Issued by the Research Division of the Foreign Ministry, marked "secret," 1937.

> This is the most detailed and generally reliable source on the Blue

Shirts that I have encountered. Iwai's authorship is indicated in the preface to this 258-page study.

Jen-ch'üan lun-chi 人權論集 (Collected essays on human rights). By Hu Shih 胡適, et al. Shanghai, 1931.
Collection of articles orginally published in *Hsin-yüeh.*

Jen-min jih-pao 人民日報 (People's daily). Foochow, November 1933.
This paper was the successor to the *Min-kuo jih-pao* (Republican daily); it commenced publication under this new name on the second day of the Fukien rebellion, Nov. 21, 1933. A few numbers are available in the Kuomintang party archives, Taiwan.

Juan Fang-hua 阮芳華. *Chung-kuo ch'ih-huo ssu-shih-nien* 中國赤禍四十年 (Forty years of red plague in China). Taipei, 1967.

Kagan, Richard Clark. "The Chinese Trotskyist Movement and Ch'en Tu-hsiu: Culture, Revolution, and Polity, with an appended translation of Ch'en Tu-hsiu's autobiography." Ph.D. diss., University of Pennsylvania, 1969.

Kan Kuo-hsün 干國勳. "Ch'ui-ssu Liu Chien-ch'ün, ping shih lan-i-she" 追思劉健群並釋藍衣社 (Recollections of Liu Chien-ch'ün and revelations regarding the Blue Shirts), *Chuan-chi wen-hsueh* 傳記文學 (Biographical literature) 21.3: 17–21 (Sept. 1, 1972).

K'an-ting Min p'an chi-lüeh 戡定閩叛記略 (Brief record of the suppression of the Fukien rebellion). N.p., n.d.
This brief account (15 double pages) contains maps and charts of the military phase of the rebellion. It is available at the Kuomintang Party Archives, Taiwan, #477/1.

Kao T'ing-tzu 高廷梓. *Chung-kuo ching-chi chien-she* 中國經濟建設 (China's economic reconstruction). Shanghai, 1937.

Kao Yin-tsu 高蔭祖. *Chung-hua min-kuo ta-shih chi* 中華民國大事記 (Record of major events in Republican China). Taipei, 1957.

Kapp, Robert A. "Provincial Independence vs. National Rule: A Case Study of Szechwan in the 1920's and 1930's," *Journal of Asian Studies* 30.3: 535–549 (May 1971).

Kennedy, Melville Talbot, Jr. "The Kuomintang and Chinese Unification, 1928–1931." Ph.D. diss., Harvard University, 1958.

Ko-ming p'ing-lun 革命評論 (Revolutionary critic). Shanghai, 1928.
Edited by Ch'en Kung-po, an organ of the Reorganization clique.

Ku-shu-chih 古述之. "Ch'en Chiang Ts'ai yü Ti-san-tang-jen te chieh-ho Min-pien yu pao-fa tao wa-chieh" 陳蔣蔡與第三黨人的結合閩變由爆發到瓦解 (The formation of the Fukien rebellion by Ch'en Ming-shu, Chiang Kuang-nai, Ts'ai T'ing-k'ai, and members of the third party, from outbreak to collapse), pts, 1–5, *Ch'un-ch'iu*, vols. 96–100 (July 1–Sept. 1, 1962).

Kuhn, Philip A. " 'Local Self-Government' under the Republic: Problems of Control, Autonomy, and Mobilization." Paper prepared for the Research Conference on Local Control and Protest during the Ch'ing Period, East-West Center, University of Hawaii, 1971. To be published in *Conflict and*

Control: Social Process in Late Imperial China, ed. Frederic Wakeman, Jr., with Carolyn Grant (Berkeley, University of California Press, in press).

Kung Ch'u 龔楚. *Wo-yü hung-chün* 我與紅軍 (I and the red army). Hong Kong, 1954.

Kung-hsien 貢獻 (The tribute). Shanghai, 1927–1928. Edited by Wang Fa-ch'in; an organ of the Reorganization clique.

K'ung Hsiang-hsi. "The Reminiscences of K'ung Hsiang-hsi (September 11, 1880————)." As told to Julie Lien-ying How. Unpub. ms. in Special Collections Library, Butler Library, Columbia University, 1961.

Kuo-wen chou-pao 國聞週報 ("Kwo-wen weekly"). Tientsin, Shanghai, 1927–1937. A major source; contained generally objective articles, collected editorials from newspapers not elsewhere easily accessible, and week-by-week surveys of political happenings.

League of Nations Archives. Geneva.

League of Nations, Council Committee on Technical Cooperation between the League of Nations and China. *Report of the Technical Agent on His Mission in China from the Date of His Appointment until April 1st, 1934*. Geneva, 1934. This "Rajchman Report" was reproduced in *China Year Book*, 1934, pp. 761–793.

Lei Hsiao-ts'en 雷嘯岑. *San-shih-nien tung-luan Chung-kuo* 三十年動亂中國 (Thirty years of China in turmoil). Hong Kong, 1955.

Levenson, Joseph R. *Confucian China and Its Modern Fate, Vol. II, The Problem of Monarchical Decay*. Berkeley, University of California Press, 1964.

Levy, Marion J., Jr. *The Family Revolution in Modern China*. New York, Atheneum, 1968 reprint of 1949 original.

Li Lu-chou 李蘆洲. *Kuo-min cheng-fu te cheng-chi* 國民政府的政績 (The achievements of the Nationalist government). Shanghai, 1934.

Lin, W. Y. *The New Monetary System of China: A Personal Interpretation*. Chicago, University of Chicago Press, 1936.

Lin Yutang. *My Country and My People*. New York, John Day, 1935.

———— *A History of the Press and Public Opinion in China*. Chicago, University of Chicago Press, 1936.

Linebarger, Paul M. A. *The China of Chiang K'ai-shek: A Political Study*. Boston, World Peace Foundation, 1941.

Liu Chien-ch'ün 劉健群. *Fu-hsing Chung-kuo ko-ming chih lu* 復興中國革命之路 (The way to regenerate the Chinese revolution). N.p., 1934.

———— Yin-ho i-wang 銀河憶往 (Memories at Yin-ho). [Taipei], preface dated 1966.

Liu, F. F. *A Military History of Modern China*. Princeton, Princeton University Press, 1956.

Liu Ta-chung [Liu Ta-chün]. *China's National Income, 1931–36: An Exploratory Study*. Washington, D. C. Brookings Institute, 1946.

———— and Kung-chia Yeh. *The Economy of the Chinese Mainland: National Income and Economic Development, 1933–1959*. Princeton, Princeton University Press, 1965.

Lo I 羅儀 and Huang Chi-ch'ing 黃楫清. *Chung-kuo fa-hsi-ssu t'e-wu chen-hsiang*

中國法西斯特務眞相 (The true picture of the fascist special services in China). N.p., 1949.

Lung-yen yüeh-k'an 龍巖月刊 (Lung-yen monthly). Lung-yen, Fukien, September 1933.
> Official publication of the Western Fukien Reconstruction Council.

Mast, Herman William, III. "An Intellectual Biography of Tai Chi-t'ao, 1890–1927: The Development of an Anti-Communist Theorist in the Kuomintang before the Purge." Ph.D. diss., University of Illinois, 1970.

Mills, Harriet Cornelia, "Lu Hsün: 1927–1936, The Years on the Left." Ph.D. diss., Columbia University, 1963.

"Min-luan ch'ien-hou chih ko-fan-tung-p'ai chien-chi" 閩亂前後之各反動派剪集 (Collected clippings on counterrevolutionary cliques before and after the Fukien disturbance). Unpub. collection.
> A collection of a series of newspaper articles, published in nine sections in an unknown newspaper. The collection is in the holdings of the Investigation Section of the Ministry of the Interior, Republic of China, Taiwan, #576.2/805/8423.

Monthly Bulletin on Economic China. Tientsin, 1934.
> Predecessor of the *Nankai Social and Economic Quarterly.*

Myers, Ramon H. "Land Distribution in Revolutionary China: 1890–1937," *The Chung Chi Journal* 8.2: 62–77 (May 1969).

—— *The Chinese Peasant Economy: Agricultural Development in Hopei and Shantung, 1890–1940.* Cambridge, Mass., Harvard University Press, 1970.

Myrdal, Gunnar. *Asian Drama: An Inquiry into the Poverty of Nations.* New York, Twentieth Century Fund, 1968.

Nankai Social and Economic Quarterly. Tientsin, 1935–1937.
> Contains numerous important articles on the economy and government by some of China's leading academicians, many associated with Nankai University. This journal was previously called the *Monthly Bulletin on Economic China.*

Nathan, James Andrew. "Factionalism in Early Republican China: The Politics of the Peking Government, 1918–1920." Ph.D. diss., Harvard Unversity, 1970.

Nature of Fascism, Ed. S. J. Woolf. New York, Vintage Books, 1969.

North China Herald. Shanghai, 1927–1938.

Nye, J. S. "Corruption and Political Development: A Cost-Benefit Analysis," *American Political Science Review* 61.2: 417–427 (June 1967).

Ou-yang Tsung 歐陽宗 et al. *Chung-kuo nei-mu* 中國內幕 (Behind the scenes in China). Shanghai, 1941.

Paauw, Douglas S. "Chinese National Expenditures during the Nanking Period," *The Far Eastern Quarterly* 12.1: 3–26 (November 1952).

—— "The Kuomintang and Economic Stagnation, 1928–1937," *Journal of Asian Studies* 16.2: 213–220 (February 1957).

Pacific Affairs. 1926–1938.

Payer, Cheryl. "Western Economic Assistance to Nationalist China, 1927–1937." Unpub. ms. (The manuscript has since been completed as a Ph.D. dissertation, Harvard University, 1971.)

P'eng Yü-hsin 彭雨新. *Hsien ti-fang ts'ai-cheng* 縣地方財政 (Local financial administration in the hsien). Chungking and Shanghai, 1945.

People's Tribune. Shanghai, 1931–1937.

Perkins, Dwight H. *Agricultural Development in China, 1368–1968.* Chicago, Aldine Publishing Co., 1969.

Problems of the Pacific, 1933: Economic Conflict and Control. Ed. Bruno Lasker and W. L. Holland. Chicago, University of Chicago Press, 1934.

Problems of the Pacific, 1936: Aims and Results of Social and Economic Policies in Pacific Countries. Ed. W. L. Holland and Kate L. Mitchell. Chicago, University of Chicago Press, n.d.

"Ranisha ni tsuite" 藍衣社に就いて (On the Blue Shirts). N.p., n.d.

> Probably a Japanese government report of 1935. It contains, inter alia, versions of the Blue Shirts "Political Program" and other documents. It is not, however, a reliable source.

"Ranisha no gainen to sono tokumu kōsaku ni tsuite" 藍衣社の概念と其の特務工作に就いて (The concept of the Blue Shirts and their special service operations). Prepared by the General Headquarters of the Expeditionary Army in China, 1940. No pagination.

> A 29-page report, quite accurate, based on a conversation with a member of Blue Shirts.

"Ranisha no kaiso shugi no tenkō narabi ni saikin no dōkō" 藍衣社ノ改組主義ノ轉向並ニ最近ノ動向 (The shift of Blue Shirt reorganizationist thought and most recent trends) (dated 1934 in pencil), in *Ranisha ni kansuru shiryō* 藍衣社に關する資料 (Materials on the Blue Shirts), a specially bound volume in the Tōyō Bunko.

"Ranisha no soshiki to hanman kōnichi katsudō no jitsurei" 藍衣社の組織と反滿抗日活動の實例 (The organization of the Blue Shirts and examples of anti-Manchukuo anti-Japanese activities), in *Ranisha ni kansuru shiryō* 藍衣社に關する資料 (Materials on the Blue Shirts), a specially bound volume in the Tōyō Bunko.

> Relatively brief (43 pp.), but an important Japanese government report probably issued in 1935.

San-min chu-i yüeh-k'an 三民主義月刊 (Three People's Principles monthly). Canton, 1933–1936.

> Edited by Hu-Han-min, it was vehemently opposed to Chiang Kai-shek and the Nanking regime.

Shanhai 上海 (Shanghai). 1936.

She-hui hsin-wen 社會新聞 ("The Society Mercury"). Shanghai, 1932–1937.

> Commentaries on people and parties in Chinese politics, it is of unreliable factual accuracy. It does, however, offer insights to the political scene that are not available elsewhere and is therefore an important source.

Hatano Ken'ichi relied heavily upon it for his writings on the 1930s—which partially explains why Hatano's publications must be used with extreme caution. For comments on the factional ties of this journal, see Chapter II, n. 20.

Shen-pao 申報 ("The Shun Pao"). Shanghai, 1927–1937.

Shewmaker, Kenneth E. *Americans and Chinese Communists, 1927–1945: A Persuading Encounter.* Ithaca, Cornell University Press, 1971.

Shih, Kuo-heng. *China Enters the Machine Age: A Study of Labor in Chinese War Industry.* Cambridge, Mass., Harvard University Press, 1944.

Shih-shih hsin-pao 時事新報 ("The China Times"). Shanghai, 1930–1934.

Regarded as the most liberal and politically outspoken among Shanghai's generally jejune and cautious newspapers. Late in the Nanking period, it fell under governmental control and thereafter had a semi-official character.

Shih-tai kung-lun 時代公論 (Contemporary forum). Nanking, 1932–1935.

Many of the contributors were members of the faculty at Nanking University. It was reputedly associated with the CC clique, although this has been denied by a former contributor.

Shina jihō 支那時報 ("The China review"). 1930–1937.

The table of contents of this journal, published 1924–1942, is reproduced in *Chūgoku kankei Nihonbun zasshi ronsetsu kiji mokuroku*, vol. II.

Shina tōmen no jūyō mondai 支那當面の重要問題 (Urgent questions confronting China). Prepared by Tōyō kyōkai chōsabu 東洋協會調査部. Tokyo, 1936.

Shirley, James Robert. "Political Conflict in the Kuomintang: The Career of Wang Ching-wei to 1932." Ph.D. diss., University of California, Berkeley, 1962.

Silin, Robert Henry. "Management in Large-Scale Taiwanese Industrial Enterprises." Ph.D. diss., Harvard University, 1970.

Snow, Edgar. *Red Star over China.* New York, Random House, 1938.

Solomon, Richard Harvey. "The Chinese Revolution and the Politics of Dependency." Ph.d. diss., Massachusetts Institute of Technology, 1966.

—— "Mao's Effort to Reintegrate the Chinese Polity: Problems of Authority and Conflict in Chinese Social Process," *Chinese Communist Politics in Action*, pp. 271–361. Ed. A. Doak Barnett. Seattle, University of Washington Press, 1969.

—— *Mao's Revolution and the Chinese Political Culture.* Berkeley, University of California Press, 1971.

Ssu-ma Hsien-tao 司馬仙島. *Pei-fa hou chih ko-p'ai ssu-ch'ao* 北伐後之各派思潮 (The doctrines of the various cliques after the northern expedition). Peiping, 1930.

State Department Archives, United States Government. National Archives, 1930–1937.

Strenuous Decade: China's Nation-Building Efforts, 1927–1937. Ed. Paul K. T. Sih. New York, St. John's University Press, 1970.

Su-ch'ü kung-jen 蘇區工人 (Soviet worker). [Juichin?], 1933–1934.

Scattered numbers are available in the "Ch'en-ch'eng Collection" (Shih-sou tzu-liao shih kung-fei tzu-liao).

Suleski, Ronald S. "The Fu-t'ien Incident, December 1930," *Early Communist China: Two Studies*, pp. 1–27. Ann Arbor, Michigan Papers in Chinese Studies, no. 4, 1969.

Sun Tso-ch'i 孫佐齊. *Chung-kuo t'ien-fu wen-t'i* 中國田賦問題 (The problem of the land tax in China). Shanghai, 1935.

Ta-kung pao 大公報 ("L'Impartial"). Tientsin, 1929–1937.

Tai Li 戴笠. *Cheng-chih chen-t'an* 政治偵探 (Political spying). N.p., Political Bureau of the Military Commission, 1938.

Tai Yü-nung hsien-sheng nien-p'u 戴雨農先生年譜 (Chronological biography of Tai Li). Comp. Intelligence Section, Defense Ministry. [Taipei], 1966.

Takayanagi Torao 高柳虎雄. *Kōnichi jimmin sensen undō no tembō* 抗日人民戰線運動の展望 (The outlook for the anti-Japanese popular front movement). Shanghai, 1936.

Tamagna, Frank M. *Bunking and Finance in China*. New York, Institute of Pacific Relations, 1942.

Tawney, R. H. *Land and Labour in China*. New York, Harcourt, Brace and Co., 1932.

Teng Yen-ta hsien-sheng i-cho 鄧演達先生遺著 (The bequeathed writings of Teng Yen-ta). Hong Kong, 1949 reprint of 1932 edition.

Thomson, James C., Jr. *While China Faced West: American Reformers in Nationalist China, 1928–1937*. Cambridge, Harvard University Press, 1969.

Ti-cheng yüeh-k'an 地政月刊 ("The Journal of Land Economics"). Nanking, 1935–1937.

        Many of the articles seem to be of dubious objectivity; was extremely critical of the current situation.

Tien, Hung-mao Harold. "Political Development in China, 1927–1937." Ph.D. diss., University of Wisconsin, 1969.

———— *Government and Politics in Kuomintang China, 1927–1937*. Stanford, Stanford University Press, 1972.

Ting, Lee-Hsia Hsu. "Government Control of the Press in Modern China, 1900–1949: A Study of Its Theories, Operations and Effects." Ph.D. diss., University of Chicago, 1969.

T'ing-chin tsa-chih 挺進雜誌 (Advance). Fukien, August–September 1933.

Tōa 東亞 (East Asia). 1933–1937.

        The table of contents of this journal, published 1928–1945, is reproduced in *Chūgoku kankei Nihonbun zasshi ronsetsu kiji mokuroku*, vol. II.

Tou-cheng 鬪爭 (Struggle). Juichin, 1933–1934.

        A considerable run of this journal is available in microfilm in the "Ch'en Ch'eng Collection" (Shih-sou tzu-liao shih kung-fei tzu-liao).

Ts'ai T'ing-kai 蔡廷鍇. *Ts'ai T'ing-k'ai tzu-chuan* 蔡廷鍇自傳 (Autobiography of Tsai T'ing-k'ai). Hong Kong, 1946.

Tso Shun-sheng. "The Reminiscences of Tso Shun-sheng." As told to Julie Lien-ying How. Unpub. ms. in Special Collections Library, Butler Library, Columbia University, 1965.

Tu-li p'ing-lun 獨立評論 (The independent review). Peiping, 1932–1937.

Tu-shu tsa-chih 讀書雜誌 ("Research Monthly"). Shanghai, 1931–1933.

Tung-fang tsa-chih 東方雜誌 ("Eastern Miscellany"). Shanghai, 1926–1938.

Van Slyke, Lyman P. *Enemies and Friends: The United Front in Chinese Communist History.* Stanford, Stanford University Press, 1967.

Wage Rates in Shanghai. By Bureau of Social Affairs, The City of Greater Shanghai. Shanghai, 1935.

Wales, Nym (pseud. of Helen F. Snow). *Notes on the Chinese Student Movement, 1935–1936.* Mimeographed, Guidance Notes prepared for the Nym Wales Collection on the Far East in the Hoover Institution on War, Revolution and Peace, at Stanford University, 1959.

Wang Cheng. "The Kuomintang: A Sociological Study of Demoralization." Ph.D. diss., Stanford University, 1953.

Wang Chien-min 王健民. *Chung-kuo kung-ch'an-tang shih-kao* 中國共產黨史稿 (Draft history of the Chinese Communist Party). Taipei, 1965.

Wang P'ei-huai 王培槐. *Ko-ming te pao-chien* 革命的寶劍 (The revolution's sword). N.p., 1936.

Wang, Y. C. "Free Enterprise in China: The Case of a Cigarette Concern, 1905–1953," *Pacific Historical Review* 29: 395–414 (November 1960).

——— *Chinese Intellectuals and the West, 1872–1949.* Chapel Hill, University of North Carolina Press, 1966.

Wen-hua chien-she 文化建設 (Cultural reconstruction). Shanghai, 1934–1937.
    A publication with ties to the CC clique; it was managed by Ch'en Li-fu and edited by Fan Chung-yün.

Wilbur, C. Martin, and Julie Lien-ying How, eds. *Documents on Communism, Nationalism, and Soviet Advisors in China, 1918–1927: Papers Seized in the 1927 Peking Raid.* New York, Columbia University Press, 1956.

Wilson, Richard W. *Learning to Be Chinese: The Political Socialization of Children in Taiwan.* Cambridge, Mass., M.I.T. Press, 1970.

Wolf, Margery. "Child Training and the Chinese Family," *Family and Kinship in Chinese Society.* Ed. Maurice Freedman. Stanford, Stanford University Press, 1970.

Wu Ching-hsiung 吳經熊 and Huang Kung-chüeh 黃公覺. *Chung-kuo chih-hsien shih* 中國制憲史 (History of constitution-drafting in China). Shanghai, 1937.
    The authors participated in the constitution-drafting of the Legislative Yüan. This is the most detailed study of the subject, the value of the work being enhanced by the inclusion of several of the draft constitutions and many other related documents. The authors have, however, avoided discussion of the political and factional aspects that affected the drafting process.

Yang, C. K. *The Chinese Family in the Communist Revolution.* Cambridge, Mass., M.I.T. Press, 1959.

——— "Some Characteristics of Chinese Bureaucratic Behavior," *Confucianism in Action*, pp. 134–164. Ed. David S. Nivison and Arthur F. Wright. Stanford, Stanford University Press, 1959.

Yang, Lien-sheng. "The Concept of *Pao* as a Basis for Social Relations in China," *Chinese Thought and Institutions*. Ed. John K. Fairbank. Chicago, University of Chicago Press, 1957.

Yang, Sueh-Chang. "China's Depression and Subsequent Recovery, 1931–36: An Inquiry into the Applicability of the Modern Income Determination Theory." Ph.D. diss., Harvard University, 1950.

Yen Chung-p'ing 嚴中平, et al. *Chung-kuo chin-tai ching-chi shih t'ung-chi tzu-liao hsüan-chi* 中國近代經濟史統計資料選輯 (Statistical materials on the history of the modern Chinese economy). Peking, 1955.

Yokota Minoru 橫田實. Newspaper Collection.

This important collection consists of eighty-nine scrapbooks of newspaper clippings covering events from 1924 to late 1930s. The clippings tend to be arranged topically, but the scrapbooks and pages of the scrapbooks are not numbered. Located in the library of the Seminar on Modern China, Tōyō Bunko.

Young, Arthur N. *China's Nation-Building Effort, 1927–1937: The Financial and Economic Record*. Stanford, Hoover Institution Press, 1971.

Yü-chou hsün-k'an 宇宙旬刊 ("The Universe"). Hong Kong, 1934–1935.

Glossary

Ch'an-kung-t'uan 剷共團
Chang Chin-chien 張金鑑
Chang Ching-yao 張敬堯
Chang-chou 漳州
Chang Fo-ch'üan 張佛泉
Chang Hsi-jo 張奚若
Chang Hung 張弘
Chang P'ei-kang 張培剛
Chang Po-chün 章伯鈞
Chang Yen 張炎
Chang Yüan-shan 章元善
Chang Yün-fu 張雲伏
ch'ang-wu kan-shih hui 常務幹事會
Ch'en Chang-heng 陳長蘅
Ch'en Chi-t'ang 陳齊棠
Ch'en Ch'i-t'ien 陳啟天
Ch'en Chih-mai 陳之邁
Ch'en Ch'iu-yün 陳秋雲
Ch'en Fu-mu 陳孚木
Ch'en Kuo-hui 陳國輝
Ch'en Ming-shu 陳銘樞
Ch'en-pao 晨報
Cheng Chieh-min 鄭介民
cheng-ch'üan 政權
cheng-kang 政綱
cheng-shui 正稅
Ch'eng T'ien-fang 程天放
Chi Fang 季方
chi-k'ou shou-t'ien 計口授田
Chi-lu yao-kang 紀律要綱

ch'i chün-tzu 七君子
Chiang Chien-jen 蔣堅忍
Chiang Hsiao-hsien 蔣孝先
Chiang Kuang-nai 蔣光鼐
Chiang-nan cheng-pao 江南正報
Chien-t'ao 檢討
chih-ch'üan 治權
chih-she 支社
chih-tui 支隊
Ch'in Te-ch'un 秦德純
Chin Tseng-ku 金增嘏
Ching-pao 京報
Chiu-wang-she 救亡社
Chou Fu 周復
Chu Wen-shan 朱蘊山
ch'u 處
chuang-shu 莊書
chung-hsin ou-hsiang 中心偶像
Chung-hsing jih-pao 中興日報
Chung-hua fu-hsing-she 中華復興社
Chung-kuo kuo-min-tang ch'ien-wei hui
  中國國民黨前衛會
Chung-kuo kuo-min-tang lin-shih hsing-
  tung wei-yüan-hui 中國國民黨臨時行動
  委員會
Chung-kuo kuo-min-tang t'ieh-hsüeh
  t'uan 中國國民黨鐵血團
chung-tui 中隊
Chung-yang jih-pao 中央日報
Chung-yang kan-shih hui 中央幹事會

ch'ü 區
ch'ü-fen hui 區分會
ch'ü-hsiao p'ai 取消派
Ch'üan-chou 泉州
chün-shih hua 軍事化
chün-shih pei-fa, kuan-liao nan-fa 軍事北伐官
　僚南伐

Fan Han-chieh 范漢傑
Fang Chen-wu 方振武
fen-hui 分會
Feng T'i 酆悌
Fu-hsing-she 復興社
fu-shui 附稅

Ho Chung-han 賀衷寒
Ho Kung-kan 何公敢
Ho Lien 何廉
hou-pu kan-shih 候補幹事
Hsia-ta chou-k'an 厦大週刊
Hsiang-tao 嚮導
Hsiao Tsan-yü 蕭贊育
hsiao-tsu 小組
hsiao-tui 小隊
hsiao-yen 硝鹽
hsien 縣
Hsin ch'ing-nien 新青年
Hsin-sheng chou-k'an 新生週刊
Hsin-sheng-hua ts'u-chin hui 新生活促進會
Hsin-shih-tai yüeh-k'an 新時代月刊
hsing-cheng tu-ch'a chuan-yüan 行政督察
　專員
hsiung-t'u 雄圖
Hsü Ch'ien 徐謙
Hsü Ch'ih-p'ing 許持平
Hsü Ming-hung 徐名鴻
Hsü T'ai-k'ung 許太空
Hu Ch'iu-yüan 胡秋原
Hu Tao-wei 胡道維
Hu Tsung-nan 胡宗南
hu-wei 滬委
Hua-pei chiu-wang hui 華北救亡會
huan-cheng yü min 還政於民
Huang Ch'i-hsiang 黃琪翔
Huang Ch'iang 黃強
Huang Hsü-ch'u 黃旭初
Huang-p'u t'ung-hsüeh hui 黃埔同學會
Huang Shao-hung 黃紹竑
hui-chang 會長
Huo-hsing-she 火星社

i-pao chih-pao 以暴制暴

I-shih pao 益世報

jen-ch'ing 人情
Jen-min ch'üan-li hsüan-yen 人民權利宣言
Ju Ch'un-p'u 茹春浦

Kan Nai-kuang 甘乃光
kan-shih 幹事
Kang-ling 綱領
K'ang Tse 康澤
Kao Ch'eng-yüan 高承元
keng-che yu ch'i-t'ien 耕者有其田
Ko-ming chan-hsien 革命戰線
Ko-ming ch'ing-nien t'ung-chih hui 革命
　青年同志會
ko-ming min-ch'üan 革命民權
Ko-ming p'ing-lun 革命評論
Ko Wu-ch'i 葛武棨
Ku Meng-yü 顧孟餘
Ku-t'ien 古田
Kua-t'ou cheng-chih 寡頭政治
Kuei Yung-ch'ing 桂永清
Kung-shang jih-pao 工商日報
kuo-chia hua 國家化
Kuo-min chün-shih hsün-lien wei-yüan-
　hui 革命軍事訓練委員會
Kuo T'ai-ch'i 郭泰祺

lan-i-she 藍衣社
Lan-i t'uan 藍衣團
Li Chang-ta 李章達
Li Chi (archeologist) 李濟
Li Chi (Trotskyite) 李季
Li Chi-shen 李濟深
Li-chih-she 勵志社
Li Ching-han 李景漢
Li-ch'üan 黎川
Li-hsing-she 力行社
li-i-lien-ch'ih 禮義廉恥
Li Ping-jo 李冰若
li-shu 里書
liang-chih 良知
Liang Kan-ch'iao 梁幹喬
lieh-teng min-tsu 劣等民族
Lin I-chin 林疑今
Liu Chien-ch'ün 劉健群
Liu Jen-ching 劉仁靜
Liu Ping-li 劉炳藜
Liu Yü-sheng 劉煜生
Lo Ch'un-i 羅純一
lo-hou 落後
Lo Lung-chi 羅隆基

Lo Tun-wei 羅敦偉
Lung-yen 龍巖

Ma Chi-lien 馬季廉
Mao Wei-shou 毛維壽
Mei Kung-pin 梅龔彬
Min-hsi shan-hou wei-yüan-hui 閩西善後
　委員會
Min-hsing pao 民興報
Min-sheng pao 民生報
min-tsu ying-hsiung 民族英雄
Ming Hsia 鳴夏
mou 畝

Nan-hua jih-pao 南華日報
nei-jung pu ch'ung-shih 內容不充實

Ou Shou-nien 區壽年

pa-hsi 把戲
P'an Han-nien 潘漢年
P'an Tzu-nien 潘梓年
P'an Yu-ch'iang 潘佑強
pao-chia 保甲
P'eng Hsüeh-p'ei 彭學沛
P'eng Shu-chih 彭述之
Pieh-tung-tui 別動隊
p'ing-chün ti-ch'üan 平均地權
pu-i t'uan 布衣團

Sa Meng-wu 薩孟武
Shang-pao 商報
She-hui tiao-ch'a 社會調查
Shen-chou kuo-kuang-she 神州國光社
Shen T'ung 沈同
sheng-ch'an hua 生產化
Sheng-ch'an-tang 生產黨
sheng-kuan fa-ts'ai 升官發財
sheng-yuan chien-sheng 生員監生
shih-kan 實幹
Shih Liang-ts'ai 史量才
shih-mou 市畝
shih-san t'ai-pao 十三太保
shu-chi 書記
shu-chi chang 書記長
shu-chi ch'u 書記處
Shun-t'ien shih-pao 順天時報
ssu-i 私意
ssu-shu 死書
Sun K'o 孫科
Sun Po-chien 孫伯騫
Sun Tien-ying 孫殿英

Ta-chung sheng-huo 大衆生活
ta-tui 大隊
Tai Chi 戴戟
Tai Li 戴笠
t'ai-tzu 太子
t'an-k'uan 攤款
t'an-p'ai 攤派
T'an P'ing-shan 譚平山
tang-pu 黨部
T'ao Hsi-sheng 陶希聖
t'e-pieh ch'ü-fen-hui 特別區分會
t'e-wu 特務
T'e-wu chü 特務局
Teng Wen-i 鄧文儀
Teng Yen-ta 鄧演達
teng-yin feng-tz'u 等因奉此
T'eng Chieh 滕傑
t'ien-fu jen-ch'üan 天賦人權
Ting Wei-fen 丁惟汾
Ting Wen-chiang 丁文江
Ts'ai T'ing-k'ai 蔡廷鍇
ts'e-shu 冊書
Tseng K'uo-ch'ing 曾擴情
Tso Shun-sheng 左舜生
Tsou T'ao-fen 鄒韜奮
Tsung-hui chien-ch'a hui 總會檢察會
tsung-tui-pu 總隊部
Tu Hsin-ju 杜心如
Tuan Hsi-p'eng 段錫朋

Wang Han-chang 汪翰章
wang-kuo 亡國
Wang Li-hsi 王禮錫
Wei Li-huang 衛立煌
Wen-hua p'ing-lun 文化評論
Wen-hua tsa-chih 文化雜誌
wen-jo 文弱
Weng Chao-yüan 翁照垣
Wong Wen-hao 翁文灝
Wu Ching-ch'ao 吳景超
Wu Ching-hsiung 吳經熊
Wu Ting-ch'ang 吳鼎昌

Yang Ch'üan 楊銓
yang-lao yüan 養老院
Yang Yu-chiung 楊幼炯
Yen Ling-feng 嚴靈峯
yu-hsin wu-li 有心無力
Yü Han-mou 余漢謀
Yü Hsin-ch'ing 余心清
Yü Hsüeh-chung 于學忠
Yü Wen-wei 余文偉

Index

Harvard East Asian Series

1. *China's Early Industrialization: Sheng Hsuan-huai (1884–1916) and Mandarin Enterprise.* By Albert Feuerwerker.
2. *Intellectual Trends in the Ch'ing Period.* By Liang Ch'i-ch'ao. Translated by Immanuel C. Y. Hsü.
3. *Reform in Sung China: Wang An-shih (1021–1026) and His New Policies.* By James T. C. Liu.
4. *Studies on the Population of China, 1368–1953.* By Ping-ti Ho.
5. *China's Entrance into the Family of Nations: The Diplomatic Phase, 1858–1880.* By Immanuel C. Y. Hsü.
6. *The May Fourth Movement: Intellectual Revolution in Modern China.* By Chow Tse-tsung.
7. *Ch'ing Administrative Terms: A Translation of the Terminology of the Six Boards with Explanatory Notes.* Translated and edited by E-tu Zen Sun.
8. *Anglo-American Steamship Rivalry in China, 1862–1874.* By Kwang-Ching Liu.
9. *Local Government in China under the Ch'ing.* By T'ung-tsu Ch'ü.
10. *Communist China, 1955–1959: Policy Documents with Analysis.* With a foreword by Robert R. Bowie and John K. Fairbank. (Prepared at Harvard University under the joint auspices of the Center for International Affairs and the East Asian Research Center.)
11. *China and Christianity: The Missionary Movement and the Growth of Chinese Antiforeignism, 1860–1870.* By Paul A. Cohen.
12. *China and the Helping Hand, 1937–1945.* By Arthur N. Young.
13. *Research Guide to the May Fourth Movement: Intellectual Revolution in Modern China, 1915–1924.* By Chow Tse-tsung.
14. *The United States and the Far Eastern Crisis of 1933–1938: From the Manchurian Incident through the Initial Stage of the Undeclared Sino-Japanese War.* By Dorothy Borg.
15. *China and the West, 1858–1861: The Origins of the Tsungli Yamen.* By Masataka Banno.
16. *In Search of Wealth and Power: Yen Fu and the West.* By Benjamin Schwartz.
17. *The Origins of Entrepreneurship in Meiji Japan.* By Johannes Hirschmeier, S.V.D.
18. *Commissioner Lin and the Opium War.* By Hsin-pao Chang.
19. *Money and Monetary Policy in China, 1845–1895.* By Frank H. H. King.
20. *China's Wartime Finance and Inflation, 1937–1945.* By Arthur N. Young.
21. *Foreign Investment and Economic Development in China, 1840–1937.* By Chi-ming Hou.
22. *After Imperialism: The Search for a New Order in the Far East, 1921–1931.* By Akira Iriye.
23. *Foundations of Constitutional Government in Modern Japan, 1868–1900.* By George Akita.